second edition

Reading with Meaning

Strategies for College Reading

Dorothy Grant Hennings

Kean College of New Jersey

PRENTICE HALL, Englewood Cliffs, New Jersey 07632

Library of Congress Cataloging-in-Publication Data

HENNINGS, DOROTHY GRANT.
 Reading with meaning : strategies for college reading / Dorothy
Grant Hennings.
  p.   cm.
 Includes index.
 ISBN 0-13-763590-7
 1. Reading (Higher education)—United States. 2. College readers.
I. Title.
LB2395.3.H46 1993
428.4'071'1—dc20
                              92-31835
                              CIP

Acquisitions editor: Carol Wada
Editorial production/supervision: F. Hubert
Prepress buyer: Herb Klein
Manufacturing buyers: Bob Anderson
Photo research: Rona Tuccillo
Cover design: Ray Lundgren Graphics, Ltd.
Cover photos: David Jeffrey/Image Bank (left); Janeart
  Image Bank (center); Jeff Smith/Image Bank (right)

In Memory of My Mother
Ethel B. Moll Grant
1896–1992

Chapter Opening Art

Contents: University of Florida. *Preface:* Cynthia Dopkin/Photo Researchers. *Chapter 1:* Public Relations Office, Kean College. *Chapter 2:* U.S. Coast Guard Official Photo. *Chapter 3:* Robert A. Issacs/Photo Researchers. *Chapter 4:* Major Morris. *Chapters 5, 7, and 8:* Laima Druskis. *Chapter 9:* Four By Five. *Chapter 10:* Laima Druskis. *Chapter 11:* Susan Rosenberg. *Chapter 12:* University of Arkansas, Division of Information. *Chapters 13 and 14:* Laima Druskis. *Summary:* Ken Karp.

Credits appear on page 352, which constitutes a continuation of the copyright page.

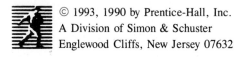 © 1993, 1990 by Prentice-Hall, Inc.
A Division of Simon & Schuster
Englewood Cliffs, New Jersey 07632

Printed in the United States of America

10 9 8 7 6 5 4 3 2 1

ISBN 0-13-763590-7

PRENTICE-HALL INTERNATIONAL (UK) LIMITED, *London*
PRENTICE-HALL OF AUSTRALIA PTY. LIMITED, *Sydney*
PRENTICE-HALL CANADA INC., *Toronto*
PRENTICE-HALL HISPANOAMERICANA, S.A., *Mexico*
PRENTICE-HALL OF INDIA PRIVATE LIMITED, *New Delhi*
PRENTICE-HALL OF JAPAN, INC., *Tokyo*
SIMON & SCHUSTER ASIA PTE. LTD., *Singapore*
EDITORA PRENTICE-HALL DO BRASIL, LTDA., *Rio de Janeiro*

Contents

PART II VOCABULARY AND READING

PART III BASIC COMPREHENSION

PART IV   EFFICIENT STUDY READING

7   Applying Systematic Study Strategies—SQ3R, Highlighting, Charting, Webbing, Outlining, Summarizing, Test Taking   140

8   Increasing Your Reading Rate   159

PART V   CRITICAL AND CREATIVE READING

9   Critical Thinking: Comparing, Inferring, Concluding, Judging   178

10   Interpreting Style, Tone, and Mood   211

PART VI   READING WITH DIVERSE PURPOSES

11   Understanding Definitions and Explanations   233

12   Understanding Descriptions and Narratives   262

13   Understanding Opinions and Persuasive Writing   292

14   Interpreting Tables, Graphs, and Diagrams   311

Preface

· Reading experts define reading as an active process of thinking. To read is to develop relationships among ideas. Reading experts also explain that what you bring to the reading of a selection is as important to your understanding of it as what the author has put into it. To the reading of a text, you bring knowledge of and attitudes toward the sciences, social sciences, and humanities. You bring a purpose for reading. You bring understanding of vocabulary, your ability to figure out meanings, and your attitudes toward reading.

PURPOSE OF THE TEXT

Maintaining the thrust of the first edition, the second edition of *Reading with Meaning: Strategies for College Reading* incorporates this interactive view of reading. It emphasizes the following:

- active reading in which you respond while reading. As you read the selections in this book, you will think, talk, and write.

- strategic reading in which you learn specific strategies for understanding the kinds of materials you will read in college. For example, you will learn to preview before reading, brainstorm what you know before reading, set purposes for reading, distinguish main from subordinate ideas, use clue words to anticipate the author's train of thought, visualize, predict, infer, compare, conclude, and judge as you read.

● vocabulary development in which you expand your vocabulary through actual reading. As you read, you will learn to use context and word-structure clues to unlock the meaning of unfamiliar words.

● expansion of your knowledge so that future reading is more meaningful.

Based on what today is called a whole language approach, *Reading with Meaning: Strategies for College Reading* contains selections similar to ones you will read in sociology, psychology, history, English, biology, earth science, and other college subjects rather than short paragraphs that drill you on specific skills. The primary purpose of this book is to prepare you to read the kinds of materials you will encounter in your courses—textbooks, other books, journals, and newspapers.

NEW DIRECTIONS

The second edition of *Reading with Meaning: Strategies for College Reading* is a bit different from the first in that there is greater attention to collaborative learning; in reading selections and responding to them, you will very often work with members of your reading class. There is also more opportunity for you to think about what you will read before reading and to use what you already know about a topic to understand it better.

More selections have been added, so there is a greater opportunity for you to practice the strategies you are learning by reading a variety of materials. The selections, too, have been chosen so that they appeal to you, the college student, as well as represent the kinds of materials you must read in college. You will read about daydreaming, human conditioning, making friends, and buying clothing as well as the lives of famous composers, the cause of eclipses, the volcanic eruption in the Philippines, and the events in Tiananmen Square.

Also, at the beginning of each chapter you will find the reading strategies you will learn in that chapter clearly outlined.

ORGANIZATION OF THE TEXT

The overall organization of *Reading with Meaning: Strategies for College Reading* reflects these emphases. Take time to study the Contents. This is something you should do before reading any college text to get an overview of it. You will see that the book starts with basic reading strategies for working with vocabulary, main ideas, and significant details, which lead into more advanced strategies for study reading and critical and creative reading.

Part I has one chapter. Its purpose is to teach you a strategy, or an approach, to use in preparing to read.

Part II focuses on vocabulary. It has two chapters. The first teaches you how to use the surrounding words in a sentence to unlock the meaning of an unfamiliar word; the second teaches you how to use word parts to figure out word meanings, especially the meanings of technical terms important in college textbooks.

Part III helps you understand what you read. The three chapters in this part teach you how to (1) find the main idea of paragraphs and selections, (2) make sense out of details, and (3) use clue words to anticipate the author's train of thought and to figure out paragraph designs.

Part IV deals with study reading. The first chapter teaches strategies like SQ3R, highlighting and notetaking in a text, webbing, data charting, outlining, and summarizing. The second chapter shows you how to increase your reading rate.

Part V involves you in critical and creative reading. The first chapter in this part introduces you to comparing, inferring, concluding, and judging. The second helps you handle style, tone, and mood in reading—elements most important in novels, short stories, plays, poems, essays, and speeches.

Part VI helps you understand the diverse selections you will read in college courses. The first chapter provides practice in comprehending definitions and explanations, which are commonly found in college textbooks in the natural and social sciences. The second introduces strategies for comprehending descriptions and narratives, which are often found in humanities as well as science textbooks. The third provides practice in reading opinions and persuasive writing, a kind of writing you will encounter in history and the humanities as well as in newspapers and magazines. The last chapter introduces strategies for reading tables, graphs, and diagrams.

At the back of the book is a glossary of words featured in the text. It contains a pronunciation guide as well as an explanation of how to use a glossary. You can use this glossary as a dictionary, checking meanings and the pronunciation of unfamiliar words just as you would use a glossary in any college textbook. There is also a reading rate chart so you can calculate your reading rate and an index so that you can look up specific strategies if you want to refer to them.

THE ORGANIZATION OF THE CHAPTERS

Very often there is a pattern to the development of chapters in a college textbook. It generally helps to identify that pattern before you start to read. To this end, turn now to Chapter 4 and identify the component parts of a typical chapter.

In *Reading with Meaning: Strategies for College Reading,* each chapter begins by asking you to look through the chapter before reading, to identify the topic, and then to jot down what you already know about that topic and what you hope to find out by reading the chapter. Each chapter then presents a statement of what you will learn through the chapter—the objective. Next comes an introductory discussion of the strategy to be taught in the chapter and practice using the strategy.

Following this instructional segment are three or more selections in which you apply what you have learned in the opening segments of the chapter. Accompanying most selections are two activities to do before reading: Expanding Your Vocabulary and Getting Ready to Read. Expanding Your Vocabulary features vocabulary from the selection so that you get continued practice in using your understanding of context and word-structure clues to unlock the meaning of unfamiliar words. Getting Ready to Read encourages you to look over a selection before reading. You can complete these activities by yourself or with class members during class time.

Next is a reading selection. Selections are from magazines, books, and textbooks. Exercises follow that you can use to check your understanding. These are either short answer or short essay. In each case, you must apply the strategies learned earlier in the chapter. Additionally, as you read, you will often be asked to record points as margin notes or to circle or underline parts of the text—something you should do in college reading. In some instances, you will find the number of words within a selection written at the end. To calculate your reading rate on a selection, you can use that number and the reading rate chart in the Appendix.

At the ends of selections, you will find exercises for reviewing featured vocabulary. In many cases, the exercises include sentences using the featured words; they provide practice in using sentence clues to unlock the meaning of words.

At the ends of selections, too, you will find suggestions for writing. Sometimes you will be asked to write using knowledge from the selection. Sometimes you will write using the same writing approaches used by the author of the selection. Research shows that writing is a good way to learn content.

A final segment of each chapter provides an opportunity for extending your understanding of the content and vocabulary and for practicing the strategies taught in the chapter.

ACKNOWLEDGMENTS

I want to thank the reviewers who read the manuscript for this book in each of its drafts and who provided suggestions that proved invaluable. I send my thanks to Linda Hatchel, McLennan Community College; Renée Price, Middlesex County College; Carolyn Smith, University of Southern Indiana; Ellen Kaiden, Ramapo College.

In addition, I would like to extend my appreciation to Barbara M. Grant of William Paterson College in Wayne, New Jersey, who has taught college reading courses for many years. She introduced me to the excitement of teaching college reading and contributed numerous ideas and suggestions.

I am grateful, too, for the careful attention to the manuscript by the professionals at Prentice Hall, especially by Frank Hubert, the production editor.

I also thank George Hennings, helpmate and husband, who contributed by locating selections, compiling the glossary, criticizing manuscript, introducing me to word processing, and providing encouragement when the work load became heavy.

DOROTHY GRANT HENNINGS

1

Getting Ready
to Read

Before reading the chapter, read the title, the stated objective, and the headings and subheadings. Ask yourself: What is the topic of the chapter? In the space above and beside the chapter number, jot down what you already know about the topic. Then in the space below the number, jot down at least two questions you hope to answer through reading the chapter.

OBJECTIVE

In this chapter, you will develop a strategy for getting ready to read. Specifically, you will learn to

1. make a general survey of a selection before reading to predict what it is about and how it is put together,
2. think about what you know on a topic before reading about it, and
3. set a purpose for your reading.

INTRODUCTION—GETTING READY TO READ

Reading is a thinking process that sets two people in action together—an author and a reader. The author has a purpose in writing and a message to communicate. In writing a piece, the author chooses the facts and ideas to include, chooses the words to express those facts and ideas, and organizes them in a clear way. In doing this, the author draws on his or her knowledge and feelings about the topic. Obviously, what the author writes in a text determines what you get out of it.

But what you get from a text also depends on what you bring to the reading of that text and your purpose for reading it (see Figure 1.1). One thing that you may bring to the reading of a selection is facts about the topic. You have lots of knowledge that you have built up through firsthand experience and through prior reading. As you read, you connect what is in the text to what you already know about the topic. The more connections you make, the more you get out of a selection when you read.

Because what you get out of a text depends on what you already know about the topic, take three steps before reading a selection.

Step 1. Preview to find out what the selection is about and how it is put together.

Step 2. Think about what you already know on the topic.

Step 3. Set your purpose for reading.

Step 1—Previewing Before Reading

The first step in reading is to preview, or look through, the selection you are going to read. Your reason for previewing is to predict what the selection is about and how it is put together. You should preview before reading informational books, chapters in your textbooks, and articles in newsmagazines, newspapers, and encyclopedias. Previewing a selection gives you a framework for understanding it when you actually begin to read.

Major questions to keep in mind as you preview a selection before reading are: What is the topic of this selection (or what is it about)? How has the author organized his or her ideas on that topic?

To answer these questions,

Figure 1.1 *Reading with Meaning*

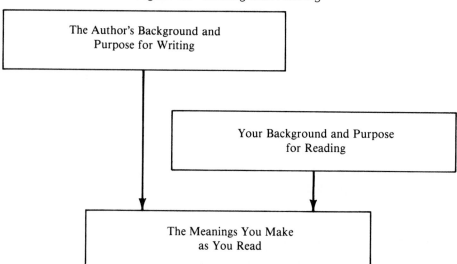

- read and think about the **title.** It often contains a clue to the topic.
- read and think about the name of the **author** if one is given. An author generally sticks to one area, such as economics, biology, history, or fiction, and if you know something about him or her, that can be a clue to the topic.
- read and think about the **headings** that may divide the piece into sections if there are any. The headings provide clues to the subtopics covered in the selection; they are good clues to the way the selection is organized, or put together.
- read and think about the **terms that the author repeats at the beginnings of paragraphs or that are in italics or in bold print.** These terms are clues to the topic, the subtopics, and the way the selection is put together, especially if there are no subheadings.

Before reading the whole selection, also

- read the **introductory paragraph or paragraphs** and the **last, or concluding, ones** if there are any. What clues do these paragraphs provide about the topic and the subtopics covered in the selection? What clues do they provide about the way the selection is put together?
- study the **illustrations**—the photographs, maps, and charts that accompany the selection. They often help you figure out the major focus of a selection. Sometimes the illustrations also give you a clue about the order in which the subtopics are explained.
- look over **margin notes** or **footnotes,** if there are any. They sometimes contain definitions of key terms, which give you a clue to what the selection is about.

Use your preview to predict what the selection is about and how the author has organized it.

Step 2—Thinking About What You Already Know

The next step is to ask yourself, "What do I already know about this topic?" To answer this question, visualize, or picture, things that are discussed in the selection and about which you already know something. For example, if an article is about cathedrals and you have seen pictures of cathedrals, you might visualize one in your head. If an article is about living cells and you have an idea about what a cell looks like, you might draw a rough picture of a cell on paper.

To get yourself ready to read, also talk to yourself in your head. Simply tell yourself what you already know about the subject of the selection. For example, if a selection you are to read is a Greek myth, you might say to yourself before reading, "A myth—that's a story where ancient people tried to explain happenings in nature. The Greeks told stories about their gods and goddesses."

When reading for a college course, you may find it helpful to jot down words that come to your mind about the topic. What you are doing at this stage is brainstorming. In brainstorming, you write down words and thoughts that come to your mind about the topic of the selection.

Step 3—Setting Your Purpose for Reading

The third step is to set your purpose for reading. At this point, knowing what the topic of the selection is and what you already know about that topic, you ask: What do I expect to learn by reading this piece?

With books you choose for personal reading, you know what you hope to get from your reading before you start. On the other hand, as a college student, you may be dealing with assigned readings. You will read these assignments to know more about the subject and to prepare yourself for tests. In this case, identifying several questions before reading guides you as you read. Answering your own questions becomes your purpose for reading.

THE GETTING-READY-TO-READ STRATEGY

In sum, a useful strategy to apply before reading includes these three steps: previewing, thinking about what you already know, and setting your purpose for reading. Figure 1.2 sums up the Getting-Ready-to-Read Strategy.

In the selections that follow, you will have the opportunity to practice the three steps of the Getting-Ready-to-Read Strategy.

---

1. **Preview the selection to predict the topic and the way the selection is put together.** Do this by

   - thinking about the title, the name of the author, and the subheadings;
   - thinking about terms that repeat at the beginning of paragraphs or that are in italics or bold type;
   - reading the first and last paragraphs;
   - studying the illustrations;
   - looking over the margin notes or footnotes, if there are any;
   - asking continuously: What is this selection about? How has the author organized the selection?

2. **Review what you know about the topic.** Do this by

   - asking: What do I already know about the topic?
   - visualizing, or picturing, what you know;
   - telling yourself what you know;
   - brainstorming words and thoughts that come to mind.

3. **Set a purpose to guide your reading.** Ask: What do I expect to learn from reading this selection?

Figure 1.2 *The Getting-Ready-to-Read Strategy*

SELECTION 1: MONEY TALKS (Personal Finance)

Previewing Before Reading

Suppose in the library you pick up a book called *Money Talks* by Bob Rosefsky published in 1989. The cover identifies Rosefsky as "host of the Emmy award winning program on personal finance." On the cover is a quotation from *U.S.A. Today* that calls the book "a comprehensive personal finance guide."

Collaborating with a classmate and based on the information just given, decide what topics you would expect to find discussed in this book. Write your expectations here.

_____

_____

_____

The title of the fourth chapter is "The Smart Shopper." The introduction to the chapter states:

You can be better off by $1000 a year, maybe even more! That's how much you, as a Smart Shopper, can save in your routine shopping for food, pharmaceuticals, clothing, and the like. Not all techniques outlined in this chapter will work for all people. But if you don't try them, you'll never know. Smart Shopper techniques that you'll learn about in this chapter include

- How to recognize built-in bad shopping habits and replace them with good, money-saving habits
- How to cut 10 percent, 20 percent, and even more from your food and pharmaceutical expenses
- How to look good without spending excessively at the clothing store
- How to get the best values for your money when shopping for furniture, appliances, and other big-ticket items

Collaborating with a classmate, decide what kind of information you would expect to find in this chapter. What specific topics do you expect Rosefsky to cover in this chapter? In your own words, write your expectations here.

_____

_____

_____

What do you already know about the topics to be covered by Bob Rosefsky in this chapter? *Brainstorming with a classmate, jot down a few things you know about being a smart shopper.* _____

_____

_____

Now pretend you are about to read a section (actually the second subsection) from "The Smart Shopper." Following are

1. the title and author of the subsection,
2. six introductory paragraphs, and
3. the subheadings.

The actual paragraphs of the selection located beneath each subheading have not been included, since you would not read them as part of your preview. Preview, or look over, the material given. As you do, predict: What is this section about? How is it put together? This section has no concluding paragraph, so you have to rely on the intro-duction and the subheadings to make your predictions.

**1. title
and author:**

SHOPPING FOR CLOTHING AND ACCESSORIES

Bob Rosefsky

". . . That looks absolutely smashing on you. Wear it anywhere, and you'll have the opposite sex enthralled."

". . . That's what absolutely everybody is wearing today. If you want to be with it, you'll buy it now before we run out of stock."

"As long as you're buying the slacks, you ought to get some nice things to go with it. Here's a nice matching sweater."

**2. introductory
paragraphs:**

Vanity, thy name is clothing shopper. Young or old, male or female, few of us are immune to the flattering persuasions of the clothing salesperson. But Smart Shopper *is* immune. Smart Shopper keeps a firm grip on his or her common sense, never letting it succumb to moods, to ego, to fads, or to impulse. Smart Shopper has carefully studied his or her practical needs for clothing and accessories and is willing to take the time to shop for those items that offer the best value (appearance considered) for the money.

Personal appearance is, needless to say, very personal. Clothing is the most costly and the most visible element of your overall personal appearance. Only you can decide how you want to look or how you should look. There's little argument that the well-dressed and well-groomed person can enjoy certain advantages over the poorly groomed or slovenly dressed person. To that extent, appropriately attractive clothing and accessories can be considered an investment in one's social and business well-being.

On the other hand, excessive spending on clothing will not necessarily produce great results. The overly dressed person can be looked upon by his or her peers as extravagant, excessive, or even in poor taste. Given your own individual circumstances—at school, at work, in social activities—you must find the balance that's right for you. And that balance must include both the desired appearance *and* the cost of creating that appearance. It's not the province of this book to suggest how you should look, but the following material can help you with the budget-balancing tricks of affording the look you do want to have.   [345 words]

3. subheadings:

Controlling Ego and Impulse

Embellishing the Simple

Finding the Good Buys

Timing Your Purchases

Buying Seconds

Considering Cleanability and Durability

Based on your preview and collaborating with a classmate, answer these questions:

● What do you predict this section is about? _____

_____

● What kind of information would you expect to find under each subheading? Jot your expectations in the middle column of the following table. Do not use complete sentences.

Subheading	What you predict the section is about	What you already know about this topic
Controlling Ego and Impulse		
Embellishing the Simple		
Finding the Good Buys		
Timing Your Purchases		
Buying Seconds		
Considering Cleanability and Durability		

Thinking About What You Already Know

Talk to a friend about what comes to your mind as you think about shopping for clothing and accessories. What do you think is important? Ask your friend to tell you what comes to his or her mind as you think about each of the subheadings. Jot a few words in the right column of the table.

Setting a Purpose for Reading

If you were to read the selection on shopping for clothing and accessories, what would you expect to learn? Discuss this with a friend who has also previewed the introduction and the subheadings. Together, write three questions that you would hope to answer if you were to read the selection.

If you are interested in this topic and want to read the actual article on shopping for clothing and accessories, get the book *Money Talks* at your library.

SELECTION 2: A NATION ON THE MOVE (History)

Getting Ready to Read

1. *Preview the selection that follows to figure out what it is about and how it is organized.* To do this, turn to pages 9–11. Quickly read, or skim, the title and

the subheadings. Read the first paragraph. Look at the photographs. Then return to this page and answer the questions in the space provided.

● What is the main topic of the selection? (What is it about?) _____

_____

● What subtopics does the selection cover? _____

_____

● In what order are these subtopics covered? _____

_____

● What clues did you use to determine the topics and subtopics? _____

_____

● What kind of information would you expect to find under each subheading? Jot your expectations in the middle column of the table.

Subheading	What you predict the section is about	What you already know about this topic
1. The National Road	_____	_____
	_____	_____
2. Canals	_____	_____
	_____	_____
3. Steamboats	_____	_____
	_____	_____
4. Railroads	_____	_____
	_____	_____

2. *Think about what you already know about the topic.* How did Americans travel west in the early 1800s? Before reading the entire selection, tell yourself or a friend what comes to your mind about westward travel in the 1800s. Talk about such questions as these: How did people travel? How did the trip differ from today? How long did it take? Was it an easy journey? Would I have wanted to make the trip? Why or why not? Then jot whatever you know about the topics identified by the subheadings in the right-hand column of the table. If you know nothing about a subtopic, leave the space blank.

3. *Set your purpose for reading.* Talking about the westward migration, you may have discovered that you know little about some aspect of the topic. What areas will you have to emphasize in your reading? What do you want to find out through reading the selection? What do you expect to learn? In this case, questions you may try to answer through your reading are: What was the National Road? When was it built? Where was it built? Why was it built?

Before reading, write at least four questions that you expect to answer through reading—one to go along with each subheading. Write your questions in the space provided here. Good questions begin with words such as *what, when, where,* and *why.* By writing questions to answer through reading, you are setting a purpose for your reading. You read to answer your questions.

Questions I hope to answer through reading:

_____

_____

_____

_____

Reading with Meaning

Now read the selection. Keep a pen in hand. When you find an answer to one of the what-when-where-why questions you wrote before reading, jot that answer in the margin.

A NATION ON THE MOVE—AMERICA MOVES WEST

Henry Graff

After the War of 1812, Americans turned their attention from the problems of Europe to the promise of a growing nation. Vast changes had begun to take place. One of the most exciting of these was the migrating of people into the region between the Appalachians and the Mississippi. One visitor to the United States said in wonder, "America seems to be breaking up and moving westward."

A problem that faced every family deciding to move west was how to go. There was no easy, direct route to follow. Recognizable roads either did not exist or were of such poor condition that after a heavy rain, wagons and horses simply bogged down in the mud.

The National Road

In 1811 the construction of a road, called the Cumberland or National Road, began. This road would stretch from Cumberland, Maryland, to

Figure 1.3   *The National Road—As each part of the National Road was finished, hundreds of families in Conestoga wagons moved farther west. The road is now called United States Highway 40.*   (Collection of the Maryland Historical Society, Baltimore)

Wheeling, a town in western Virginia. When the road opened seven years later, people by the thousands traveled on it, seeking a new life farther west. Conestogas, or covered wagons, filled with goods bound for market used the road in both directions.

Canals

In the early 1800s shipping goods from one section of the country to another was expensive. The National Road had helped to lower this cost. Still, American businesspeople searched for ways to move freight across the country even more cheaply. A way truly to link the East and the West had to be found. The answer, some thought, was the *canal,* a waterway dug across land for ships to sail through.

DeWitt Clinton, the governor of New York, began in 1817 to push for the construction of a canal linking the Great Lakes with the Atlantic Ocean. Many people considered Clinton's "Big Ditch," as the project was nicknamed, doomed to failure. Finally the massive project got underway. Eight years later the canal stretched from Buffalo, New York, to Albany, New York, on the Hudson River. The Erie Canal, costing $7 million, paid for itself within nine years. Its immense success encouraged other states to begin canal projects.

Steamboats

Americans had always used the natural waterways to transport themselves and their goods from one place to another. When a boat was forced to sail against the current of a river, however, it was impossible to be sure how long the trip would take.

Figure 1.4 *The Erie Canal—Boys walked alongside boats in the Erie Canal, guiding them with ropes to keep them from hitting the banks.*   (I. N. Phelps Stokes Collection Miriam and Ira D. Wallach Division of Art, Prints and Photographs, the New York Public Library, Astor, Lenox and Tilden Foundations)

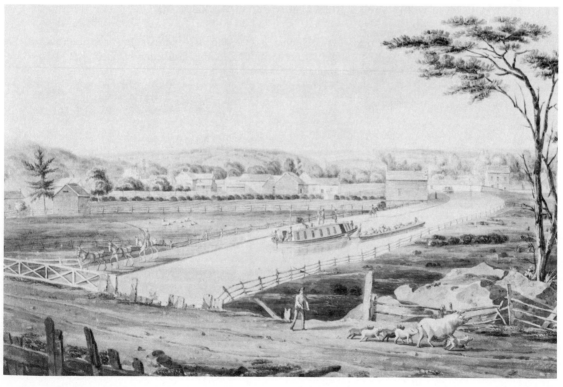

Several Americans worked on an invention—the steamboat—that would greatly aid river travel. They believed that a boat powered by steam engines would be able to move upstream readily against a strong current. When Robert Fulton's *Clermont* sailed up the Hudson River from New York City to Albany in 1807, a new age in travel and transport was born. What was also needed was a faster means of transportation across land.

Railroads

Some Americans were convinced that steam engines could also be used to move wagons faster on land. In 1828 investors in the city of Baltimore began to build a railroad to the Ohio River. The first spadeful of earth was turned by Charles Carroll, the last surviving signer of the Declaration of Independence. The merchants of Baltimore hoped that the railroad would give faster, cheaper service to the West than was then available.

By the 1840s railroad building was going on everywhere. During the 1850s, the amount of railroad track in the United States increased from 9021 miles (14,434 kilometers) to 30,626 miles (49,002 kilometers). The East Coast was now joined to the land beyond the Appalachian Mountains by the iron rails.   [594 words]

Checking for Understanding

Select the best answer to each question. As you answer, feel free to refer to the notes you wrote in the margin while reading. When you have finished, compare your answers with those of a friend. Explain to him or her why you answered as you did.

1. The National Road stretched from
    a. Maine to California.

Figure 1.5   *The First Passenger Railroad in the United States—With the connection between Baltimore and Wheeling, West Virginia, completed in 1853, the Baltimore & Ohio became the first passenger railroad in America. No north-south line was built until after the Civil War.*
(Chicago Historical Society Photo, Baltimore and Ohio R.R. "Atlantic" showing engine and two cars. ICH: 09067)

b. Maryland to western Virginia.

c. Maine to Florida.

d. Albany, New York, to Buffalo, New York.

2. Why was the National Road important?

a. Thousands of people traveled west on it in search of a new life.

b. Goods bound for market were carried west on it.

c. Goods bound for market were carried east on it.

d. All of the above are true.

3. The Erie Canal stretched from

a. Maine to California.

b. Maryland to western Virginia.

c. Maine to Florida.

d. Albany, New York, to Buffalo, New York.

4. Of the following, which is true about the Erie Canal?

a. It was an idea that paid off.

b. It was an idea that never came into being.

c. It was a bad idea that never paid off.

d. It was a project that was stopped before it was completed.

5. What was a disadvantage of boats not powered by steam?

a. They would not go against the current of a river.

b. It was impossible to be sure how long a trip would take when boats were forced to go against the current.

c. They were much more unstable especially when forced to go against the current of a river.

d. They used much more coal than a steamboat.

6. Who was Charles Carroll?

a. the inventor of the steamboat.

b. the inventor of the railroad.

c. the person who developed the idea for the Erie Canal.

d. the person who turned the first spadeful of earth in the building of the railroad that joined the East Coast to the land beyond the Appalachians.

7. In the period from 1840 to 1860, railroad building was

a. almost nonexistent.

b. taking place, but on a very limited scale.

c. taking place on a large scale.

8. Of the following, which came last?

a. the East Coast connected to land beyond the Appalachian Mountains by a railroad.

b. the Erie Canal completed connecting Buffalo, New York, to Albany, New York, on the Hudson River.

c. the first trip by a steamboat.

d. the completion of the National Road.

9. Of the following, which came first?

a. the East Coast connected to land beyond the Appalachian Mountains by a railroad.

b. the Erie Canal completed connecting Buffalo, New York, to Albany, New York, on the Hudson River.

c. the first trip by a steamboat.

d. the completion of the National Road.

Thinking and Writing About What You Have Learned

Answer the following in complete sentences. Think (or talk about the questions with a classmate) before writing.

1. Which do you think was the biggest accomplishment: the building of the National Road, the building of the Erie Canal, or the building of the railroad between Baltimore and Wheeling, West Virginia? Give your reasons.

2. On the map in Figure 1.6, circle the following sites: Cumberland, Maryland; Wheeling, West Virginia; the Great Lakes; Buffalo, New York; Albany, New York; New York City; and Baltimore, Maryland. Label the Appalachian Mountains, which extend from West Virginia into Pennsylvania, and the Atlantic Ocean. Label the Hudson River than runs from Albany to New York City. Plot the locations of the Erie Canal and the National Road. Refer back to the selection to help you plot the locations.

3. Study the locations you have circled on the map. Then use what you have learned from the selection and your map study to answer this question. Why was each of the following important to the growth of our country?

   a. the National Road

   b. the Erie Canal

   c. the steamboat

   d. the railroad across the Appalachians

Figure 1.6   *The Northeastern United States*

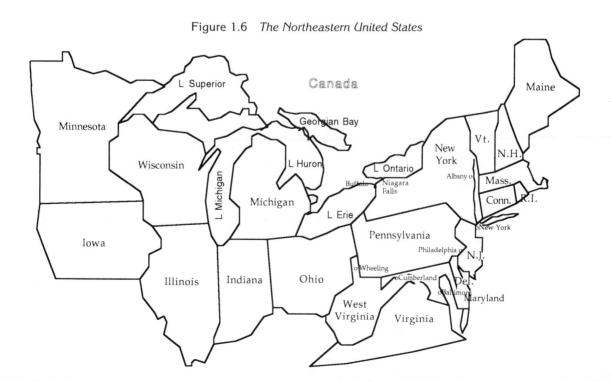

SELECTION 3: FOR HEAVEN'S SAKES, CHOOSE A JOB YOU ENJOY! (Career Planning)

Getting Ready to Read

1. *Preview the selection that follows to figure out what it is about and how it is organized.* Read the title and the first paragraph. Read the subheadings, given in bold. Read the concluding paragraph. Think about the footnote information. Then return to this page and answer the questions in the space provided.

   ● What is the main topic of the selection? (What is it about?) _____

   _____

   ● What kind of information do you expect to learn from the article? _____

   _____

   _____

   ● How many tips does the author supply? How do you know? _____

   _____

   ● What is the author's background? _____

2. *Think about what you already know about the topic.* What do you think is important in choosing a job? Before reading the entire selection, tell yourself or a friend what you already know. Talk about this question. What are some things to keep in mind when you look for a job? Jot a few thoughts here. _____

   _____

   _____

3. *Set your purpose for reading.* Do you have any questions that came to mind as you previewed the article and you thought about the topic?

   Before reading, write several questions to answer through reading. Answering your questions is your purpose for reading.

   _____

   _____

   _____

Reading with Meaning

Now read the selection. Keep a pencil in hand. Write information that answers your purpose-setting questions directly in the margin. A helpful question to answer through reading is: What are seven tips for finding a job I enjoy?

FOR HEAVEN'S SAKES, CHOOSE A JOB YOU ENJOY!

Pat McKinney Sleem*

The Greeks bequeathed to us the wise philosophy *nosce teipsum,* "Know thyself." And since graduating from the Harvard Business School nearly ten

*Pat McKinney Sleem is a Harvard MBA (Master of Business Administration), and a partner in the firm Professional Résumé and Employment Placement (PREP). PREP specializes in résumé preparation by mail.

years ago, I have become convinced of the absolute necessity to apply that wise counsel in one's job choices.

What do you like to do?

As the co-owner of a leading firm in the résumé preparation/career counseling/job placement business, I see a number of people daily making dramatic "career transitions." Most of them tell me they feel they have wasted their time by taking and staying in jobs that were the "wrong fit" for them. Although they had the skills to do the job, they say, they weren't in a job doing the things they liked to do. Eventually they came face-to-face with the grim reality that people can truly excel—and be happy—only when they are doing things that interest them.

Don't ignore what you know about yourself.

A fellow classmate of mine comes to mind. He knew he wanted to work for the auto industry. He knew his goal was line management. He *knew* what he liked to do and what his interests were. But when the consulting companies came courting in the Spring, he got seduced by the big bucks and smitten by the prestige of consulting. When I see him now, he seems dissatisfied. Now, 10 years later, he feels "stuck" and unfulfilled working for a great company in a job he's good at but doesn't particularly enjoy. And the sad part of this story is that even though he knew what his real interests were, he chose a job that didn't "fit" his interests and goals.

Seven Tips for Finding the Job You Enjoy

1. *Do some self-assessment.*

Your interests can change over time. To figure out what interests you now, ask questions that will lead you in the direction of the right job. What gives you the most satisfaction? What is your greatest achievement? Who are the three people whose careers appeal to you most? Name your talents. List the subjects that interest you so much that you have read quite a lot about them.

2. *Forget about money for a moment.*

If your main objective in your job hunt is to sell yourself to the highest bidder, you're likely to end up disappointed with your job. Financial reward will be a natural byproduct of excelling in a job you really enjoy. So identify your real interests and you'll find that monetary rewards will happen.

3. *Who can you talk to who might be a wise sounding board for your ideas?*

Talk to someone who knows you well enough to give you a "second opinion" about what you seem best suited for.

4. *Given what you know about yourself, what specific careers hold the most appeal?*

5. *What is the current job market like in the fields that interest you?*

6. *Get an effective résumé.*

If you decide you want to enter a new field, you may not have the experience required for the job you want. A creative, interest-sparking résumé that "sells" your interests, enthusiasm, and potential will be a necessity.

7. *Finally, take a risk if you have to.*

Successful executives say that "taking risks" has been critical to their job satisfaction. A sobering statistic: only 10% of American workers find their jobs meaningful and more important than their leisure time. Leaving the familiar rut requires bravery, a skill not necessarily refined in classrooms.

In summary, remember too that no job is interesting all the time. A company personnel director told me this once: "Sometimes I think I'd hire someone sight unseen who didn't want a challenging job, because there's lots of unchallenging work to be done around here too!" But take some time to "know yourself" and you *can* find the job that is the "best fit" with your interests.   [690 words]

Checking for Understanding

Once you have read the selection, answer these questions in collaboration with a classmate.

1. What is the topic of this selection? _____

2. During your preview, how accurately did you predict what the author was going to say? _____

3. Pat Sleem gives seven tips for finding an enjoyable job. List here the four you think are the most important.

   a. _____

   b. _____

   c. _____

   d. _____

4. List here the one you think is least helpful to you. _____

SELECTION 4: THE SIGNS OF LIFE (Biology)

Getting Ready to Read

1. *Preview the selection that follows to figure out what it is about and how it is put together.* Read the title, the first paragraph, and the last. Since there are no subheadings to guide your reading, look over the first lines of the other paragraphs looking for words that repeat (which is a good strategy to use when there are no subheadings). Then return to this page and answer these questions.

   ● What words do the authors repeat at the beginning of most paragraphs that are clues to the topic? _____

   ● What is the main topic of the selection? _____

   ● How many characteristics of living things are the authors going to discuss? _____ How do you know? _____
   _____

2. *Think about what you already know about living things.* What makes living things different from nonliving things? Think in specific terms, about living things you know. This is always more helpful than thinking in very general terms.

For example, is a rooster a living thing? Why? What does a rooster have that all living things have? What can a rooster do that all living things can do? Is a rock alive? Why not? In the chart—based on what you already know about living things—write down things about a rooster that make it a living thing. Then write down why you think a rock is not alive—what it cannot do that a rooster can. Make your predictions by talking or collaborating with a friend or two. There are seven slots in the chart because Curtis and Barnes are going to tell you about seven characteristics. If you cannot fill in the seven slots before reading, do just what you can. The rest you will learn by reading the selection.

Characteristics of a Rooster That Make It a Living Thing	Characteristics of a Rock That Make It a Nonliving Thing
1.	
2.	
3.	
4.	
5.	
6.	
7.	

3. *Now set your purpose for reading.* Write a question that you expect to answer by

reading the selection. To do this, start your question with the words "What are . . . ?" Record your question here:

What are _____

Reading with Meaning

Read Selection 4 keeping a pen in hand. You may want to read the selection aloud, taking turns with a friend in your class. Underscore the sentences in the text that tell you the characteristics of living things. You should underscore approximately seven sentences. As you read, put a number in front of each paragraph to indicate the number of the characteristic the authors are discussing at that point. For example, put a number 1 next to the paragraph that begins, "The first characteristic of living things. . . ." This will help you organize your reading because there are no subheadings. As you read, also keep relating what the authors say to the rooster and to the rock we talked about earlier. Although the authors do not mention roosters and rocks, what they say applies to them.

THE SIGNS OF LIFE

Helena Curtis and N. Sue Barnes

Biology is the "science of life." But what do biologists mean when they use the word "life"? Actually, there is no simple definition for this common word. Life does not exist in the abstract. There is no "life," only living things. And living things come in a great variety of forms, from tiny bacteria to giant sequoia trees. All of these, however, share certain properties that, taken together, distinguish them from nonliving objects.

The first characteristic of living things is that they are highly organized. In living things, atoms—the particles of which all matter is composed—are combined into a vast number of very large molecules called macromolecules. Each type of macromolecule has a distinctive structure and a specific function in the life of the organism. Some macromolecules are linked with other macromolecules to form the structures of an organism's body. Others participate in the dynamic processes essential for the continuing life of the organism; among the most significant are the large molecules known as enzymes. Enzymes, with the help of a variety of smaller molecules, regulate all of the processes occurring within living matter. The complex organization of both structures and processes is one of the most important properties of living things.

The second characteristic is closely related to the first: living systems maintain a chemical composition quite different from that of their surroundings. The atoms present in living matter are the same as those in the surrounding environment, but they occur in different proportions and are arranged in different ways. Although living systems constantly exchange materials with the external environment, they maintain a stable and characteristic internal environment.

A third characteristic of living things is the capacity to take in, transform, and use energy from the environment. For example, in the process of photosynthesis, green plants take light energy from the sun and transform it into chemical energy stored in complex molecules. The energy stored in these molecules is used by plants to power their life processes and to build the characteristic structures of the plant body. Animals, which can obtain this stored energy by eating plants, change it into still other forms, such as heat, motion, electricity, and chemical energy stored in the characteristic structures of the animal body.

Fourth, living things can respond to stimuli. Bacteria move toward or away from certain chemical substances; green plants bend toward light; cats pounce on small moving objects. Although different organisms respond to widely varying stimuli, the capacity to respond is a fundamental and almost universal characteristic of life.

Fifth, and most remarkably, living things have the capacity to reproduce themselves so that, generation after generation, organisms produce more organisms like themselves. In each generation, however, there are slight variations between parents and offspring and among offspring.

Most organisms have a sixth characteristic: they grow and develop. For example, before hatching, the fertilized egg of a frog develops into the complex, but still immature, form that we recognize as a tadpole; after hatching, the tadpole continues to grow and undergoes further development, becoming a mature frog. Throughout the world of living things, similar patterns of growth and development occur.

A seventh characteristic of living things is that they are exquisitely suited to their environments. Moles, for instance, are furry animals that live underground in tunnels shoveled out by their large forepaws. Their eyes are small and sightless. Their noses, with which they sense the worm and the other small animals that make up their diet, are fleshy and enlarged. This most important characteristic of living things is known as adaptation.

These characteristics of living things are interrelated, and each depends, to a large extent, on the others. At any given moment in its life, an organism is organized, maintains a stable internal environment, transforms energy, responds to stimuli, and is adapted to its external environment; the organism may or may not be reproducing, growing, and developing, but it possesses the capacity to do so.   [660 words]

Checking for Understanding

Go back to the data chart about the rooster and the rock on page 17. Collaborate, or work together, with your reading partner to correct the predictions you made. Add points that you learned through reading so you have seven reasons why a rooster is a living thing and some reasons why a rock is nonliving. Also answer the question you wrote before reading.

*Collaborating with a partner, use your data chart to answer the following questions. Talk together about each item. Decide if each is a characteristic of living things. Put a check in front of the items that are characteristics of **all** living things. Be ready to support your decision by reading a sentence from the selection. **Do not try to do this from memory.** Use your notes in your data chart.*

_____   1. They are highly organized.

_____   2. They maintain a chemical balance similar to that of their surroundings.

_____   3. They can take in, transform, and use energy from their environment.

_____   4. They transform light energy from the sun into chemical energy.

_____   5. They can respond to stimuli.

_____   6. They respond to the same stimuli.

_____   7. They can reproduce themselves.

_____   8. Offspring do not vary at all from their parents.

_____   9. They are well suited to their environments.

_____   10. They can travel from location to location.

_____   11. They have feelings.

_____   12. They are very happy.

Thinking and Writing About What You Have Learned

Answer the following in complete sentences. Think (or talk about the questions with a classmate) before writing.

1. In reading textbooks with technical terms, the reader sometimes has to work on understanding the meanings of those terms. This is especially true when the author does not provide definitions of technical terms in the margins. A good strategy is to make your own glossary of terms with definitions to use in study. Write definitions of the following terms directly in the margin in the appropriate location just as you would in studying a textbook. Refer to the selection in writing your answers:

   a. atoms   b. enzymes   c. macromolecules   d. photosynthesis

2. In your reading notebook write a paragraph in which you explain in your own words one characteristic of living things. Pick the characteristic that to you is the most striking one. You may be asked to read your paragraph to the class and tell why you picked that characteristic as the most striking one.

SELECTION 5: THE NEW COLOSSUS
(American Literature—Poetry)

Getting Ready to Read

1. *Preview the selection to figure out what it is about. First, read the title and answer the questions in the space provided.*

   ● What is the meaning of the adjective *colossal?* If you do not know its meaning, check in the glossary before reading. _____

   _____

   ● Check the glossary (under the term *colossus*) to find out about the Colossus of Rhodes. What was it? Where did it stand? _____

   _____

   Read the paragraph that introduces the poem.

   ● Who wrote the poem? What was her background? _____

   _____

   _____

   ● Predict: What is the "New Colossus"? _____

- What is the topic of the selection? _____

2. *Next think about what you already know about the topic.* Picture the "New Colossus" in your mind. What does she hold in her hand? Why does she hold this? What does she have on her head? Why does she have this? How big is she? Tell yourself: What does the statue mean to people? What does the statue mean to me?

   With a classmate create a simple idea web, which is a good way to think about a selection that does not have subheadings. To make a web, simply draw lines outward from the central topic word, and jot down several words about the statue, its meaning to you, and its meaning to peoples of the world. Do not write complete sentences—just doodle. Connect related ideas to one another with lines. One or two thoughts are given to get you started.

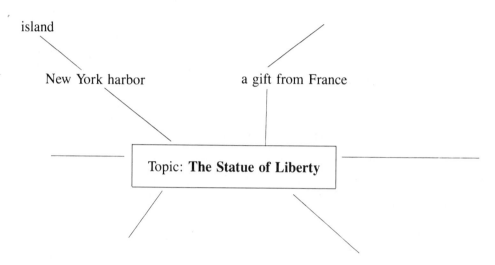

   Making an idea web like this is a useful way to think about what you already know about any subject you will read.

3. *Set your purpose for reading.* Remember that this is a poem, and in writing poetry rather than prose, authors are often more concerned about expressing feelings rather than facts. Because the author's purpose is different, your purpose may be something other than to get information. Write your purpose for reading.

   _____

   Listen as your instructor reads "The New Colossus" aloud to you. Or read the poem aloud to yourself or to a classmate. As you listen or read, keep your purpose in mind.

Reading with Meaning

THE NEW COLOSSUS

Emma Lazarus

Emma Lazarus was born in New York City in 1849. Throughout her life, which was short, Lazarus had two major interests: the Jewish people who had come to America and poetry. Her poem, "The New Colossus," is engraved on the base of the Statue of Liberty, which is located in New York Harbor near Ellis Island.

Not like the brazen giant of Greek fame,
With conquering limbs astride from land to land;
Here at our sea-washed, sunset gates shall stand
A mighty woman with a torch, whose flame
Is the imprisoned lightning, and her name
Mother of Exiles. From her beacon-hand
Glows world-wide welcome; her mild eyes command
The air-bridged harbor that twin cities frame.
"Keep, ancient lands, your storied pomp!" cries she
With silent lips. "Give me your tired, your poor,
Your huddled masses yearning to breathe free,
The wretched refuse of your teeming shore.
Send these, the homeless, tempest-tost to me.
I lift my lamp beside the golden door!"

Checking for Understanding

Answer these questions either by yourself or with a classmate.

1. Who is the "mighty woman with a torch"? _____

2. Why do you think Emma Lazarus called the "mighty woman" the Mother of Exiles? Think about Lazarus's background and interests as you answer this question. _____

   _____

   _____

3. To whom is Lazarus referring when she writes about the "huddled masses yearning to breathe free"? _____

4. How does the poet feel about those "huddled masses"? _____

   _____

5. How do those "huddled masses" feel as they approach the shores of their new land? _____

   _____

6. What does the Statue of Liberty mean to new immigrants? _____

   _____

7. What does the Statue of Liberty mean to you? _____

   _____

Thinking and Writing About What You Have Learned

In the poem, "The New Colossus," Emma Lazarus spoke for the Statue of Liberty. Try your hand at poetry. Collaborating with a friend, write a few lines in which you pretend to be an inanimate, or nonliving, object, such as Niagara Falls, the Golden Gate Bridge in San Francisco harbor, the ship *Queen Elizabeth II,* the faces cut in the rock at Mt. Rushmore, or Mt. St. Helens. Do not worry about rhyming or producing a perfect poem; just get down some thoughts and feelings.

EXTENDING WHAT YOU HAVE LEARNED

Reviewing the Strategies

In this chapter, you have been applying the three steps of the Getting-Ready-to-Read Strategy. What are those three steps? Tell yourself the steps. Then outline them here.

1.

2.

3.

Reread the directions beneath the title on the first page of this chapter. If you follow those directions before reading the chapter, you are applying the Getting-Ready-to-Read Strategy. You will find similar directions at the beginning of each chapter to help you preview before reading.

Incidentally, most college textbooks have blank space at the beginning of chapters. Use that space to jot down what you know about the topic before reading. Use it, too, to write down questions you hope to answer through your reading. Also keep a pen in hand to jot down points as you read. Jotting down points as you go along helps you keep your mind on the topic.

Applying the Strategies to Your Independent Reading

Find a selection that you want to read or one that has been assigned to you in a course you are taking. Apply the three steps of the Getting-Ready-to-Read Strategy. Before you read, in your reading notebook

- Record your predictions about what the selection is about.
- Tell yourself what you already know about the subject. Then in your notebook, write a few words that come to your mind on that topic.
- Establish a purpose before reading; write in your notebook some questions you hope to answer by your reading.
- Bring your notebook to class so that you can share your predictions and thoughts.

2

Unlocking the Meaning of Words: Using Context Clues

Before reading the chapter, read the title, the stated objective, and the headings and subheadings. Ask yourself: What is the topic of the chapter? In the space above and beside the chapter number, jot down what you already know about the topic. Then in the space below the number, jot down at least two questions you hope to answer through reading the chapter.

OBJECTIVE

In this chapter, you will develop strategies for figuring out the meaning of an unfamiliar word through the use of context clues, or the surrounding words in a sentence. Specifically, you will learn how to use

1. definitions built directly into a sentence, or given in a margin note or footnote in a textbook,
2. synonyms placed near the word,
3. explanations and descriptions given in the paragraph,
4. words that express contrasting, or opposite, meanings,
5. the overall sense, or meaning, of a sentence.

INTRODUCTION—
UNLOCKING THE MEANING OF UNFAMILIAR WORDS

As you read, you may meet unfamiliar words. What can you do to figure out their meaning?

When you encounter an unfamiliar word in reading, you should look at the surrounding words in the sentence, or the **context clues.** You should study

- definitions, synonyms, and explanations built directly into a sentence or placed in the margin;

- contrasting phrases and words of opposite meaning (**antonyms**) found close by; and

- the overall meaning of the sentence in which the word occurs.

Context clues
Surrounding words in a sentence

Synonym A word with almost the same meaning as another

Antonym A word with the opposite meaning from another

If you can't get the meaning of a word from the context, check the glossary found at the back of the book or a dictionary.

Sometimes context clues are very explicit; the author defines a difficult term in the sentence. To help the reader, the author may set technical terms in italics or boldfaced type. The author may also use a **synonym** (a word with almost the same meaning) near the unfamiliar term. In textbooks, the author may provide a definition as a footnote or in the margin as we have done here. If there are definitions in the margin, read them during your preview. If there are not, you may make your own margin notes of technical terms after you have read a paragraph. Just write the definitions of key terms in the margin as you read.

How do you think about context clues? Take, for example, the word *synonym*. In the previous paragraph, the phrase "a word with almost the same meaning" defines the term *synonym*. The definition is also in the margin. Similarly, the definition of the word *context* is built into the text—"the surrounding words in the sentence." It is also in the margin.

Sometimes, context clues are not so clear. You must consider an entire sentence and even surrounding sentences to figure out the meaning of an unfamiliar word.

For example, study the sentence in the third paragraph in which the word *explicit* is used. The sentence reads, "Sometimes context clues are very explicit; the author defines a difficult term in the sentence." What does that explanation tell you about the meaning of the word *explicit?* It hints that when things are explicit, they are very clear.

But there is another clue to the meaning of *explicit* in the text. The fifth paragraph begins, "Sometimes, context clues are not so clear." Here is a contrast to the sentence, "Sometimes context clues are very explicit." Thinking about the two sentences, you can figure out that *explicit* means the opposite of "not so clear." *Explicit* means "clearly set forth."

Sometimes the only clue to the meaning of a word is the overall meaning of the sentence. In that case, you should try to substitute a word that you know for the unfamiliar one to see if it makes sense. What you are doing is seeing if the word you know works in that context. If it does, you have a clue to the meaning of the unfamiliar word.

The Clue	An Example	Notes About the Example
Definition	*Archaeology* is the scientific study of prehistoric cultures by excavation of their remains.	Definition is given directly in the sentence.
	Through *archaeology,* the scientific study of prehistoric cultures by excavation of their remains, we have learned much about our human ancestors.	Definition is given next to the term, set off by commas.
	Through *archaeology*—the scientific study of prehistoric cultures by excavation of their remains—we have learned much about our human ancestors.	Definition is given next to the term, set off by dashes.
	Through *archaeology* (the scientific study of prehistoric cultures by excavation of their remains), we have learned much about our human ancestors.	Definition is given next to the term, set off in parentheses.
Description	A *paramecium* is a microscopic organism. Made up of one small cell, the paramecium is shaped like a slipper and has a deep groove down its side. It lives in fresh water.	A complete description is included that gives a complete picture of the object being defined.
Synonym (word with the same meaning)	Reducing the blood cholesterol has a number of *beneficial* results. One positive outcome is a lessening of the chances of heart attack.	The word *positive* is set near its synonym, *beneficial.* You can relate *beneficial* to *positive,* and in that way figure out the meaning of *beneficial.*
Antonym (word with the opposite meaning)	Her taste tends toward *pastels.* In contrast, I prefer sharp colors like bright red or deep purple.	The word *pastels* is set near a phrase with nearly the opposite meaning. Using the words *in contrast,* you can pick up the contrast and reason that pastels are less bright, more muted.

Figure 2.1   *Context Clues*

For example, in the sentence "The thirsty man yearned for a drink of water," you might think: "I can substitute the word *craved* for *yearned.* Therefore, *yearned* may mean the same as *craved.* The thirsty man wanted a drink very much."

Figure 2.1 summarizes types of context clues and examples of each. In each example sentence in Figure 2.1, circle the word or words that define the italicized term.

PRACTICING USE OF CONTEXT CLUES

Use the context of these sentences to figure out the meaning of each italicized word. Circle the term that is closest in meaning to the italicized one. Jot down next to each item the sentence clue you used to find the meaning (e.g., definition, synonym, or explanation given in the text; word of opposite meaning found close by; the overall meaning of the sentence). Reread Figure 2.1 if you have trouble using context clues.

1. She took some deep breaths to *alleviate* the nervousness she felt before the swim meet.
   a. lessen   c. elevate
   b. motivate   d. evoke

2. He *brooded* over the loss of his summer job, wondering if anything he said could have made a difference.
   a. forgot   c. worried
   b. paid a great deal of money   d. hatched

3. He felt *contempt* for all those who would not stand up for their beliefs.
   a. respect   c. love
   b. scorn   d. concern

4. She did her exercises each day at the hour *designated;* when she got sick, however, she could not exercise when she was supposed to.
   a. that was assigned   c. that was best for her
   b. that she requested   d. that was part of her design

5. It's hard to do an *improvisation* in drama class because you have to make up your lines as you go along.
   a. a bad performance   c. a performance without preparation
   b. a good performance   d. a performance done alone

6. The shy boy spoke so softly that his voice was practically *inaudible*.
   a. unable to be heard   c. unable to be seen
   b. unable to be enjoyed   d. without variation

7. We saw the axe neatly *cleave* the board in two.
   a. make into something else   c. hold up
   b. split   d. make clean

8. When she first began training, she was a *novice* at the sport, and her movements were awkward.
   a. an expert   c. a beginner
   b. a young woman   d. a helper

9. As the wind grew even stronger, the mountain climber came *perilously* close to losing his grip.
   a. dangerously   c. permanently
   b. practically   d. ridiculously

10. Because his movements were so *subtle*, I was hardly aware he was moving at all.
    a. clear   c. extreme
    b. slight   d. wonderful

11. The paintings in her collection appealed to my *aesthetic* sense.
    a. philosophical   c. scientific
    b. mathematical   d. artistic

12. The cat jumped from one window ledge to the next with amazing *agility;* we were impressed at the ease with which the animal made the difficult jumps.
    a. nimbleness   c. clumsiness
    b. speed   d. care

SELECTION 1: ON GEOLOGY (Earth Science)

Here are some sentences from the introduction to a college physical science textbook. In each sentence, there is an italicized word or phrase. Use the context to figure out the meaning of the word. Then write down how you unlocked the meaning. Finally, write the meaning in the space provided. The first two are completed as a model of how to do it.

ON GEOLOGY

Charles Cazeau, Robert Hatcher, and Francis Siemankowski

1. It is morning and you are having breakfast in the kitchen. You test your cup of coffee to see how hot it is and *leisurely* unfold the newspaper.

> "Leisurely — it is breakfast time, morning. It appears you are getting ready to drink your coffee and you are relaxing, since you are going to read the newspaper. <u>Leisurely</u> must mean 'taking your time' — in a relaxed, unhurried way."

2. As usual, you think, there is bad news in the world. An earthquake in Chile has left many dead and thousands homeless. They say the *intensity* of the earthquake was 8.1 on the Richter scale, whatever that means.

> "The Richter scale must be a scale for measuring earthquakes. The intensity on this scale was 8.1. The 8.1 must tell how great the earthquake was — how powerful. <u>Intensity</u> must mean strength."

3. Hawaii is *bracing* for the arrival of large sea waves triggered by the quake.

4. Another item catches your eye. "Flooding in the Midwest. Several towns *inundated,* and men paddling boats through the streets."

5. At the bottom of the page the newspaper notes that scientists are still observing a new volcano that appeared a few days ago in the north Atlantic. The volcano is *spewing* out ash and cinders amid thunderous explosions.

6. You turn the page and take another sip of coffee. Ah, here are, perhaps, more *relevant* matters on the local news front.

7. In addition to the *furor* over the severe pollution of the lake, a manufacturer is accused of polluting the groundwater supply by pumping acids and other wastes into a disposal well.

8. In this *hypothetical* situation you started your day, perhaps without realizing it, by reading a series of geological reports.

9. All the items noted share one thing in common. They involve geology. *Geology* is the study of the earth.

10. The *overall* objective of the geologist is to try to answer questions concerning the earth's physical nature, both past and present.

11. Of equal concern to the geologist is the application of this knowledge to certain problems that beset human beings as they *wrest* from the earth the things that they need (e.g., oil, gas, water, metals, construction materials).

12. In attempting to understand the nature of the earth, geologists study the rocks that make up its outer *crust.*

13. These rocks might be thought of as documents that have *survived* through millions of years yet carry within them the clues to past events.

14. Geologists seek to unlock these secrets by careful study of rock records, not only in their natural outdoor settings, but by subjecting samples of these rocks to further *scrutiny* in the laboratory.

15. In addition the geologist must pay close attention to forces *operative* at the earth's surface (e.g., wind, wave, and stream action) and forces *operative* within the earth.

In the next three sections of this chapter, you will read selections that contain some words that may be new to you. Use the context in which these words are used to figure out, or analyze, their meanings as you read.

SELECTION 2: THE COMPUTER AS A MIND TOOL
(Computer Science)

Getting Ready to Read

Look over the following selection before reading. Quickly read the title and first paragraph. Then return here and answer these questions.

● What is the selection about? _____

● Have you ever used a computer? If so, for what purpose? Was it a help to you? What thoughts come to your mind when you think about a computer? How do

you feel about computers? _____

_____

_____

Reading with Meaning

Now read the selection, keeping this special question in mind: What is the meaning of each technical term used? To answer this question, relate the term to the context in which it occurs.

THE COMPUTER AS A MIND TOOL
Patrick McKeown

In *Megatrends,* his popular book on the direction of Western society, John Naisbitt discusses the many trends that currently affect our lives. One important concept that he presents is the **information society**—that is, a society in which the majority of the workers are involved in the transmittal, or sending, of information. Naisbitt notes that we have undergone a transition from an agrarian society to an industrial society to the current information society.

The tools for such a society have existed for some time. These tools include the adding machine, the typewriter, the file cabinet, the television, and the telephone. The adding machine helps us work with numbers, the typewriter facilitates our work with characters, the file cabinet stores information in an easily retrievable fashion, the television portrays our ideas in pictures, and the telephone allows us to communicate with others instantaneously.

However, the key element in the transition from an industrial society to an information society is a "wonder" called a computer. The agrarian society depended on the metal plow and wheel, and the industrial society depended on the steam engine. The information society depends on the computer. Because the computer facilitates the work of the mind rather than manual labor, we refer to it as a mind tool—that is, a tool that extends, but does not replace, the human mind.

The key idea behind the computer as a mind tool is that it performs all of the operations performed by the adding machine, typewriter, file cabinet, television, and telephone. On a computer, we can manipulate numbers as we do on a calculator (add, subtract, divide, multiply, and so on), we can manipulate letters of the alphabet as we do on a typewriter, and we can have the computer draw pictures based on these manipulations. Any of these symbols may be stored within the computer. Finally, we can communicate with other computer users over a telephone line. If a computer can do all of these things, just exactly how would it be described? Briefly, a **computer** is a machine that stores and manipulates symbols based on a series of user instructions called a program. This ability to execute a list of instructions differentiates the computer from a calculator or other office machines.

In addition to the computer's ability to perform all these tasks, two important characteristics of the computer make it the catalyst that generated the information society. These characteristics are speed and accuracy. The speed of a computer's operations is measured in *nanoseconds*— billionths of a second—and the computer does *exactly* what it is instructed to do. These two characteristics can also lead to problems when the computer is given the wrong instructions. In this case, the computer quickly performs incorrect operations!　　[464 words]

Checking for Understanding of Words

In the selection, underline the nine words or phrases listed here. Then circle the phrases in the selection that give you clues to the meaning of each of the underlined items. Write the definitions on the lines provided. If you are unsure of a meaning, check the glossary. Be ready to tell how you unlocked the meaning of each word or phrase.

1. an information society _____

_____

2. a mind tool _____

_____

3. manipulate numbers _____

_____

4. a computer _____

_____

5. nanosecond _____

_____

6. a computer program _____

_____

7. agrarian (The definition is not given explicitly. You must figure it out from

words used in relation to it—"plow and wheel.") _____

_____

8. manual labor (The definition is not given explicitly. You must figure it out by contrasting manual labor with "the work of the mind.") _____

_____

9. catalyst (Figure this one out based on the meaning of "generated." If you run into problems, check the glossary.) _____

_____

Being able to figure out the meanings of technical terms is very important as you read college texts. You can use this same strategy in your college reading:

- Underline each unfamiliar technical term.
- Circle words or phrases that are clues to the meaning of the term.
- Check the glossary or a dictionary when you are uncertain.
- Write in your notebook or in the margin of your textbook definitions of words you will need to know.

SELECTION 3: PRENATAL DEVELOPMENT
(Developmental Psychology)

Getting Ready to Read

Preview the selection by reading the title, the first paragraph, and the margin notes. Then answer the following questions.

- What is the selection about? _____

- What do you think contributes to a child's healthy development during the period before he or she is born? _____

_____

- Predict: What kind of information will this article give you about the topic?

_____

- For what purpose does this author use margin notes? _____

_____

Reading with Meaning

Read this selection from a psychology textbook. Think about the italicized words as you read. Use the context in which the words are used to predict their meaning. The names and dates in parentheses tell who the author is quoting and when the research quoted was published. This material takes the place of footnotes that are sometimes used to give this same information.

PRENATAL DEVELOPMENT

Charles Morris

Scientists once thought that the development of the child before birth was simply a process of physical growth. Only at birth, they believed, did experience and learning begin to influence psychological development. Today, we know that the unborn baby is *profoundly* affected by its environment. Some experts, such as psychologist Leni Schwartz, have even gone so far as to say that "the most important time in our lives may well be the time before we were born." (Spezzano, 1981)

The Prenatal Environment

During the earliest period of *prenatal* (before birth) *development,* survival is the most important issue. Immediately after *conception,* the fertilized egg divides many times, beginning the process that will change it from a one-celled organism into a highly complex human being. The cell ball implants itself in the uterus, and around it grows a *placenta,* which carries food to it and waste products from it as the organism grows. In time, the major organ systems and physical features develop. If all goes well, by the end of this stage of development the organism is recognizably human and is now called a *fetus.* The fetal period begins in the eighth week after conception and lasts until birth. (It is usually early in this period that a woman discovers that she is pregnant.) The important role of this period is the preparation of the fetus for independent life.

From the second week after *conception* until birth, the baby is linked to its mother, and thus to the outside world, through the placenta. Many changes in the mother's body chemistry, whether as a result of nutrition, drugs, disease, or *prolonged* stress or excitement, affect the fetus directly through the placenta. However, the placenta is not merely a *passive* tube connecting mother and fetus; it is an active organ with some ability to select and provide

Prenatal development Physical and psychological changes in an organism before birth

Placenta Organ that connects the developing fetus to the mother's body, providing nourishment to it and filtering out some harmful substances

Fetus An unborn infant at least eight weeks old

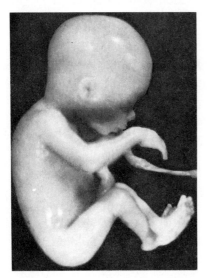

Figure 2.2   *A Five-month Old Human Fetus.*
(Dr. Landrum Shettles)

substances that the developing fetus needs. Unfortunately, although it can filter out some harmful substances, it cannot protect the fetus from the *toxic* effects of alcohol, narcotics, medications, and a variety of other chemicals.

Good nutrition is at least as important for the fetus as it is for us. Yet many mothers, especially in developing countries, *subsist* on diets that are not substantial enough to nourish them or their babies properly. Even in the United States, expectant mothers' diets are often inadequate. Malnutrition in the prenatal period can result in seriously deprived babies and often permanent damage. These babies may have smaller brains and bodies and be weak, listless, and disease-prone (Stechler & Halton, 1982). During childhood, they often show *impaired* intellectual functioning that is usually difficult or impossible to improve.

Besides malnutrition, drugs *constitute* a particular threat to the unborn child. If the mother is a heavy drinker, her baby may be born mentally retarded, be unusually small and slow to develop, and suffer from other serious *abnormalities* (Clarren & Smith, 1978). If the mother is a heavy user of drugs, her baby may be born with an addiction and may experience withdrawal symptoms immediately after birth. If she smokes, the baby may be premature, underdeveloped, or deformed (Evans, Newcombe, & Campbell, 1979).

Certain diseases can also injure the fetus, particularly early in pregnancy. German measles (rubella) is especially dangerous and leads to eye damage, heart malformations, deafness, and mental retardation. Other diseases, such as syphilis and diabetes, can also produce defects in the fetus.

Moreover, prolonged stress or excitement on the part of the mother can directly affect the health of the fetus. There is some evidence that when pregnant women experience emotional stress, their fetuses move more frequently and forcefully than usual (Sontag, 1964). In one study, it was found that women who were under severe stress (most often from extremely unhappy marriages) gave birth more often to children who were sickly and slow to develop and whose behavior was *abnormal*. Critics of these and similar studies have pointed out, however, that the connection between maternal stress and developmental problems in children is by no means clear. For example, since many of the mothers under stress in their studies were also poor, it may have been that growing up in a deprived household was more responsible for the children's problems than was prenatal stress (Sameroff & Chandler, 1975).

It is possible to detect many fetal disorders before the baby is born, using the technique of *amniocentesis* (the technique of collecting cells cast off by the fetus into the fluid of the womb and testing them for genetic abnormalities). Moreover, it should be kept in mind that despite the hazards to the fetus that we have mentioned, most babies develop normally. If a pregnant woman is careful to eat well, maintain her health, and avoid exposure to harmful substances and communicable diseases, she should not worry about whether stress at home or on the job will harm her child. Young children are *resilient* and with proper care can often recover completely from minor problems related to prenatal development. As human beings, we have a long period of childhood, and most of our development occurs after we have been born.   [847 words]

Checking for Understanding of Featured Words

Underline these terms in the selection and circle the words in the selection that are clues to their meaning. Then circle the definition for each item listed here. Check the glossary if you are uncertain. You may collaborate with a friend.

1. prenatal
   a. related to nations or governments
   b. related to the period before birth
   c. related to a premonition, or prethought
   d. related to natural events
2. profoundly
   a. very sincerely   c. very greatly
   b. very tenderly   d. very slightly
3. conception
   a. point at which a woman becomes pregnant
   b. point at which a ball of cells becomes a fetus
   c. point at which a woman knows she is pregnant
   d. point at which a woman gives birth
4. fetus
   a. an unborn child
   b. an unborn child at least three weeks old
   c. an unborn child at least eight weeks old
   d. a newly born child
5. placenta
   a. the cell ball that implants itself in the uterus
   b. the fertilized egg
   c. a one-celled body
   d. the organ that connects the fetus to the mother's body and provides nourishment to it
6. prolonged
   a. extended over a period of time
   b. slight
   c. personal
   d. intense, impossible to endure
7. passive
   a. not active   c. passing materials through
   b. connecting   d. in a position to get excited
8. toxic
   a. alcoholic   c. medical
   b. poisonous   d. chemical
9. subsist
   a. keep alive   c. nourish
   b. continue   d. conceive
10. impaired
    a. impossible   c. improved
    b. damaged   d. thoughtless
11. constitute
    a. threaten   c. make up
    b. cause   d. warn of

12. abnormalities
    a. deviations from the standard
    b. impossible happenings
    c. permanent changes
    d. physical and psychological changes in an organism before birth
13. amniocentesis
    a. the organ that nourishes the developing fetus
    b. abnormalities that appear at birth
    c. the technique of collecting cells cast off by the fetus into the fluid of the womb and testing them for genetic abnormalities
    d. physical and psychological changes in an organism before birth
14. resilient
    a. passive   c. residual
    b. underdeveloped   d. able to spring back

SELECTION 4: PERSON MARKETING (Business)

Getting Ready to Read

Preview the selection that starts on this page. Read the title and the first paragraph. Then answer these questions.

- What is the selection about? _____

- What do you think "marketing a person" means? What does the word *marketing* mean in this context? _____

  _____

- Predict: What kinds of things can be done to market a person? _____

  _____

Read on to see if your prediction is right.

Reading with Meaning

Think about the italicized words as you read this selection from a marketing textbook. Use the context in which the words are used to predict their meaning.

PERSON MARKETING

Philip Kotler and Gary Armstrong

People are marketed. Person *marketing* consists of activities undertaken to create, maintain, or change attitudes or behavior toward particular people. All kinds of people and organizations practice person marketing. Politicians market themselves to get votes and program support. Entertainers and sports figures use marketing to *promote* their careers and improve their incomes. Professionals such as doctors, lawyers, accountants, and architects market themselves in order to build their reputations and increase business. Business leaders use person marketing as a tool to develop their company's fortunes as well as their own. Businesses, charities, sports teams, fine arts groups, religious groups, and other organizations also use person marketing. Creating, *flaunting,* or associating with well-known personalities often helps these organizations to better achieve their goals.

Here are two examples of successful person marketing:

● Lee Iacocca, the heavily marketed chairman of Chrysler Corporation, is highly visible. His direct, dramatic, and blunt style commands attention and respect. In Chrysler ads, Iacocca levels with consumers, *conveying* confidence and trust. In a typical press conference, he might attack the timid U.S. trade policy toward Japan, praise Chrysler cars and workers, speak out on the federal deficit, advise broadly on how to tackle tomorrow's business problems, and again deny that he will run for president. Iacocca's *visibility* helps Chrysler sell cars and gain the support of important consumer, financial, employee, government, media, and other publics. Iacocca's visibility is no accident; his *transformation* into a celebrity was as *deliberate* as the manufacture of his cars.

● Michael Jordan, star of the Chicago Bulls, possesses remarkable basketball skills—great court sense with quick, fluid moves and the ability to *soar* above the rim for dramatic dunks. And he has an appealing, unassuming personality to go along with his *dazzling* talents. All of this makes Michael Jordan very marketable. After graduating from college, Jordan signed on with ProServ Inc., a well-known sports management agency. The agency quickly negotiated a *lucrative* five-year contract with the Bulls, paying Jordan some $4 million. But that was just the beginning. ProServ decided to market Jordan as the new Dr. J. of basketball—a supertalented good guy and solid citizen. Paying careful attention to placement and staging, the agency booked Jordan into the talk-show circuit, accepted only the best products to *endorse,* insisted on only high-quality commercials, arranged appearances for charitable causes, and even had him appear as a fashion model. Jordan's market *soared,* and so did his income. Person marketing has paid off *handsomely* for Michael Jordan. . . . Jordan recently signed a new eight year, $25 million contract with the Bulls and current *endorsements* for Nike, Wilson, Coca-Cola, Johnson Products, McDonald's, and other companies earn Jordan an additional $4 million a year.

The objective of person marketing is to create a "celebrity"—a well-known person whose name *generates* attention, interest, and action.   [479 words]

Checking Your Ability to Use Context Clues

Find each of these words in the selection on person marketing. Using context clues, figure out the meaning of each. In many cases, you can substitute a word you know for the highlighted word. Write a very short definition or a synonym for each word. That definition can be one or two words. If you have trouble, check the glossary or a dictionary, as you would have to do if there were no glossary.

1. marketing

2. promote

3. flaunting

4. conveying

5. visibility

6. transformation

7. deliberate

8. soar

9. dazzling

10. lucrative

11. endorse

12. handsomely

13. generates

REVIEWING CHAPTER VOCABULARY

Using Context Clues

Select the word from the list that best fits the context of each sentence. Use each word only once. Consult the glossary for help if you need it.

a. abnormalities	d. passive	g. resilient
b. constitutes	e. profoundly	h. subsist
c. impaired	f. prolonged	i. toxic

1. Many environmentalists are concerned about the masses of _____ wastes that humankind is producing.

2. Because of the mother's _____ exposure to radioactive materials, the fetus was malformed.

3. The child's vision was _____ because he looked directly into the sun.

4. Children are very _____; they bounce back quickly even after a prolonged illness.

5. There is much controversy over what _____ child abuse.

6. Citizens should not remain _____ onlookers; they should take an active role in the community.

7. I was _____ affected by what I saw; as a result, I now take a less passive role in school activities.

8. Doctors are seeing _____ that are a result of a mother's drug dependency.

9. The explorers had to _____ on berries and roots when they lost all of their supplies.

Using More Context Clues

Use each of these technical terms in the appropriate sentence.

a. amniocentesis   c. fetus   e. prenatal
b. conception   d. placenta

1. _____ occurs when the sperm unites with an egg.

2. _____ is a technique for determining genetic abnormalities before the birth of a baby.

3. The _____ period is the period before birth.

4. The _____ is an unborn infant at least eight weeks old.

5. The _____ is the organ that connects the fetus to its mother.

Using Words in Sentences

Try to write a sentence with a context clue that hints at the meaning of the word. If you have a problem, model your sentences after the ones on pages 27–28 or those in the glossary.

1. alleviate

2. brooded

3. contempt

4. designated

5. improvisation

6. inaudible

7. cleave

8. novice

9. perilously

10. subtle

11. aesthetic

12. agility

Doing More with Context

Put these words into the sentence blanks. Use the context to decide. Use each word only once. Be ready to explain the sentence clue you used.

a. bracing	d. inundated	g. relevant	i. spewing
b. hypothetical	e. leisurely	h. scrutiny	j. wrest
c. intensity	f. operative		

1. Our trip was a _____ one; we took our time. As a result we returned home relaxed and full of energy.

2. Make sure that all the information you put into your report is _____; unrelated ideas will confuse the reader.

3. The weather reporter predicted a storm of great _____ with much rain and wind.

4. Because the volcano was _____ out lava, we could not go near it.

5. The professor subjected the students' papers to careful _____ before assigning a grade.

6. I tried to _____ the gun from his hand, but I could not get it away.

7. Because we were _____ for a severe storm, we were pleasantly surprised when there was only a little shower.

8. On the exam we had to devise a _____ plan telling what we would have done if we had been there.

9. Near the end of the semester, students often feel _____ with work; so much work comes their way that they do not know where to begin.

10. We studied the forces _____ within society during the Civil War.

Reviewing More Words

Put these words into the sentence blanks. Use the context to decide. Use each word only once. Be ready to explain the sentence clue you used.

a. convey	e. flaunt	h. lucrative	k. transform
b. dazzle	f. generate	i. market	l. soared
c. deliberate	g. handsomely	j. promoting	m. visibility
d. endorsed			

1. Today there are companies such as ProServ Inc. that attempt to _____ celebrities such as Michael Jordan.

2. One outcome of person marketing is increased _____ of the person, who may now be seen very commonly on TV.

3. His purpose for appearing on TV was to _____ the message that he was a warm and human person.

4. One side effect was that he was able to _____ considerable interest in the charity that he was _____.

5. When the celebrity _____ the product, sales _____. They climbed to unprecedented heights.

6. The marketing agency was able to _____ her image. She went from being thought of as a shy person to being considered an outgoing, interesting woman.

7. The outcome was that she won several very _____ contracts that made her a multimillionaire. In short, her efforts paid off _____.

8. What she did was a _____ effort to promote herself. Everything she did was intentional.

9. The star basketball player would _____ his success by bragging about how much he earned.

10. But on the court, he would _____ everyone with his speed, accuracy, and skill.

EXTENDING WHAT YOU HAVE LEARNED

Reviewing Your Understanding of Context Clues

In your notebook, write a brief paragraph in which you present at least three steps to use in attacking new words you meet in reading. Be sure to tell something about context clues.

Applying the Strategies to Your Reading

1. Read a column from the editorial page of a newspaper. As you read, underline three or four words that are rather new to you. In the margin of the article jot down the meanings of the words as you figured them out from the context. Be ready to share your new words with the class and tell how you figured out the meanings.

2. Starting in Chapter 4, before each reading selection you will find sentences with new words from the selection. Use your understanding of context clues to unlock the meanings of these words as you work through the text during the semester.

3

*Unlocking
the Meaning
of Words:
Using Word-Structure Clues*

Before reading the chapter, read the title, the stated objective, and the headings and subheadings. Ask yourself: What is the topic of the chapter? In the space above and beside the chapter number, jot down what you already know about the topic. Then in the space below the number, jot down at least two questions you hope to answer through reading the chapter.

OBJECTIVE

In this chapter, you will develop strategies for figuring out the meaning of an unfamiliar word through the use of word structures, or the parts that make up the word. Specifically, you will learn how to use

1. roots (or basic word parts), and
2. affixes (suffixes and prefixes).

INTRODUCTION—
UNLOCKING THE MEANING OF WORDS

Understanding how words in our language are constructed, or structured, can help you become a better reader, especially when you deal with content loaded with technical terms. That is because the English language contains many words built from roots and affixes. A **root** is a basic unit of meaning in the language. Some English roots—*sing,* for example—can function as a word. From that root word, we can build *singing* and *singer.* Some word parts come from other languages, such as Latin and Greek; we generally do not use these roots as words in our language, but we put them together to form words. Affixes include both **prefixes** (meaningful units added to the beginnings of words and roots) and **suffixes** (meaningful units added to the ends of words and roots).

As you read and encounter unfamiliar words, especially technical terms, you should apply a basic word-structure strategy:

● Break words into component parts—roots, prefixes, and suffixes.

● Use the meanings of the component parts you know to figure out the meanings of words you do not know.

For example, a commonly used root that is from Latin is *astro,* which means "star." Words formed from *astro* include the following:

astronomy—the scientific study of the heavens;

astronaut—a traveler beyond the earth;

astrology—the pseudoscientific study of the effects of heavenly bodies on people's lives;

asterisk—the star-shaped symbol (*);

aster—the star-shaped flower.

Based on your understanding of the root *astro* and your ability to use context clues, you can figure out the meaning of the italicized word in this sentence: He asked an *astronomically* high price for towing my car to the garage.

To figure out the meaning of *astronomically,* you might reason: *Astro* means "star." Stars are very high in the sky. *Astronomically* must mean "high as the stars." That fits the context of the sentence. An astronomically high price is a very, very high one. Both word-structure and context clues help you unlock the meaning of *astronomically.*

What is the meaning of the word *astronomer?* Analyzing the structure of the word, you might reason: *Astro* means "star"; *astronomy* is the "study of stars and heavenly bodies"; *-er* is a suffix that sometimes means "a person who." An *astronomer* is someone who studies the stars and heavenly bodies. Analyze the word *astrologer.* What is its meaning?

A widely used root is *graph* or *grapho.* It means "drawn or written." Predict the meanings of the italicized words using both word-structure and context clues.

1. She described the accident in such *graphic* terms that I felt I had been there.
   Graphic means
   a. clear or vivid.   c. boastful.
   b. terrible.   d. unpleasant.

2. Her brother decided to study *graphic arts* because he could draw well. The *graphic arts*
   a. involve physical activity.   c. relate to drawing, etching, painting.
   b. relate to driving a car.   d. relate to a mathematical graph.
3. Guglielmo Marconi was the inventor of the first successful wireless *telegraph*. The *telegraph* is
   a. a device for sending messages or signals over a distance.
   b. a picture tube.
   c. a computer.
   d. a television set.

In figuring out the meaning of *telegraph,* you may use the meaning of a very commonly used root—*tele.* It means distant, or sent over a distance. Other words that are built with *tele* include *telegram* (a message sent by telegraph), *telescope* (an instrument for making distant objects appear nearer), and *television* (the broadcasting of a moving image over a distance). Think about the meanings of these words: *telethermometer, telepathy, teletypewriter.*

In the next section, you will become familiar with other common word-building elements.

COMMON WORD-BUILDING ELEMENTS

Memorizing word parts and their meanings will not help you become a better reader. Being aware that words are made up of meaningful parts and using that awareness to figure out the meaning of words as you read will increase your comprehension.

Increasing Your Awareness of Word Parts

Here are some commonly used word parts and their meanings as well as the definition of one word built from the part. In the blank column, write the word that fits the definition. Remember that you have already learned that bio- *means "life."*

Word Part	Meaning of Part	Word	Meaning of the Word
1. -scope	instrument for viewing	_____	an instrument for viewing the heavens
2. micro-	very small	_____	an instrument for viewing small things
3. -ology	the study of	_____	the study of living things
4. -ologist	one who studies	_____	one who studies small living things (Note: You must use both *bio-* and *micro-*)
5. anthropo-	human person	_____	study of the development of humankind
6. archeo-	ancient times	_____	one who studies life in ancient times
7. astro-	star	_____	study of heavens to predict human events

8. chrono-	time	_____	study of time
9. geo-	earth	_____	one who studies the earth and its forms
10. hydro-	water	_____	study of water
11. neuro-	nerves	_____	a doctor who specializes in study of the nervous system
12. patho-	disease	_____	a person who studies tissues for evidence of disease
13. psycho-	mind	_____	study of human behavior
14. socio-	social	_____	a person who studies human society
15. theo-	god	_____	study of religion

Working with Word Parts

Some word elements are clues to number meanings. For example,

mono-	means	one	*deca-*	means	ten
bi-	means	two	*cent-*	means	hundred
tri-	means	three	*mille-*	means	thousand
quadri-	means	four	*multi-*	means	many
quint-	means	five	*omni-*	means	all

Based on the meanings just given, circle the meaning of each italicized word.

1. In feudal times, the king was *omnipotent.*
   a. everywhere   c. respected
   b. all powerful   d. feared
2. In 1876, the United States celebrated the nation's *centennial.*
   a. tenth-year anniversary   c. two-hundredth-year anniversary
   b. hundredth-year anniversary   d. thousandth-year anniversary
3. In 1976, the United States celebrated the nation's *bicentennial.*
   a. tenth-year anniversary   c. two-hundredth-year anniversary
   b. hundredth-year anniversary   d. thousandth-year anniversary
4. How many *centimeters* are there in a meter?
   a. one   c. hundred
   b. ten   d. thousand
5. How many *milliliters* are there in a liter?
   a. one   c. hundred
   b. ten   d. thousand
6. The decade ending in 1870 saw the end of the Civil War. How long is a *decade?*
   a. one year   c. twenty years
   b. ten years   d. forty years
7. Because my friend was *bilingual,* he got a job as a translator. *Bilingual* means
   a. able to speak two languages.   c. very intelligent.
   b. able to travel.   d. born outside the country.

8. Great Britain, France, and the United States entered into a *trilateral* trade agreement. *Trilateral* means
   a. having to do with business.
   b. three way.
   c. having to do with war.
   d. having to do with a triumphant victory.

9. Mr. Fitzpatrick fainted when he heard his wife had given birth to *quintuplets*. How many children were born?
   a. three   c. five
   b. four   d. six

10. The *quadricentennial* of the United States will take place in
    a. 2076   c. 2276
    b. 2176   d. 2376

11. The popular leader had a *multitude* of friends.
    a. ten   c. a thousand
    b. a hundred   d. a great number

12. No one can live for a *millennium*. How long is a *millennium?*
    a. ten years   c. two hundred years
    b. a hundred years d. a thousand years

13. For each of the word parts given, write a word based on the part and the definition of the word. Use a dictionary if you have trouble building words. Do not use words from the sentences in the exercise.

Part	Word	Meaning
a. mono-	_____	_____
b. bi-	_____	_____
c. tri-	_____	_____
d. quadri-	_____	_____
e. quint-	_____	_____
f. deca-	_____	_____
g. cent-	_____	_____
h. mille-	_____	_____
i. multi-	_____	_____
j. omni-	_____	_____

COMMON PREFIXES

A prefix is a letter or group of letters added to the beginnings of words. An example of a common prefix is *re-*, which means "again." To *reconsider* is simply to consider again. What meanings do you assign to these words?

Readjust   _____

Reappoint   _____

Reattach   _____

Reassure   _____

Seeing the prefix at the beginning of these words and assigning the meaning of *again* to it helps you unlock the meaning of the whole word. However, not all words that begin with *re-* are built from the prefix. Cases in point are *read, ready,* and *reason.*

Seeing Prefixes in Words

See if you can figure out the meanings of the prefixes italicized in these sentences:

1. Astrology is often considered a *pseudo*science because astrologers try to predict human events based on the stars.
    a. before   c. against   e. not
    b. after   d. false

2. As part of his *pre*operative treatment, he had to take antibiotics so that he would be ready for surgery.
    a. before   c. against   e. not
    b. after   d. false

3. During the *post*war period, many people joined in to clear away the rubble.
    a. before   c. against   e. not
    b. after   d. false

4. The man joined the *anti*war movement because he was against violence in any form.
    a. before   c. against   e. not
    b. after   d. false

5. Because of his illness, he was *un*able to come.
    a. before   c. against   e. not
    b. after   d. false

6. Two-year-old children are often *hyper*active.
    a. between   c. over
    b. within   d. not

7. Although I wanted to go, it became *im*possible; I had to stay home.
    a. between   c. over
    b. within   d. not

8. Because she was so unfriendly, I began to *dis*like her.
    a. between   c. over
    b. within   d. not

9. When I traveled from New Hampshire to Massachusetts, I took the *inter*state highway.
    a. between   c. over
    b. within   d. not

10. Because he hauled products from Los Angeles to San Francisco, he was said to be involved in *intra*state commerce.
    a. between   c. over
    b. within   d. not

11. Because the ship was completely *sub*merged, we could not see it.
    a. under   c. around   e. before
    b. above   d. across

12. The *trans*continental railroad connected the West and East coasts.
    a. under   c. around   e. before
    b. above   d. across

13. The Revolutionary War *ante*dates the Civil War.
    a. under   c. around   e. before
    b. above   d. across

14. The *super*intendent was in charge of the entire operation.
    a. under   c. around   e. before
    b. above   d. across
15. Magellan's ship was the first to *circum*navigate the globe.
    a. under   c. around   e. before
    b. above   d. across

Making a Table of Prefixes

Using the answers to the previous exercise, complete this summary chart of prefixes. Make your sample word one not used in the previous sentences.

Prefix	Prefix Meaning	Sample Word	Word Meaning
1. pseudo-	_____	_____	_____
2. pre-	_____	_____	_____
3. post-	_____	_____	_____
4. anti-	_____	_____	_____
5. un-	_____	_____	_____
6. im-	_____	_____	_____
7. hyper-	_____	_____	_____
8. dis-	_____	_____	_____
9. inter-	_____	_____	_____
10. intra-	_____	_____	_____
11. sub-	_____	_____	_____
12. trans-	_____	_____	_____
13. ante-	_____	_____	_____
14. super-	_____	_____	_____
15. circum-	_____	_____	_____

COMMON SUFFIXES

A suffix is a letter or a group of letters that is added to the end of a word and may change the part of speech of that word. An example of a common suffix is *-ness.* It means "the state of." You have seen it on nouns formed from adjectives, such as *loveliness* (the state of being lovely), *thoughtfulness* (the state of being thoughtful), and *softness* (the state of being soft).

A second suffix you probably know is *-ical* or *-al,* which simply turns a noun into a word that can serve as an adjective. You have seen it on adjectives such as *practical* (adapted for actual use), *societal* (pertaining to society), and *theoretical* (based on theory).

Another common suffix is *-ize,* which means "to make." You have seen it on verbs such as *civilize* (to make civil), *personalize* (to make personal), and *categorize* (to put into categories).

Still another very common suffix is *-ion,* which means "state of" or "process of." You have seen it on nouns such as *invention* (the process of inventing), *limitation* (the state of being limited), and *innovation* (the process of innovating, or creatively changing).

Here are a few other suffixes. For each give the meaning of the sample word, reasoning from the meaning of the suffix. Then give an example of another word that contains the suffix.

Suffix	Meaning	Word	Meaning	Another Word
-able	able to be	likable	_____	_____
-ous or -ious	full of	joyous	_____	_____
-ful	full of	peaceful	_____	_____
-y	state of being	rainy	_____	_____
-ify	to make	simplify	_____	_____
-er or -or	a person who	banker	_____	_____
-ist	one who does, is concerned with, or holds certain beliefs	communist	_____	_____

As you read, keep alert for suffixes that may give you a clue to the meaning of an unfamiliar word. Try to see the component parts of the word.

Circle the suffixes in the italicized words. Then write the definition of each word using word-structure and context clues.

1. It was a *memorable* occasion. I will always remember it.

2. Without *innovation* the world would stand still. Progress is dependent on *innovation*. (Reminder: You already know the meaning of *novice*.)

3. There must be some way of joining the work of the two committees. Good *articulation* is necessary.

4. The oval arch was a *radical* departure from the way it was done before. In that respect it was an innovation.

5. Surface changes are not enough. Deep *structural* changes are required.

6. Scientists are concerned with *theoretical* ideas as well as with practical applications.

7. Do not confuse him. Try to *clarify* the situation instead.

In the next part of this chapter, you will read three selections. The first deals with word roots used in science. The second is a general selection that includes many words built from roots. The third is a selection from a biology textbook that also has many words built from roots. In reading the last two selections, use your growing familiarity with word parts to unlock words as you meet them in context.

SELECTION 1: ATTACKING WORDS IN SCIENCE
(Language)

Getting Ready to Read

Read the title, the first paragraph, and the subheadings of this selection, which is from a paperback from the National Science Teachers Association called The Language of Science.

- What is this selection about? _____
- What do you already know about words and how they are put together? Add words, phrases, and ideas you already know about the topic to this idea web, or cluster. One idea has been given to get you thinking.

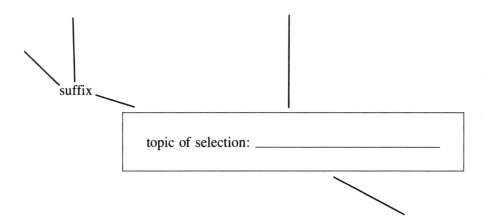

suffix

topic of selection: _____

Reading with Meaning

Now read the selection, looking particularly for examples of how word meanings can be unlocked through understanding of word parts.

ATTACKING WORDS IN SCIENCE

Alan Mandell

To unlock the meanings of complex scientific words, such as *infraphotodensitometer* and *bathythermograph,* or even to learn to spell them correctly, may appear to be a nearly impossible task. Yet, using some of the clues and word-attack skills to be discussed in this article, you should be able to conquer words such as these and most of the other scientific words you encounter.

Analyzing Words for Meaning

You are familiar with root words, prefixes, and suffixes from your language studies. Most science terms are words composed of a root word and prefixes or suffixes or both. Consider the word *photosynthesis*. Here the root "photo," meaning light, and the root "synthesis," meaning to put together, are combined to produce a term which signifies "putting together through the use of light." You probably know photosynthesis as a term which describes the processes by which green plants make food materials in the presence of light. If you didn't know that, the word itself, thus analyzed, would give you a clue to its meaning.

Think of some other "photo" words. *Photograph* implies writing (graphein = to write) by light; add an "er" and we have *photographer*. *Photometer* suggests a device to measure (meter = measure) light. Indeed, a photometer is used by photographers (people who write or record with light) to determine the amount of light available in order to take a good picture. Going back to *infraphotodensitometer,* we identify "infra" as near the limits of the light spectrum (i.e., infrared) and "density" as referring to the thickness or denseness of a material. Our word then becomes an understandable term which describes a device that measures the density of a material to infrared light energy.

When we look again at *bathythermograph,* we get a clue to "thermo" from the word *thermometer,* which we know is a temperature-measuring instrument. If we know that "bathy" refers to depths under water, we can see that bathythermograph signifies a device that records (writes) the temperature in deep waters.

From these examples, it should be apparent that knowing the meanings and uses of some of the more commonly used scientific root words, prefixes, and suffixes is of primary importance in becoming adept with the scientific vocabulary. Figure 3.1 lists some common combining terms, their meanings, and uses.

Analyzing the Sequence of Word Parts

The arrangement of the parts of a complex word is often an important clue to its meaning. Consider, for example, *photomicrography* and *microphotography.* Knowing the meanings of "photo" and "graphy" and adding that "micro" pertains to very small objects, we can see that both terms are concerned with written records of light energy on a very small scale. Word analysis, using the relative positions of the parts of the word, suggests that microphotography means "small, light-written, recording." It is the process of making extremely small photographic records (on microfilm) of normal-size materials. Photomicrography, on the other hand, indicates "light-written records of tiny materials" and is used generally to describe taking pictures through the microscope.

Origin of Word Parts

Scientific terms and symbols come from Greek, Latin, Arabic, and many other languages. Historically, Greek and Latin were the languages of the learned world, so it is not surprising that much scientific terminology derives from word roots of these languages. Some scientific terms have mixed Greek and Latin roots.

Term[a]	Meaning	Example of Use
alb	white	albino
anti	against	antitoxin (opposes poisons)
anthrop	human being, man	anthropology (study of man)
aqua	water	aqueous (watery)
archeo	ancient	archaeology (study of ancient remains)
bar	weight, heaviness	barometer (measures weight of atmosphere)
bio	life	biology
centr	center	centrifuge
claus	an enclosed place	claustrophobia (fear of being confined)
dem	people	demography (study of human populations)
derm	skin	ectodermis
ect	outer	ectodermis (outer skin layer)
end	inner	endodermis (inner skin layer)
ep	upon, atop	epicenter (above the center)
gene	birth, descent	genealogy
ge	earth	geography (mapping of the earth)
graph	write	geography
hydr	water	hydrometer (water meter)
is	equal	isotope (same place in atomic table)
logy	study of	biology, anthropology
lun	moon	lunar (pertaining to the moon)
mes	middle	mesodermis (middle skin layer)
meter	measure	metrology (study of measurement)
muta	change	mutate, mutation
morph	shape, form	morphology (study of form and structure)
nym	name	pseudonym (false name)
omni	all, total	omniscient (all-knowing)
phil	love	aquaphila (love of water)
phob	fear	claustrophobia (fear of being confined)
phon	sound	phonograph
phot	light	photograph
phyt	plant	epiphyte (a plant growing upon another)
pod	foot	pseudopodium ("false foot" of single-celled animal)
prot	early, first	protozoa (first animals)
pseud	false	pseudonym
scien	knowledge	science, omniscient
therm	heat	thermometer
top	place	topography
tox	poison	toxic (poisonous)
zo	animal	zoology

[a]In forming words from these terms, connecting vowels are often used, as will be clear from the examples given. Dictionaries and various authorities may give slightly different forms for terms or roots.

Figure 3.1   *Some Common Combining Terms Used in Science.*   (Chart courtesy of Alan Mandell and the National Science Teachers Association)

Checking for Understanding

Using the information in Figure 3.1, circle the root or roots in each word, indicate the meaning of each root, and propose the meaning of the term.

1. anthropologist

2. antibiotic

3. genetic

4. geology

5. aquaphobia

6. photometer

7. antonym

8. prototype

9. dermatology

10. omnipresent

SELECTION 2: BRUSHING UP ON DINOSAURS
(Paleontology)

Expanding Your Vocabulary for Reading

In the next selection, you will meet some interesting words. You probably already know the word *dinosaur.* It is made up of two Greek roots, *dino* meaning "terrible" and *saur* meaning "lizard." You can see how that prehistoric animal (an animal living before the days of written records) received its name.

In the selection, you will meet *Tyrannosaurus rex,* who also has an appropriate name. *Tyranno* is a Greek root, which means "absolute ruler." *Rex* means "king." Can you define the word *tyrant?* Check the glossary to be sure.

Another root important to your understanding of the selection is *paleo.* It means "ancient," or "old." You already know that the suffix *-ology* means "the study of." Based on the meaning of the root and the suffix, you can figure out the meaning of *paleontology.* Again, check the glossary to be sure. Why would someone who studied dinosaurs be called a paleontologist?

Another root is *eco.* It means "home," "abode," or "habitat." *Ecology* is the branch of biology that focuses on relations between organisms and their environment. An *ecologist* is a person who studies ecology. *Ecological* means "of or relating to organisms and their environment." *Ecological niche* refers to the role of an organism in a community of plants and animals.

Getting Ready to Read

Preview this selection by reading the title, introductory sentence, and first paragraph.

● What does the title "Brushing Up on Dinosaurs" and the first paragraph tell you about the topic of the selection? _____

_____

● What does the phrase *brushing up* suggest? _____

_____

● What comes to mind when you think about dinosaurs? _____

_____

● Read the selection to see if you can use your understanding of word parts to figure out the meanings of complex words in the selection.

Reading with Meaning

Now read the selection. Keep your purpose in mind: to use your understanding of word parts to increase your comprehension. Also read to find out how scientists of today view the dinosaur as compared to the way scientists of the past viewed the animal.

BRUSHING UP ON DINOSAURS

Stefi Weisburd

When art and science combine, the result can be a remarkably vivid and accurate glimpse into prehistoric life.

Robert Bakker met his first dinosaurs in the spring of 1955 in his grandfather's sun room, and he fell in love. There on the coffee table, a terrifying *Tyrannosaurus rex* glowered at a long-necked *Apatosaurus* supping in a swamp—both surrounded by a menagerie of wonderfully exotic creatures that roamed the prehistoric landscape hundreds of millions of years ago. Ten-year-old Bakker had discovered Rudolph Zallinger's Pulitzer-prize-winning mural, reproduced that week on the cover of *Life*.

"As soon as I saw it I decided I was going to spend the rest of my life studying dinosaurs," says Bakker, who went on to do just that, becoming a renowned paleontologist and artist in his own right. "That was the first really great color dinosaur mural. It launched an awful lot of careers, including mine."

While many, like C. P. Snow in *The Two Cultures,* have lamented the growing abyss between science and the arts, the two are merged in paleontology, particularly in the reconstruction of dinosaurs and their habitats and behavior. This union of art and science is what makes ancient bones of long-extinct animals come alive. Paintings and sculptures not only spark the public imagination and inspire new ranks of paleontologists, but for scientists they are also an effective means of communicating ideas and exploring new theories.

"Paleontology is a very visual inquiry," notes Bakker. "All paleontologists scribble on napkins at coffee breaks, making sketches to explain their thinking." If they are not artists themselves, most dinosaur paleontologists work closely with artists, some of whom have published scientific works of their own.

Museums have presented displays of dinosaurs. In many of the early displays, dinosaurs were portrayed as violent, clumsy and slovenly beasts, dressed in drab greys, browns and dark greens and standing by themselves. Newer paintings and sculptures project quite a different image of sleeker, more varied and lively animals that lived in socially complex communities and had adapted to almost every ecological niche now occupied by modern mammals and birds.

One of the most important changes that has taken place in the portrayal of dinosaurs is in their posture. Until fairly recently, the convention was to draw many large dinosaurs with their front legs splayed out and bent at the elbows like lizards. But in pictures today, the elbows are straight and the front legs have been pulled under the body, closer to the animal's center of gravity.

The physical portrayal of many dinosaurs has changed in other ways as well. Recent studies have shown that the *Stegosaurus,* which had been portrayed with two rows of bony plates down its back for 100 years, really had just one row. And contemporary illustrators have started to use more vivid colors: mauve, pink, metallic blues and reds. While there is no direct physical evidence to show that dinosaurs were indeed colorful creatures, "this makes a

Figure 3.2   *One of the Great Dinosaurs—Tyrannosaurus rex and the other great dino-saurs of prehistoric times became extinct. Scientists disagree as to why these mighty reptiles died out.*   (American Museum of Natural History, New York)

lot of sense," says Bakker, "because dinosaurs are closely related to birds. Colors were undoubtedly used, especially in the mating season."

By studying the mass and distribution of muscles, the mechanics of limbs, fossilized footprints and the newly characterized posture of the dinosaurs, some scientists have concluded that the animals could move at greater speeds than once thought. Bakker, in particular, has championed the idea that dinosaurs were much nimbler than earlier paleontologists believed. His 1969 drawing of a running *Deinonychus* (or "terrible claw," for the lethal, sickle-shaped claws on its feet) shows a very sleek, fast-moving animal.

Bakker has presented evidence that some dinosaurs averaged a walking speed of about 3 miles per hour—about four times as fast as that of present-day lizards and turtles, and comparable to the speeds of moose, deer, bulls and other warm-blooded animals. Because the average cruising speed reflects an animal's metabolism, Bakker argues that many dinosaurs were warm-blooded.

Another perception that has evolved dramatically is that of the social behavior of dinosaurs, which paleontologists have inferred from various kinds of physical evidence. These clues—such as bone beds, created when a group of animals was killed *en masse* by a flood, volcano, or other catastrophe, and fossilized trackways—suggest that both predators and prey traveled in packs or herds. One painting by a Baltimore artist, Gregory Paul, illustrates that the prey were by no means defenseless: A herbivorous *Diplodocus* is rearing up like an elephant to protect the rest of its herd against a carnivorous *Allosaurus,* and is swinging a thick, very lethal, whip-like tale. Trackways also show that some dinosaurs walked side by side as they traveled. Other tracks indicate that meat-eating dinosaurs could swim, leaving the herbivores little chance of escaping in the water, as some scientists had once believed they could.

There is also growing evidence that dinosaurs, like present-day crocodiles, cared for their young after they hatched. Dinosaur eggs were first discovered in the 1920s in the Gobi desert, but it wasn't until a few years ago that communal nesting grounds were found. Paleontologist John Horner discovered a series of nests in Choteau, Montana, that had belonged to duckbilled *Maiasaura*. Because young *Maiasaura* of different ages and sizes were found in nests, some scientists have concluded that parents were protecting and feeding their young until they were large enough to fend for themselves.   [891 words]

Checking for Understanding

Give the meaning of each term, based on its structure.

a. Paleontology

b. Ecology

c. Prehistoric

d. Dinosaur

e. Carnivore

f. Reconstruction

SELECTION 3: FOOD CHAINS (Ecology)

Learning New Words

As you read the next selection, you will notice some words that are built from affixes and roots. An example is the word *biological* built from *bio* meaning "life" and *ology* meaning "the study of." Another example is *photosynthesis* built from *phot* meaning "light" and *synthesis* meaning "the combining of parts."

As you read, look out for technical words, especially those made up of affixes and roots. Circle the technical terms as you read. Using both context and word structure, figure out their meaning. In the margin write the meanings of words you circle.

This selection is typical of what you will find in college science texts. Such texts are often heavy with technical vocabulary. In reading, you have to work on unlocking the meanings of the technical terms.

Getting Ready to Read

Preview this selection, which is from an environmental science book, by reading the title and first sentence and by studying the illustrations.

● What is this selection about? _____

● What, if any, do you already know about that topic? _____

_____

● What two questions do you expect to answer by the time you finish reading the selection? Use the title to help you write the questions.

_____

_____

Reading with Meaning

Now read the selection keeping in mind your purpose: to figure out the meaning of technical terms through use of word-structure clues.

FOOD CHAINS

*Daniel D. Chiras**

In the biological world you are one of two things, either a producer or a consumer. (Only rarely can you be both.) **Producers** are the organisms that support the entire living world through photosynthesis. Plants, algae, and cyanobacteria are the key producers of energy-rich organic materials. They are also called **autotrophs** (from the Greek root "troph"—to feed, nourish),

*From *Environmental Science,* Third Edition, by Daniel D. Chiras (Redwood City, CA: Benjamin/Cummings Publishing Company; 1991), pp. 54–55.

because they literally nourish themselves photosynthetically, that is, by using sunlight and atmospheric carbon dioxide to make the food materials they need to survive. **Consumers** feed on plants and other organisms and are called **heterotrophs** [*hetero = other*], because they are nourished by consuming other organisms.

Consumer organisms that feed exclusively on plants are called **herbivores.** Cattle, deer, elk, and tomato hornworms are examples. Those consumers that feed exclusively on other animals, such as the mountain lion, are **carnivores.** Those consumers that feed on both plants and animals, such as humans, bears, and raccoons, are **omnivores.**

The interconnections among producers and consumers are visible all around us. Mice living in and around our homes, for example, eat the seeds of domestic and wild plants and, in turn, are preyed on by cats and hawks.

A series of organisms, each feeding on the preceding one, forms a **food chain.** Two basic types of food chains exist in nature: grazer and decomposer. **Grazer food chains,** like the one discussed above, are so named because they start with plants and with grazers, organisms that feed on plants. . . . In the second type—the **decomposer,** or **detritus, food chain**—organic waste material is the major food source. **Detritus** is organic waste which comes from plants and animals. . . .

Food chains are conduits for the flow of energy and nutrients through ecosystems. The sun's energy is first captured by plants and stored in organic molecules, which then pass through the grazer and decomposer food chains. In addition, plants incorporate a variety of inorganic materials such as nitrogen,

Figure 3.3 *The Autotrophs—Plants such as these are autotrophs; they make their own food through photosynthesis.* (Weyerhaeuser Company)

Figure 3.4   *The Heterotrophs—Animals such as these are heterotrophs; they get their energy by consuming organic matter.*   (National Dairy Council)

phosphorus, and magnesium from the soil. These **chemical nutrients** become part of the plant's living matter. When the green plant is consumed, these nutrients enter the food chain. They are eventually returned to the environment by the decomposer food chain.   [366 words]

Checking Your Understanding of Word Parts

1. *Here is a list of roots from words in Selection 3. Next to each is the meaning of the root. In the third column, write a word from the selection that contains the root. In the fourth column, write the meaning of the word based on the context and the word structure. You may complete this activity with another member of your class.*

Root	Meaning of Root	Word with the Root	Meaning of the Word
auto	self	_____	_____
troph	feed	_____	_____
hetero	other	_____	_____
herb	grass	_____	_____
vore	eat, devour	_____	_____
carn	flesh, meat	_____	_____
omni	all	_____	_____
synthetic (synthesis)	make, or place together	_____	_____
phot	light	_____	_____
bio	life	_____	_____
inter	between	_____	_____

2. *Complete the following chart. You may reread the article if you need to and again you may work with a classmate.*

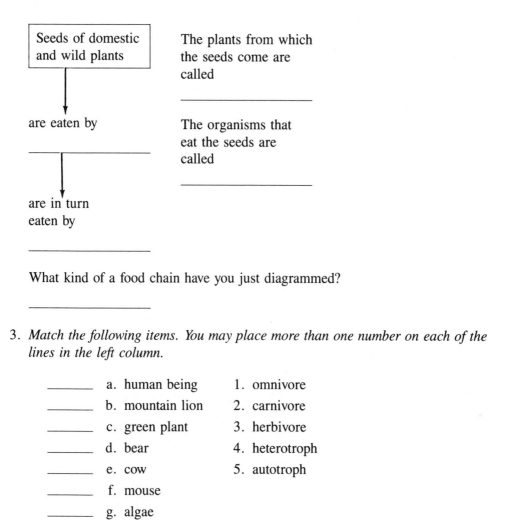

Seeds of domestic and wild plants

The plants from which the seeds come are called

_____

are eaten by

_____

The organisms that eat the seeds are called

_____

are in turn eaten by

_____

What kind of a food chain have you just diagrammed?

_____

3. *Match the following items. You may place more than one number on each of the lines in the left column.*

_____ a. human being	1. omnivore	
_____ b. mountain lion	2. carnivore	
_____ c. green plant	3. herbivore	
_____ d. bear	4. heterotroph	
_____ e. cow	5. autotroph	
_____ f. mouse		
_____ g. algae		

Writing About What You Have Learned

Write two sentences in your notebook, one in which you tell about autotrophs and one in which you tell about heterotrophs. Writing after reading is an effective way to review what you have read and to firm up your understanding of new terms.

EXTENDING WHAT YOU HAVE LEARNED

Handling Unfamiliar Words in Reading

In Chapters 2 and 3, you have been learning ways of handling unfamiliar words in reading. Here, in summary, are the steps in a strategy for unlocking the meaning of new words.

1. Look at the unfamiliar word in relation to the sentence in which it appears. Ask: Is there something in the sentence that provides a clue to the meaning of the word?
   ● Is there a definition built directly into the sentence? If so, what does it say?
   ● Is there a synonym in the sentence that provides a clue to the meaning? If so, what is it?

- Are there explanations or descriptions that relate to the unfamiliar word? If so, what do they tell you about the meaning of the unfamiliar word?
- Are there words in the sentences that express contrasting meanings? If so, what do they tell you about the unfamiliar word?
- Is there a clue that you can get from the overall sense of the sentence?
2. Look at the word itself. Can you break the word into parts? If so, do you know any of the word parts? Do the word clues give you a clue to meaning?
3. Ask yourself whether you need to check the glossary or a dictionary.

The word-unlocking strategy just outlined is particularly important as you read textbooks that contain technical terms. You need to know those terms to understand important ideas. This is especially true when you read science textbooks. In contrast, in doing recreational reading, you do not need to know the meaning of all the terms used; you often can get the main ideas without considering the meaning of almost every word.

Applying the Strategy

Read three editorials in your local newspaper. Locate six words from the editorials that you can define based on your understanding of roots, prefixes, and affixes. Circle them. In the margin of the article, note the meanings of the circled words. Your instructor may ask you to share an editorial and the circled words with the class.

Building Your Vocabulary

Because a large vocabulary is important in reading, you should also develop a strategy for building your personal vocabulary. The strategy that we introduced in this chapter is keeping a vocabulary notebook.

As you read and encounter a new word that has general usefulness, record it in a personal vocabulary notebook. Record also the meaning of the word and a sample sentence using that word. For example, you could begin your vocabulary notebook with the words *clarify* and *innovation* from this chapter. As you add words to your notebook, you may find it helpful to section it alphabetically. Keep a page for words that begin with the letter *a,* another page for *b* words, and so forth.

This vocabulary-building strategy will work only if you think about the words you record after you have entered them in your personal notebook. For example, today as you walk around, consider where you might apply the word *innovation*. Where do you see examples of innovation? When have you been innovative?

If you record and keep thinking about two new words each day, your vocabulary will grow. Research shows that one or two encounters with a word are not enough for you to learn a word. To own a word—to make it yours—you must encounter that word many times. Therefore, from time to time, thumb through your personal vocabulary notebook and think about your entries. Make an effort to use those words when appropriate in speaking and writing.

The design of the paragraph is shown here:

Supporting detail sentence
Supporting detail sentence
Supporting detail sentence
Supporting detail sentence
Supporting detail sentence

Main idea (or topic sentence)

This design is an inductive one. An *inductive paragraph* provides a series of details and gives the general, or main, idea at the end.

When you read a paragraph in which the main idea is not stated in the first sentence, your job as a reader is more difficult. You must keep relating each new piece of information to those already given in the paragraph. Sifting through each new sentence, you must ask yourself: In what way is this new piece of data like the ones that have gone before it? What are the sentences saying about the topic? A repeating term (in this case the word *Virginia*) may hint at the main idea as you read through the paragraph. The last sentence—the topic sentence—confirms the main idea.

Finding the Main Idea When It Is Not Stated

Very often in college texts, the author does not state the main idea. He or she leaves it to the reader to figure out.

Study this chart. As you look at it, ask yourself. What is the topic of the chart? (Clue: The topic is stated directly.) What point is it making about the early presidents of the United States? (Clue: The point is not stated directly.)

Early Presidents of the United States

Name	Number of President	Birthplace	Other Data
George Washington	1	Westmoreland Co., Virginia, 1732	Called the "father of our country"; lived at Mt. Vernon in Virginia
Thomas Jefferson	3	"Shadwell" in Goochland (now Albermarle) Co., Virginia, 1743	Founded the University of Virginia at Charlottesville, Va.; lived at Monticello in Virginia
James Madison	4	Port Conway, Va., 1751, member of the Virginia planter class	Helped to draft the Constitution for the state of Virginia
James Monroe	5	Westmoreland Co., Va., 1758	Educated at the College of William and Mary in Williamsburg, Va.; studied law under Jefferson

What is the topic of the chart? Write down the topic before continuing to read.

_____ The topic of the chart is given in the title, "Early Presidents of the United States."

What is the chart saying about those early presidents? In answering that question, you will have identified the main—but unstated—idea of the chart. Write down what you think the main idea is before continuing.

_____

Sifting through the data in the chart, did you see a way in which most of the data are related? How were these early presidents similar? What feature of their background was the same?

One clue to noting relationships within a body of data like this (or within a paragraph, which is like a body of data) is to identify words or phrases that repeat. In the data chart on the early presidents, the word *Virginia* repeats. The main idea is that these four presidents were Virginians.

Some paragraphs are like the chart about the early presidents; they have no topic sentence. Such a paragraph is simply a string, or lineup, of interrelated sentences. You, the reader, must figure out what the main idea is. You must reason from the specific details to understand the general point the paragraph is making. This is what you actually did when you interpreted the chart about the early presidents on page 69. You had to put together the main idea because it was not explicitly stated.

Here is the same paragraph about early presidents of the United States written without a topic sentence.

> George Washington, the father of our country and the first president, was born in Westmoreland County, Virginia, and spent his later years at his estate in Virginia, Mt. Vernon. Thomas Jefferson, the third president, was also a native Virginian. Raised in what is now Albermarle County, Virginia, he founded the University of Virginia and his home in later years was Monticello near the university. James Madison, the fourth president, was born in Port Conway, Virginia, and helped draft the Constitution for the State of Virginia. James Monroe, the fifth president, was born, like Washington, in Westmoreland County; he was educated at the College of William and Mary in Williamsburg and studied law under Thomas Jefferson.

To get the main idea of this paragraph, you must sift through each piece of data as it is presented and ask these questions: How does this sentence relate to the ones before it? What point is this sentence making about the topic?

The linear design of the paragraph is simply this:

> Supporting detail sentence
> Supporting detail sentence
> Supporting detail sentence
> Supporting detail sentence
> Supporting detail sentence

Writing Paragraphs with Main Ideas and Topic Sentences

Here is another data chart. Study it to determine the main idea, or point. The point is not stated. You must figure it out.

Name	Number of President	Birthplace	Other Data
John Adams	2	Born in Braintree, Mass., 1735	Graduated from Harvard in Cambridge, Mass.; on the drafting committee of the Declaration of Independence
John Quincy Adams	6	Born in Braintree, Mass., 1767	Son of John and Abigail Adams

What is true of the second and sixth presidents of the United States? Think about that question before continuing, and write your answer here.

_____

Can you see from the chart that both men were from the same state and the same family? They were both Adamses from Massachusetts.

Write a paragraph in your notebook which makes that point. Begin with a topic sentence. You may model it after the topic sentence about the presidents from Virginia. Follow your topic sentence with one or two sentences giving details about John Adams. Follow that with a sentence or two about John Quincy Adams. Doing this, you will be writing a deductively designed paragraph.

Revise your paragraph so that it is structured inductively. Begin with some details about John Adams. Follow with details about his son. Then write a sentence at the end that states the main idea, the important relationship you are stressing in your paragraph. Again, record your paragraph in your notebook.

Share your paragraphs with a classmate. See whether he or she can identify the topic sentence with the main idea.

SELECTION 1: SUMMER OF DESTINY (Political Science)

The paragraphs in the next section are from an article about the drafting of the U.S. Constitution. It is titled "Summer of Destiny," and was written by Hubert Pryor.

Expanding Your Vocabulary for Reading

The italicized words in the following sentences are from the selection. Think about them before reading. Use both context and word-structure clues to unlock their meanings. Where the context is unclear to you, check the glossary. Record the meanings in the space provided. Select one or two to add to your personal vocabulary list in your notebook.

1. In our *bicameral* legislature there is a Senate and a House of Representatives.

_____

_____

2. Twenty-one members out of a total membership of forty came to the meeting. Because there was a *quorum,* we were able to vote. _____

   _____

3. Because she is a member of the *legislative* branch, rather than the *executive* branch, of government, her daily activities relate to making the laws rather than administering them. _____

   _____

4. As a member of the *electorate,* he had the right to vote. _____

   _____

5. The vote was *unanimous;* everyone agreed. _____

6. When she *presided* over the convention, she made sure everyone had an opportunity to express his or her opinions. _____

   _____

Identifying Main Ideas

Now read this paragraph, the first in Pryor's article. As you read it, think about the topic of the paragraph—what it is about. Think also about the main idea of the paragraph. Keep asking yourself: What is the paragraph saying about the topic? What point is the author trying to make? Where are all the details leading?

The United States of America, many contend, was born, not in 1776, but in the summer of 1787. It was in the late spring of 1787 that delegates from 11 of the original states gathered in the Pennsylvania State House in Philadelphia, then America's largest city. (The New Hampshire delegation arrived in late July.) In the paneled assembly room of the graceful red-brick building topped by white clock tower and steeple—the place we now call Independence Hall—they sweated through four months of arduous, inspired, sometimes bitter, and almost disastrous deliberations. The result: the most brilliant document for human government in world history.

What is the topic? If you said the paragraph was about the birth of our nation or about the birth of the Constitution of the United States, you were correct. What is the paragraph saying about the topic? What is the main idea of it? The main idea is that our country was born in the summer of 1787 with the writing of the Constitution. Where was that idea stated? The first sentence comes rather close to stating that main idea.

As you read earlier, the paragraph is the first one in an article called "Summer of Destiny." Why is it a good title for an article that starts this way? How would thinking about the title help you get the main point of the article?

Practicing Finding the Main Idea of a Paragraph

Here are other paragraphs from Pryor's article. Read each paragraph. Identify the topic. Then write down the main idea.

1. Topic:

Some of the 55 men who took part in the Constitutional Convention bore legendary names: George Washington, James Madison, Alexander Hamil-

ORDINANCES, *&c.*

A DECLARATION *of* RIGHTS *made by the reprefentatives of the good people of* Virginia, *affembled in full and free Convention; which rights do pertain to them, and their pofterity, as the bafis and foundation of government.*

1. THAT all men are by nature equally free and independent, and have certain inherent rights, of which, when they enter into a ftate of fociety, they cannot, by any compact, deprive or diveft their pofterity; namely, the enjoyment of life and liberty, with the means of acquiring and poffeffing property, and purfuing and obtaining happinefs and fafety.

2. That all power is vefted in, and confequently derived from, the people; that magiftrates are their truftees and fervants, and at all times amenable to them.

3. That government is, or ought to be, inftituted for the common benefit, protection, and fecurity, of the people, nation, or community, of all the various modes and forms of government that is beft, which is capable of producing the greateft degree of happinefs and fafety, and is moft effectually fecured againft the danger of mal-adminiftration; and that whenever any government fhall be found inadequate or contrary to thefe purpofes, a majority of the community hath an indubitable, unalienable, and indefeafible right, to reform, alter, or abolifh it, in fuch manner as fhall be judged moft conducive to the publick weal.

4. That no man, or fet of men, are entitled to exclufive or feparate emoluments or privileges from the community, but in confideration of publick fervices; which, not being defcendible, neither ought the offices of magiftrate, legiflator, or judge, to be hereditary.

Figure 4.2 *An Early Bill of Rights from Virginia—The Constitution and the Bill of Rights drew upon ideas from previous documents such as this one.*

ton, Benjamin Franklin. But, except for Madison, their names are known more for other achievements than for what they did in Philadelphia. Others with names as legendary, including Thomas Jefferson and John Adams, were occupied with other duties so never attended. And a few with names not widely known, notably James Wilson and Gouverneur Morris of Pennsylvania, won their special place in history for the way they helped forge the framework for the nation we have been for the past 200 years.

Despite the glorious strike for freedom of 1776 and the victorious end of the War of Independence in 1781, the Articles of Confederation governing our land were "nothing more than a treaty of amity and alliance between independent and sovereign states." The words are those of James Madison. Working perhaps more than anyone else to bring the states together in the Constitutional Convention, he faced a land with no President, no national courts. The only central body was the Continental Congress, in which each state had one vote, which had no power to impose taxes or coerce states to raise an army.

Main idea (what the author is saying about the topic):

2. Topic:

Main idea:

3. Topic:

   Main idea:

   By the 1780s, the lack of national purpose and direction had brought economic depression and even talk of war between states. There was no uniform currency, foreign trade was regulated by individual states, and trade barriers were being erected between states. By 1785, General Washington, looking sadly at the land he had led to freedom so recently, declared, "The wheels of government are clogged."

4. Topic:

   Main idea:

   As Virginia delegate Washington arrived in Philadelphia on Sunday, May 13, 1787, from Mount Vernon, where he had retired, thousands of citizens turned out excitedly to meet him. When at last the convention met with a quorum present—11 days later than scheduled—the delegates unanimously paid him the honor due him as America's liberator by naming him to preside.

5. Topic:

   Main idea:

   The choice contributed mightily to the ultimate success of the long, hot weeks and months that were to follow, often in perilous disagreement. And yet Washington spoke out only once—at the end. The General's commanding presence was such that all were simply awed into persisting in their work.

6. Topic:

   Main idea:

   And so the gathering set to work, on track from the start thanks to Madison. The soft-spoken but brilliant young Virginian—he was 36—had outlined a proposed system of government in informal talks with other delegates during the days they were awaiting a quorum. His so-called Virginia Plan, presented by Virginia Governor Edmund Randolph, called for a national government split three ways, with legislative, executive, and judicial branches.

7. Topic:

   Main idea:

   The plan envisioned a bicameral Congress with two houses whose members would be in proportion to the general electorate. A curious mechanism was proposed by which Senators would be elected by the House of Representatives "from persons nominated by the individual legislatures" of the states. And as a counterbalance to the Congress and the states, veto power would be given to a council formed by the executive branch and "a convenient number of the national judiciary."

8. Topic:

   Main idea:

   After agreeing to two houses of congress, the delegates squared off on the issue of membership in the lower chamber, or House of Representatives. Delegates from smaller states wanted the states represented equally there. But delegates from the larger states pushed through representation in proportion to the population. They insisted on the same rule in the Senate and won their point—for the moment—by one vote.

9. Topic:

   Main idea:

   A whole new debate followed on the make-up of the executive branch. It should consist, some said, of three men. Others wanted a council headed by one man. The idea of one man alone was finally adopted with a big "but": The executive should be chosen, not by the people, but by the national legislature. And he could serve only one term of seven years.

Vocabulary Review

Complete the following sentences.

1. A *bicameral* legislature has
   a. one house.   c. three houses.
   b. two houses.

2. A *quorum* generally consists of
   a. one less than half.   c. one more than half.
   b. half.

3. The *legislative branch* of government is responsible for
   a. running the courts.   c. administering the government.
   b. making the laws.
4. The *electorate* are the people who
   a. are elected to office.
   b. have the franchise, or the right to vote.
   c. have the franchise but who cannot run for office.
   d. do not have the franchise.
5. An *unanimous* vote is one in which
   a. a majority, or more than half, of voters agree.
   b. fewer than half the voters agree.
   c. all voters agree.
6. To *preside* over a meeting or convention is to
   a. chair it.   c. speak at it.
   b. attend it.   d. send a letter to it.

SELECTION 2: JAMES MICHENER
(Literature—Biography)

In this section of the chapter, you will have the opportunity to use your main idea strategy as you read an article.

Expanding Your Vocabulary for Reading

The italicized words in the following sentences are from the selection. Think about them before reading. Use both context and word-structure clues to unlock their meanings. Check the glossary if you are unsure of a meaning. Record the meanings in the space provided. Select one or two to add to your personal vocabulary notebook.

1. The difference between the two versions of the story was practically *imperceptible.* I could hardly tell that any changes had been made. (Use word-structure clues: *im-* means "not"; *-ible* means "able.")

2. That writer *eschews* publicity. He avoids it at all costs. (Use a synonym clue.)

3. I try to be *objective,* but unfortunately I end up letting my own viewpoint take over. (Use a phrase of opposite meaning as a clue.)

4. The Pulitzer Prize is one of the most *prestigious* awards in this country. People look up to writers who receive this award for writing. (Use the meaning of the word *prestige* to help. Check the glossary.)

5. Michener's voice is *resonant;* his words roll through the room like organ notes in a cathedral. (Use context clues, especially the description.)

6. *Fortuitously,* I found my lost term paper one hour before it was due.

Getting Ready to Read

Preview the selection by reading the title and first paragraph.

● What is the topic? _____

● What, if anything, do you already know about this topic?

_____

_____

● Michener is a writer. What would you like to find out about him through your reading? Write two questions you would like to answer.

_____

_____

Reading with Meaning

Now read the selection, keeping your two purpose-setting questions in mind. As you read each paragraph, write the topic and main idea in the outer margin. The first paragraph has been done as a model for you. Review the main idea strategy before beginning.

JAMES MICHENER

William Ecenbarger

1. Topic: America's most popular serious novelist.

Main idea: America's most popular serious novelist is a very ordinary man who acts in an ordinary way.

2. Topic:

Main idea:

The lobby of the hotel just outside Washington, D.C., is teeming with purposeful name-tagged men and women awaiting the beginning of the afternoon convention schedule. Outside, motorists are locking horns on the busy street, and a taxi breaks free and sprints to the hotel entrance. A man in a rumpled blue suit emerges, fumbles for the fare and steps through the door. He is bespectacled and looks like a college professor, which he once was. He carries a small overnight bag and is not wearing a name tag. He walks, with an almost imperceptible limp, to the registration desk and hands a piece of paper to the clerk, who advises him, "Your room is ready, Mr. 'Mikener.' " America's most popular serious novelist eschews an offer to carry his bag and walks to the elevator alone. None of the crowd in the lobby has noticed him.

Later, James Albert Michener (MITCH-ner) shrugs off his suit coat, squeaks into a leather chair, and responds to the first question: "No, I'm never noticed anywhere. I even did one of those American Express commercials because of it. I guess when you look at it objectively, there are at least 30 countries in which it is better to be a writer than the United States. The best are Russia, France, Germany and China. They revere their writers. America is still a frontier country that almost shudders at the idea of creative expression.

Michener has come to Washington for a meeting of a national commission studying the problems of UNESCO. It is one of three such groups of which he is now a member. Over the past decade he has served on the boards of a dozen prestigious organizations, including the advisory board of the National Aeronautics and Space Administration while he was writing his 1982 novel *Space*.

"If you last into your 70s, you get a lot of breaks that you're not entitled to. Almost every week I'm invited to participate in something at a level at which young men just don't get asked. These meetings are very intense and real, and just being around a lot of brilliant people keeps me young. I should have to pay to attend them." Michener's voice is resonant, and his words roll through the room like organ notes through a cathedral.

Michener follows a seven-day-a-week routine, which he follows with the persistence of gravity. He rises at 7:30 A.M., drinks a glass of grapefruit juice, which he calls battery acid, and within five minutes is at his desk and typing with two fingers until 12:30, when he usually has completed six pages. He never works in the afternoon and works only two or three evenings a month.

Michener was 40 years old before he settled on a literary career, but in the 37 years since then he has written 33 books that have sold 21 million copies, been translated into 52 languages, inspired 12 films and one smash Broadway musical. All but a few of his books are still in print and readily available. The popularity of such novels as *The Bridges at Tokori, Hawaii, The Source, Chesapeake,* and *Centennial* have made him America's most popular serious novelist—a distinction he views with considerable humility.

While Michener, in keeping with a longstanding practice, will not discuss the content of his new novel, there are threads running through his previous fiction that are not likely to be absent here. His women are strong, resourceful, independent. There is a great deal of scholarly instruction for the reader. And nearly every Michener book deals at least once with interracial or intercultural marriage. The central theme of Michener's work is the destructiveness of injustice and prejudice—a subject that he, making a temple of his fingers, is willing to discuss.

"When you grow up at the bottom of the totem pole, you see things in a different perspective, and with me there's the circumstance of my birth." His eyes crinkle sagely. "If I really don't know who I am, I can hardly look down on anyone. I seem to have a Germanic turn of mind, but I may be Jewish or Lithuanian or part black. With that uncertain background, one's attitude becomes quite tolerant very early."

Michener is not the real name of the man who created Bali-ha'i and Bloody Mary—it's the name of the woman who found him on her doorstep in Doylestown, Pennsylvania, and adopted him.

"I've been led to believe for various reasons that I was born somewhere near Mount Vernon, New York. There's never been any doubt that the year was 1907 because I turned up almost immediately in Pennsylvania. It was a matter of weeks." Two extensive investigations into Michener's origins—one by the State

3. Topic:

   Main idea:

4. Topic:

   Main idea:

5. Topic:

   Main idea:

6. Topic:

   Main idea:

7. Topic:

   Main idea:

8. Topic:

   Main idea:

9. Topic:

   Main idea:

10. Topic:

    Main idea:

Department when he applied for a passport, the other by the U.S. Navy when he was commissioned—failed to solve the mystery of his biologic origins. He does not know for sure where or exactly when he was born, and he has no idea who his natural parents are.

11. Topic:

    Main idea:

Mable Michener was a widow when she took in the waif she named James Albert. She had one son of her own and raised five or six other children at various times. She scratched out a living as a laundress and seamstress, but when times were bad, as they often were, young Jim had to weather the storm in the Bucks County Poorhouse.

12. Topic:

    Main idea:

"My mother did absolutely backbreaking, sweatshop labor, but there were still times when we had nothing. Zero! Money was absolutely all-important to me when I was young, simply because I never had any. This tightens you inside. I've had one success after another, but don't forget that it came very late. I have a very hard inner consciousness. I'm tougher inside than people think."

13. Topic:

    Main idea:

The chance adoption by Mabel Michener was fortuitous for a future writer because she loved literature, especially Dickens, and she read aloud from the classics to her children nearly every night. "It was an absolutely formative part of my life," Michener recalls. "I remember it most vividly today. We would all gather around and she would read from *Oliver Twist* or *David Copperfield*. From this I learned that there were certain conventions to use to make things happen and move the narrative along."

14. Topic:

    Main idea:

Michener began reading himself at an early age. At 14, he chanced upon an issue of *National Geographic*—and was instantly beset by a thirst for travel that he has never managed to slake. By the time he finished high school in 1925, young Michener had visited 45 of the then 48 states—mostly by hitchhiking.

15. Topic:

    Main idea:

"I usually got a ride within 15 minutes. I was young and had a lot of blond hair and kept myself neat. I could always find someone to feed me and bed me down for the night, and I had no hesitation whatever about leaving for a month with 85 cents in my pocket. The whole experience left me very optimistic about the human race."

16. Topic:

    Main idea:

Today Michener is probably the most traveled writer in history. He estimates he has been to Singapore 50 times, Burma 20 times and Bora Bora eight times. He has lived and worked for extended periods in Afghanistan, Australia, Fiji, Hawaii, India, Israel, Japan, Mexico, Portugal, Samoa, Spain, Tahiti, Thailand and Vienna.

17. Topic:

    Main idea:

A dazzling academic high school record won Michener the first full four-year scholarship ever awarded by Swarthmore College, where he graduated summa cum laude in 1929. He spent the next decade traveling, teaching and studying at nine universities in the United States and Europe.

18. Topic:

    Main idea:

He volunteered for the U.S. Navy in 1942 during World War II and was signed to the South Pacific, where as an island-hopping aircraft maintenance officer he was given wide latitude, partly because it was sometimes assumed that he was related to an admiral named Mitscher—an impression he did nothing to clarify. He came to know the area intimately, and on lonely afternoons at a cacao plantation on the island of Espiritu Santo, he began plotting a novel.

At night he battled mosquitoes and humidity in an abandoned building and typed his material. He completed *Tales of the South Pacific* after his discharge. It was not and never has been a bestseller, but it won the 1947 Pulitzer Prize and came to the attention of Richard Rodgers and Oscar Hammerstein, who transformed it into a Broadway musical with staggering success.

Unfortunately, Mabel Michener never was able to enjoy James's literary rewards. She died on March 22, 1946, while he was still in the South Pacific, 11 months before publication of his first novel. [1,458 words]

19. Topic: _____

Main idea: _____

Checking for Understanding

Place a T (true) or F (false) on the line before each statement based on the main idea notes you jotted in the margin during reading. You may look at your notes as you answer the questions.

_____ 1. Michener is a brash and self-important man.

_____ 2. Michener believes that Americans revere their writers.

_____ 3. Michener serves on national boards and commissions.

_____ 4. Michener enjoys his work on national commissions.

_____ 5. Michener has a daily writing schedule that he sticks to.

_____ 6. Michener is America's most popular serious novelist.

_____ 7. The central theme of Michener's novels is the horror of war.

_____ 8. Michener's background may have affected his attitude toward people.

_____ 9. Michener was raised by a sister named Mary.

_____ 10. Michener was born on June 8, 1907.

_____ 11. His mother was a writer.

_____ 12. Michener was raised in a well-to-do home.

_____ 13. Literature was important to him in his youth.

_____ 14. Michener began to travel when he was 40.

_____ 15. He is very pessimistic, or negative, about the human race.

_____ 16. Michener has not had much opportunity to travel although he enjoys traveling.

_____ 17. Michener was an average student.

_____ 18. Michener plotted out his first novel while in the South Pacific during World War II.

_____ 19. Michener's mother read all of his books.

Reviewing Basic Vocabulary

Circle the word that is closest in meaning to the italicized one.

1. She was chairperson of the most *prestigious* committee.
   a. high standing, or honored   c. hardworking
   b. responsible   d. productive
2. Try to be *objective*. Don't let your feelings color your decision.
   a. prestigious   c. impartial
   b. thoughtful   d. subjective

3. My friend had an almost *imperceptible* flaw in his character, but I recognized it after knowing him for two years.
   a. recognizable   c. very slight
   b. serious   d. terrible
4. His voice was *resonant.* I thought he was a singer.
   a. soft   c. wonderful
   b. serious   d. full and vibrant
5. That man *eschews* all offers to pay him for his work.
   a. avoids   c. accepts
   b. criticizes d. rewards
6. My meeting her was *fortuitous.* She drove me home and I avoided a long bus ride home.
   a. sad   c. lucky
   b. happy d. unpleasant

IDENTIFYING THE MAIN IDEA
OF AN EXTENDED SELECTION

You know now that when authors write a paragraph, they have an idea in mind they are trying to tell their readers. The same is true when writers compose an entire selection. They generally have a major idea, or **thesis,** that is at the core of the piece.

A strategy to identify the major thought of an entire selection or chapter is to

● think through the main idea of each paragraph as in the example just given, asking yourself the major idea question: What big thought is the author trying to tell me in this selection? What general point is he or she making about the topic?

Let's apply that strategy to the selection about James Michener that you have just read to figure out the author's thesis. Review the selection, studying the main ideas of the individual paragraphs as you recorded them in the margin. Think about the major thought the author is communicating. Here is a model of what you might say to yourself in your head to identify the main idea of the piece.

The article starts out by saying that Michener is America's most popular author, but one who goes unrecognized. The first part of the article tells me about his work on committees, his daily routine, and his many books. The next part tells about Michener's youth when he was adopted by a poor woman who loved books. It tells about his early interest in books, his early travels, and his service in the navy. All of these experiences must have affected his writing. The major idea seems to be that Michener, America's most popular author who often goes unrecognized, had many varied experiences as a young man—experiences that made him the writer he is today.

In some instances, authors directly state the major point they are making. They can do this anywhere in a selection or textbook chapter. Sometimes authors state their thesis at the beginning to help guide your reading. In other instances, authors state the thesis at the end. Sometimes they do it twice, at the beginning and at the end. In still other instances, authors express their thesis somewhere in the middle.

Reread the selection on pages 14, 15, and 16 of Chapter 1 called "For Heaven's Sakes, Choose a Job You Enjoy!" The author stated her thesis in the first paragraph and again in the last. What is it? Underline it wherever the author states it. Write the thesis of the selection here. _____

_____

Reread the selection on pages 18 and 19 of Chapter 1 called "The Signs of Life." The author states her thesis in the first paragraph. Underline it. Then write the thesis of the selection here. _____

_____

Often authors of articles and sections of a textbook do not state their main point; they suggest it only indirectly. You, the reader, must figure out the thesis from the paragraphs of the selection and from what you already know about the subject. In these cases, which occur more often than not, you must keep asking the major idea question as you read: What is the main point this author is trying to tell me?

In Selections 3 and 4, you will have the opportunity to identify the main ideas of paragraphs and the thesis of an entire selection. In each case, the author did not state his or her thesis directly.

SELECTION 3: THE SECRET OF AMERICA
(Political Science)

Extending Your Vocabulary for Reading

The italicized words in the following sentences are from the selection. Use both context and word-structure clues to figure out their meanings. Record the meanings in the space provided. Select one or two to add to your personal vocabulary notebook.

1. In the *intervening* years, from 1787 to now, the Constitution has served us well. (Note the prefix *inter-*) _____

_____

2. The chairman took measures to *ensure* that all members of the committee had equal opportunity to present their options. (Note the root *sure;* it is a clue to meaning.) _____

_____

3. The most *salient* feature of the building was a large wall projecting out in front. (Note how the word is used in the sentence. Check the glossary.)

_____

_____

4. The document is a *testament* of what free people can do. (Relate this word to the word *testify.* What does one do when one testifies?) _____

_____

5. A *stalwart* nation is firm, steadfast, and uncompromising. (Here is a definition of

the term given in context.) _____

_____

Getting Ready to Read

Preview the selection.

1. *Read the title of the next selection and the information about the author. Run your eyes over the article, looking for key words that give you a clue to the topic. This is necessary here because there are no subheadings. Based on your preview, predict what the article is about.*

    ● The topic is _____

2. What do you already know about this author? What do you already know about the topic? Having just read an article about the author and another on the same topic, you should have considerable background to bring to bear in reading the selection.

    Record what you already know about the Constitution on the following idea web. Note that the idea web includes what, why, who, when, and where questions, which is a good way to organize your thinking before reading.

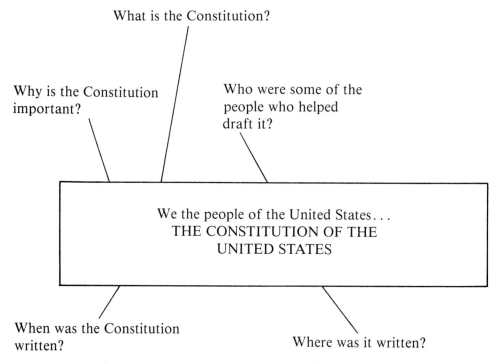

What is the Constitution?

Why is the Constitution important?

Who were some of the people who helped draft it?

We the people of the United States. . .
THE CONSTITUTION OF THE
UNITED STATES

When was the Constitution written?

Where was it written?

Based on what you already know about Michener, what do you expect him to say about the Constitution? How do you think he feels about this document?

Record your predictions here. _____

_____

3. *Set a purpose for reading. Using the words of the title, write a question you expect to be able to answer by reading the piece.* _____

_____

Reading with Meaning

As you read, keep your pen in hand. Do not use a yellow marker. Record the main idea of each paragraph in the margin. As you read, also keep asking: What is Michener saying about the Constitution? What is the major point he is trying to make about it? How does this author feel about the Constitution?

THE SECRET OF AMERICA

James A. Michener *

In the closing years of the 18th century the American colonies in North America won two stunning victories. In 1781 on the battlefield at Yorktown they sealed a military victory which ensured their freedom, and during the summer of 1787 in the debating halls of Philadelphia they won a political struggle which enabled them to survive triumphantly until today.

The writing of the Constitution of the United States is an act of such genius that philosophers still wonder at its accomplishment and envy its results. Fifty-five typical American citizens met and argued for 127 days during a ferociously hot Philadelphia summer and produced one of the magisterial documents of world history. Almost without being aware of their great achievement, they fashioned a nearly perfect instrument of government, and I have studied it for nearly 70 years with growing admiration for its utility and astonishment at its capacity to change with a changing world. It is a testament to what a collection of typical free men can achieve.

I think this is the salient fact about our Constitution. All other nations which were in existence in 1787 have had to alter their form of government in the intervening years. France, Russia and China have undergone momentous revolutions. Stable nations like Sweden and Switzerland have had to change their forms radically. Even Great Britain, most stalwart of nations, has limited sharply the power of its monarch and its House of Lords. Only the United States, adhering to the precepts of its Constitution, has continued with the same form of government. We are not of the younger nations of the world; we are the oldest when it comes to having found the government which suits it best.

It is instructive to remember the 55 men who framed this document. Elder statesmen like George Washington and Benjamin Franklin contributed little to the debate but greatly to the stability and inspiration of the convention. Thomas Jefferson, perhaps the most brilliant American of those days, missed the meetings entirely; he was on diplomatic duty in France. The hard central work of determining the form of government seems to have been done by a handful of truly great men: James Madison and George Mason of Virginia, Roger Sherman of Connecticut, James Wilson and Gouverneur Morris of Pennsylvania. Alexander Hamilton of New York did not speak much but did exert considerable influence.

The 55 contained a college president, a banker, a merchant, a great teacher of law, a judge, a major, a clergyman, a state governor and a surgeon. One-sixth of the members were foreign born. Two were graduates of Oxford University, one of St. Andrews in Scotland. But the group also contained some real nonentities, including a military man who had been court-martialed for

---

*Born in 1907, James Michener is an American novelist whose books include *The Bridges at Tokori, Hawaii, Chesapeake, Texas,* and *Centennial.* If you like stories with considerable historical detail, you will enjoy reading a novel by Michener.

cowardice during the Revolution, some who contributed nothing to the debate, and some who were not quite able to follow what was being debated.

What this mix of men did was create a miracle in which every American should take pride. Their decision to divide the power of the government into three parts—Legislative, Executive, Judicial—was a master stroke, as was the clever way in which they protected the interests of small states by giving each state two Senators, regardless of population, and the interest of large states by apportioning the House of Representatives according to population.

But I think they should be praised mostly because they attended to those profound principles by which free men have through the centuries endeavored to govern themselves. The accumulated wisdom of mankind speaks in this Constitution.   [641 words]

Checking for Understanding

1. Think about the main idea of each paragraph you have just read. Do this by telling each main idea to yourself or a classmate or two. Using a pencil, revise the main idea you wrote down as you read.
2. Now think about what Michener was trying to say about the Constitution of the United States. To guide your thinking, answer these questions:
   ● What does Michener mean by "The Secret of America"? _____

   _____

   ● On a scale of 1 to 5, with 1 very negative and 5 very positive, how does Michener feel about the Constitution of the United States? _____

   _____

   ● What words give you a clue about his feelings? _____

   _____

   ● What is the thesis of the article? What is the major point that Michener is trying to communicate about the Constitution? _____

   _____

   ● Do you agree with Michener about the Constitution? Why or why not?

   _____

   _____

   _____

3. Once you have written your answers to question 2, discuss them with a classmate or two. In this case, there is no single right answer. Your own background determines what you make of the selection. Having discussed your answers, you may want to revise them. Record here what you now think is the main thesis of the article. _____

   _____

Circle the answer that is closest in meaning to the italicized term.

4. When we talk about *intervening* years, we are talking about the years that
   a. have gone by.   c. come between.
   b. will come.   d. have just ended.
5. If we *ensure* the freedoms of all people, we
   a. make sure of.   c. forget about.
   b. do away with.   d. handle thoughtfully.
6. When we say of a person that he was our most *stalwart* supporter, we mean that he was
   a. forgiving.   c. firm and steadfast.
   b. helpful.   d. understanding.
7. Michener says that the Constitution is a *testament* to what free people can achieve. By this he means that it is a/an
   a. legal document.   c. essay.
   b. written report.   d. piece of evidence.
8. A *salient* feature is one that is
   a. unimportant.   c. unhelpful.
   b. conspicuous.   d. related.

SELECTION 4: TIME MANAGEMENT: A GUIDE FOR PERSONAL PLANNING (Management Science)

Extending Your Vocabulary

The italicized words are from the selection. Use context and word-structure clues to figure out their meanings. Record the meanings in the space provided. If you have trouble, check the glossary or a dictionary. Select one or two of the words to add to your personal vocabulary list.

1. The *interval* between the beginning of the college year and midterms is a frightening time for some freshmen. _____

2. During that time, you have to get your *priorities* straight. You must decide what is most important to you—doing well in your courses, going out and having a good time, or meeting a lot of people. _____

3. I have a major *objective*. My goal is to achieve at least a B average in college.
   _____

4. When you are a college student, you cannot *delegate* your responsibilities to someone else. You take care of them yourself. _____

5. I found it *cumbersome* to travel with two suitcases, a tote bag, and a briefcase.
   _____

Getting Ready to Read

Preview the selection.

1. *Read the title of the next selection, the introductory paragraphs, the margin note, and the subheadings. Based on your preview, predict what the article is about.*

   ● The topic is _____

2. What do you already know about managing your time? What can you do to use your time wisely? Discuss these questions with a classmate. Then jot down a few words or phrases that come to mind. _____

   _____

   _____

3. Set a purpose for reading. Read to find out the main idea, or thesis, this author is trying to communicate.

Reading with Meaning

Read the selection. It is from a college textbook on management. If you take courses in management science, this is the kind of material you will read. As you read, note in the margin the main idea of each paragraph. Notice, too, the helpful way this text provides definitions of technical terms in the margin.

TIME MANAGEMENT: A GUIDE FOR PERSONAL PLANNING

Stephen Robbins

Do any of the following describe you?

> You do interesting things before the uninteresting things?
> You do things that are easy before things that are difficult?
> You do things that are urgent before things that are important?
> You work on things in the order of their arrival?
> You wait until a deadline approaches before really moving on a project?

time management A personal form of scheduling time effectively

If you answered yes to one or more of these questions, you could benefit from time management. In this section, we'll present some suggestions to help you manage your time better. We'll show you that **time management** is actually a personal form of scheduling. Managers who use their time effectively know what activities they want to accomplish, the best order to take the activities in, and when they want to complete those activities.

Time as a Scarce Resource

Time is a unique resource in that, if it's wasted it can *never* be replaced. While people talk about *saving time,* the fact is that time can never actually be saved. It can't be stockpiled for use in some future period. If wasted, it can't be retrieved. When a minute is gone, it is gone forever.

The positive side of this resource is that all managers have it in equal abundance. While money, labor, and other resources are distributed unequally in this world, thus putting some managers at a disadvantage, every manager is allotted twenty-four hours every day and seven days every week. Some just use their allotments better than others.

Focusing on Discretionary Time

Managers can't control all of their time. They are routinely interrupted and have to respond to unexpected crises. It's necessary, therefore, to differentiate between response time and discretionary time.

The majority of a manager's time is spent responding to requests, demands, and problems initiated by others. We call this **response time** and treat it as uncontrollable. The portion that *is* under a manager's control is called **discretionary time.** Most of the suggestions offered to improve time management apply to its discretionary component. Why? Because only this part is manageable!

response time
Uncontrollable time spent responding to requests, demands, and problems initiated by others.

Unfortunately, for most managers, particularly those in the lower and middle ranks of the organization, discretionary time tends to become available in small pieces—five minutes here, five minutes there. Thus it is very difficult to use effectively. The challenge, then, is to know what time is discretionary and then to organize activities so as to accumulate discretionary time in blocks large enough to be useful. Those who are good at identifying and organizing their discretionary time get significantly more accomplished, and the things they accomplish are more likely to be high-priority activities.

discretionary time The part of a manager's time that is controllable.

How Do You Use Your Time?

How do managers, or anyone for that matter, determine how well they use their time? The answer is that they should keep a log of daily activities for a short period of time, then evaluate the data they gather.

The best log is a daily diary or calendar broken into fifteen-minute intervals. To get enough information from which to generalize, you need about two weeks' worth of entries. During this two-week period, you enter everything you do in the diary in fifteen-minute segments. To minimize memory loss, post the entries as you do them. Keep in mind that honesty is important. You want to record how you actually spend your time, not how you *wished* you had spent your time!

When the diary is complete, you have a detailed time and activity log. Now you're ready to analyze how effectively you use your time. Rate each activity in terms of its importance and urgency (see Table 4.1). If you find that many activities received C's or D's, you'll find the next sections valuable. They provide detailed guidelines for better time management.

Five Steps to Better Time Management

The essence of time management is to use your time effectively. This requires that you know the objectives you want to accomplish,

---

Table 4.1 Analyzing Activities for Importance and Urgency

Rate Each Activity for
Importance
A. Very important: must be done
B. Important: should be done
C. Not so important: may be useful, but is not necessary
D. Unimportant: doesn't accomplish anything

Urgency
A. Very urgent: must be done now
B. Urgent: should be done now
C. Not urgent: can be done sometime later
D. Time not a factor

---

the activities that will lead to the accomplishment of those objectives, and the importance and urgency of each activity. We've translated this into a five-step process.

1. *Make a list of your objectives.* What specific objectives have you set for yourself and the unit you manage?

2. *Rank the objectives according to their importance.* Not all objectives are of equal importance. Given the limitations on your time, you want to make sure you give highest priority to the most important objectives.

3. *List the activities necessary to achieve your objectives.* What specific actions do you need to take to achieve your objectives?

4. *For each objective, assign priorities to the various activities required to reach the objective.* This step imposes a second set of priorities. Here, you need to emphasize both importance and urgency. If the activity is not important, you should consider delegating it to someone below you. If it's not urgent, it can usually wait. This step will identify activities that you *must* do, those you *should* do, those you'll get to *when you can,* and those that can be *delegated to others.*

5. *Schedule your activities according to the priorities you've set.* The final step is to prepare a daily plan. Every morning, or at the end of the previous work day, make a list of the five or so most important things you want to do for the day. If the list grows to ten or more activities, it becomes cumbersome and ineffective. Then set priorities for the activities listed on the basis of importance and urgency.   [920 words]

Checking for Understanding

1. Think about the main idea of each paragraph in the selection. Do this by telling each main idea to yourself or a classmate or two. Using a pencil, revise the main ideas you wrote down in the margin as you read.
2. What is Stephen Robbins trying to say about time management? To guide your thinking, answer these questions:

● What does Robbins mean by "time management"? _____

_____

● On a scale of 1 to 5, with 1 very negative and 5 very positive, how does Robbins feel about time management? _____

_____

● What is the thesis of the selection? What is the major point that Robbins is trying to communicate about time management? _____

_____

3. Once you have written your answers to question 2, discuss them with a classmate or two. Having discussed your answers, you may want to revise them. Record here what you now think is the main thesis of the article.

_____

_____

Reviewing New Vocabulary

Insert each of these words in the sentence where it fits best.

a. delegate   c. interval   e. priorities
b. cumbersome   d. objective

1. You must learn to _____ responsibility to those who work for you. You can't do everything yourself.

2. What is your primary _____ in taking a course in time management?

3. You must let a decent _____ elapse before you get married again.

4. What are your _____? What is most important to you? What is the least important?

5. If a box is overly large, you may find it _____ to carry.

EXTENDING WHAT YOU HAVE LEARNED

Reading for Main Ideas

In this chapter you have been learning a strategy for identifying main ideas as you read paragraphs. List the steps you use to find the main idea of a paragraph.

1.

2.

3.

Applying the Strategy to Your Reading

Find an article in a newsmagazine such as *Newsweek* or *Time*. Preview the article to identify the topic. Then think about what you know on the topic. Read the article to identify the main point the writer is making about the topic. Finally, record the title of the article, the date when written, the topic as you identified it, and the major idea, or thesis, of the article on an index card.

Applying the Strategy to Textbook Reading

Read a two- or three-page section from a textbook you are using in another course. Use the main idea strategy to identify the main idea of each paragraph. Record the idea in the margin as you read along. When you finish reading, review the ideas you have written down, and in the bottom margin, write the major point, or thesis, of the entire section.

Building a Knowledge Base for Future Reading

Geographic sites mentioned in this chapter include Washington, D.C., Massachusetts, Virginia, and Philadelphia, Pennsylvania. Circle the names of these places on the map on page 13.

5

Thinking About Details

Before reading the chapter, read the title, the stated objective, and the headings and subheadings. Ask yourself: What is the topic of the chapter? In the space above and beside the chapter number, jot down what you already know about the topic. Then in the space below the number, jot down at least two questions you hope to answer through reading the chapter.

OBJECTIVE

In this chapter, you will learn strategies for thinking about details as you read. Specifically, you will learn to

1. sort details to identify the more significant ones, and
2. rely on approximations when reading numerical details.

INTRODUCTION—THINKING ABOUT DETAILS

In developing the main idea of a paragraph, a writer generally includes considerable detail. Some details relate directly to the main idea; these help support the point the writer is making. Other details relate in some way to the main idea, but they are not essential to the point the writer is making. In a way, these details are icing on the cake; they add interest and flavor.

Identifying Significant Details

In reading it is important to identify the significant details that support the point a writer is making. A basic strategy for doing this is to ask yourself:

- How does this detail relate to the main idea?
- Does this detail support the main point, or is it icing on the cake?

Ask these questions as you read a paragraph. Do not wait until the end. Sorting significant from less essential details is a continuous process; you do it all the time as you read.

Let's apply this strategy to the details in the first paragraph of the selection about James Michener from Chapter 4. Reread it, recalling the main idea as you do.

> The lobby of the hotel just outside Washington, D.C., is teeming with purposeful, name-tagged men and women awaiting the beginning of the afternoon convention schedule. Outside, motorists are locking horns on the busy street, and a taxi breaks free and sprints to the hotel entrance. A man in a rumpled blue suit emerges, fumbles for the fare and steps through the door. He is bespectacled and looks like a college professor, which he once was. He carries a small overnight bag and is not wearing a name tag. He walks, with an almost imperceptible limp, to the registration desk and hands a piece of paper to the clerk, who advises him, "Your room is ready, Mr. 'Mikener.' " America's most popular serious novelist eschews an offer to carry his bag and walks to the elevator alone. None of the crowd in the lobby has noticed him.

The point the writer is making is that Michener is a humble man. What details from the paragraph support this picture of Michener? Before reading on, write down three details that support this main idea.

1. _____

2. _____

3. _____

Essential details include the fact that Michener carries his own bag, wears a rumpled suit, does not wear a name tag, and does not correct the clerk who mispronounces his name. These details support the idea of the paragraph—Michener is a humble man.

What about the less significant details in the paragraph about Michener? Write down at least one detail that has little bearing on the main idea:

_____

One rather insignificant detail is that motorists are locking horns. Another is that the street is busy. Even the fact that the lobby of the hotel is filled with people has little bearing on Michener's natural humility.

What function do these details have in the paragraph? They are the icing! They make an interesting beginning and add style to the writing. They also provide a contrast. Here are all these purposeful, name-tagged men and women, probably dressed for success. In contrast is this rumpled and fumbling man, America's most popular serious novelist.

Is it important to remember the lesser details? In most cases, no. As readers we move our eyes over them, getting the flavor of the writing and going on to details that support the main idea.

Approximating Numerical Detail

Some paragraphs are filled with numerical detail—lots of numbers given in support of the main idea. A strategy to use here is to

● Look at the precise details and approximate a ballpark figure.

Let's apply this strategy to the following paragraph from the Michener article. Reread it, asking two questions: What is the main idea? How will I handle all those numbers that relate to the main idea?

Michener was 40 years old before he settled on a literary career, but in the 37 years since then he has written 33 books that have sold 21 million copies, been translated into 52 languages, inspired 12 films and one smash Broadway musical. All but a few of his books are still in print and readily available. The popularity of such novels as *The Bridges at Tokori, Hawaii, The Source, Chesapeake* and *Centennial* have made him America's most popular serious novelist—a distinction he views with considerable humility.

The main idea is that Michener is a prolific author; he has written many books. But what do you do with the numbers that support the main point?

Unless you have a reading purpose that requires knowing these details, typically you generalize based on the numbers. You do not try to remember that Michener wrote 33 books but think in terms of *more than 30 books*. Notice that this is a ballpark figure—in other words, an approximation. Similarly, you generalize that the books have been translated into *lots of languages,* and *some films* have been based on the books.

Reread this paragraph from the Michener article. As you read a detail, do not try to remember it. Try for a ballpark approximation:

Today Michener is probably the most traveled writer in history. He estimates he has been to Singapore 50 times, Burma 20 times and Bora Bora eight times. He has lived and worked for extended periods in Afghanistan, Australia, Fiji, Hawaii, India, Israel, Japan, Mexico, Portugal, Samoa, Spain, Tahiti, Thailand and Vienna.

The main point of the paragraph is that Michener is widely traveled. Write two details from the paragraph—in ballpark terms—to support the point.

1. _____

2. _____

From the data, you may have generalized that Michener has visited some locations from 8 to 50 times. You may have noted that he has traveled all over the world—from Spain to Tahiti. It probably is not essential to remember all the places mentioned.

In the remainder of this chapter, you will have the opportunity to practice your strategy for identifying significant details.

SELECTION 1: GREAT CONSTRUCTIONS OF THE PAST
(History)

Getting Ready to Read

To handle main ideas and details with any degree of proficiency, you must be able to identify whether details support a main idea. For example, read this statement of a main idea:

> **Main Idea:** The Great Pyramids of Gizeh are the most famous of the pyramids of Egypt.

Now read these statements of detail, asking yourself: Which of the statements provides a detail that supports the main idea—the idea that the Gizeh Pyramids are the most famous? Which are about the pyramids but do not relate directly to the fame of the pyramids?

a. The Step Pyramid is older than the Pyramids of Gizeh.
b. The Great Pyramid at Gizeh is one of the Seven Wonders of the Ancient World.
c. The Mayans also built pyramids.
d. The Pyramids of Gizeh are located near the city of Cairo.

All of the details are true, but only one supports the idea of the fame of the pyramids: The Great Pyramid at Gizeh is one of the Seven Wonders of the Ancient World. The Gizeh pyramids must have been outstanding and famous to be so designated. The other facts—that the Step Pyramid is older, that the Mayans built pyramids, and that the Gizeh pyramids are located near Cairo—are true but do not relate directly to or support the main idea—the fame of the Pyramids of Gizeh.

Reading with Meaning

Read the following main idea statements. For each, circle the detail that most strongly supports the main idea. All of the items deal with great engineering accomplishments of the past.

1. **Main Idea:** The Great Sphinx is a colossal sculpture set like a guard near the Pyramid of Khafre in Egypt.
   a. The Great Sphinx has the head of a human and a body of a lion.
   b. Thousands of sphinxes were built in ancient Egypt.
   c. The sphinx is part of Greek mythology.
   d. In Greek mythology, the sphinx was a winged monster with the head of a woman and the body of a lion.
2. **Main Idea:** The Colossus of Rhodes was a large bronze statue that once stood in the harbor of Rhodes, an island in the eastern Mediterranean Sea.

    a. Legend says that the Colossus stood across the harbor and ships passed between its legs.

    b. A famous American colossus is the Statue of Liberty.

    c. The human mind has always been intrigued by great statues.

    d. The Mediterranean Sea separates Europe from North Africa and has always been important in the trade of this area.

3. **Main Idea:** Some astronomers propose that the standing stones of Stonehenge in England were built by ancient people to measure solar and lunar movements.

    a. There are some similarities between Stonehenge and another ancient monument of stones near Avebury in England.

    b. So many visitors now come to Stonehenge that it is no longer possible to wander among the upright stones.

    c. The astronomer Gerald Hawkins used computers to test his belief, or hypothesis, that the stones related to astronomical movements.

    d. Stonehenge is a short day trip from London.

4. **Main Idea:** The term *romanesque* describes the style of architecture that was seen in western Europe between the end of the ninth and the twelfth centuries.

    a. Architects who worked during the ninth and twelfth centuries were considered of low social status.

    b. The church was a dominant force during the ninth and twelfth centuries.

    c. The Durham Cathedral, begun in Durham, England, in 1093, is considered one of the outstanding examples of romanesque architecture.

    d. Few romanesque cathedrals remain today exactly as they were originally constructed.

5. **Main Idea:** The gothic age (1150–1300) was a period of great cathedral building in France.

    a. The ribs on a gothic vault are primarily there for aesthetic purposes.

    b. People harnessed themselves to carts to pull the limestone building blocks from the quarry to the cathedral site.

    c. The people of the period felt that the cathedral belonged to them; they took pride in their gift to God.

    d. French cathedrals built during this period include Notre Dame de Paris, Rheims, Chartres, Amiens, Le Mans, Beauvais, and many others that are lesser known.

6. **Main Idea:** The Suez Canal is an important navigational link that facilitates world trade.

    a. The Suez Canal connects the Mediterranean Sea with the Gulf of Suez and then with the Red Sea.

    b. The Suez Canal was constructed in the period between 1859 and 1869.

    c. The modern-day canal was planned by a French engineer; the British underwrote much of the cost of the canal.

    d. The Suez Canal is a sea level canal that is more than 100 miles long; it is longer than the Panama Canal.

7. **Main Idea:** Mount Rushmore is a national shrine that honors great American presidents.

    a. The same sculptor who worked on Stone Mountain in Georgia conceived of Mount Rushmore.

    b. Mount Rushmore is located in the state of South Dakota in the Black Hills.

    c. It took fourteen years to carve the faces in the stone; the sculptor, Gutzon Borglum, died before the carving was completed.

    d. Carved in the rock of the mountain are the faces of four great presidents.

8. **Main Idea:** The Verrazano-Narrows Bridge is the longest suspension bridge in the United States.
   a. The Verrazano-Narrows Bridge was designed by O. H. Ammann.
   b. The Verrazano-Narrows Bridge is 4,260 feet long and spans the Narrows at the entrance to New York harbor.
   c. The Verrazano-Narrows Bridge was named for Giovanni da Verrazano, an Italian sailing in the service of France, who possibly was the first European to enter New York Bay.
   d. The Verrazano-Narrows Bridge has two levels; each holds six lanes of traffic.

SELECTION 2: HE'S MY SON! (Sociology)

Expanding Your Vocabulary Through Reading

Here are five words from the selection you will read: *assumption, expectation, contradiction, situation, interaction.* These nouns have been formed from verbs to which the suffix *-tion* has been added. An assumption is something we assume, or take for granted. A contradiction is something that contradicts, or goes against another piece of evidence. An expectation is something that we expect, or anticipate. A situation is something that is situated somewhere. Interaction occurs when people interact with one another. Write two other words that have the suffix *-tion* in them. From what verb was each constructed?

_____   _____

word with -tion   verb   *word with -tion   verb*

When you read a noun with the suffix *-tion,* identify the verb from which it was constructed. You can use your understanding of the verb to figure out the meaning of the noun.

Getting Ready to Read

Read the title and the first sentence of the selection, which is from a college sociology text. Then predict: What do you anticipate is going to happen next? Write

your expectation here. _____

_____

Reading with Meaning

Read to find out what actually happened, to find out the main idea of the piece (the thesis), and to be able to retell the story giving only the details that relate to the main idea.

HE'S MY SON!

John Macionis

The automobile roared down the mountain road, tearing through sheets of windblown rain. Two people, a man and his young son, peered intently through the windshield, observing the edge of the road beyond which they could see only a black void. Suddenly, as the car rounded a bend, the headlights shone upon a large tree that had fallen across the roadway. The man swerved to the right and braked, but unable to stop, the car left the road, crashed through some brush, turned end upon end, and came to rest on its roof. Then a bit of good fortune: the noise of the crash had been heard at a nearby hunting lodge, and a telephone call from there soon brought police and a rescue crew. The driver, beyond help, was pronounced dead at the scene of the accident. Yet, the boy was still alive, although badly hurt and unconscious. Rushed by ambulance to the hospital in the town at the foot of the mountain, he was taken immediately into emergency surgery.

Alerted in advance, the medical team burst through the swinging doors ready to try to save the boy's life. Then, with a single look at his face, the surgeon abruptly exclaimed: "Oh, no! Get someone to take over for me—I can't operate on this boy. *He's my son!*"

How can the surgeon's reaction be explained?

This situation appears to contain a contradiction: if the boy's father died in the crash, how could the boy be the surgeon's son? The contradiction, however, exists only in the reader's *assumption* that the surgeon must be male. Inconsistency is resolved if we conclude that the surgeon is simply the boy's *mother.*

Social interaction is the process by which people act and react in relation to others. Through social interaction human beings create meaning in any situation. Every situation, however, is also shaped by assumptions and expectations rooted in the larger society of which we are a part.   [330 words]

Checking Your Understanding

1. What is the big idea, the thesis, which the sociologist is trying to communicate

   through this story? _____

   _____

2. Turn to a classmate and tell him or her the story, leaving out the unessential facts and including only those necessary to get the tale across. Then together study the story and identify the details you left out. Why were those details not essential to

   the telling of the tale? _____

   _____

3. Mark the following as either an essential (E) detail or an unessential (U) detail—icing on the cake that adds interest.

   _____   a. The car came to rest on its roof.

   _____   b. There was a lodge nearby.

   _____   c. The father was killed.

   _____   d. The boy was injured.

   _____   e. The team burst through the swinging doors.

   _____   f. The surgeon said, "He's my son!"

   _____   g. The hospital was at the foot of the mountain.

   _____   h. The medical team was alerted in advance.

Reviewing Key Vocabulary

Place each word in the sentence where it best fits the context. Use each word only once.

a. assumption   c. expectation   e. situation

b. contradiction   d. interaction

1. The _____ was resolved when the judge pointed out the inconsistency in the evidence.

2. He was operating under an unwarranted _____ that he later learned was totally untrue.

3. In that _____ there was only one thing that we could do—run for safety.

4. Professors try to encourage _____ among members of a class.

5. I bought the book with the _____ that it was a novel. I discovered immediately upon opening it that I was in error.

SELECTION 3: WHAT DOES McDONALD'S PAY?
(Economics)

Getting Ready to Read

Read the title and the first paragraph of this selection from a college economics text.

● What do you think determines what McDonald's pays? _____

_____

Reading with Meaning

Read the selection to test your prediction. Read also to pick out the most essential details.

WHAT DOES McDONALD'S PAY?

Karl Case and Ray Fair

At two locations about 40 minutes apart in the Boston area, McDonald's hires workers at very different wage rates. At one franchise, a small sign on the counter reads "Help wanted, full or part time." If you ask about a job, however, you will find that they have only one part-time opening, and that the wage rate offered is the minimum wage, $3.35 per hour. At the other location, a large sign says "Full-time or part-time positions available, day or night shifts, excellent benefits and $7.00 per hour." The location has six openings.

Why would one restaurant pay wages nearly twice as high as an identical place with identical jobs in the same metropolitan area? The franchise owner simply finds that she has no applicants at lower wages, and even at the higher rates, she has a very difficult time keeping her available positions filled.

Clearly the two restaurants are buying labor in different labor markets. If people could move at no cost from one point to another, such wage differences would disappear. But there are costs. Neither of these restaurants is accessible by public transportation. Thus to take a job at one of them, you must live nearby or have a car. Restaurants such as McDonald's draw much of their labor from the supply of high-school students who want to work part time. Most of them don't have cars. The high-wage franchise is on a major highway at some distance from local high schools and residential areas; the low-wage franchise is in the center of a town.

Other facts as well probably affect the available labor supplies at the two locations. The median income of the four towns surrounding the high-wage franchise is 50 percent higher than the median income of the four towns surrounding the low-wage franchise. To the extent that the labor supply is made up of students, parents' income may well have an effect. Higher-income families may spend some of their money buying leisure for their children. Many lower-income families expect older children to contribute to the family income.

The data support this argument. In one of the lower-income towns, 82 percent of all high-school students held at least one part-time job during the school year. In one of the high-income towns, only 24 percent of high-school students held part-time jobs.

In the high-wage area, the demand for labor in general is also higher. A number of major employers relatively close by pay high wages and hire part-time workers. In addition, workers, whether or not they are students, are more likely to have cars in the high-wage area. Cars give them the ability to search for work over a wider geographical area.

This example illustrates at least three important points. First, labor supply depends on a number of factors including wage rates, nonlabor income, and wealth. Second, individual firms have very little control over the market wage; firms are forced to pay the wage that is determined by the market. Finally, because people cannot be moved free of charge, and because people do not reside at their workplaces, there is an important spatial dimension to labor markets. Different supply and demand conditions can and do prevail at different geographical locations. This is true across regions as well as within cities. Labor markets in different regions of the country—Northeast, South, and so forth—are very different.   [572 words]

Checking Your Comprehension

In the last paragraph, the authors sum up their major ideas, or points. For each point, give one or two details from the selection that support it. When working with numbers, use a ballpark figure. Perhaps collaborate with a classmate.

1. **Main Idea:** Labor supply depends on a number of factors, including wage rates, nonlabor income, and wealth.

   Supporting Details: _____

   _____

2. **Main Idea:** Individual companies have little control over the wages they must pay.

   Supporting Details: _____

   _____

3. **Main Idea:** Because people cannot be moved free of charge, location influences what wages a company must pay.

Supporting Details: _____

_____

SELECTION 4: THE DREAM AT PANAMA
(Geography and History)

Expanding Your Vocabulary Through Reading

Determine the meaning of the italicized terms by using context and word structure clues. Where you are uncertain, check the glossary for a definition. Record the definition in the space provided. The italicized words are from the selection you will read shortly.

1. The *isthmus,* the narrow strip of land between the two islands, was visible only at low tide.

2. *Devastating* winds roared over the countryside destroying everything in sight.

3. The situation that existed after World War II was *akin* to the situation after World War I.

4. All the energy he could *muster* was not enough for him to move the boulder.

5. For Washington, the Battle of Long Island was a *debacle.* He was forced to retreat with his troops.

6. The wagons became *mired* in the mud. We had no way to pull them out.

7. During the war, we had to endure *horrific* conditions—lack of food, medicine, adequate shelter, and even pure water.

8. The *incumbent* judge—the one currently in office—will try the case.

9. He was a *virtual* prisoner of the rebels for two months; there was a guard at his door, and he could not leave his home.

10. At the end of the month we were *inundated* with bills. There were so many we could not pay them.

11. The *continental divide* is a ridge of mountains that separates rivers flowing into one ocean from those flowing into the other. In North America, the continental divide is the ridge of the Rocky Mountains, which separates westward-flowing streams from eastward-flowing ones.

Getting Ready to Read

Preview the selection.

● Read the title, the italicized introductory section, and the first paragraph. Study the illustration in Figure 5.1. What is the topic of the selection? Write the topic in the center of the idea web below.

● What do you already know about the Panama Canal? Talk about what you know with a classmate or two. Then working together, add what you know to the web. On your web, include your own opinion about the importance of the Panama Canal.

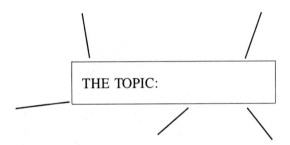

THE TOPIC:

● What questions do you want to answer based on your preview of the selection? Write two questions here. _____

_____

_____

Reading with Meaning

Read the selection, keeping your purpose-setting questions in mind and visualizing what is being described. Then reread the article; for each paragraph record significant details that support, or substantiate, the main idea. If your instructor permits it, complete the activity with a classmate. The first two paragraphs are done as a model.

THE DREAM AT PANAMA

George Cruys

Perhaps there is only the moon to compare with it. Of all the achievements of American engineering, only the landing on the

1. **Main idea:** The building of the Panama Canal is an accomplishment that equaled the landing of astronauts on the moon.
Supporting detail: Building the canal is akin to building the pyramids.

2. **Main idea:** People had long dreamed of a canal in Panama.
Supporting detail: A Panama Canal was proposed as early as the 1500s.

3. **Main idea:** The canal required great creativity.
Supporting detail:

4. **Main idea:** Geographic relationships are important at the canal.
Supporting detail:

5. **Main idea:** The first path across the isthmus was Las Cruces Trail.
Supporting detail:

6. **Main idea:** Railroad was built and encouraged the French to try to build a sea level canal.
Supporting detail:

moon and the planting there of a wrinkled flag can rival the construction of the Panama Canal as an epoch-making accomplishment. The Suez Canal, the trans-Siberian Railroad and the Taj Mahal all pale beside it. The canal's construction is more closely akin to the pyramids of Egypt in its scope and difficulty of execution, but in the modern era, there is only the moon.

Like the landing on the moon, the construction of a canal across the narrow Isthmus of Panama was a dream long before it became reality. As early as 1534, Charles I of Spain proposed a canal at Panama, but it would take nearly 400 years for builders to catch up with his imagination.

When the canal finally was proposed, it required all the creativity the twentieth century could muster. It was the largest public work ever attempted. Its engineers had to control a wild river, cut the continental divide, construct the largest dam and man-made lake known to that date and swing the largest locks ever constructed from the biggest cement structures ever poured. Along the way, two of the world's most devastating diseases had to be wiped out in one of their greatest strongholds. And all of this was to be done without the airplane or the automobile: Kitty Hawk rose into the headlines in 1903—the same year the U.S. signed a treaty with Panama—and there was no road across the isthmus until World War II.

If Panama has had an unusual role in bygone dreams, it most certainly has a startling relationship to the hard facts of geography. The country is farther east than most people imagine—the canal and about half of Panama actually lie east of Miami. Because of the country's shallow "S" shape and east-west orientation, it has places where the sun rises in the Pacific and sets in the Atlantic. More significantly, Panama is squeezed into the narrowest portion of Central America. At the canal, just 43 miles of land separate Atlantic and Pacific shores. Perhaps even more important, Panama offers the lowest point in the North American continental divide—originally 312 feet above sea level at the canal's Culebra Cut. By comparison, the lowest pass in the United States is nearly 5,000 feet.

Spanish & French Era

The first path across the isthmus was Las Cruces Trail. A winding, difficult tunnel through the jungle from Panama City to Portobelo, it was built by slaves to transport riches to the Spanish Main. At the edge of the narrow trail a tangled mass of strange plants issues threatening noises even today. "It's O.K. in the daytime," said guide José Turner during a recent visit, "but imagine it at night."

California's gold rush sent thousands of prospectors to Panama in search of a quick crossing to the Pacific. By 1855, a small railroad operated between coasts and some prospectors paid $25 in gold just to walk along its tracks. Today the train costs $1.75 to ride and takes about an hour and a half to cross the continent. The new railroad encouraged engineers toward one of the greatest peacetime debacles in human experience: the ill-fated French attempt to build a sea level canal at Panama.

Figure 5.1   *Views of the Panama Canal Being Built.*   (Panama Canal Company)

7. **Main idea:** It is hard to imagine today what it was like then.
Supporting detail:

8. **Main idea:** Excessive rainfall was a major problem.
Supporting detail:

9. **Main idea:** Threatening vegetation and creatures were a problem.
Supporting detail:

10. **Main idea:** The worst problem was the mosquito.
Supporting detail:

11. **Main idea:** Many people lost their lives to diseases.
Supporting detail:

12. **Main idea:** French canal builders faced problems that made them give up the project.
Supporting detail:

13. **Main idea:** The French had actually done fine work.
Supporting detail:

Crossing the canal today, it is hard to imagine the impossible challenge Panama presented just a century ago. Today's transit is so smooth and the surrounding grounds so park like, the stories of horror in the jungle sound like tropical exaggerations. But in 1881, when the first party of French engineers arrived to dig the canal, the Isthmus of Panama was—as an American senator would later put it—"death's nursery."

Panama is inundated by seventy inches of annual rainfall on the Pacific side, and an improbable 144 inches on the Atlantic side. Up to six inches can fall in a single day. Fed by this rain, the Chagres River, which empties into the Atlantic just west of modern Cristobal, could rise more than forty-five feet. During one storm it rose ten feet in just twenty-four hours.

The rain forest is a threatening wall of vegetation inhabited by all manner of equally threatening creatures. On Barro Colorado—a single island in modern Gatun Lake—there are twenty-two species of alligators, two species of crocodiles and thirty-seven species of serpents, while area mammals include the jaguar, puma and ocelot.

But the most formidable creature of Panama, when the French were deciding to build a canal there, was one of its smallest. The clean, soft skins of engineers and laborers were about to be welcomed by clouds of mosquitoes—and at the time that the French arrived, nobody knew that they carried disease.

Malaria and yellow fever were the worst diseases, but others included nearly all of the bad ones: cholera, typhoid, dysentery, tuberculosis, smallpox, and—for a frightening interlude during the American era—black plague. In the twenty years that the French would labor to build their hopeless canal, roughly 20,000 people would perish—most of them from disease. Jules Dingler, the director of the French excavations in 1883, lost his entire family in Panama to disease—wife, son, daughter and prospective son-in-law. After two crushing years, he went home to France.

The French canal, spearheaded by Suez builder Ferdinand de Lesseps, became mired in mud, jungle, disease, rising costs, corruption and controversy. Leaders of the private undertaking were sentenced to prison; 25,000 Jamaican laborers were stranded when the company went bankrupt. In 1904 the French sold their interest in the canal to the United States for $40 million—a sum considerably short of the $287 million they had invested and vastly less than it had cost them in lives and broken dreams.

In spite of all their difficulties, the French had done excellent work. In 22 years of labor, they excavated 78 million cubic yards of earth under the most horrific conditions. Sadly, due to the different nature of the American canal, most of the French work was useless. Today, if you want to see what the French sacrificed so much to accomplish, you must watch carefully on the western bank, moving toward the Atlantic from Gatun Locks. There by a red buoy, number sixteen, there is a wide channel that disappears quickly into the jungle. It is the only section of the French canal that is left.

The American Era

In 1906, when the bespectacled Theodore Roosevelt came to Panama to see the "Big Ditch" for himself, the occasion marked the first visit of an incumbent president to a foreign country in the history of the United States. It was a clear sign of the importance Roosevelt would place on the canal's construction.

At the turn of the century Panama was part of Colombia, ruled by Bogotá. When negotiations with Colombia for U.S. rights to build a canal came to a standstill, Panama proclaimed its independence in 1903 with key U.S. support. Less than a month later, a treaty with the Panamanian Republic established a Panama Canal Zone to be controlled by the U.S. "in perpetuity," extending five miles on either side of the proposed waterway.

The Americans arrived in 1904 equipped with several advantages over their French predecessors. Larger steam shovels, bigger train cars, a huge national effort supported by a closer home country and an astonishingly corruption-free administration all favored the American attempt. The new engineers, it was noted, were particularly adept at using the rails to transport excavated material.

The key initial accomplishment was the virtual elimination of disease by Dr. William Gorgas, a U.S. Army physician who had already survived a yellow fever attack in Texas and one of malaria in Panama. With exacting and lifesaving thoroughness, Dr. Gorgas wiped out the breeding grounds of mosquitoes in the construction area. In an immense effort which at times included as many as 4,000 sanitation laborers, Gorgas eliminated yellow fever by the end of 1905 and radically reduced malaria.

With disease on the wane, engineers set to work. By 1907 some 30,000 men had arrived, primarily from Barbados, Jamaica and the U.S. Due to a shortage of available labor, Panama itself supplied just 357 workers for the canal.

The solution for the flooding Chagres River was to build an enormous dam that would create a lake over which ships could sail. Locks would raise ships to lake level, reducing the dig at Culebra on the continental divide to a conceivable scale. Ironically, both solutions had been previously suggested by Frenchmen.

The troublesome Chagres River was turned on itself. At the town of Gatun, engineers built what was, in its day, the largest earth dam ever constructed. One and a half miles long, half a mile wide at its base, Gatun Dam rose to 105 feet above sea level. Behind it gathered the waters of what was then the largest man-made lake in the world, 163-square-mile Gatun Lake. The massive waterway inundated several towns, rerouted the Panama Railroad, completely changed the geography of the canal area and furnished 23.5 navigable miles of the canal itself. The engineers had saved themselves a lot of digging, but there was still the question of the continental divide.

14. **Main idea:** President Roosevelt recognized the importance of building a Panama Canal.
Supporting detail:

15. **Main idea:** U.S. signed a treaty with Panama in the early 1900s to establish a Canal Zone.
Supporting detail:

16. **Main idea:** The Americans had advantages that the French did not have.
Supporting detail:

17. **Main idea:** The key advantage was the virtual elimination of disease.
Supporting detail:

18. **Main idea:** Workers were brought into Panama.
Supporting detail:

19. **Main idea:** Solution to the construction problem was a series of locks that raised ships and the formation of a lake.
Supporting detail:

20. **Topic:** The Gatun Dam
Main idea:

Supporting detail:

21. **Topic:** Getting across the continental divide
Main idea:

Supporting detail:

22. **Topic:** The Culebra solution
Main idea:
Supporting detail:

23. **Topic:** The canal locks
Main idea:
Supporting detail:

24. **Topic:** Completion of the canal
Main idea:
Supporting detail:

25. **Topic:** Landslides
Main idea:
Supporting detail:

26. **Topic:** Results of the canal
Main idea:
Supporting detail:

27. **Topic:** Change to Panamanian control
Main idea:
Supporting detail:

28. **Topic:** Traveling the canal today

There are seventy hill formations along the canal route, but the cut across the continental divide at Culebra was the deepest and most difficult. The deeper the men dug, the more the mountains fell into the hole around them—sometimes burying steam shovels and railroad equipment. In 1912 alone, four and a half months were spent removing landslides from Culebra Cut. At one point, engineers discovered to their astonishment that the bottom of the excavation actually was rising under pressure from the surrounding mountains. In one place the ground rose six feet in five minutes.

The solution at Culebra was to keep removing dirt. Originally expected to require a 670-foot width, the final excavation grew to more than a quarter of a mile across and nine miles in length. Lt. Col. David Gaillard—the engineer in charge and the person who later would give his name to Culebra—would have been amused to note that the astronauts who returned from the moon brought with them just forty-seven pounds of lunar rocks.

The ditches at sea level and at eighty-five feet that crossed the continental divide were connected by the largest canal locks ever attempted. Radical in scale, they were reliable in operation. Seventy-two years after the opening of the canal, the same locks and seven-story, 700-ton lock gates are still in use, still activated by the same forty-horsepower motors. Nearly three quarters of a century after their construction, the tower control panels look almost exactly the same as the day they were built. It has proven to be a very workable design.

The Modern Era

The Panama Canal was completed under budget at $387 million. The *SS Ancon* made the first transit ahead of schedule on August 15, 1914, a landmark event overshadowed by the outbreak of World War I.

Since the canal's opening, work has continued at a surprising rate. In 1915 the channel was closed for eight months due to landslides, twenty-six of which fell into the canal in that year alone. The last major landslide occurred in 1970.

In all, 262 million cubic yards of earth were removed from the canal—enough to fill a twelve-foot hole through the center of the earth. As a result, the sea route from New York to San Francisco is reduced by roughly 8,000 miles. Since its opening, more than 650,000 vessels have taken the shortcut, carrying everything from oil and grains to elephants, giraffes, and London Bridge. Admittedly a miracle of engineering, the canal also has proven to be a marvel of operational efficiency. Tolls have been raised just four times since the waterway was completed.

In 1977, the United States signed two new treaties with Panama which provided for the gradual transition of canal operations into Panamanian hands by the year 2000. With the tenth anniversary of the treaty's signing . . . , about eighty percent of today's canal workers are Panamanians, more than thirty of whom are canal pilots.

The transit of the canal today holds a special fascination for anyone who enjoyed the amusement park water slide as a kid. The ship is raised and lowered eighty-five feet via six pairs of chambers. Each lock chamber is 1,000 feet long and 110 feet wide. When the chambers fill with water there is no sensation of movement but you are readily aware that something amazing is underway. The passage through the Gaillard Cut is a narrow, steep-walled slot. In the two-hour crossing of Gatun Lake you are sailing over what were once the most feared jungles of the American coast. Average transit time for the entire canal is about nine hours.

When you are sailing through the Panama Canal there is ample time to stand at the ship's rail and reflect. The deep green hills still look rugged, the thick clot of the jungle has not changed. Admittedly, there are no more pirate treasure mules, the French left long ago with their sad story, and the astronauts have been to the moon and back. But the canal—the realization of so many dreams—is there and it is working. It is probably the most fascinating place you can go to revel in the genius of first rate engineering until that day, far in the future, when you can stand by the flag on that distant lunar plain and stir up the dust with your boot.

Main idea:
Supporting detail:

29. **Topic:** The dream at Panama
Main idea:
Supporting detail:

Checking for Understanding of Supporting Detail

Discuss the building of the Panama Canal with a classmate or two. Talk about why the construction of the canal was so important and why it was so difficult to achieve. Talk also about what this achievement indicates about human beings' will to overcome obstacles.

Circle the best response. Do not rely on your memory. Use your margin notes to check your answers.

1. In scope and difficulty, the canal's construction was more closely akin to the
   a. Suez Canal.
   b. trans-Siberian Railroad.
   c. Taj Mahal.
   d. pyramids.
2. A canal in Panama was first proposed in the
   a. 1300s.
   b. 1500s.
   c. 1600s.
   d. 1700s.
3. The canal was built with the help of
   a. the airplane.
   b. the automobile.
   c. both the plane and the automobile.
   d. neither the plane nor the automobile.
4. Which of these statements is true?
   a. About half of Panama lies east of Miami.
   b. Panama is squeezed into the narrowest portion of Central America.
   c. Panama offers the lowest point in the North American continental divide.
   d. All are true.
   e. Both b and c are true.
5. A small railroad operated across the isthmus by
   a. the beginning of the 1700s.
   b. the middle of the 1700s.
   c. the beginning of the 1800s.
   d. the middle of the 1800s.
6. Today's transit of the canal is
   a. scary.
   b. a challenge.
   c. smooth.
   d. horrific.

7. The annual rainfall on the Atlantic side is closest to
   a. 50 inches.   c. 150 inches.
   b. 100 inches.   d. 200 inches.
8. Which of these are found in Panama?
   a. crocodiles   c. serpents
   b. alligators   d. all of the above and then some
9. The worst diseases were
   a. malaria and yellow fever.   c. smallpox and black plague.
   b. cholera and typhoid.   d. smallpox and dysentery.
10. According to treaty, the Panama Canal Zone was to be controlled by
    a. Panamanians.   c. Bogotá.
    c. Colombia.   d. the United States.
11. Gorgas attacked malaria and yellow fever by
    a. changing the breeding patterns of mosquitoes in the area.
    b. wiping out the breeding grounds of mosquitoes there.
    c. interbreeding the mosquitoes to get a new breed.
    d. all of the above.
12. The large Gatun Lake was formed by
    a. building locks.   c. rerouting the railway.
    b. building a dam.   d. building a roadway.
13. The major construction problem at Culebra Cut was
    a. landslides.   c. the flooding river.
    b. lack of money.   d. weak concrete.
14. The locks used today are the
    a. same ones built initially.   c. third set built.
    b. second set built.
15. The first transit of the Panama Canal occurred at the time of the
    a. Spanish-American War.   c. Second World War.
    b. First World War.   d. Korean War.
16. The average transit time through the canal today is about
    a. 15 minutes.   c. 9 hours.
    b. 2 hours.   d. 2 days.

Checking Your Word Power

Circle the response that comes closest to the meaning of the italicized term.

1. The *isthmus* of Panama is a
   a. canal.   c. kind of crocodile.
   b. narrow strip of land.   d. man who once ruled Panama.
2. A *devastating* storm is one that
   a. brings destruction.   c. is accompanied by thunder.
   b. comes and goes quickly.   d. occurs only at night.
3. I felt something *akin* to love.
   a. actual   c. similar, or related
   b. foreign   d. funny about
4. The building of the canal required all the creativity its builders could *muster.*
   a. play with   c. pull
   b. carry   d. call forth
5. The French *debacle* occurred because they tried to build a sea level canal.
   a. debate   c. complete breakdown
   b. departure   d. happening

6. Their plan became *mired* in red tape.
    a. stuck   c. married
    b. mixed with   d. manufactured
7. They plodded on despite *horrific* problems—floods, landslides, and disease.
    a. causing honor   c. causing sadness
    b. causing pleasure   d. causing horror
8. I will vote for the *incumbent* governor.
    a. one who is coming   c. one who is running for
    b. one holding office   d. one who is living in the state
9. The key accomplishment of the period was the *virtual* elimination of malaria.
    a. nearly complete   c. partial
    b. absolute   d. parallel
10. The waters of the overflowing river *inundated* the surrounding countryside.
    a. flooded   c. irrigated
    b. watered   d. washed
11. The *continental divide* is a
    a. railroad that divides the continent.
    b. mountain range that divides the continent.
    c. river that divides the continent.
    d. canal that cuts across the isthmus.

Writing with Significant Details

According to the selection you just read, the construction of the pyramids of Egypt was an engineering feat akin to the construction of the Panama Canal. Read a brief selection in an encyclopedia about the pyramids. Then decide on the main idea you want to express and some details you can use to support that idea. Map the main idea and the details on Figure 5.2. Using your idea map, write one paragraph about

Figure 5.2 *A Guide for Plotting Main Idea and Supporting Details of a Paragraph Before Writing. Jot your thoughts directly on the guide before you begin to draft your paragraph.*

Main Idea:

Supporting Detail:

Supporting Detail:

Supporting Detail:

Supporting Detail:

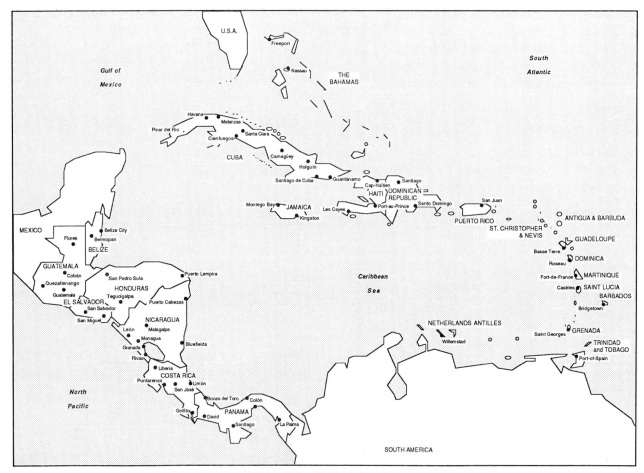

Figure 5.3 *Central America*

the pyramids. Start with a topic sentence that communicates the main point. Then write several sentences with details that support the main point you make in the topic sentence.

EXTENDING WHAT YOU HAVE LEARNED

Building Your Knowledge Base

Circle or plot these locations on the map in Figure 5.3.

Central America	Pacific Ocean	North America
South America	Isthmus of Panama	Atlantic Ocean

Building Your Personal Vocabulary

Select several words emphasized in this chapter to add to your personal vocabulary list. Record the chosen words as well as a model sentence using each word.

Reviewing Your Strategy for Working with Details

What two questions should you ask yourself to determine if a detail is significant?

1. _____

2. _____

How should you generally handle dates and numbers as you meet them in reading?

_____

_____

Practicing Your Strategy

Locate an article that describes an event, person, or place that interests you. Read the article. As you read, focus on the main idea and those details you need to remember to support that idea. On paper, record the title and author as well as the source; record the main idea and the details you feel are significant.

6

Using Clue Words to Follow an Author's Thoughts

Before reading the chapter, read the title, the stated objective, and the headings and subheadings. Ask yourself: What is the topic of the chapter? In the space above and beside the chapter number, jot down what you already know about the topic. Then in the space below the number, jot down at least two questions you hope to answer through reading the chapter.

OBJECTIVE

In this chapter, you will learn a strategy for using clue words to perceive relationships among ideas so that you can anticipate what is going to happen next in a sentence or paragraph. You will learn to use clue words such as these:

1. *one, two,* and *three,* which indicate the number of items to be enumerated (or named one by one) and discussed.
2. *for example* and *such as,* which indicate an example is coming.
3. *also* and *furthermore,* which indicate more on the same idea is coming, and *but, however,* and *yet,* which indicate ideas in opposition.
4. *similarly* and *on the other hand,* which indicate a comparison or contrast is on the way.
5. *if/then, hence,* and *consequently,* which indicate a conditional relationship (a condition followed by an outcome).
6. *because* and *for this reason,* which indicate a reason is coming.

INTRODUCTION—USING CLUE WORDS

In previous chapters, you learned that writing has structure. For example, deductive paragraphs have a topic sentence followed by sentences that provide supporting details. Being able to perceive this kind of paragraph structure aids in comprehension; your perception gives you a framework for understanding the paragraph.

Writers also rely on clue words to give structure to their writing and to help you—the reader—predict, or anticipate, what will happen next in a sentence or paragraph. If you know the way clue words function in writing, you can better understand important sentence relationships. In this chapter, you will learn to use clue words to anticipate what kinds of thoughts are coming next.

PARAGRAPHS OF ENUMERATION

A basic reading strategy is to use number words such as *first, second, third* to guide your reading.

Preview the selection by skimming the title, the first sentence, and the italicized words. Then read the selection. As you do, keep alert for number words that tell you how many items the writer is going to discuss. Circle the number words. The word *abrasion* in the selection means "the wearing down or away by friction."

THE THREE CLASSES OF ROCKS

George Hennings

All the rocks in the earth's crust are grouped into three classes. When magma (the molten material beneath the earth's crust) and lava (the molten rock coming out on the earth's surface) cool, they harden and become *igneous rocks,* the first class. The word *igneous* comes from the Latin word for fire. As the molten mass loses heat, minerals harden into a crystalline igneous rock.

As rocks are exposed to a variety of forces (water, lower surface temperatures, lower surface pressures, and abrasion), the igneous rocks start to come apart both chemically and physically. The broken rock particles may be carried downgrade by wind and water. They may come eventually to rest as sediments. As time passes, sediments cover other sediments, layer on layer. Particles are compacted together; grains fit more tightly. Dissolved chemicals form cement, and particles turn into stone. Thus we have the formation of the second class of rock—*sedimentary rocks.*

Deeply buried sedimentary and igneous rocks are heated and squeezed together by enormous pressures. They change in form as grains rearrange themselves and minerals change their composition. The change in form is called metamorphism. The result is the third class of rock, the *metamorphic rocks.*

Did you circle the word *three* in the first paragraph? When you came to that word, did you predict and say to yourself, "This is going to be about three classes of rock. The author will probably start by describing the first class, go on to the second, and finish with the third"? Did you circle the word *first* in the first paragraph, *second* in the second, and *third* in the third? Those words are clues to the framework the author is using to develop his ideas: The author is enumerating, or naming, three items and discussing them in order, one after the other.

History and science writers often use this pattern to organize their writing. In the first sentence of their first paragraph, they tell the number of items they are going to enumerate and discuss. In this respect, that first sentence serves as the topic sentence for the series of paragraphs to follow. In the first paragraph and perhaps in others that follow, they then name and discuss the first item—in this case igneous rocks. In the next paragraph or two, they name and discuss the second item. Completing the discussion of the second item, they move to a discussion of the third. At each transition, the reader, who is wise to the ways of writers, says to him or herself: "Now the author is moving to the next point."

The writer of the geology paragraphs built a second organizing clue into the paragraphs. He italicized the names of the rock classes. A reader who realizes the importance of previewing before reading may pick up this clue during the preview. Learning in the first sentence that there are three classes of rocks, the reader quickly scans the paragraphs to come, noting the three italicized rock types. The reader then knows that the first paragraph is about igneous, the second about sedimentary, and the third about metamorphic; and the reader knows all that even before he or she has actually read the material. Here previewing has paid dividends; it provides a framework for anticipating while reading.

Now reread the selection on page 113 and complete the idea map in Figure 6.1 that clarifies the structure of the selection.

Also reread the six objectives on the first page of Chapter 6. In this case, the objectives enumerate, or name in order, the items to be discussed. Many textbook authors use their introductory section to name the items they will discuss in the

Figure 6.1 *An Idea Map of a Passage. Map the passage by recording the thesis, or main point, of the entire passage about rocks in the top box. Record the main ideas of the individual paragraphs in the connecting boxes.*

Thesis of the Entire Passage:

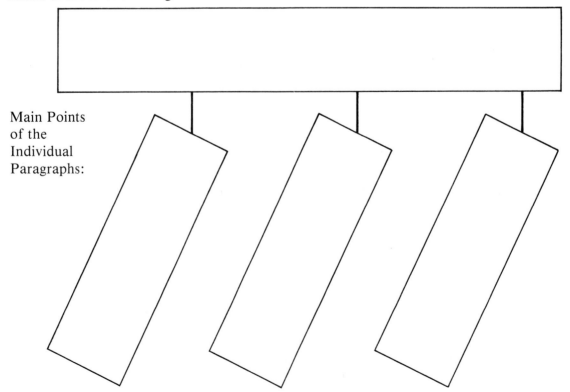

Main Points of the Individual Paragraphs:

chapter or in a section of the chapter. If that material is available, give it some attention, since you can use it to guide your reading.

PARAGRAPHS WITH EXAMPLES

A second basic reading strategy is to use words to guide your reading that hint that an example is coming.

Read this short passage. As you read, circle any word or phrase that gives you a clue that the author is going to give an example.

Cities have been completely destroyed by volcanic eruptions. A famous example is the destruction of the city of Pompeii in Italy by the eruption of Mt. Vesuvius. On the morning of August 24, A.D. 79, horrific explosions broke the stillness of the day. Columns of smoke, gases, and steam rose into the air. A rain of ash and glowing debris fell on Pompeii. Within several hours of the first volcanic rumblings, Pompeii was inundated under twenty feet of volcanic ash. Roofs collapsed, and people were suffocated by poisonous gases.

Did you circle the phrase *A famous example?* That phrase is a clue to the design of the paragraph. The first sentence states the main idea. But then the writer shifts gears slightly. She supports the main idea with an example of one well-known volcanic

Figure 6.2   *An Idea Map to Show Relationships in a Paragraph. Map the paragraph to show the relationship between the main idea and the supporting example. Record the main idea in the top box and the supporting example in the connecting box.*

Main Idea:

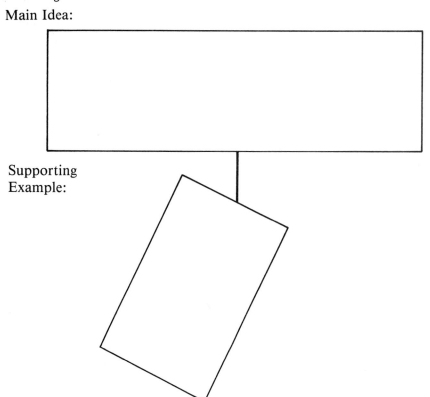

Supporting
Example:

eruption. Figure 6.2 helps you visualize the relationship among main and supporting ideas in the paragraph. Complete it by adding the main idea and the supporting example.

Phrases like *a famous example* are clues you can use to predict what is coming. Reading it, you get ready to handle the example. You predict: "The author is going to give an example." Similar phrases that tell you that you can anticipate an example are *such as, for example,* and *for instance.* Sometimes a writer provides more than one example and introduces it with the phrase *Another example* or *Another instance.*

Read this paragraph, and compare it to the structure of the one about Vesuvius. Ask yourself as you read: How is it similar in design to the previous paragraph? How is it different? The word *pertinacious* used in the first (and topic) sentence means "extremely persistent, clinging tightly to a purpose."

> The human race is extraordinarily pertinacious in continuing to live around volcanoes and even high up on their slopes. Vesuvius, "the pride and terror of Naples," is thickly surrounded by towns and villages and is covered with gardens, groves, and vineyards that extend far up toward its summit. Etna, a volcanic peak in Sicily, is cultivated up to an altitude of 4000 feet, intensively below an elevation of 1500 feet. On the slopes, there are orange and lemon groves, vineyards, and oleanders, all in vivid contrast to the black lava flows. Mount Rosso, the largest cinder cone on Etna, built in 1669 during the most disastrous eruption in the history of Etna, is now green with vineyards halfway to its summit.

1. What is the main idea of the paragraph? _____

_____

2. How is the paragraph similar to the previous one about Vesuvius?

_____

_____

3. How is it different? _____

_____

If you said that both paragraphs start with a topic sentence, you recognized a basic element in their design. If you said that the pattern was topic sentence supported by example, you recognized a second element in their design. Both paragraphs rely on examples to support the main idea.

Now consider the differences. The first paragraph contains a single example—Vesuvius. The second paragraph contains two examples—Vesuvius and Etna. Also the first paragraph provides a clue phrase *(a famous example)* that helps you anticipate a paragraph containing an example. The second paragraph does not. In the later case, you must figure out as you read about the towns and villages surrounding Vesuvius that this is an example. When you get to the sentence on Etna, you must figure out that this is a second example. In this case, what helps you predict during reading is your knowledge of the way authors develop their paragraphs.

PARAGRAPHS WITH ADDITIONAL INFORMATION—
A CONTINUATION OF OR A CHANGE IN THE TOPIC

A third ongoing reading strategy is to look for words hinting that the author is getting ready to give more information in support of the topic or supply information in opposition to the topic. Some words or phrases are clues about what the writer is going to do next.

Some words tell you that the author is going to provide more details about the same idea. They are the *and*-words; *and*-words include

and	also
too	additionally
in addition	furthermore
moreover	

Other words tell you that the author is going to change direction and provide details on the opposite side of the topic. They are the *but*-words; *but*-words include

but	yet
however	on the other hand
nevertheless	instead

Read this short paragraph:

Many people are familiar with the recent violent volcanic eruption that occurred at Mt. St. Helens in Washington State. In addition, people know about the 1991 eruption at Mt. Pinatubo in the Philippines, which threatened the U.S. military installations at Clark Air Base and Subic Bay Naval Station. In the case of Mt. Pinatubo, more than 20,000 American military personnel and their families had to be evacuated on warships and cargo planes and Clark Air Base had to be shut down. The Filipinos, however, had no way of escaping and were in a state of panic.

1. What do you anticipate when you read the words *In addition?* What do you know is going to happen next in the paragraph? _____

_____

2. What do you anticipate when you read the word *however?* What do you know is going to happen next in the paragraph?_____

_____

Read the following paragraphs that are adapted from a college geology text, actively picturing in your mind what the authors are describing. The word *eject* in the first paragraph means "to throw out." *Viscous* means "sticky, or adhesive"; pancake syrup is viscous. *Fluid* means "liquidy, able to flow"; water is very fluid and can flow rapidly downhill.

Figure 6.3 *Mount St. Helens volcano in Washington state.* (UPI/
Bettmann Newsphotos)

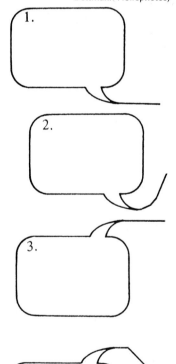

A. Volcanic Lavas

Different volcanoes erupt lavas of different kinds. Vesuvius erupts one kind, *and* Etna spews out another. More remarkable still, neighboring volcanoes may erupt very different lavas. Stromboli and Vulcano are in the Lapari Islands north of Sicily, only 25 miles apart: Stromboli is ejecting basalt, *but* Vulcano in the recent past has ejected rhyolite—lavas about as different as you can get.

Furthermore, a volcano during its lifetime may erupt lavas of several kinds. For example, as many as five kinds of lavas were erupted from San Francisco Mountain, a large extinct volcano rising 5000 feet above the plateau of northern Arizona.

B. Lava Flows

Very fluid lavas flow rapidly, especially on steep slopes. Some, like the Hawaiian Island flow from Mauna Loa in 1850, average 10 miles an hour. *However,* speeds of more than 5 miles an hour are rare. As the lava flows cool and become viscous, they move much more slowly, creeping onward, possibly for several years.

C. Volcanic Eruptions and Bodies of Water

From the presence of lots of volcanic islands in the sea, it is evident that vast outpourings of lava have occurred on the seafloor. The volcanic chain of the Hawaiian Islands is an example of this. Eruptions occurring beneath the sea have been recognized by the pouring out of vapors and ash from the water.

Eruptions occur *also* on the floors of bodies of fresh water. *Moreover,* streams of lava flow from the land into the sea or into lakes. The resulting lava flow resembles a pile of pillows. Such lavas are called "pillow lavas."

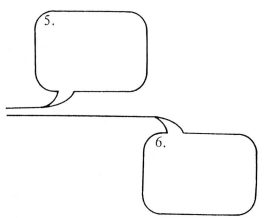

Reread paragraphs A through C. Think about how the authors use clue words either (1) to maintain the same direction and add more details about the topic, or (2) to change direction and add details on the opposing side of the topic. Some of the words in the paragraphs have been italicized. In the balloons connected to these words, write what the authors are doing at that point—giving an opposite point or adding more information on the topic.

As a review, underline the topic (or main idea) sentence in each of the preceding paragraphs A through C if there is one. Then put a check by each example in the paragraphs.

PARAGRAPHS WITH COMPARISONS AND CONTRASTS

A fourth ongoing reading strategy is to look for words that hint that the author is getting ready to make a comparison or contrast. In comparing, writers tell how things or events are the same. In contrasting, writers generally tell how they differ. Here are some words and phrases that hint that an author is comparing or contrasting items:

Comparisons	Contrasts
similarly	on the other hand
as in the case of	on the contrary
like the	unlike the
the same as	in contrast to
in comparison to	whereas or whereas others

Read these two paragraphs. As you read, put an X at the point where the authors begin to make a comparison or contrast. Ask yourself: What are they comparing or contrasting? Are they giving similarities or differences? The word *solidify* means "harden, or turn into a solid."

When the lava first flows out, it is red or white hot and very fluid. The lava soon cools on the surface, darkens, and crusts over. As it cools, it becomes more and more viscous. When the flow becomes very viscous, the under part may still be moving while the upper part crusts over and breaks up into jagged blocks, which are carried as a tumbling mass on the surface of the slowly moving flow. When eventually the flow comes to rest and solidifies, the resulting lava sheet is extremely rough. Its top is a mess of blocks and fragments, with many sharp points. Such lava flows are termed *block lava*. In Hawaii they are called *aa* (ă ă).

In marked contrast to the block lava, other flows harden with smooth surfaces, which have curious ropy, curved, and billowy forms. This is corded lava. The Hawaiians call it *pahoehoe* (pă-hō ā-hō ā).

1. In the two paragraphs, what two kinds of things are the authors describing?

   _____

   _____

2. Are they telling how the items differ or are the same? _____

   _____

3. What phrase do the authors use as a clue to tell you there is going to be a

   contrast? _____

4. How does the paragraphing help you make sense of the contrast?

   _____

The English language provides another clue that writers are developing a contrast in a paragraph—the use of the ending *-er* or the word *more*. For example, an author may begin one paragraph with the phrase *In older volcanoes* and begin the follow-up paragraph with the phrase *In younger volcanoes*. The use of the comparative *-er* helps you figure out that the author is contrasting the two.

Read these paragraphs. Circle the clue words that tell you that a comparison or contrast is being developed. Ask: What is being compared or contrasted? Are similarities or differences being developed? To help you understand these paragraphs, picture in your mind what the authors are describing.

Lavas, even after they have come out of a volcano, still contain dissolved gases. This is shown by the clouds of steam that escape from volcanoes for weeks and months. It is also shown by the bubble-like structures that result as the lava solidifies into rock. Viscous lava may become blown up by the expansion of many, many bubbles of gas. Each bubble hole is a vesicle (like a sac). It is spherical if the lava was stationary while the hole was forming. In contrast, it is almond shaped if the lava was moving and drawing out the vesicle while the hole was forming. The upper portion of a flow, especially of a viscous lava, may contain so many holes that it has become a froth, like whipped cream. Rock froth is known as *pumice*.

In more fluid lava, the gas cavities, or vesicles, are much larger. In this case, the holes are very irregular in shape and size. They are so abundant that there is as much empty space as solid matter. The resulting rock is *scoriaceous*.

1. What is being compared or contrasted? _____

   _____

2. Are similarities or differences being stressed? _____

3. What clues do the authors use to let you know there is to be a contrast?

_____

4. How does the design of the paragraphs help you to understand the contrast?

_____

PARAGRAPHS WITH CONDITIONAL RELATIONSHIPS ("What-Then?" Paragraphs)

A fifth ongoing reading strategy is to look for words that hint that a conditional relationship is being developed. Conditional relationships are common in scientific writing, both in the natural and social sciences. When authors express conditional relationships, they state a condition and then tell what happens, or results, when that condition is met. A common language pattern for doing this is an *if* clause followed by a *then* clause, as in this sentence:

> **If this condition exists,**   **then this results**
>
> If the rocks are radioactive, ⟶ then heat will build up.

1. What happens if the rocks are radioactive? What then? Write the outcome, or

   results here. _____

   _____

Often the word *then* is left out; you must mentally add it in reading. You must think to yourself: If this happens, what then? Asking the "what-then" question is a simple strategy for interpreting a conditional relationship. Ask that question as you read this example.

> **If this condition exists,**   **then this results**
>
> If magma reaches the Earth's
> surface and is discharged
> from an opening,   ⟶ it flows out on the
>   surface where it cools
>   rapidly and solidifies.

2. What happens if the magma is discharged from the volcano? If this happens (if

   the condition is met), what is the outcome, or effect? _____

   _____

Read the following paragraph. Whenever you run into an if clause, ask the "what-then" question to keep you on track. Ask: If this happens, what then? The word *edifice in the paragraph means "a building, especially a large one."*

The shape of the edifice that builds up around the mouth of a volcano depends on the material that formed it. If the edifice is made entirely of fragments, a steep cone is built. Slopes of 30 degrees or more are built up before the accumulating mass begins to slide. Volcanic edifices of this kind are called *pyroclastic cones*. A pyroclastic cone built of huge blocks forms the summit of Etna. If a pyroclastic cone consists totally of cinders, it is called a *cinder cone*. Cinder cones are relatively small.

3. If the cone is made totally of fragments, what then? What is the effect, or result? _____

   _____

4. If a cone consists of cinders, what then? What is the effect, or outcome?

   _____

Other words that are clues to a conditional relationship include *consequently, therefore, thus,* and *hence.* Here are some examples:

If this condition exists	Effect, or result
At the time the lava comes from the earth, it may be too thick to flow readily. ⟶	Consequently a sluggish pasty mass piles up over the mouth of the volcano as a great dome.

5. What happens if the lava is too thick, or viscous, to flow readily?

   _____

   _____

6. What word warns you that an effect may be coming? _____

7. Rewrite the two sentences substituting another clue word for *consequently* so that you get the feel for how this kind of conditional writing operates. Perhaps use *hence* or *thus* to express the conditional relationship.

   _____

   _____

If this condition exists	Effect, or result
Sometimes the magma cools in the ground under a thick jacket of rocks; ⟶	hence its dissolved gases cannot escape easily.

8. What happens when the magma cools under a thick jacket of rocks?

   _____

9. What word warns you that an effect may be coming? _____

10. Rewrite the sentence substituting another clue word for *hence* so that you better understand how this kind of conditional thinking operates.

    _____

    _____

    _____

CAUSE/EFFECT PARAGRAPHS

A sixth ongoing reading strategy is to look for words that hint that a cause/effect relationship is being developed. Writers of social and natural science content often give reasons why things happen or are as they are. You can predict when writers are getting ready to provide causes and effects by looking out for these word clues:

because	for	as a result
for this reason		since

Here is an example:

Reason, or cause	What happens, or the effect
Because rocks conduct, or carry, heat very poorly, ⟶	the magma loses heat slowly and solidifies slowly.

1. What clue word introduces the reason? _____

2. Why does the magma lose heat slowly? Complete this sentence in answering:

   The magma loses heat slowly and solidifies slowly because _____

   _____

Did you notice that in the model sentence the reason (Because rocks conduct, or carry, heat very poorly) comes before what happens? In the sentence you just wrote, the happening (the magma loses heat slowly and solidifies slowly) comes before the reason. This indicates that reasons can come before or after the related event or happening as shown in these two sentence maps:

Reason ⟶	What happens as a result
What happens ⟶	The reason for it

Read this paragraph, and use the clue words that warn of "reason-giving" to figure out the points where the author is going to give reasons. Also ask: Why does this happen? The why question is a key one to ask when handling reasons.

Because the Hawaiian volcano, Mauna Loa, is about sixty miles long and thirty miles wide and because it rises from a base 15,000 feet below sea level to 13,680 feet above sea level, it is known as the "Monarch of Mountains." Since Mauna Loa is the world's largest active volcano, each year many tourists visit the island of Hawaii to view it.

3. Why is Mauna Loa known as the "Monarch of Mountains"? _____

_____

_____

4. What word introduces the reason? _____

5. Why do tourists visit Mauna Loa? _____

_____

6. What word introduces the reason? _____

7. Rewrite the first sentence in the paragraph, placing the reasons after the happening they explain. Start the sentence: Mauna Loa is known as the "Monarch of

Mountains" _____

_____

Here is one caution before going on. Remember that when writers are giving reasons, they are telling you why something is as it is or why something happened as it did. The key question to ask as you interpret reasons is, Why? In contrast, when writers are expressing an if-then relationship, they are telling the conditions under which events occur. The key question to ask in handling if-then relationships is, If that is true, then what?

In the next sections of this chapter, you will read three selections, one from a text on human sexuality, one about astronomy, and one from a physical science text. Use the clue words to help you follow the points the authors are making.

SELECTION 1: FORMING A FRIENDSHIP
(Human Sexuality)

Expanding Your Vocabulary for Reading

Use word-structure and context clues to determine the meaning of each italicized term. Write a definition for each featured word in the space provided.

1. The research *affirms* what I always knew—that success in college generally requires work. _____

_____

2. Despite outside influences, she *consistently* held to the principles in which she

believed. _____

_____

3. When they didn't do well in the game, the children's *compensatory* behavior was to refuse to play. _____

_____

4. Sarah's personal *attributes* overcame her plain appearance. _____

_____

5. The government was *stable* and not likely to be overturned by revolution.

_____

_____

6. Their affection for each other was *overt;* they made no attempt to find privacy.

_____

_____

7. The teams worked out a *reciprocity* whereby they took turns practicing on the small basketball court. _____

_____

8. The artist placed all the parts of his drawing in a *configuration* that was most pleasing to the eye. _____

_____

Getting Ready to Read

Preview the next selection. Read the title, author, and introductory paragraph.

● What is the topic of the selection? _____
● What do you already know about the way people form friendships?

_____

_____

● Now study the three headings that introduce the main sections of the article. Choose one and write a question you expect to get answered by that section.

_____

_____

● Predict which one will surprise you with ideas you had not thought about.

_____

Reading with Meaning

Read the selection, which is from a college text in human sexuality. Use the author's clue words such as *and, however, if . . . then,* and *because* to guide your reading.

FORMING A FRIENDSHIP

Kathryn Kelley and Donn Byrne

1. How many factors will the author discuss?

   What are they?

2. If we respond positively, what then?

Once two people meet and begin to interact several factors come into play, influencing how the relationship develops. First, our initial impressions of others depend in large part on appearance. If our reactions are negative, the process stops. If we respond positively, the second factor comes into play: the extent to which we discover that we share similar beliefs and attitudes with the other person. Third, the final step in forming a close friendship occurs when we and the other person each feel and express a positive evaluation of the other. We will now examine these three factors in greater detail.

Physical Attractiveness: Life as a Beauty Contest

3. Nevertheless, what happens?

On first coming in contact with someone, we have a strong tendency to respond to **physical attractiveness**—that combination of facial features, body configuration, and general appearance that our culture defines as pleasing. We all have learned that "Beauty is only skin deep" and "You can't judge a book by its cover"; nevertheless, most people respond most positively to those they perceive as attractive. Even in childhood, attractive preschool girls are treated better than their less attractive peers by other children; the physically attractive children are helped more and hurt less. Also, attractiveness and unattractiveness remain as fairly stable characteristics throughout childhood and adolescence.

Other species also respond to overt physical characteristics—a peacock's tail, a deer's antlers, a swordtail fish's tail fin—suggesting an inherited tendency to attract mates on the basis of such clues.

4. What is an example of our culture's emphasis on beauty?

Our culture also emphasizes the value of beauty. For example, advertisements instruct women to cover their embarrassing age spots, lose weight, change their hairstyle and color, wear the right makeup, and so on. The mass media are found to stress slimness for women much more strongly than for men. Men, too, are told to take steps to avoid gray hair, dandruff, insufficiently white teeth, underdeveloped muscles, and a host of other "defects." One result is that both men and women focus on the attractiveness of the opposite sex in most of their interactions. Not surprisingly, then, attractive men and women receive more invitations for dates in a video-dating service than unattractive ones. Women are, however, able to overlook male unattractiveness if the men possess compensatory attributes such as status, money, power, or prestige.

5. What does the word *however* tell you that the author is going to do here?

Physical attractiveness creates a halo around those who possess it. Both men and women assume that good-looking people also have a great many positive personal qualities. Our inflated view of attractive people can best be overcome if we learn to pay more attention to their behavior than to their appearance.

6. If we learn to pay more attention to behavior, what then?

Altogether, beauty has a number of benefits, however unfair this may be. Attractive men and women have more success with the opposite sex, including more dates, and they succeed in many other social situations as well. One explanation is that those who are attractive behave differently than those who are unattractive. For example, attractive males are relatively assertive and unafraid of rejection, and attractive women are relatively unassertive, and these are precisely the qualities each sex most prefers in the other in a dating situation. Beyond the dating age, the greater a person's physical attractiveness, the better off he or she is in educational level, income, status, and mental health.

Because of the value we place on attractiveness, it follows that self-perceptions of deficiencies in appearance lower self-esteem and lead to efforts to improve how we look.

Similarity: Seeking Those Most Like Ourselves

Attraction toward a similar partner goes beyond physical appearance. Once we begin interacting with someone new, we try to discover as much as possible about his or her likes and dislikes. Throughout history it has been observed that people respond most positively to other individuals who are most similar to themselves, especially those who hold similar attitudes, beliefs, and values.

Research consistently finds that **attitude similarity** leads to attraction. You may hear that "opposites attract," but such mismatching works better in fiction than in real life. Attraction is a direct consequence of similar attitudes. Thus, friends, lovers, and spouses have similar views on most issues.

Matching occurs between friends whose daily habits are similar. We like friends who behave as we do and who make decisions similar to our own. High school friends resemble each other in drug use, for example. At least among women, patterns of smoking, drinking, and premarital sexual activity are more similar among groups of friends than among classmates in general. People who live together are more satisfied with the relationship if they have similar preferences about when to sleep and when to be active. For most characteristics that have been studied, similarity leads to attraction.

Why is similarity so crucial in relationships? It appears that similarity has a positive effect because it helps confirm our judgments about the world. When another person agrees with us, he or she affirms or "validates" our view about politics, religion, and so on and also provides evidence that our judgments, tastes, and style of behavior are reasonable, normal, and wise. We find it rewarding when others provide this positive information.

Reciprocity of Positive Evaluations: If You Like Me, Let Me Know

If someone is really your friend and if your interactions are positive, would you expect that person to evaluate you positively, help you whenever possible, and let you know you are liked? Many studies indicate that the communication of such positive evaluations between partners is the most crucial characteristic of a successful relationship.

7. What important clue phrase is used here? What does it tell you the author is going to do in this part?

8. Why do our perceptions of deficiencies lower self-esteem?

9. Do opposites really attract? What clue word tells you that is not true?

10. Why do friends, lovers, and spouses have similar views?

11. Give an example of matching between friends.

12. If someone is really your friend, what then?

13. What contrasting point is made in this paragraph?

Even when two people are dissimilar in their attitudes, a man will be attracted to a woman if she shows interest in him by maintaining eye contact, talking to him, and leaning toward him. When reciprocity of positive reactions occurs, either verbally or nonverbally, the relationship is strengthened for both individuals. Flattery, a desire to be together and to communicate, and any sign of affection indicate clearly that positive affect is operating in the friendship. In contrast, hostility, negative evaluations, or refusal to be helpful to one another, creates negative affect, which clearly endangers the relationship.

Checking Your Understanding

Answer the questions in the margin by referring to the text at that point. Use the author's clue words to help you answer.

Reviewing the Featured Vocabulary

Place each word in the sentence in which its meaning is most appropriate.

a. affirmed   c. compensatory   e. consistently   g. reciprocity
b. attributes   d. configuration   f. overt   h. stable

1. The young man had a very _____ relationship with his girlfriend; he had been seeing her for over two years.

2. I was attracted to him because of his social _____ and his physical characteristics.

3. The president _____ scored at the top of her class; she always got A's.

4. The agreement of _____ between the two clubs made it possible for a member of one club to eat in the dining room of the other.

5. During halftime, the band lined up in a _____ that spelled out the name of the university.

6. There was nothing underhanded in what the team captain did; he was always _____ and above board in his actions.

7. The captain of the team _____ that he had never taken drugs.

8. In _____ education a person learns things to make up for his or her deficiencies.

SELECTION 2: THE SUN DISAPPEARS— A SOLAR ECLIPSE (Astronomy)

Expanding Your Vocabulary for Reading

Use word-structure and context clues to figure out the meanings of the italicized words, which are from the selection you will read next. If you are not sure of the meanings of the terms, check the glossary. Write the meaning of each italicized term in the space provided.

1. The fighting armies saw a raven flying over the battlefield and decided it was an *omen* of bad things to come.

2. The power of the Netherlands was gradually *eclipsed* by the growing influence of Great Britain.

3. The Vikings *terrorized* the people living to the south by killing, raping, and stealing.

4. My grandmother only had to have *partial* dentures because some of her teeth were still in good condition.

5. The sun, when viewed from afar, has the shape of a *disk*. It appears to be round with a flat surface.

6. Because of the breeze, first the candle *flickered*. Then it went out.

7. The view of Victoria Falls in Africa is *awesome*. It makes us feel the power and beauty of nature.

Getting Ready to Read

Preview the following selection by reading the title.

● Write the topic of the selection. _____

● What do you already know about the cause of an eclipse? Jot some ideas here.

_____

_____

● Write at least one question that you hope to be able to answer after reading.

_____

_____

Reading with Meaning

Read the selection to get a general idea of what it is about. Then, working with a classmate, reread the article. Together, study the way the italicized words are used to show relationships among ideas within the sentences. Explain to each other what the italicized clue words tell you. In the balloon connected to each of the italicized words, write down what that clue word tells you. For example, the clue word may tell you that the author is going to do one of the following:

1. write about a specific number of items;
2. provide an example;
3. add more information on the same aspect of the topic;
4. add more information, but on a different aspect of the topic;
5. make a comparison or contrast;
6. state a condition and the effect of that condition (if . . . then);
7. give a reason.

You may refer to Figure 6.4 for help. The first word is done for you.

THE SUN DISAPPEARS—A SOLAR ECLIPSE

George Hennings

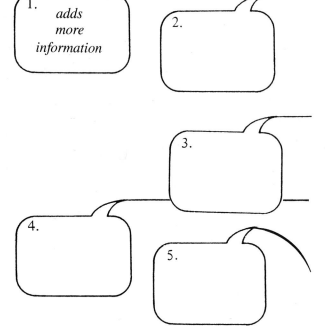

1. Suppose that you lived in a long ago time when few people could read or write and when people knew little or nothing about the sun and the planets. Suppose, *too,* that suddenly on a lovely sunny day the sun disappeared *and* the world turned dark. What would you think? Would you think that the world was coming to an end? Would you think that this was a sign from an angry god? Over the centuries, day turning to night has terrorized, or frightened, people who saw the sun suddenly disappear from the sky.

2. *For example,* on May 28 in 585 B.C. the Medes—who were from what is now northern Iran—were in battle with the Lydians who lived in what is now Turkey. To the horror of both sides, the sun disappeared. The war had been going on for five years, *but* the Medes and Lydians were so frightened at this ill omen that they made peace.

3. Today, astronomers are able to explain such disappearances of the sun. On its trip around the earth, *if* the moon passes directly between the sun and the earth, then it prevents rays of the sun from reaching the earth and causes a temporary darkening.

Figure 6.4   *Diagram of an Eclipse*

Total Eclipse of the Sun

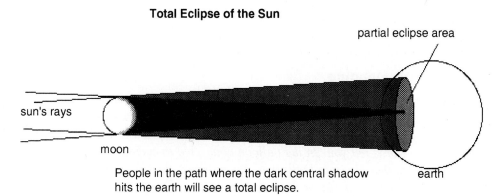

People in the path where the dark central shadow
hits the earth will see a total eclipse.

This is what is known as a solar eclipse. A solar eclipse can last as long as seven and a half minutes.

4. You can do a simple experiment to show how the sun with a diameter 400 times wider than that of the moon can be blocked out, or eclipsed, by the moon. Close one eye. Hold up one finger in front of a large object across the room or out the window. Your finger represents the moon. The blocked object is the sun. Your finger has "eclipsed" the larger object. However, *if* your finger is too far from your eye and closer to the object, you can see part of the object around your finger. In this case, you have made a partial eclipse. Part of the object is visible.

5. *Because* a total eclipse of the sun by the moon requires that the disk of the moon exactly cover the disk of the sun, *two* conditions must be met for a total eclipse to occur. First, *since* the sun is 400 times wider than the moon, the sun must be 400 times farther away than the moon *if* the disk of the moon is to cover the disk of the sun. And it is! Second, the moon must be directly in the line of sight between the earth and the sun. This does happen, but not very often.

6. In 1991 there was a total eclipse of the sun. *Because* the moon passed directly in the line of sight between the sun and the earth, its shadow spread a path of darkness across the land. This path extended from Hawaii to South America in what astronomers called "the eclipse of the century."

7. *Instead of* being frightened by the eclipse as had ancient peoples, Americans flocked to Hawaii and Mexico to view the awesome sight. Scientists viewed the eclipse from an observatory on Hawaii's 13,796 foot Mauna Kea, a volcanic peak. In the continental United States, *however,* only a partial eclipse occurred. Unfortunately, *as a result of* a cloud cover, this partial eclipse was barely visible.

8. Interesting things happened during the 1991 eclipse. *For example,* animals in a zoo in Mexico City headed into their dens when the eclipse began. When the sun reappeared, roosters crowed as if it were morning. *And* light-sensitive lamps flickered on at the beginning of the eclipse and flickered off at the end.

9. The next total eclipse visible in the United States will occur in August 2017. How old will you be then? What will you think if you see it? Will you shake with fear, as did the peoples of the past? *Or, in contrast,* will you be able to explain to your children what causes a solar eclipse?

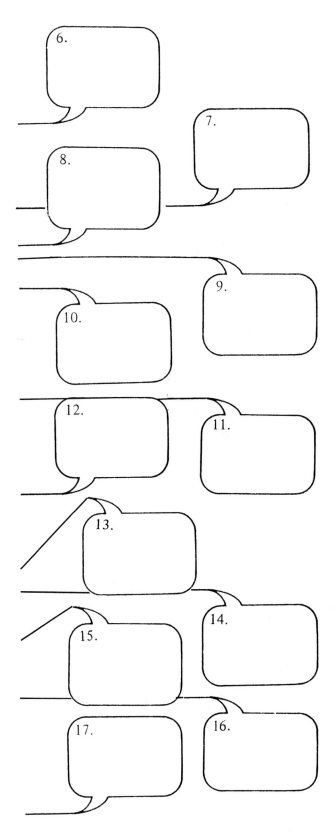

Checking for Understanding

Explain to a classmate what causes a solar eclipse. Incidentally, when you study for other college courses, you may find it helpful to explain what you have read to someone you know. In explaining ideas to someone, you clarify your own understanding. Then mark the following items either T (true) or F (false).

_____ 1. In Mexico City, animals headed into their dens at the end of the 1991 eclipse.

_____ 2. For there to be a total solar eclipse, the moon must be directly in the line of sight between the sun and the earth.

_____ 3. A total solar eclipse happens at least once a year in the continental United States.

_____ 4. People have always understood the cause of a solar eclipse.

_____ 5. In the past people have been frightened by solar eclipses.

_____ 6. The moon never moves.

Working with a classmate, reconsider the selection about the solar eclipse and then answer these questions. Be ready to explain your reasoning.

7. Which sentence in the first paragraph comes closest to stating the main idea?
   a. the first
   b. the second
   c. the next to last
   d. the last
8. The purpose of the second paragraph is to
   a. give an example of the idea stated in the first paragraph.
   b. explain the cause of an eclipse.
   c. provide a contrasting idea to that expressed in the first paragraph.
   d. give details about eclipses, in general.
9. The purpose of the third paragraph is to
   a. give an example of the idea stated in the first paragraph.
   b. explain the cause of an eclipse.
   c. develop in more detail the idea expressed in the second paragraph.
   d. describe a specific eclipse.
10. In the third paragraph, the words "if the moon passes directly between the sun and the earth" tell
    a. the reason for an eclipse.
    b. an example of an eclipse.
    c. a condition under which an eclipse will occur.
    d. a contrasting idea.
11. The general purpose of the fourth paragraph is to
    a. provide an opposite idea to that stated in the third paragraph.
    b. expand on the ideas given in the third paragraph.
    c. take off in a totally different direction than that of the third paragraph.
12. In the fifth paragraph, the words "since the sun is 400 times wider than the moon," give
    a. the reason that the sun must be 400 times farther away than the moon if there is to be a total eclipse.
    b. an example of an eclipse.
    c. a contrasting idea.
    d. the conditions under which an eclipse will occur.

13. In the sixth paragraph, the word *because* tells you to expect
    a. an example.   c. an effect.
    b. a reason.   d. a contrasting idea.
14. In the seventh paragraph, the words *instead of* tell you to expect
    a. an example.   d. a contrasting idea.
    b. a reason.   e. the main idea.
    c. an effect.
15. The first sentence in the eighth paragraph (Interesting things happened during the 1991 eclipse) gives
    a. an example.   d. a contrasting idea.
    b. a reason.   e. the main idea.
    c. a condition.
16. In the eighth paragraph, the next sentence (For example, animals in a zoo in Mexico City headed into their dens when the eclipse began) gives
    a. an example.   d. a contrasting idea.
    b. a reason.   e. the main idea.
    c. a condition.
17. In the last paragraph, the words *Or, in contrast,* introduce
    a. the main idea.
    b. an opposite idea from that just expressed.
    c. an example.
    d. a reason.
    e. a condition.

Reviewing New Vocabulary

Select from the list the word that best fits the meaning of each sentence. Use each word in only one sentence.

    a. awe   d. flickered   f. partial
    b. disk   e. omen   g. terrorized
    c. eclipse

1. As a result of the storm, the lights _____; however, the lights did not go off.

2. Some people look upon a rainbow as a good sign for the future. On the other hand, some people think of a rainbow as a bad _____.

3. If you shine a light through a transparent red _____ that is placed on a transparent yellow one, then you will see orange.

4. In contrast to a solar _____, a lunar _____ occurs when the earth passes directly between the moon and the sun.

5. She had only _____ vision. Consequently, she needed glasses.

6. The vandals _____ the community. As a result, the community rose up and formed a citizens' watch force.

7. If you stand and look up at the great vaulting roof of the cathedral of Notre Dame in Paris, you will be filled with _____.

Now reread the sentences in this exercise and circle the clue words you have learned in this chapter. In the margin, explain what each clue word tells you.

SELECTION 3: ELEMENTS KNOWN TO ANCIENT CIVILIZATIONS (Physical Sciences)

Getting Ready to Read

In this section you will read some paragraphs titled "Elements Known to Ancient Civilizations." The title gives you the topic of the selection. An element is a substance, or material, like gold, iron, oxygen, and hydrogen, which cannot be separated into simpler parts by chemical means.

Before you read, name some other elements that you know.

_____

Then predict: What elements were known to ancient people? Write your prediction here. _____

_____

Reading with Meaning

Now read to see if your prediction is correct and if you can recognize sentence relationships. Later you will be asked to answer questions about the main idea and sentence relationships very similar to questions that are asked on some standardized reading tests.

ELEMENTS KNOWN TO ANCIENT CIVILIZATIONS

Jay Pasachoff

Paragraph A

Not many of the elements occur in nature as pure substances, lying around waiting for someone to pick them up. A few do, and it is not surprising that these were known and collected for various uses in societies around the globe as far back as several thousand years B.C. *Sulfur* is one of those elements. It was known to burn with smelly results and have an odd appearance. Its use was probably confined to religious ceremonies. *Carbon* was also known since antiquity, because the charred bones of animals and portions of partially burned trees consist largely of carbon in the form of charcoal. Although we don't know all the uses primitive peoples made of charcoal, we do know that it was the key to releasing many other elements from their chemical combination in rocks. For example, if a copper-containing rock was heated in a hot fire with charcoal present, the carbon in the charcoal would combine with the other elements in the rock, leaving free metallic copper. In ways like this people were able to discover the elements *copper, iron, lead, tin,* and *zinc,* although they didn't necessarily appreciate that these substances were elements. They just knew that they were useful.

1. What is the main idea of this paragraph?
   a. Not many elements occur in nature as pure substances, but ancient peoples made use of the few that do.
   b. Ancient peoples found copper, iron, lead, tin, and zinc very useful.
   c. If a copper-containing rock was heated in a hot fire with charcoal present, the carbon in the charcoal would combine with the other elements in the rock, leaving free metallic copper.
   d. Sulfur and carbon are two elements found free in nature.

2. What is the purpose of the sentence "*Sulfur* is one of those elements"?
   a. It states the main idea.
   b. It supports the main idea by providing a reason.
   c. It supports the main idea by providing an example.
   d. It states an idea that is in contrast to the main idea.
3. What is the purpose of the sentence "*Carbon* was also known since antiquity"?
   a. It states the main idea.
   b. It supports the main idea by providing a reason.
   c. It supports the main idea by providing an example.
   d. It states an idea that is in contrast to the main idea.
4. What is the purpose of the group of words "if a copper-containing rock was heated in a hot fire with charcoal present"?
   a. It provides an example of carbon combining with other elements.
   b. It states the condition under which carbon combines with other elements.
   c. It contrasts carbon with other elements found free in nature.
   d. It states the main idea of the paragraph.
5. Which word or words in the paragraph introduce a reason?
   a. and   c. also
   b. because   d. for example
6. The word *although* is used twice in the paragraph. In both cases the word introduces a/an
   a. reason.   c. opposite idea.
   b. example.   d. condition.

Paragraph B

Iron also arrived occasionally from the heavens in the form of iron-containing meteorites. Because of this, one might think that iron would have been thought of as a "heavenly" element, a gift from the gods. Instead, this honor has always fallen to the element *gold*. Gold doesn't fall from the skies, but it is found in its pure state in some places. It has the unusual property of never tarnishing like other metals do. Gold objects don't rust, as iron does, nor do they turn green or black on the surface, as do many other metals.

1. The main idea of the paragraph is that
   a. iron arrived from the heavens and for this reason ancient people considered it a heavenly gift.
   b. ancient people did not consider iron a gift from the gods.
   c. ancient people considered gold, not iron, as a gift from the gods because it never tarnishes or rusts.
   d. gold objects are very valuable because they do not tarnish or rust.
2. What is the purpose of the sentence "Instead, this honor has always fallen to the element *gold*"?
   a. It states the main idea.
   b. It provides an example of the idea stated in the previous statement.
   c. It states an opposite point from that given in the previous statement.
   d. It develops the idea stated in the previous statement.
3. What is the purpose of the sentence "It has the unusual property of never tarnishing like other metals do"?
   a. It states a contrast.
   b. It provides an example of the idea stated in the previous statement.

c. It states an opposite point from that given in the previous statement.

d. It develops the idea stated in the previous statement.

4. What word or words set up a comparison in the paragraph?

   a. also   c. nor

   b. because   d. like

5. What kind of relationship does the word *but* establish in this sentence: "Gold doesn't fall from the skies, but it is found in its pure state in some places"?

   a. It changes the direction of the thought.

   b. It introduces an example.

   c. It indicates that more on the same thought is coming.

   d. It indicates that the writer is going to enumerate, or list, several points on the same topic.

6. What kind of relationship is established in the last sentence by the group of words, "as do many other metals"?

   a. example   c. condition

   b. reason   d. comparison

Paragraph C

The ancient Egyptians used gold for jewelry and for coins. Gold is still used for jewelry, although pure gold is too soft for this purpose. Coins and jewelry, instead, are made of *alloys*. These are metals made by melting two or more metals in a pot together in such a way that they dissolve in one another. Gold coins are usually 90 percent gold and 10 percent copper. An alloy of gold and silver is called *white gold*.

1. The main idea of the paragraph is that

   a. coins and jewelry are and have been made from alloys of gold.

   b. an alloy of gold and silver is white gold.

   c. an alloy is made by melting two or more metals in a pot together so that they dissolve in one another.

   d. the ancient Egyptians used gold for jewelry and for coins.

2. The word *instead* in the third sentence suggests a/an

   a. example.

   b. continuation of the thought.

   c. change in the direction of the thought.

   d. reason.

3. What is the purpose of this sentence: "These are metals made by melting two or more metals in a pot together in such a way that they dissolve in one another"?

   a. It states the main idea.

   b. It gives a detail to support the idea in the previous sentence.

   c. It provides an example in support of the idea in the previous sentence.

   d. It lists, or enumerates, several points relative to the main idea.

Paragraph D

Silver was one of the first metals to be used by human beings; alloys of silver continue to be used today in a variety of products, including jewelry and coins. Unlike gold, silver tarnishes to become blackish in color. On the other hand, silver is like gold in that it is melted with other elements to form alloys. One alloy is coin silver, consisting of 90% silver and 10% copper. A second alloy is sterling silver, which contains 92.5% silver and 7.5% copper. Other silver alloys today are used in dental fillings and for electrical contacts.

1. What is the main idea of the paragraph?
   a. Silver tarnishes to become blackish so that it is necessary to use silver alloys instead of pure silver.
   b. Alloys of silver continue to be used today in a variety of products.
   c. Silver alloys are formed by melting silver with other elements such as copper.
   d. Sterling silver has a larger percentage of silver than coin silver.
2. What is the purpose of this sentence: "Unlike gold, silver tarnishes to become blackish in color"?
   a. to establish a contrast between gold and silver
   b. to give a reason for the tarnishing of silver
   c. to show that gold is better than silver
   d. to give the condition under which silver will tarnish
3. What is the purpose of this sentence: "On the other hand, silver is like gold in that it is melted with other elements to form alloys"?
   a. to compare gold and silver
   b. to give an example of how an alloy is formed
   c. to give a reason for making alloys of silver
   d. to give a weakness of silver
4. What is the purpose of this sentence: "One alloy is coin silver, consisting of 90% silver and 10% copper"?
   a. to provide a comparison   c. to provide a reason
   b. to provide an example   d. to provide a condition
5. What is the purpose of this sentence: "A second alloy is sterling silver, which contains 92.5% silver and 7.5% copper"?
   a. to provide a comparison   c. to provide a reason
   b. to provide an example   d. to provide a condition

APPLYING WHAT YOU KNOW IN WRITING

In the previous sections, you have seen how writers structure their writing to express relationships and how they choose words and phrases that provide clues to the relationships they are developing. Using those clue words in reading, you can predict where a particular writer is going next in a selection. Figure 6.5 is a composite chart of clue words writers use.

To help you gain control over these words that provide clues to relationships being expressed, next you will write sentences and paragraphs using them.

Study the following chart of data:

The Three States of Matter

The State	Characteristics	Relation to Heat	Examples
Solid	retains its volume (how much space it occupies) and shape.		ice below 0 °C; gold and silver at room temperature.
Liquid	retains its volume but takes the shape of its container.	may be formed by heating the solid form.	water above 0 °C; mercury at room temperature.
Gas	takes the shape and volume of its container.	may be formed by heating the liquid form.	water vapor above 100 °C; oxygen and hydrogen at room temperature.

Using the data in the chart, write a three-paragraph article about the states of matter. Model your paragraph after the one about the three classes of rocks that opens this chapter. Use the idea map in Figure 6.1 as a guide.

1. Start with a topic sentence that tells there are three states of matter. Then in the same paragraph tell about solids and give some examples.

2. Shift to a new paragraph about liquids. Perhaps use the phrase *In contrast* to make the transition. Again, include examples.

3. Shift to a third paragraph about gases. Include examples.

4. Take data from the chart on page 137 in constructing your paragraphs.

5. Remember to use clue words to show key relationships. In this case, number words may be useful in identifying the three kinds of matter. Phrases like *for example . . .* or *an example of . . .* may be useful when presenting examples. Phrases like *If . . . then* may be useful in talking about conditions under which matter exists as a solid, liquid, or gas.

Go back and circle the key words you used to clarify relationships you are expressing in your paragraphs. Note in the margin the kind of relationship you are establishing in each case. Use Figure 6.5 as a guide in doing this. Share your para-

Figure 6.5   *Clue Words*

What Is Going to Happen	Clue Words	Strategy for Handling the Clues
A. Writer is going to enumerate or discuss a number of items.	*three* kinds, *two* problems, *four* reasons, the *first,* the *second,* the *third . . .*	Ask: How many items is the author going to enumerate (list) or talk about?
B. Writer is going to enumerate or describe examples to support a point.	*An example* of this is, *For example, such as, For instance.*	Ask: Is this an example of the point?
C. Writer is going to provide more on the topic or change the direction.	More on the topic: *and, also, in addition, moreover, furthermore, additionally.*	Ask: Does this relate to what went before?
	Change of direction: *but, yet, however, on the other hand, nevertheless.*	Ask: Does this present the other side of the point?
D. Writer is going to compare or contrast.	Similarities are to be presented: *similarly, as in the case of, like the, the same as, like . . . .*	Ask: Is the author stating the way things are the same?
	Differences are to be presented: *on the other hand, on the contrary, unlike the, in contrast to, whereas, while.*	Ask: Is the author stating the way things differ?
E. Writer is going to set up a conditional relationship.	*If . . . then, consequently, hence, thus.*	Ask: If *x,* then what?
F. Writer is going to give reasons.	*Because, for, as a result, since, for this reason.*	Ask: Why?
G. Writer is going to indicate "in spite of the fact that . . . ."	*Although, even, though.*	Ask: In spite of what?

graphs with another student. Have him or her help you edit the paragraphs so they express your ideas as clearly as possible.

EXTENDING WHAT YOU HAVE LEARNED

Applying the Strategies as You Read

Review the word clues contained in Figure 6.5. Then read an article from a science magazine such as *Scientific American* or a section from a biology or earth science text. As you read, write on a card several sentences with clue words that help you grasp what is happening in the article. On the card next to each clue word, write what you learned from that clue word: The author is going to enumerate the number of items to be considered, change the direction of the thought, continue with the thought, present an example, compare/contrast, give an if . . . then relationship, give a reason. Be ready to share your findings with classmates.

Extending Your Vocabulary

Select several words from those emphasized in the chapter to use in writing and speaking. Record these in your personal vocabulary list. Include a model sentence for each.

Building Your Knowledge Base

Locate the Hawaiian Islands on a globe. Would you like to go there? What would you expect to see? Locate the following places on the map in Figure 12.1: Mt. Etna in Sicily and Mt. Vesuvius in Italy.

7

Applying Systematic Study Strategies— SQ3R, Highlighting, Charting, Webbing, Outlining, Summarizing, Test Taking

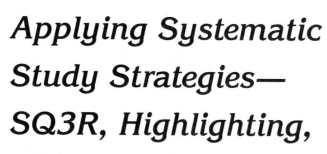

Before reading the chapter, read the title, the stated objective, and the headings and subheadings. Ask yourself: What is the topic of the chapter? In the space above and beside the chapter number, jot down what you already know about the topic. Then in the space below the number, jot down at least two questions you hope to answer through reading the chapter.

OBJECTIVE

In this chapter, you will learn to use several systematic study strategies. Specifically, you will learn how to use

1. SQ3R,
2. highlighting and recording notes directly in a text,
3. data charting, data webbing, and outlining, and
4. summarizing.

You will also learn strategies to help you study for and take tests.

SQ3R—A SYSTEMATIC STUDY STRATEGY

SQ3R is a popular strategy for systematically studying a textbook or a textbook-like article that has subheadings.

Step 1 in SQ3R is to survey, or preview, a chapter to be read and studied. The *S* stands for *survey*. When you survey, you

- read the title, author, and any introductory and summary paragraphs including focusing questions, statements of objectives, and review questions. You (1) identify the topic, (2) tell yourself what you already know about that topic, and (3) set your general purpose for reading the selection.
- check the introduction to see if it provides clues to the main point of the chapter and the organization of it (for example, does it say, "In this section you will read about two ways. . . ." or "In this section, we will consider four events . . ."?).
- survey the subheadings, using them to predict what each subsection is about and to spark in your mind things you already know about the topic. As you do this, scan related illustrations, boldface terms, and margin notes (if there are any) and *keep telling yourself what you already know.*

Step 2 in SQ3R is to turn the major subheadings of a chapter into questions to answer while reading. The *Q* in SQ3R stands for *question*. For example, the heading that introduces this section of text is "SQ3R—A Systematic Study Strategy." If you were to compose questions based on that heading to guide your reading of the section, you might think, "What is SQ3R? What do I do when I use SQ3R to study? What do all those letters and the number mean?"

Step 3 is to read the chapter, keeping your questions in mind. That is the first *R* in SQ3R; the R means to *read* to find answers to your own questions. As you read, also keep sifting through details to get the main idea of the section and keep alert for clues to tell you where the author is going. Clues, as you remember, include organizing words such as *first, second,* and *finally.*

Step 4 is to *recite*—the second *R* in SQ3R. After reading each major subdivision of a chapter, you stop to tell yourself the answers to the questions you made up earlier. Also tell yourself

- the main idea of that part of the text,
- the important points the author made to support the main idea,
- the points explained in the graphs, charts, or other visuals that accompany that part of the text,
- the meanings of key terms defined in that subsection.

If you have trouble talking to yourself about what you have just read, reread.

Step 5 is to *review*—the third *R* in SQ3R. You review when you finish reading a chapter and on several occasions thereafter as you prepare for a test on the material. You review by again telling yourself the answers to the questions you made up before reading, at times by writing down the answers, and sometimes by rereading when you know you do not understand.

In sum, SQ3R is a five-step study plan that includes these components:

Survey	Question	Read	Recite	Review

In the next selection, taken from a popular book on personal finance, you will have an opportunity to try out SQ3R.

SELECTION 1: GAMES DEALERS PLAY (Personal Finance)

Expanding Your Vocabulary Through Reading

As you read, watch for words that are new to you. Circle them. Use word-structure and context clues to figure out their meaning. Write a definition of new words in the margin.

Getting Ready to Read

1. **SURVEY**   *Preview the selection by reading the title, author, first paragraph, the headings, and the concluding paragraph.*
   - What do you think this selection is about? _____

   - What do you already know on this topic? What experiences have you had nego-tiating for a car that you wanted to buy? Write some phrases that come to your

     mind when you think about the games car dealers play. _____

     _____

     _____

   - Do you recognize the name of this author? What kind of writing does this man

     do? (Look back to Chapter 1 to refresh your memory.) _____

     _____

2. **QUESTION**   *In the margin of the selection next to each of the four subheadings, write a question that you will answer through your reading. Answering these questions will be your reading purpose.*

Reading with Meaning

READ   *As you read the selection, try to answer the questions you just wrote in the margin. Since this book does not provide any end-of-chapter questions, you must provide your own questions for study. After each subsection of text, stop and tell yourself the answer to your question based on that heading.*

GAMES DEALERS PLAY

Bob Rosefsky

The automobile business is extremely competitive. Competitiveness breeds anxiety and that in turn may cause car salespeople and dealerships to now and then bend the ethics of good business practices in order to win a sale. Some of these practices are illustrated in the following tale. Try to spot the pitfalls as they occur.

You're planning to buy a car, and you've set your heart on a Rammer-Jammer XJKB. You've priced it at two dealerships, who are within a few dollars of each other: About $4000 in cash will be required over your old trade-in. You want to try one more dealership, which advertises heavily that they will "meet or beat any deal in town."

You and your spouse [or friend] take a drive to that dealership one evening after dinner. A pleasant young chap takes you under his wing and suggests that you test drive the model you've been admiring. While you're driving around, you're very impressed with the seeming honesty and candor of this nice fellow, and you're particularly intrigued when he suggests that the trade-in value of your old car might be $1000 more than what other dealers have quoted you! He explains that this dealer's inventory of used cars is very low, and he's offering better deals on trade-ins to build up his inventory. What's more, the salesman confides, he thinks the boss has been overcharging too many customers, and he, as a bright honest young man, doesn't like people to get a raw deal. Thus, he tells you, he's going to take it upon himself to see that you get the best possible deal available, and the boss won't know the difference.

Back at the showroom, he takes you into his little office to do some calculating. After a few moments, he looks up at you with a smile. "If I can get the boss to agree on a deal that would take $3000 plus your trade-in, would you sign the deal tonight?"

Wow! $3000! You were willing to pay $4000 for exactly the same car at a different showroom. Of course you'd be willing to take a deal for $3000 if the boss will go along with it. The well-trained salesman spots your enthusiasm and proceeds.

"Look," he says, "the boss doesn't like me to approach him with proposed deals unless he's sure that the customer will take the deal. He doesn't like to waste his time haggling back and forth. If he knows he has a firm deal right at the outset, that means he's saving time and he'll give you a better price. Let me do this: Let me fill out the contract showing a $3000 trade difference, and you give me a good faith check for $50. That way, he knows he's got a firm deal *if* he signs the contract. If he doesn't go for the deal, he won't sign the contract and you're not obligated for anything. If he doesn't go for it, I'll give you back the contract and your check, and you can rip them both up. What have you got to lose?"

You've got nothing to lose, or so you think. You're sitting there planning on how you can spend the $1000 you've just saved and itching to get behind the wheel of the new car that's just a signature away. You review what the salesman has just said. He's right. If the owner doesn't sign the contract, there's no deal.

"O.K.," you say, "fill out the contract and I'll sign it."

He leaves the room with the signed contract and the check, and you and your spouse [or friend] sit and snicker over the tremendous deal you're getting. "I was ready to pay $4000, and we're stealing it for $3000," you say. (There's a little bit of larceny in all of us.)

You sit and wait for ten, then twenty minutes. You're getting impatient because you want that contract to come back signed by the owner so you can hop in your new Rammer-Jammer and be off, before they realize how you've taken them.

Just as you're about out of patience, the young man sticks his head in the door, smiles at you, and says, "I think everything is going to be O.K. I'm going to take the car around to the service department and get it ready for you so you can take it home tonight if you want."

Your motor starts racing, and you lean back to wait some more. Another ten minutes pass, and an older man enters the room. He tells you he is the assistant boss. Very understandingly, he tells you that he appreciates how anxious you are to get into that new car. But, sadly there seems to have been a snag. The pleasant young man whom you were so fond of, it seems, has been doing a lousy job for the dealer. He makes mistakes on his estimates, and he's trying to cut the prices lower than the dealer can afford. Very likely, the young man isn't long for this kind of business. As a matter of fact, the assistant boss continues, it seems as though the young man was off by $1000 on your deal. He vastly overestimated the value of your trade-in. "We'd love to have you in this car, because I know you want to be in it," the assistant boss says, "but we've just got to talk about a $4000 trade difference, not $3000." The bubble has burst.

"In the first place," the assistant boss goes on, "we didn't even give your trade car a test drive. Let me have the keys to it so our service manager can check it out and give you a fair trade-in price." Bewildered, you hand over your keys and he disappears with them.

You're confused and dejected. You want to get back the contract and your check, and though some suspicions are beginning to grow in your mind, there's still a glimmer of hope that you can correct this foul-up and still get the deal you had already set your heart on. You and your spouse [or friend] debate the matter in the privacy of the closing room and tentatively agree that if you can strike a deal somewhere between $3500 and $4000, maybe you'd still go for it since it would be better than any of the other quotes you'd been given.

The assistant boss reappears momentarily with your contract, which he hands over to you; and you tear it up. "Where's my $50 check?" you ask. He looks a little bewildered and guesses that it must still be in the boss's office. "Don't worry about it," he says, "I'll get it for you in just a few minutes. Now about your deal," he begins. "We've given your trade-in a good look, and it needs a lot of work and new tires. A good deal for us would be $4300 plus your trade-in, but since you've been here so long and have been so patient, since you were misled by the young fellow, we can bend some and let you have the new Rammer-Jammer for $4100."

You've been there over an hour already, and the grind is beginning to wear you down. You finally concede, "$3900, not a penny more," knowing that he's winning. You're starting to wonder when you're going to get your $50 check back and what they are doing with your old car. You finally tell him that you think you had best go home and talk about the matter before making a decision, and you demand your check and your car keys. He promises that he will try to locate them right away, and he leaves the room. You're getting tense now, but you still feel that you can get the deal for $3900, which is still a $100 better than the next best deal. You discuss it with your spouse [or friend] and decide that since you've been here this long you might as well hang around a little longer and hope the deal can be wrapped up for $3900.

A few minutes later, salesman number three comes in. This is the boss, and he's high pressure all the way. The hour is getting later and you're getting more and more tired. The boss now is pushing hard to close you at $4050, which, as he says, "I'm losing money on."

Then comes the clincher. You again demand your check and your keys, and he comes back from a quick search to inform you sadly that the cashier has left for the night and the check has been locked up in the register. "Don't worry, it's perfectly safe there. If we don't close on the deal tonight, you can come back and pick it up in the morning."

Furthermore, the used car appraiser has also left for the night and thinking that your old car had been accepted as a trade-in, he parked it in the lot and locked the keys in his office. "Don't worry," says the boss, "we can give you a ride home tonight and pick you up in the morning to get your old car. I assure you, there's absolutely no problem. Now about this deal . . ."

The final thrust: "Look folks, I know how late it's getting, and I want to get out of here as badly as you do. Let me ask you this—if I give you the deal for $4000, will you take it, then we'll all go out and have a drink?" Resignation has finally set in, and you agree to the deal. After all, it's still as good as the best deal you had any other place. Wearily, you reach for your pen.

Interwoven throughout this intrigue are four types of sales tactics (Did you recognize them?) that have brought a poor reputation to a small segment of the automobile sales industry.

The Highball Trick

The first salesman used the highball trick, in which he quoted a much higher trade-in value on your old car than was reasonable. Indeed, it sounds too good to be true, which causes the first strong opening pull on your purse strings. The opposite of the highball is lowball, where the salesperson looks at the sticker price on the new car and suggests a too-good-to-be-true discount from that price. The obvious tactic here is to lead you to believe that you're going to get a better deal than you thought possible, all the quicker to get you into the showroom where the heavy pressure can be applied.

The Takeover Operation

The "takeover" ploy involves a succession of salespersons ranging from low pressure to high pressure. The first one's job is to soften you and win your confidence. Subsequent salespeople increase the pressure until the closer takes over. The process is designed to wear down your resistance gradually. The first salesperson's job is accomplished when he gets you to sit down in the closing office, not just in a mood to buy, but with a raging desire to buy, albeit at a price that would later turn out to be impossible. The success of the takeover operation depends on the next tactic.

The Bugged Closing Room

Unless you are an electronics whiz, you would probably not be able to determine whether a room is bugged. This indeed is a devious trick not generally employed by a legitimate dealer, but you never know what you're up against. By listening in to your conversations, the salespeople know just where your soft spots are and how far they can take you. If they determine that you are really thin skinned and have strong sales resistance, they can always fall back on the next sales tactic.

The "Disappearing Check" Trick or the "Keys Are Locked Up for the Night" Gambit

This is the last straw. By claiming to have "misplaced" something of value, such as a check or car keys, they are, in effect, nailing you to the wall until your resistance finally breaks. The best way to avoid being trapped in this manner is not to write any checks and to stand by as they test your trade-in car so you can retain the keys until the deal is either made or not made.

If you spot any of the tactics noted above in operation in your car shopping, you can be relatively sure that you're in for a high-pressure pitch that might lead you to signing a contract you otherwise wouldn't sign. Even though, in the above case, you thought you got away with the same deal you could have had elsewhere, that isn't necessarily so. Had you gone back to the other dealers for a follow-up bargaining session, you might have gotten a still better deal. Awareness of these tricks and a willingness to walk away from shady tactics when you spot them are necessary weapons when shopping for a car. Dealers sell hundreds of cars each month. You buy only one every few years. They know a lot more about tricks of bargaining and striking a deal than you do. They're entitled to a fair profit for whatever work they're involved in, just as you are, but that doesn't give them the right to take advantage of you—all of which leads back to the most important point: Know whom you are dealing with. There's no substitute for a reputation of integrity.   [2,238 words]

Checking for Understanding

RECITE   Now go back and tell yourself the answers to the questions you wrote in the margin before you began to read. In this instance, do not just give a definition to each of the terms used in the subheadings, but tell yourself an example.

REVIEW   Come back to this selection after some time has passed. Again tell yourself the answers to the questions you wrote before reading. If you have trouble, reread the appropriate sections and write out the answers to the questions. Then tell yourself the answers in your head. In class, your instructor will ask you to tell the answers to your questions. He or she may also give you a short quiz on the important material from the selection.

HIGHLIGHTING AND NOTETAKING DIRECTLY IN A TEXTBOOK

Many college students make marks and notes directly in their textbooks. For example, as they survey a chapter before reading, they build an outline right into the text. Surveying the first major heading (e.g., "The Highball Trick" in the selection "Games Dealers Play"), they put a number 1 in front of that heading. Reaching the second heading (e.g., "The Takeover Operation"), they put a number 2 before it. Go back to the selection "Games Dealers Play," and put a number in front of each of the tricks. If you do this as a part of a survey, it clarifies that there are four tricks you will be reading about. In addition, some students find it helpful as part of the survey stage of SQ3R to write their questions directly in the margin. If you do this as part of your survey, when you go back to recite and review after reading, you can use your margin questions as a guide.

You may also find it helpful to make other kinds of notes in your textbooks after reading a paragraph.

1. If there is a main idea, or topic, sentence, underline that sentence with a pen. Do the same with definitions you will need to remember. In the margin (or in a special vocabulary section of your notebook) write the definition of a key term in abbreviated form to use in future study of the text. Using a pen for making in-text notes generally takes less time than using a highlighting marker.

2. If the author makes a series of related points within a paragraph, insert numbers in front of the points to keep track of them. This is helpful if the author talks about "first," "second," and so on. Insert directly into the text a number 1, a number 2, and so forth, at such sites. Or you may want to list main points in the margin, listing a key word for each point to remind you of it. That is another advantage of using a pen rather than a colored highlighting marker. You can write clearer notes with a pen.

Generally you will want to underline points and make notes *after* rather than while reading a paragraph. In that way you know what is important in the paragraph and avoid marking sentence after sentence. There is not much sense in marking almost every line of text as many students do while reading. And marking too many lines wastes your time.

Here is a paragraph from a college business text, with in-text notes made by a student. Study the notes to decide why that reader underlined and made notes in the margin as she did.

Purpose and Objectives of Business

Why do businesses exist? A business has one main purpose: to serve the public. Any business that does not serve the public will not exist for long. However, if a business is striving to operate at maximum production and efficiency, serving the public is often not enough. Generally, a business owner will strive to accomplish two major objectives. First, the owner will try to provide a specific service and/or good that will satisfy human needs and wants. For example, your local clothing store provides a service by selling consumer goods such as coats, shoes, pants, and other related clothing articles. These are products that you need and want for everyday use. Second, the owner will strive to operate at a profit. In other words, an important objective of business is to generate income that exceeds the expenditures it incurs for such things as salaries, rent, and the cost of goods, and at a rate that will satisfy the risk.

A. main purpose

B. objectives

Why did the student underline the words she did? Why did the student jot those terms in the margin? _____

_____

_____

Reread the four paragraphs that describe the four types of sales tactics given in "Games Dealers Play." After you reread each paragraph, use a pen to underline the definition of the trick or tricks described. Then in the margin, jot down the intent of the salesperson using that trick. Do not write in complete sentences.

DATA CHARTING, WEBBING, AND OUTLINING

Data charting is another systematic study strategy that can help you read a college textbook. As with SQ3R and highlighting the text, the first step in using data charting is to survey the selection you are going to read. You look at the same kinds of things as with SQ3R—the introductory and concluding paragraphs, the headings, and so forth—predict what the section is about, and think about what you already know on the topic. (*If you own the textbook,* you may also highlight at this stage by building an outline directly into the text by numbering the main headings.)

Step 2 is to use the subheadings to create a data chart for taking notes while reading. You do this before you read the selection. For example, surveying the selection "Games Dealers Play," you would quickly sketch a chart like this:

Games Dealers Play

Highball Trick	
Takeover Operation	
Bugged Closing Room	
Disappearing Check Trick or Keys Are Locked Up for the Night	

Or, you could have prepared a web for taking notes. In that case, your preliminary web might have looked like this:

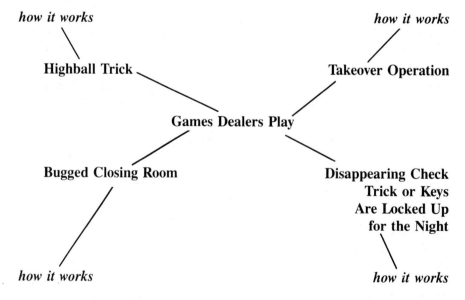

Or you could have begun a formal outline of the material by listing the main subheadings:

I. The Highball Trick
   A.
   B.
       etc.

II. The Takeover Operation
   A.
   B.
    etc.
III. The Bugged Closing Room
   A.
   B.
    etc.
IV. The Disappearing Check Trick or Keys Are Locked Up
   A.
   B.
    etc.

Step 3 is to read the selection. As you finish the segment of text under a subheading, you stop and write down the main idea and important details of that section in the appropriate slot of your data chart or in the appropriate area of your data web, using key words and phrases. You do this for the material under each subheading. In the case of a formal outline, you would use the traditional capital letters, numbers, and lower-case letters to list subpoints under the headings you previously listed.

Step 4 is to reread the material on your data chart, your web, or your outline, and then to recite it to yourself in your head until you can do this without looking at your notes.

Step 5 is to review the material several times by reciting it to yourself in your head.

The data charting, webbing, or outlining strategy is particularly useful when you are reading in a library textbook and you cannot make notes directly in it. Working with two of your friends, go back and fill in the data chart, the data web, and the formal outline based on "Games Dealers Play." Each one of you use one of the techniques. Compare your results. Decide which technique is the most useful for you.

Here is a selection from a college music textbook. Try using the data-charting strategy to study it.

SELECTION 2: AFRICAN-AMERICAN FOLK MUSIC
(Music)

Expanding Your Vocabulary Through Reading

As you read, watch for words that are new to you. Circle them. Use word-structure and context clues to figure out their meaning. Write a definition of new words in the margin.

Getting Ready to Read

1. **SURVEY**   *Preview the selection by reading the title, author, first paragraph, and headings.*
   - What is the topic of the selection? _____
   - What do you already know on this topic? Write some phrases that come to your
     mind about African-American music. _____
     _____

- Now go back and build an outline directly into the text by putting a number (1, 2, 3, etc.) before each major subheading.
2. **DATA CHART** *Make the outline of a data chart based on the major subheadings from the selection.* You will read this selection to identify important ideas and supporting details.

Reading with Meaning

READ *As you read the selection, stop and write down main ideas and supporting details on your data chart under the appropriate subheading label.*

RECITE *After each subsection of text, stop and tell yourself the material you have recorded on the chart. Also review in your head the meaning of any italicized terms. You may prefer to work with a friend, reading each subsection to yourself and then deciding together what to record on your data chart.*

AFRICAN-AMERICAN FOLK MUSIC, THE BLUES, AND AFRICAN-AMERICAN SPIRITUALS

Daniel Politoske

African-American Folk Music

Of all the ethnic influences that have gone into the creation of popular music in America, probably the most important has been that of black Africa. West African music, though very different from European music, shared with it certain basic characteristics of harmony. Thus, when the two traditions were brought together in America by slavery, it was possible for them to blend. African-American folk music was just the first of many important and widely influential results.

Generally pressed into slavery by European adventurers on the west coast of Africa, the hundreds of thousands of African-Americans who began arriving in America in 1619 brought with them a highly developed musical tradition and a habit of incorporating music into every activity of life. Religion, dance, and work were some of the main functions it served. Much of their music came to America intact. Once here it was gradually altered to meet new needs. The banjo, unique to America, is thought to have African roots. The use of drums, the most important instrument of West Africa, was continued in the New World.

Field Holler

African-Americans developed a wide repertory of songs, both secular and religious. One early type of secular song, perhaps the closest of all to African prototypes, was the *field holler* that slaves often sang while working. A field holler was the yearning cry of a slave working alone, a sound midway between a yell and a song, whose words determined the tone. It began with a high, long-drawn-out shout and then glided down to the lowest note the singer could reach. Such songs were characterized by falsetto tones, swoops and slides from note to note, complicated and unexpected changes of rhythm, and an occasional line of melody from Anglo-American ballads or hymns. They were heard not only in the fields but wherever an African-American worked at hard, lonely tasks. When slavery ended, the songs were taken onto the docks, into the railroad camps, and onto the Mississippi River.

Group Work Song

Related to the field holler was the *group work song.* This, too, was close to African sources, for whenever Africans worked together at a task they found it natural to pace their labor with a song. Field hands sang as they hoed or picked the cotton. Rowing songs were used to time the strokes on the flat-bottomed boats of the South. Later on, work songs were chanted by chain gangs and by railroad workers, whose backbreaking, dangerous labor was regulated by the rhythmic chanting of the song leader. The leader played a very important part in the group work song, choosing the song to be sung, setting the pace, adjusting it to the feel of the work being done, and improvising catchy lyrics and musical byplay to fire the energies of the other workers. A good song made the work go faster and better and relieved the weary monotony of it.

Although there was great variety in their lyrics and uses, the earliest work songs were almost entirely African in sound and structure. They made use of the African call-and-response pattern, expressive African vocal techniques such as those used in the field holler, and occasional syncopated African rhythms built around a steady meter. Most work songs were sung with the leader and chorus responding to each other, but some were performed almost in unison, with incidental improvised variants.

Ring Shout

Another musical style that closely resembled its African counterparts was the *ring shout,* a shuffling dance with chanting and handclapping. To an African, dancing was a natural part of worship, but as the Bible was thought to prohibit dancing in church, slaves had to be content with a short shuffling step executed counterclockwise in a ring. This circular movement was accompanied by excited clapping and a kind of *shout song* that provided more rhythm than melody. Biblical stories supplied the words for the shout songs, which were chanted in the customary leader-chorus fashion. Starting slowly, the music gathered speed and intensity with the hypnotic repetition of body movements and musical phrases.

Song Sermons

In many African-American religious services, the sermon also took on some of the qualities of song, generally with a driving, hypnotic rhythm. Delivering such a *song sermon,* the preacher would at different times speak, chant, or sing, steadily increasing speed and passion as the song proceeded. The congregation, caught up in the pulse of the rhythm, would interject rhythmic cries or abbreviated lines of melody, using words such as "Amen!" or "Yes, my Lord!"

Lining Out

Lining out was a technique borrowed from white colonial churches. In many of these churches hymn books were in short supply; in others many of the people of the congregation were illiterate. Thus, it was common practice for the preacher to sing each line of a hymn or psalm and then wait for the congregation to repeat it. This technique adapted itself perfectly to the African call-and-response pattern.

The Blues

The invention of the *blues* represents a major contribution of African-American folk music. Its influence on popular music has been notable, even since 1960. The blues style is characterized by distinctive *blue notes* produced by slightly bending the pitch of certain tones of the major scale. The style was somehow right for plaintive songs of sadness. A whole repertory of such songs grew up, created by unrequited lovers, prisoners, lonely people far from home, and thousands of others who needed to ease their pain by expressing it.

African-American Spirituals

In many respects, the religious counterpart of the blues was the *spiritual*. Developed largely in rural areas in the mid-nineteenth century, spirituals did not receive much public attention until they were made popular after the Civil War by groups who performed harmonized arrangements such as the Fisk University Jubilee Singers. *Nobody Knows the Trouble I've Seen* and *Steal Away* are among the most familiar examples. The African-American spiritual was superficially similar to spirituals written early in the nineteenth century. However, it is the African-American spiritual that has remained important to the present day. The music of the African-American spiritual was in effect an extremely successful mixture of church melodies and harmonies and West African rhythms and styles of performance.   [1,046 words]

Checking Your Understanding

REVIEW   When you have read the entire selection, go back and tell yourself or a colleague the ideas, facts, and definitions you wrote on your chart.

Be ready to take a test on what you have read. Before studying for and taking that test, read the section of this chapter (pp. 155–157) that deals with test-taking strategies.

WRITING SUMMARIES

Research shows that writing summaries of content you have read is one of the best ways to learn it. In writing a summary, you generally start by writing a sentence that states the thesis, or main point, of a section of text you have just read. Chapter 4 explains how to identify the thesis. Then using the subheadings as a guide, you write some sentences providing details that support the main point. Here is a model summary based on the selection, "Games Dealers Play." Notice that the first sentence states the main point and successive sentences explain each of the "tricks." Notice that the final sentence is based on the conclusion offered in the selection.

Sometimes car salespeople bend the ethics of good business practice to win a sale. They may at first quote a much higher trade-in value on your old car than is reasonable (the highball trick) or suggest a too low discount from the sticker price (the lowball trick). They may play the takeover ploy in which you are moved from low pressure to high pressure salespersons. They may listen in on your conversations by placing you in a bugged room. Or they may "disappear" something of yours—a check or your car keys—to increase the pressure. If you spot any of these tricks, you probably are better off buying from another dealer.

Study the notes you made on your data chart as you read the selection about African-American folk music. Then in your notebook write a summary paragraph. Start by composing a topic sentence based on the two introductory paragraphs about the importance of black folk music in America. Then compose a sentence based on each subsection to provide supporting detail. In other words, write a sentence about the field holler, the group work song, and so on. Your summary paragraph will have about eight sentences.

STUDYING MATERIAL WITHOUT HEADINGS

In some college courses, especially in the humanities when you are studying literature, you will have to read selections in which there are no subheadings and no illustrative charts or pictures. In such cases, the strategies discussed so far in this chapter are difficult to use, and you must modify them. Of course, you should start by previewing the material—looking over the title, the author, and any introductory paragraphs. Before reading, you need to predict what the selection is about and think about what you already know on the topic. Then, compose several general questions you hope to answer through reading the selection.

As you read, keep your questions in mind. As with SQ3R, do not try to read the entire selection nonstop. Stop periodically to tell yourself the answers to your questions and to tell yourself the important ideas and supporting details. When you finish the selection, review by telling yourself the main points. Review also by writing a summary of the article as described in the previous section.

SELECTION 3: THE ACHIEVEMENT OF DESIRE
(Literature—Autobiography)

Expanding Your Vocabulary Through Reading

As you read, circle words that are new to you. Using word-structure and context clues, figure out the meanings of your circled words. Write their definitions in the margins.

Getting Ready to Read

1. **SURVEY** *Preview the selection by reading the title, author, and introductory note. Skim the first paragraph as part of your prereading survey.*

   ● What is the topic of the selection? _____

   ● What thoughts come to your mind as you begin to read? _____

   _____

2. **QUESTION** Write two or three general questions you hope to answer through reading. This selection, as you see, does not come from a text. It is from an autobiography of a type you may well have to read in a college humanities course. There are no subheadings.

   _____

   _____

   _____

Reading with Meaning

READ/RECITE   *As you read this section, stop at the end of each paragraph. Ask yourself: What is the main idea Rodriguez is trying to get across? What points does he use to support that idea? Recite the answers to yourself at the end of each paragraph.*

THE ACHIEVEMENT OF DESIRE
*Richard Rodriguez**

OPEN THE DOORS OF YOUR MIND WITH BOOKS, read the red and white poster over the nun's desk in early September. It soon was apparent to me that reading was the classroom's central activity. Each course had its own book. And the information gathered from a book was unquestioned. READ TO LEARN, the sign on the wall advised in December. I privately wondered: What was the connection between reading and learning? Did one learn something only by reading it? Was an idea only an idea if it could be written down? In June, CONSIDER BOOKS YOUR BEST FRIENDS. Friends? Reading was, at best, only a chore. I needed to look up whole paragraphs of words in a dictionary. Lines of type were dizzying, the eye having to move slowly across the page, then down, and across. . . . The sentences of the first books I read were coolly impersonal. Toned hard. What most bothered me, however, was the isolation reading required. To console myself for the loneliness I'd feel when I read, I tried reading in a very soft voice. Until: 'Who is doing all that talking to his neighbor?' Shortly after, remedial reading classes were arranged for me with a very old nun.

At the end of each school day, for nearly six months, I would meet with her in the tiny room that served as the school's library but was actually only a storeroom for used textbooks and a vast collection of *National Geographics.* Everything about our sessions pleased me: the smallness of the room; the noise of the janitor's broom hitting the edge of the long hallway outside the door; the green of the sun, lighting the wall; and the old woman's face blurred white with a beard. Most of the time we took turns. I began with my elementary text. Sentences of astonishing simplicity seemed to me lifeless and drab: "The boys ran from the rain. . . . She wanted to sing . . . the kite rose in the blue." Then the old nun would read from her favorite books, usually biographies of early American presidents. Playfully she ran through complex sentences, calling the words alive with her voice, making it seem that the author somehow was speaking directly to me. I smiled just to listen to her. I sat there and sensed for the first time some possibility of fellowship between a reader and a writer, a communication, never *intimate* like that I heard spoken words at home convey, but one nonetheless *personal.*

One day the nun concluded a session by asking me why I was so reluctant to read by myself. I tried to explain; said something about the way written words made me feel all alone—almost, I wanted to add but didn't, as when I spoke to myself in a room just emptied of furniture. She studied my face as I spoke; she seemed to be watching more than listening. In an uneventful voice she replied that I had nothing to fear. Didn't I realize that reading would open

*Richard Rodriguez is the son of working-class Mexican immigrant parents. He spoke Spanish as a child. He graduated from Stanford and Columbia universities, did graduate work at the Warburg Institute in London and the University of California at Berkeley, and today works as a writer and lecturer.

up whole new worlds? A book could open doors for me. It could introduce me to people and show me places I never imagined existed. She gestured toward the bookshelves. (Bare-breasted African women danced, and the shiny hubcaps of automobiles on the backcovers of the *Geographic* gleamed in my mind.) I listened with respect. But her words were not very influential. I was thinking then of another consequence of literacy, one I was too shy to admit but nonetheless trusted. Books were going to make me 'educated.' *That* confidence enabled me, several months later to overcome my fear of silence.

In fourth grade I embarked upon a grandiose reading program. 'Give me the names of important books,' I would say to startled teachers. They soon found out that I had in mind 'adult books.' I ignored their suggestion of anything I suspected was written for children. (Not until I was in college, as a result, did I read *Huckleberry Finn* or *Alice's Adventures in Wonderland.*) Instead, I read *The Scarlet Letter* and Franklin's *Autobiography* and whatever I read I read for extra credit. Each time I finished a book, I reported the achievement to a teacher and basked in praise my effort earned. Despite my best efforts, however, there seemed to be more and more books I needed to read. At the library I would literally tremble as I came upon whole shelves of books I hadn't read. So I read and I read and I read. . . . Librarians who initially frowned when I checked out the maximum ten books at a time started saving books they thought I might like. Teachers would say to the rest of the class, "I only wish the rest of you took reading as seriously as Richard does." [851 words]

Checking Your Understanding

REVIEW   Review on your own until you can tell yourself the main point, or thesis, and some supporting details from the selection. Share the thesis and details with a classmate. Together write a summary, which includes the thesis and the supporting details. Your instructor will give you a short quiz later to check your understanding, just as an English instructor might quiz you on your reading. Before studying for and taking that quiz, read the next section of this chapter that deals with test-taking strategies.

TAKING AN EXAMINATION ON WHAT YOU HAVE READ

Having read a selection such as those in this chapter, you may be tested on what you have learned from it. In some instances, your instructor may give you an essay examination in which you must respond by writing out your answers. In other instances, your instructor may give you a short-answer examination. Generally it pays to ask the instructor what kind of examination he or she plans to give.

Preparing for and Taking Essay Examinations

The best way to prepare for an essay examination is to review your textbook and your class notes by systematically reciting main ideas and supporting details to yourself as described in the preceding section. Do not merely reread the text or your notes. Test yourself by asking yourself: What is the main idea? What are the important facts? What is the significance of these ideas and facts? Follow your "explaining-to-yourself" study with writing. Compose questions that you believe the instructor may ask. Write out possible answers.

Instructors tend to ask these kinds of questions.

- *Definition questions,* which ask you to give the precise meaning of a term. (Example: Define the word *theory.*) To answer this kind of question, start with the term and state: "A theory is. . . ."

- *Give-an-example questions,* which ask you to provide an example, or a specific instance. (Example: Give an example of a theory that made a radical difference in the way scientists viewed the earth.) To answer this kind of question, begin: "An example of a theory that made a radical difference in the way scientists viewed the earth is. . . ."

- *Enumeration or listing questions,* which ask you to give a series of items. (Example: List the names of four scientists who contributed to that discovery.) To answer this kind of question, do not give an extended explanation. Make a *(1), (2), (3), (4)* list of the names, or whatever the question asks for.

- *Explanation questions,* which ask you to explain *how* or *why.* (Example: Explain why the Puritans left England to come to America.) To answer an explain-why question, start: "The Puritans left England to come to America because. . . ." If you want to give more than one reason, continue: "A second reason the Puritans came to America. . . ." The word *because* is useful in writing an answer to an explain-why question. To answer an explain-how question—(Explain how iron ore is made into steel)—give the steps in the process. Start: "There are four steps in the process in which iron ore is transformed into steel. The first is. . . . The second is. . . ." It helps to use number words—*four steps, the first, the second—* to answer explain-how questions.

- *Evaluation questions,* which ask you to judge something. (Example: Give your opinion of the word processing capabilities of a computer.) To answer this kind of question, state what you think. Then give some facts to support your opinion.

- *Discussion questions,* which ask you to talk about a particular topic. (Example: Discuss the causes of the Civil War.) These are generally the most difficult questions to answer because they are vague. Do not answer by simply listing. You must include an analysis in your answer, suggesting why events happened as they did and how they happened.

- *Description questions,* which ask you to tell about the main characteristics of an event or item. (Example: Describe a plant cell.) To answer this kind of question, talk about the key aspects of the plant cell. Sometimes you can use a diagram to clarify your written description.

- *Comparison/contrast questions,* which ask you to tell how two things are the same and different. (Example: Compare a plant cell to an animal cell.) In this case, first describe the animal cell; then talk about the plant cell, telling how it is the same as and different from the animal cell.

- *Summarization questions,* which ask you to give the main points. (Example: Summarize the important points about natural selection.) This is another vague kind of question. To answer a summarization question, think in terms of main ideas, or big points.

Interpreting Essay Questions

The following are examples of essay questions. Circle the word that tells you the task you must do. Then explain what kind of answer you would give in each case. (Note: Do not answer the questions as stated.)

1. List the three branches of the federal government. _____

   _____

2. Explain how a bill becomes a law. _____

   _____

3. Compare a horse to a zebra. _____

   _____

4. Discuss the events leading up to the American Civil War. _____

   _____

5. Define the word *protoplasm*. _____

   _____

Preparing for and Taking Short-Answer Examinations

In preparing for a short-answer examination—multiple choice, fill-in-the-blanks, matching—you should rely on your talking-to-yourself-in-your-head strategy. As with essay exams, tell yourself the main points. Go over significant facts: names, dates, definitions, items in a sequence. Keep telling yourself this information until you can remember it without looking at your notes or your textbook.

Here are some clues for taking an examination:

- Place your answer sheet near the hand you write with, so that you do not waste time by crossing that hand over the examination paper.
- Put your name on your paper immediately.
- Read the directions carefully. Ask: How am I supposed to respond to the questions—by circling, underlining?
- Preview the entire examination before beginning, to get a general sense of what is being asked and how long the exam is.
- Read each question carefully. Ask yourself: What is the question asking?
- Pace yourself while taking the test. Do not spend too much time on any one question. If you find a question that is difficult for you, put a check on the test paper at that point, continue with the next question, and go back to the difficult questions after finishing the others.

You will have an opportunity to practice these strategies when your instructor gives you an examination on the selections in this chapter.

EXTENDING WHAT YOU HAVE LEARNED

Applying SQ3R, Highlighting, Data Charting, Webbing, Outlining, and Summarizing to Your College Reading

Select a chapter from another textbook—perhaps one that you are reading in a course you are currently taking. On a piece of paper, record the name of the text and its author. Then survey a chapter and on the paper write a series of questions to be answered through reading. Base your questions on the major headings. Read the chapter, stopping at the end of each subsection to make in-text notes and to recite the answer to the question you wrote before reading. When you have read the entire chapter, go back and review what you have read to the extent that you will be able to share your new understandings orally with classmates. Select a second chapter from the textbook. Use another strategy, such as outlining or summarizing, to study it. Be ready to give your opinion of the strategy that works best for you.

Making Vocabulary Your Own

Select several words from those you circled in the two selections of the chapter to make your own. Record them and a sample sentence or two in your personal vocabulary list.

8

*Increasing Your
Reading Rate*

Before reading the chapter, read the title, the stated objective, and the headings and subheadings. Ask yourself: What is the topic of the chapter? In the space above and beside the chapter number, jot down what you already know about the topic. Then in the space below the number, jot down at least two questions you hope to answer through reading the chapter.

OBJECTIVE

In this chapter, you will practice a strategy for increasing your reading rate. Specifically, you will learn to

1. block out unrelated thoughts;
2. concentrate on getting the gist as you go along;
3. read in chunks of meaning, moving your eye quickly across the lines and pausing only two or three times on each line to pick up a "mindful" at each pause;
4. vary your reading rate based on the kind of material you are reading.

You will also learn to calculate your reading rate.

INTRODUCTION—INCREASING YOUR READING RATE

Faced with extended reading assignments, do you complain that you read too slowly? Do you know that it takes you longer to complete reading assignments than it takes your friends? Here are some ideas for increasing the rate at which you read.

Developing Your Powers of Concentration

You must concentrate on the task at hand if you are to read rapidly with a high level of comprehension. For rapid reading, you must block out external distractions—movements of other students in the room, the noise of people talking, the noise of cars in the distance. You must look for a quiet place to study, without loud music and radio talk in the background. You must block out thoughts that do not relate to the reading task—fears of not doing well, thoughts about other events, thoughts about how other people are doing. How do you do this?

Some of the strategies you have already learned will help you concentrate. With longer selections, one of those strategies is previewing the selection by running your eyes over it quickly before beginning, noting the title, introductory and concluding words, and headings and italicized words, if there are any. Based on your preview, you make predictions of what is to come and phrase questions you will answer through reading. As you learned in the first chapter of this book, having a purpose in mind helps you to understand what you are reading. It also helps you to concentrate.

With longer selections, too, it pays to stop after reading sections of text to recite to yourself what you have read. At first you may think this slows you down. It does not. It makes you think about what you are reading.

With some selections that are preceded or followed by questions, it helps to survey those questions before reading the selection. Previews of this kind should be rapid, but research indicates that your ability to answer those questions is increased if you know them ahead of time. That makes sense, doesn't it? So where it is allowed, before reading, quickly skim the questions you must answer after reading.

Reading in Chunks of Meaning

It is important to read in "chunks of meaning" rather than to focus on every word. Reading in chunks, or *chunking*, not only helps you understand what you read but also increases your reading speed.

Practice Exercise 1:
Rapid Reading (Learning Theory)

Preview the following selection by reading the title and predicting what you will learn through reading it. Based on the title, devise a purpose-setting question. Notice that the selection is set on the page in a narrow column to help you fixate on chunks that have meaning. Record in this fashion the time when you start reading:

9 o'clock   10 minutes   10 seconds

For this purpose you will need a watch with a second hand. Before reading the selection that follows, record your starting time here:

_____ o'clock   _____ minutes   _____ seconds

Next read the selection. Be prepared to record your ending time as soon as you finish the selection and before you answer the follow-up questions.

WHAT'S INVOLVED IN RAPID READING

Nila Smith and H. Alan Robinson

Investigations of eye movements have shown
that the rapid reader's eyes
move fleetingly across the lines,
pausing briefly two or three times on each line,
picking up an "eyeful" of words at each pause,
while the eyes of the poor reader
pause on every word
or on small word units.
    It is the mind, of course,
that controls the eye movements.
    The great value
of eye-movement investigations
is that they furnish us
a picture of the different ways
in which the mind works
in perceiving reading symbols.
    They tell us
that the mind of the poor reader loafs along,
picking up very small units at a time,
while the eyes of the excellent reader
race over the lines,
gathering an entire, meaningful idea at a glance.
    Cultivating the habit of reading for *ideas* not only increases speed;
but also increases understanding.
    A person who reads one word at a time
thinks in terms of the meanings
of these separate words
and thus 'can't see the woods for the trees.'
    The first and most important instruction is,
'Read for Ideas!'
If you can cultivate the habit
of rapidly picking up one complete thought unit
after another,
the eye movements
will take care of themselves.

Record the time when you stopped reading here:

_____ o'clock   _____ minutes   _____ seconds

Now based on your reading of the passage, select the best answer.

1. Most important in rapid reading is
   a. keeping the eyes moving.
   b. reading for ideas.
   c. keeping the lips still.
   d. keeping the head still.

2. How do rapid readers move their eyes in reading?
   a. They pause two or three times per line.
   b. They never pause while reading.
   c. They look primarily at the first words on a line.
   d. They look primarily at the last words on a line.
3. What controls eye movements?
   a. the body   c. the hand
   b. the eyes themselves   d. the mind
4. What is the meaning of the phrase "can't see the woods for the trees" in this selection?
   a. There are many woods in a forest.
   b. The trees get in the way of seeing the forest.
   c. In reading, it is important to focus on the big ideas rather than on the individual words.
   d. In reading, it is important to focus on individual words rather than on the big ideas.
5. The authors of the selection believe that eye movement investigations are
   a. worthless because they tell us little about how expert readers function.
   b. worthless because eye movements have nothing to do with skillful reading.
   c. valuable because they provide a picture of the ways the mind works in perceiving word symbols.
   d. valuable because they tell us much about the way the eye is put together.

Next determine your reading rate by first subtracting your starting time from your ending time.

Ending time: _____ o'clock _____ minutes _____ seconds

Starting time: _____ o'clock _____ minutes _____ seconds

_____

Reading time: _____ minutes _____ seconds

Use the directions in the appendix to determine your reading rate on this practice passage. The number of words in it is 202.

Reading rate is measured in words per minute—for example, 110 words per minute, 320 words per minute. Most readers vary their reading rate depending on the topic of the selection, on what they know about that topic, and on the complexity of the sentences.

Practicing Reading in Chunks of Meaning

Efficient reading requires that you *not* dwell on individual words. Pointing your finger at or focusing your eyes on each word slows down your reading. So does moving your lips to say each word as you read and moving your head from left to right as you read lines.

Here is a summary of "Don'ts" to help you read more rapidly:

● Do not point at each word as you read.

● Do not move your head or lips while reading. Reading is thinking, not mouthing individual words.

● Do not focus on individual words. Rather keep your eyes moving across lines and down the page, and focus on meaningful chunks.

Determine your reading rate for the selection by referring to Table A in the appendix. There are 591 words in the selection.

In the next section are four selections. One is from an autobiography of a writer (Eudora Welty), the second from a computer magazine, the third from a professional booklet, and the fourth from a best-selling book. Comparing your reading rate on these selections to your rate on the practice exercises you have just completed will give you a general idea of how fast you read different kinds of materials.

SELECTION 1: ONE WRITER'S BEGINNINGS
(Literature—Autobiography)

Getting Ready to Read

Before you begin, read the title. From it, predict what the selection will be about—given the fact that you know it is autobiographical. Ask yourself: What will I learn through reading this selection? Record your starting time here:

_____ o'clock _____ minutes _____ seconds

Reading with Meaning

ONE WRITER'S BEGINNINGS

Eudora Welty

Jackson's Carnegie Library was on the same street where our house was, on the other side of the State Capitol. "Through the Capitol" was the way to go to the Library. You could glide through it on your bicycle or even coast through on roller skates, though without family permission.

I never knew anyone who'd grown up in Jackson without being afraid of Mrs. Calloway, our librarian. She ran the Library absolutely by herself, from the desk where she sat with her back to the books and facing the stairs, her dragon eye on the front door, where who knew what kind of person might come in from the public? SILENCE in big black letters was on signs tacked up everywhere. She herself spoke in her normally commanding voice; every word could be heard all over the Library above a steady seething sound coming from her electric fan; it was the only fan in the Library and stood on her desk, turned directly onto her streaming face.

As you came in from the bright outside, if you were a girl, she sent her strong eyes down the stairway to test you; if she could see through your skirt she sent you straight back home: you could just put on another petticoat if you wanted a book that badly from the public library. I was willing; I would do anything to read.

My mother was not afraid of Mrs. Calloway. She wished me to have my own library card to check out books for myself. She took me in to introduce me and I saw I had met a witch. "Eudora is nine years old and has my permission to read any book she wants from the shelves, children or adult," Mother said. . . .

Mrs. Calloway made her own rules about books. You could not take back a book to the Library on the same day you'd taken it out; it made no difference to her that you'd read every word in it and needed another to start. You could take out two books at a time and two only; this applied as long as you were a child and also for the rest of your life, to my mother as severely as to me. So two by two, I read library books as fast as I could go, rushing them home in the basket of my bicycle. From the minute I reached our house, I started to read. Every book I seized on, from *Bunny Brown and His Sister Sue at Camp Rest-a-While* to *Twenty Thousand Leagues Under the Sea*, stood for the devouring wish to read being instantly granted. I knew this was bliss, knew it at the time. Taste isn't nearly so important; it comes in its own time. I wanted to read immediately. The only fear was that of books coming to an end.

My mother was very sharing of this feeling of insatiability. Now, I think of her as reading so much of the time while doing something else. In my mind's eye *The Origin of Species* is lying on the shelf in the pantry under a light dusting of flour—my mother was a bread maker; she'd pick it up, sit by the kitchen window and find her place, with one eye on the oven. I remember her picking up *The Man in Lower Ten*, while my hair got dry enough to unroll from a load of kid curlers trying to make me like my idol, Mary Pickford. A generation later, when my brother Walter was away in the Navy and his two little girls often spent the day in our house, I remember Mother reading the new issue of *Time* magazine while taking the part of the Wolf in a game of "Little Red Riding Hood" with the children. She'd just look up at the right time, long enough to answer—in character—"The better to eat you with, my dear," and go back to her place in the war news.   [671 words]

Record your ending time here:

_____ o'clock   _____ minutes   _____ seconds

Checking for Understanding

Select the best answer without looking back at the selection.

1. As a child, Eudora Welty felt that reading was
   a. a wonderful thing to do.
   b. a very difficult task, especially for herself.
   c. something best left to librarians like Mrs. Calloway.
   d. a weekend pastime.
2. What word best describes Mrs. Calloway, as Eudora Welty perceived her?
   a. a warmhearted person   c. a mother substitute
   b. a dragon   d. a fellow reader
3. How did Mrs. Calloway "test" the girls coming into the library?
   a. She checked that they did not coast through the Capitol building on roller skates.
   b. She checked that they had their own library cards.
   c. She checked that they were over nine years of age.
   d. She checked that they wore enough petticoats so she could not see through their skirts.
4. Which statement best describes Eudora Welty as a reader?

a. She read everything she could get her hands on.

b. She had a high degree of literary taste even as a child.

c. She followed the dictates of the librarian as to which books to read.

d. She read very few books—only the best.

5. Which of the following was a rule in Mrs. Calloway's library?

a. Children could check out only two books at a time, but adults could take four books.

b. Children and adults could check out only four books at a time.

c. Children and adults could check out only two books at a time.

d. Children could check out books only when accompanied by an adult.

6. Eudora Welty remembered seeing *The Origin of Species* under a light dusting of flour. This came about because

a. Eudora's mother was a poor housekeeper.

b. Eudora's mother would read as she baked bread.

c. Eudora read the book as her mother baked bread.

d. Eudora read the book as she herself baked bread.

7. How did Eudora get to the library?

a. by walking   c. by bicycle

b. by bus   d. by a car driven by her mother

8. Eudora Welty's attitude toward reading was probably influenced most strongly by the fact that

a. her mother loved to read.

b. her house was located near the library.

c. she liked going to the library.

d. she liked the librarian.

Checking Your Reading Rate

Subtract your starting time from your ending time.

Ending time: _____ o'clock _____ minutes _____ seconds

Starting time: _____ o'clock _____ minutes _____ seconds

_____

Reading time: _____ minutes _____ seconds

Determine your reading rate for the selection by referring to Table A in the appendix.

There are 671 words in the selection. Record your reading rate here: _____

SELECTION 2: BIG BROTHER IS WATCHING YOU
(Personal Finance)

Getting Ready to Read

This selection is from a computer magazine (MacUser). *First read the title. Predict what the article is about. What do you hope to learn from the article? Record your starting time here:*

_____ o'clock   _____ minutes   _____ seconds

Reading with Meaning

BIG BROTHER IS WATCHING YOU
Robert Wiggins

In his book *1984*, George Orwell envisioned a future society where every aspect of a person's life was watched and controlled by the evil Big Brother. We are now several years past that infamous year, and have avoided the dismal fate Orwell had in store for us. Or have we?

When you walk into a store and purchase a product with a credit card, most of the time the credit card company is immediately informed of the purchase (and makes the decision to accept or deny the charge) via telecommunications. As point-of-sale terminals become more sophisticated, you may not even know it is happening.

When you apply for a loan, a credit card or try to rent an apartment, a computerized credit check is usually run on you, and almost every aspect of your financial life is scrutinized. Thanks to federal legislation, there are now ways to see your credit report and offer rebuttals for inaccuracies that may have gotten into your report. Prior to these laws, there were many horror stories about false and even malicious information that had been carried in some credit reports and widely circulated. TRW, the largest credit reporting service, in a brilliant marketing move, is even selling a service to allow you to periodically review and update your credit history (something you can do for free if you are denied credit based on a TRW report).

When you have a brush with the law, no matter how minor, they can tap into the FBI's National Crime Information Center (NCIC) computer and instantly find out if you've ever been arrested or otherwise managed to get into any law enforcement files. The FBI Advisory Policy Board last year approved proposals to link NCIC to IRS, INS, Social Security, SEC and several other data bases and to create a system to track anyone *suspected* of a crime. More and more organizations, including private companies, are pushing to gain access to this system and, in the absence of legislation, the same excesses that used to be possible in credit reporting will be extended to law enforcement. Orwell may not have been so far off.   [363 words]

Record your ending time here:

_____ o'clock   _____ minutes   _____ seconds

Checking for Understanding

Mark the following items T (true) or F (false) based on the information from the article. Do not reread or look back.

_____   1. George Orwell envisioned a world in which people's lives were watched by an evil power.

_____   2. The article suggests that some aspects of the world envisioned by Orwell have come to be.

_____   3. Federal legislation prevents your seeing your credit report if you have been denied credit.

_____   4. Usually when you try to rent an apartment, a credit check is run on you.

_____ 5. You can only see your credit report by paying for the service.

_____ 6. The National Crime Information Center is under the control of TRW.

_____ 7. Today there are federal laws that determine who can tap into NCIC data banks.

_____ 8. Private companies are pressing to gain access to the data in the National Crime Information Center.

_____ 9. George Orwell's prediction was for the world in 2001.

_____ 10. Every time you buy anything with a credit card, the credit card company is immediately informed before credit is granted.

Determining Your Reading Rate

Subtract your starting time from your ending time.

Ending time: _____ o'clock _____ minutes _____ seconds

Starting time: _____ o'clock _____ minutes _____ seconds

_____

Reading time: _____ minutes _____ seconds

Now use the table in the appendix to find your reading rate on this selection. There are 363 words in the selection. Record your rate here. _____

SELECTION 3: LANGUAGE AND COMMUNICATION (Biology)

Getting Ready to Read

This selection is from a booklet published by a professional organization. Before reading, read the title. Predict what the article is about. What do you hope to learn by reading the article? Record your starting time here:

_____ o'clock _____ minutes _____ seconds

Reading with Meaning

LANGUAGE AND COMMUNICATION

Alan Mandell

One of the characteristics that distinguishes human beings from the other animals is their highly developed ability to communicate—that is, to transfer ideas from one individual to another through abstract visual or oral symbols, and especially to record these symbols so that they can communicate with individuals far away in place or time. Many of the other animals also communicate with each other in a less complex but nevertheless interesting fashion. Some birds have a repertoire of calls, each of which appears to have a significant meaning to other birds. Worker bees have a sign system, by which they inform other bees in the hive of the direction and distance to a food supply. Some animals communicate by using a chemical language; the odors they produce may attract or repel other animals. Still others project messages by gestures, facial expressions, or body attitudes. Communication by use of a language composed of abstract symbols—particularly recorded symbols—appears, however, to be confined to the human animal.   [168 words]

Record your ending time here:

_____ o'clock   _____ minutes   _____ seconds

Checking for Understanding

Select the best answer.

1. The main idea of this selection is that
    a. although other animals can communicate, only humans have a language composed of abstract symbols that they can record.
    b. all animals have a system of communication.
    c. worker bees communicate with one another.
    d. to be abstract is to be better.
2. According to the selection, bird calls
    a. are simply pleasurable sounds that enrich the environment.
    b. have a meaning to other birds.
    c. have no meaning.
    d. are part of the chemical language birds use to communicate.
3. Which is an example of chemical language?
    a. body attitudes
    b. gestures that animals use to communicate
    c. facial expressions
    d. the odors animals produce that attract or repel other animals.
4. When the article talks about "recorded symbols," it is talking about
    a. speech.   c. writing.
    b. sounds.   d. computer activity.
5. Worker bees use their sign system to tell other bees of
    a. impending danger.
    b. the direction and distance to food.
    c. changes in the weather.
    d. ways to improve the structure and design of the hive.

Determining Your Reading Rate

Calculate your reading time by subtracting your starting time from your ending time.

Ending time: _____ o'clock   _____ minutes   _____ seconds

Starting time: _____ o'clock   _____ minutes   _____ seconds

_____

Reading time: _____ minutes   _____ seconds

Use the chart in the appendix to find your rate for reading scientific content. There are 168 words in the selection. Write your reading rate here. _____

SELECTION 4: LOVE ISN'T EASY (Literature—Essay)

Getting Ready to Read

The next selection is an essay from the bestseller, *All I Really Need to Know I Learned in Kindergarten: Uncommon Thoughts on Common Things* by Robert Fulghum. In it, Fulghum uses humor to reflect on the meaning of life and to get across some basic truths about life. One reviewer (in *Washington* magazine) wrote about the author, "Fulghum is a natural-born storyteller who can pluck your heartstrings, tickle your funny bone and point up a moral all at the same time."

Preview the essay by reading the title and thinking about what it means to you. Then record your starting time here:

_____ o'clock   _____ minutes   _____ seconds

Reading with Meaning

LOVE ISN'T EASY

Robert Fulghum

This is about a house I once lived in. An elderly lakeside cottage built at the end of the road at the end of the nineteenth century. A summer place for a family who traveled by horse and buggy out from Seattle through deep woods and over steep hills on logging trails. It was wild there, then, and it is wild there still.

The house was off the ground on bricks, surrounded by thickets of blackberry bushes and morning-glory vines bent on a struggle to the death. And even though it is only minutes, now, from downtown, squirrels, rabbits, feral pussycats, and "things" I never saw but only heard had long established squatters' rights on the property.

And raccoons. We had raccoons. Big ones. Several.

For reasons known only to God and the hormones of raccoons, they chose to mate underneath my house. Every spring. And for reasons known only to God and the hormones of raccoons, they chose to mate underneath my house at three A.M.

Until you have experienced raccoons mating underneath your bedroom at three in the morning, you have missed one of life's more sensational moments. It is an uncommon event, to say the least. If you've ever heard cats fighting in the night, you have a clue. Magnify the volume and the intensity by ten. It's not what you'd call a sensual and erotic sound. More like a three-alarm fire is what it is.

I remember the first time it happened. Since conditions were not conducive to sleep, I got up. When I say I got up, I mean *I GOT UP.* About three feet. Straight up. Covers and all.

When I had recovered my aplomb and adjusted to the new adrenaline level, I got a flashlight and went outside and peered up under the house. This lady raccoon and her suitor were squared off in a corner, fangs bared, covered with mud and blood, and not looking very sexy at all.

Neither my presence nor the beam of light could override what drove them on. With snarls and barks and screams, the passionate encounter raged on. While I watched, the matter was finally consummated and resolved. They had no shame. What had to be done was done. And they wandered off, in a kind of glazy-eyed stupor, to groom themselves for whatever might come next in the life of a raccoon.

I sat there in the rain, my light still shining into the trysting chamber. And I pondered. Why is it that love and life so often have to be carried forth with so much pain and strain and mess? I ask you, why is that?

I was thinking of my own sweet wife asleep in the bed right above me, and our own noises of conflict mixed with affection. I wondered what the raccoons must conclude from the sounds a husband and wife make at night—the ones that sound like "If-you-really-loved-me-you-would-not-keep-making-such-a-mess-in-the-bathroom," followed by "OH, YEAH? WELL LET ME TELL YOU A FEW THINGS. . . ."

Why isn't love easy?

I don't know. And the raccoons don't say.   [534 words]

Record your ending time here. _____

_____ o'clock   _____ minutes   _____ seconds

Checking for Understanding

Answer the questions by placing T (true) or F (false) on the line.

_____   1. The house that is the setting of this story is somewhere near Seattle.

_____   2. The raccoons that lived on the property were rather small.

_____   3. The raccoons chose to mate under Fulghum's house in mid-afternoon.

_____   4. Fulghum describes the experience of having raccoons mate under one's house as one of life's sensational moments.

_____   5. The first time raccoons mated under his house, it was raining.

_____   6. The mating raccoons wandered off when Fulghum flashed a light at them.

_____   7. When the raccoons had mated, they simply fell asleep on the spot.

_____   8. When the raccoons had mated, Fulghum sat there and thought about life.

_____   9. Fulghum compared the noises of the raccoons mating to the noises of conflict that occur between husbands and wives.

_____   10. Fulghum concluded by saying that love is easy.

Determining Your Reading Rate

Calculate your reading time by subtracting your starting time from your ending time.

Ending time: _____ o'clock   _____ minutes   _____ seconds

Starting time: _____ o'clock   _____ minutes   _____ seconds

_____

Reading time: _____ minutes   _____ seconds

Use the chart in the appendix to find your reading rate for popular material. There are 534 words in the selection. Write your reading rate here. _____

EXTENDING WHAT YOU HAVE LEARNED

Think about your reading rates on the four practice exercises and the four selections. Do they vary? They should. Most people slow down when they read a technical selection in a textbook such as a passage about the germ theory of disease. They read more quickly when faced with general articles in magazines and newspapers and light content as in some bestsellers.

Expert readers also vary their reading rate depending on their familiarity with the content they are reading. They read quickly on topics with which they are familiar; they read slowly when faced with material that is new to them. For example, if you already knew the story about "The Hare and the Tortoise," you probably breezed through it when you read it again in this book. Try to vary your rate based on these factors.

This chapter has proposed a number of strategies for increasing your rate of reading. Perhaps the best single way of improving your reading efficiency, however, is practice. You must spend time reading to become a better reader. Spending spare time reading rather than viewing television as a "couch potato" is essential. To this end, make a visit to a library to select a book for recreational reading. Make your selection a book on a topic that really interests you. For example, if you enjoyed reading the humorous story by Robert Fulghum, you may select his book to read. Once you have chosen a book, carry it with you. Whenever you have a spare moment, read that book. Set a time limit for finishing it. Then return to the library for another book. You should try to read at least one book for recreation during every three-week period. If you do that and vary the kinds of books you read, you will find your reading speed increasing.

Also buy yourself a stenographer's notebook. As you read, write brief summaries and reactions to what you read in your notebook. Periodically go back and read what you have written. Writing summaries is one of the best ways to increase your reading comprehension.

9

Critical Thinking: Comparing, Inferring, Concluding, Judging

Before reading the chapter, read the title, the stated objective, and the headings and subheadings. Ask yourself: What is the topic of the chapter? In the space above and beside the chapter number, jot down what you already know about the topic. Then in the space below the number, jot down at least two questions you hope to answer through reading the chapter.

OBJECTIVE

In this chapter, you will refine your strategies for thinking critically as you read. You will refine your ability to

1. compare,
2. infer,
3. conclude, and
4. judge.

INTRODUCTION—
COMPARING, INFERRING, CONCLUDING, JUDGING

As you learned in Chapter 1, reading is an active process in which you think about and expand on ideas from a selection. Of course, to get involved while reading, you must be able to

- find the main idea,
- sort significant from less significant details,
- follow the author's train of thought, and
- figure out sentence relationships.

But to read with full understanding, you must leap beyond the text. You must analyze relationships and come up with your own ideas.

Comparing

One way to get involved while reading is to make comparisons. In *comparing,* you consider two or more items and determine how those items are similar and how they are different. The items can be people, events, ideas—almost anything, for that matter.

Your strategy for comparing is

- Identify the significant features of each item you are comparing.
- Ask: What features do the items share, or have in common?
- Ask: How do the items differ?

Sometimes in reading a selection, you find a description or explanation of only one item. You still can and should make comparisons. You compare the item described or explained in a passage to ones with which you are already familiar.

- Ask: What does this remind me of? How is it like what I already know? How does it differ?

Read the following two paragraphs. Of course, start by previewing. Your purpose for reading is to compare the two experiments. How are they the same? How are they different? To this end, complete the data chart in Figure 9.1 as you read.

CAN CHIMPANZEES LEARN TO SPEAK?

Jean Berko Gleason

In 1931 Professor and Mrs. W. N. Kellogg became the first American family to raise a chimpanzee and a child together. The Kelloggs brought into their home Gua, a seven-month-old chimpanzee, who stayed with them and their infant son Donald for nine months. No special effort was made to teach Gua to talk; like the human baby she was simply exposed to a speaking household. During this period, Gua came to use some of her natural chimpanzee cries rather consistently; for instance, she used her food bark not just for food but for anything else she wanted. Although Gua was rather better than Donald in most physical accomplishments, unlike Donald she did not babble and did not learn to say any English words.

	Gua	Viki
When was the experiment done?		
Who did the experiment?		
What procedure did the investigator use?		
What was the outcome?		
What did the investigation seem to prove?		

Figure 9.1   *A Chart for Gathering Data*

In the 1940s psychologists Catherine and Keith Hayes set out to improve upon the Kellogg's experiment by raising a chimpanzee named Viki as if she were their own child. They took her home when she was six weeks old, and she remained with them for several years. The Hayeses made every effort to teach Viki to talk; they had assumed that chimpanzees were rather like retarded institutionalized children and that love and patient instruction would afford Viki the opportunity for optimal language development. After six years of training, Viki was able to say four words: "mama," "papa," "cup," and "up." She was never able to say more, and the words she did say were very difficult to understand: in order to pronounce a *p,* she had to hold her lips together with her fingers.   [266 words]

Review the data you organized in Figure 9.1. In what ways were the two experiments similar? In what ways were they different? Complete Figure 9.2.

Before reading the next section, study the two charts you just completed based on the Gua/Viki passage. You can use them as models for your own charts to collect and analyze data for comparing while reading.

Inferring

A second way you can get actively involved while reading is to read between the lines and infer relationships not stated directly by the author. In *inferring,* you pick up

| How the experiments were similar: |
| How the experiments were different: |

Figure 9.2   *A Chart for Making Comparisons*

hints or clues from the passage. You relate those clues to things you already know and come up with an idea that the author has only alluded to, or suggested indirectly.

The key strategy question in this case is this:

● What is the author suggesting (or hinting at) through the facts he or she is giving? What can you "read into" what he or she is saying?

Here is an example. What inference do you make when you read the line, "When she saw him, her lips tightened"? Having seen people tighten their lips when they are angry (or when they are uptight about something), you may infer that the person was not pleased at all; she was angry. That is an inference because the writer does not come right out and state, "She was angry." You must figure that out from the clues given.

What inferences do you draw from the statements in Figure 9.3? Complete the chart by filling in the cells.

Having completed the chart, you can draw a conclusion about kinds of inferences you can make. You can make inferences about the age of a person, the kind of person he or she is, the kind of relationship that exists between people, a person's feelings, the season of the year, the time of day, the place where a story is set, or the date when an event took place.

Concluding

A third kind of thinking that you should do as you read is *concluding*—developing conclusions based on information given. A conclusion is a generalization about a topic. It is a big idea that you put together based on the facts. Very often your conclusions flow out of the comparisons you have made and the inferences you have drawn. Reread the last paragraph of the preceding section. That paragraph states a conclusion about kinds of inferences. The examples in the chart support the generalization. Can you see how?

In formulating conclusions, the main question to ask yourself is this:

● What big idea or ideas can I put together based on the facts given in the selection?

Reread the paragraphs about Gua and Viki. What conclusion can you draw about whether chimpanzees are capable of humanlike speech? Write your conclusion here. _____

_____

Did you conclude that chimpanzees cannot learn to speak as humans do, even when given explicit instruction? That would be an acceptable conclusion based

Statement	Question	Inference	Clue in the Sentence That Helps You Infer
His face was lined with wrinkles.	How old was he? What else might you infer?		
He had a scowl on his face as he passed me without speaking.	How did he feel about me? What else might you infer?		
The fellow and girl were holding hands as they strolled through the mall.	What can you infer about their relationship?		
It was snowing heavily and the light had almost disappeared from the heavens.	What season of the year was it? What else can you infer?		
The car was swerving from one side of the road to the other.	What can you infer was wrong here?		
A man remarks, "I do not believe a woman should serve on the Supreme Court."	What kind of man is he?		
She had straight black hair done up in a bun.	What kind of woman was she?		
There were tears running down his face.	What can you infer?		
I gave the grocer a quarter for the quart of milk.	What can you infer?		

Figure 9.3 *A Chart for Making Inferences*

on the facts given. What details from the selection support that conclusion? Write

some supporting facts here. _____

_____

In drawing conclusions, you are really getting at the ultimate meaning of things—what is important, why it is important, how one event influenced another, how one happening led into another. To simply get the facts in reading is not enough. You must think about what those facts mean.

Judging

A fourth kind of thinking to do while reading is *judging*—developing judgments of your own about the content you are reading and reasons to support that judgment. In making a judgment, you decide whether an act is right or wrong, good or bad, fair or unfair.

A strategy for rendering a judgment includes asking these questions:

- Do I agree with the point of view expressed in the selection? Why? Why not?
- Do I believe the action described in the selection is right or wrong? Good or evil? Fair or unfair?
- Are the facts in the selection accurate?
- Is the selection clearly written? Or is the phrasing awkward and the organization illogical?

Again go back to the selection about Gua and Viki. Do you believe that it is right to experiment with animals in the way described in the passage? In your notebook, write a topic sentence that states your opinion. Then write a sentence or two with points that support your opinion.

Thinking and Reading

What the introduction to this chapter has been saying is that you should be thinking about ideas continuously as you read. Generally you do this by asking and answering questions as you go along. These questions include the following:

- *Comparing.* What does this (person, place, event, etc.) remind me of? How are these two things similar? Different? How does this event, person, or place relate to other events?
- *Inferring.* What does this clue—hidden between the lines—tell me? What does it hint about the feelings involved, the age of the person, the kind of person he or she is, the kind of relationship that exists between people, the season of the year, the time of day, the place where the story is set, the date when the event took place?
- *Concluding.* Why is this important or significant? Why did this happen? What is the ultimate meaning of these events?
- *Judging.* Do I agree or disagree? Why? Is this accurate? Is this good or bad? Why?

In the selections you will read next, you will have the opportunity to compare, infer, conclude, and judge.

SELECTION 1: THE BRIDGE THEY SAID COULDN'T BE BUILT (History)

Getting Ready to Read

Read the title, the introductory paragraph, and the headings.

- What is this selection about? _____

- What do you already know about this bridge? _____

   _____

- What do you think you will learn from reading the selection? Write two questions
   that you hope to answer by reading it. _____

   _____

Reading with Meaning

Read the following segments from a selection titled "The Bridge They Said Couldn't Be Built." When you have read each segment, you will answer questions that require an inference.

THE BRIDGE THEY SAID COULDN'T BE BUILT

Lee Sheridan

New York in the Winter of 1866–1867

The winter of 1866–1867 was one of the worst ever recorded in the history of New York. Snow covered most of the area, and great blocks of ice clogged the East River between Manhattan and Brooklyn. Often the Fulton Street ferryboat was unable to cross the East River. So people trying to get to work in Manhattan or return home to Brooklyn were jammed up at each riverbank. What's more, with no electricity and no telephones, there was no way of even communicating across the river except by boat.

What the East River needed was a bridge. Many people thought so, but most said building a bridge would be impossible: the river was too wide; the currents, winds, and ocean tides were too powerful.

Select the most probable inference.

1. The Brooklyn Bridge that spans the East River was completed
   a. before the winter of 1866–1867.   c. after the winter of 1866–1867.
   b. during the winter of 1866–1867.
2. The telephone was invented
   a. before the winter of 1866–1867.   c. after the winter of 1866–1867.
   b. during the winter of 1866–1867.
3. Before the construction of the Brooklyn Bridge,
   a. many bridges had successfully been built across distances as great as the East River.
   b. few bridges had successfully been built across distances as great as the East River.
   c. no bridges had successfully been built across distances as great as the East River.

Figure 9.4   *The Brooklyn Bridge*

John A. Roebling

One person who didn't think a bridge was impossible was an engineer named John A. Roebling. Roebling was known throughout the world as the expert bridge builder of the day. Suspension bridges were his specialty. A suspension bridge is a bridge suspended by wire cables hung over towers and fastened on the land at both ends.

Roebling had founded his own Wire Rope Company to manufacture the cables for suspension bridges. In 1866 he had just completed the longest suspension bridge ever built—a bridge in Cincinnati over the Ohio River. If anyone could build a suspension bridge over the East River—a length of half a mile—John A. Roebling was the one to do it.

Several years earlier, Roebling had submitted a plan for a suspension bridge connecting Manhattan and Brooklyn. No other kind of bridge could be built across an area as wide as the East River and also allow ships to pass underneath. Still, the officials of both New York and Brooklyn had doubts. They rejected Roebling's first plan as impossible.

Select the most probable inference.

4. Before designing the Brooklyn Bridge, Roebling had designed
   a. no other suspension bridges.   c. several suspension bridges.
   b. one other suspension bridge.
5. The distance across the Ohio River at Cincinnati was probably
   a. less than half a mile.   c. greater than half a mile.
   b. a half a mile.
6. Shipping was of
   a. no importance to people living in this area.
   b. little importance to people living in this area.
   c. considerable importance to people living in this area.

Roebling's New Design

Roebling persisted in presenting his plan for a bridge across the East River. He assured people that he had added something new to suspension bridges to make them safer. He had designed a series of diagonal supports running downward from the top of the two towers to points on the suspenders. (Look at Figure 9.4.) With the added strength of these diagonal supports, he said, the bridge was guaranteed to withstand strong winds and last for generations.

Still, Roebling's design might never have been accepted if it hadn't been for the harsh winter of 1866–1867. By then, the people of Brooklyn and New York were willing to take any chance on a bridge, if it meant an easier way to get across the river. In the same year the bridge project was begun. John A. Roebling gladly took up his appointment as chief engineer of the project.

Select the most probable inference based on what you know so far.

7. What phrase best sums up the way people in 1866–1867 viewed long suspension bridges?
   a. Very, very safe   c. Not too safe
   b. Safe

8. What word best sums up the feelings of the people of Brooklyn and New York during the winter of 1866–1867?
   a. calm
   c. unconcerned
   b. desperate

Accident on the Ferryboat

Unfortunately, John Roebling, who had designed most of the details for the project was not able to see his great bridge even begun. In the summer of 1869, he was riding on the Fulton ferry to locate the exact spot for the Brooklyn tower of the bridge. His foot was accidentally crushed between some loose logs as the ferry slammed into the Brooklyn dock.

Such an injury alone is not enough to kill a person, but John Roebling would not rest as the doctors told him. He was so concerned about his bridge that he refused medicine and wouldn't even stay in bed. Within sixteen days of the accident, John A. Roebling, the master bridge builder, was dead.

Select the most probable inference based on what you know so far.

9. What kind of engineer was Roebling?
   a. a designer who got directly involved in bridge-building projects
   b. a designer who left the details to other more practical engineers
   c. a designer who was primarily concerned with putting ideas together
10. If Roebling had obeyed the doctor's orders, he probably would have
    a. lived to see his bridge finished.
    b. died anyway because medical science then was not what it is today.
    c. never completed the bridge.

(*Note: The Brooklyn Bridge was completed in May 1883. Roebling's son, also an engineer, became the chief engineer on the project after the death of his father.*)

Answer these questions that require you to make inferences and comparisons, draw conclusions, and render judgments. You may talk with a classmate before writing your answers.

11. What kind of person was Roebling? _____

    _____

    _____

12. Of whom does Roebling remind you? In what ways is Roebling similar to the

    person you have identified? How is he different? _____

    _____

    _____

13. Name another event that is similar in some way to the building of the Brooklyn Bridge. Tell why the events are similar. Tell why they are different.

    _____

    _____

14. Why do you think people living in New York in 1866 thought a bridge across the East River was impossible to build? _____

_____

15. Why do you think that Roebling did not believe such a bridge was impossible?

_____

_____

SELECTION 2: MORAL POWER OR GUN POWER
(Sociology)

Expanding Your Vocabulary for Reading

Use word-structure and context clues to unlock the meanings of the italicized words. If you are uncertain of the meaning, check the glossary. Write the definition of the italicized words in the space provided.

1. The weather that winter was *unprecedented;* we had far colder weather than ever before. _____

_____

2. The *reformers* wanted change. _____

_____

3. There were, however, many *hard-liners* who strongly advocated keeping things as they were. _____

_____

4. *Repression* was severe. If anyone stepped out of line, he or she was immediately jailed. _____

_____

5. We heard *ominous* rumblings of thunder in the distance and knew we were in for a terrible storm. _____

_____

6. *Turmoil* resulted when the alarm sounded and the electricity went out.

_____

_____

7. The two knights *dueled* over a minor disagreement that had turned into a major confrontation. _____

_____

8. The wealthy woman spent her money *indiscriminately* until she had very little left for important purposes. _____

_____

9. Students from all over the United States *converged* on Florida during spring
break. _____

Getting Ready to Read

*Read the title and the first sentence or two of the following selection, which is
from a college sociology textbook.*

● What is this selection about? _____

● What do you already know about Tiananmen Square? Share what you know with
a classmate. Collaborate by writing down a few phrases that come to mind.

Reading with Meaning

*Read this selection to find out the major idea, or thesis, the author is trying to
communicate and to think critically about the ideas presented.*

MORAL POWER OR GUN POWER

John Macionis

Not since the revolution that brought the communists to power in 1949
has the People's Republic of China experienced anything like the events of the
spring of 1989. Tiananmen Square—the central landmark of the capital city of
Beijing—was the scene of an unprecedented five-week demonstration in support
of greater political democracy. The demonstrators, numbering in the thousands,
were initially mostly students encouraged by recent economic reforms to
demand a greater voice in government. Clustered together in the shadow of the
Great Hall of the People, some began a hunger strike; others resolutely
displayed banners and headbands that proclaimed their goals. As the days
passed, their numbers steadily increased, until more than 1 million of
the city's people mixed uneasily with a growing number of soldiers around
the square.

Reformers among the country's leaders supported the demonstration.
Hard-liners strongly opposed it, urging the use of force to crush the protest.
The balance of power slowly shifted toward a policy of repression. Ominous
signs appeared: troops from other regions of China (denied news of how
popular the protest had become) were trucked to the outskirts of the city. Waves
of soldiers periodically tried to clear sections of the square; each time, the
demonstrators held their ground. Premier Li Peng then announced that the
"turmoil" was to be swiftly ended. Anxiety rose as the government ordered
satellite dishes and other communication links operated by foreign news
agencies shut down.

About 2 A.M. on the morning of Sunday, June 4, the political dueling
ended in convulsions of violence and horror. From three sides, a fifty-truck
convoy of ten thousand troops converged on the square. Soldiers leveled AK-47
assault rifles and began firing indiscriminately at the crowds. Tanks rolled over
makeshift barriers, crushing the people behind them. Some demonstrators
bravely fought back, but their fate had already been sealed. Within three hours,

the pro-democracy movement had ended, and Tiananmen Square was awash with the blood of thousands of people.

Events such as those in Tiananmen Square make clear a lesson often lost in the concerns of daily life: the operation of every society is shaped by those who have the power to control events. Power, of course, takes many forms, but all are not necessarily equal. As they occupied the center of their nation's capital city, the Chinese people claimed the moral power to direct their own lives. The response of their government, in words once used by Chinese leader Mao Zedong, was: "Political power grows out of the barrel of a gun."

Checking Your Understanding

Collaborate with a classmate to answer these questions.

1. What is the main idea, or thesis, of this selection? _____

   _____

2. Why do you think the students were at the forefront of the demonstrations?

   _____

   _____

3. Why do you think that troops from outside the city were trucked in to control the

   demonstrators? _____

   _____

4. Who won the political duel—the hard-liners or the reformers? _____

   What evidence in the selection supports your answer? _____

   _____

5. Of what other events from the past or present do the events in Tiananmen Square remind you? In what ways are the events the same? Different?

   _____

   _____

6. Do you agree with the Chinese people's claim that they had the moral power to direct their own lives? Talk about reasons to support your opinion.

   _____

   _____

7. What is the meaning of the statement, "Political power grows out of the barrel of

   a gun"? _____

   _____

8. Do you agree or disagree with the statement in question 7? Explain your answer.

   _____

   _____

   _____

9. What has happened politically in China since the events in Tiananmen Square?

_____

_____

Reviewing Vocabulary

Place each of these words into the sentence where it best fits the context.

a. converged   d. indiscriminately   g. repression

b. dueled   e. ominous   h. turmoil

c. hard-liners   f. reformers   i. unprecedented

1. The veterans _____ on the White House to bring their demands directly to the president.

2. _____ was everywhere at that time; no one was allowed to speak out on an issue in a way that differed from the government.

3. There were _____ shouts from the crowd indicating that turmoil could break out at any moment.

4. The situation was _____. Nothing like it had ever happened before.

5. The soldiers fired _____ into the crowds, striking anyone who happened to be there.

6. Alexander Hamilton _____ with Aaron Burr in a gunfight that stands out in American history.

7. The _____ wanted to keep things just as they were. The _____ wanted change. The result was an unsettled situation with lots of _____ that lasted many years.

SELECTION 3: NATIVE AMERICAN MYTHS AND LEGENDS
(Literature—Legend)

Expanding Your Vocabulary for Reading

Determine the meaning of the italicized words by using word-structure and context clues. Use the glossary to check your prediction. Write the meaning in the space provided.

1. His achievements became *legendary;* they have been celebrated and described over and over again.

2. The general *rallied* the army after the defeat and later led the army to victory.

3. The *keening* of the women for the dead general filled the air; their wailing could be heard through the village.

4. The workmen erected a *scaffold* to display the golden ornaments so all could see them.

5. His first name is Grant and his last name is Evans, or *vice versa*.

6. In the United States a ring on the third finger of the left hand *signifies* that the wearer is married.

7. She *aspires* to be a lawyer. She aims at this vocation because her mother is a lawyer.

8. My *coup* for the year is getting the contract to build the shopping center. I count it as one of my greatest accomplishments.

9. A peace-loving person, my grandmother *abhorred* war. She regarded it with extreme loathing.

10. No one knows the real reason for the *extinction* of the dinosaur; we only know that dinosaurs ceased to be.

Getting Ready to Read

Survey the selection by reading the title, author, headings, and introductory section.

● What is the selection about? _____

● What kind of selection is it? _____

● What do you already know about the topic and this kind of selection?

_____

_____

Reading with Meaning

Read the following Native American legends. As you read, keep in mind the following questions:

1. How are the two stories similar? How are they different? (comparison)

2. What do the legends tell you about the White River Sioux and the Cheyenne? (inference)

3. What conclusions can you develop about the Sioux and the Cheyenne and the way they view courage? (conclusion)

4. Do you view courage in the same way? If not, why not? (judgment)

NATIVE AMERICAN MYTHS AND LEGENDS: THE WHITE RIVER SIOUX AND THE CHEYENNE

Richard Erdoes, as Told by Jenny Leading Cloud at White River, Rosebud Indian Reservation, South Dakota, 1967

War for many Indians was an exciting but dangerous sport. In a way it resembled a medieval tournament, governed by strict rules of conduct. The battlefield became an arena for an intensely personal competition of honor in which a young man might make a name for himself and earn the eagle feathers which signified adulthood. One could be killed in this game, but killing enemies was not the reason why men went to war. Total war resulting in the extinction of a tribe was almost unknown and generally abhorred.

The conduct of war was a ceremonial affair, full of magic and ritual. Men rode to war with protective medicine bundles, miracle-working pebbles, or medicine shields, their horses covered with sacred gopher dust or painted with lightning designs—all intended to make the wearer arrow- or bulletproof, and to give his horse supernatural speed.

The main object in any battle—and the only way to gain honors—was to "count coup," to reckon one's brave deeds. Killing a man from an ambush with a gun was no coup because it was easy—even a coward could do it. But riding up on an unwounded and fully armed enemy and touching him with the hand, or with one's coupstick, was a great feat. Stealing horses right under the enemy's nose was also a fine coup. Coups were proudly boasted of around campfires, their stories and details told and retold. In some tribes a young man could not aspire to marry unless he had counted coup.

Here are two stories that show how the Sioux and Cheyenne viewed war.

Chief Roman Nose Loses His Medicine

The Lakota and the Shahiyela—the Sioux and the Cheyenne—have been good friends for a long time. Often they have fought shoulder to shoulder. They fought the white soldiers on the Bozeman Road, which we Indians called the Thieves' Road because it was built to steal our land. They fought together on the Rosebud River, and the two tribes united to defeat Custer in the big battle of the Little Bighorn. Even now in a barroom brawl, a Sioux will always come to the aid of a Cheyenne and vice versa. We Sioux will never forget what brave fighters the Cheyenne used to be.

Over a hundred years ago the Cheyenne had a famous war chief whom the whites called Roman Nose. He had the fierce, proud face of a hawk, and his deeds were legendary. He always rode into battle with a long warbonnet trailing behind him. It was thick with eagle feathers, and each stood for a brave deed, a coup counted on the enemy.

Roman Nose had a powerful war medicine, a magic stone he carried tied to his hair on the back of his head. Before a fight he sprinkled his war shirt with sacred gopher dust and painted his horse with hailstone patterns. All these things, especially the magic stone, made him bulletproof. Of course, he could be slain by a lance, a knife, or a tomahawk, but not with a gun. And nobody ever got the better of Roman Nose in hand-to-hand combat.

There was one thing about Roman Nose's medicine: he was not allowed to touch anything made of metal when eating. He had to use horn or wooden spoons and eat from wooden or earthenware bowls. His meat had to be cooked in a buffalo's pouch or in a clay pot, not in a white man's iron kettle.

One day Roman Nose received word of a battle going on between white soldiers and Cheyenne warriors. The fight had been swaying back and forth for over a day. "Come and help us; we need you" was the message. Roman Nose called his warriors together. They had a hasty meal, and Roman Nose forgot about the laws of his medicine. Using a metal spoon and a white man's steel knife, he ate buffalo meat cooked in an iron kettle.

The white soldiers had made a fort on a sandspit island in the middle of a river. They were shooting from behind and they had a new type of rifle which was better and could shoot faster and farther than the Indian's arrows and old muzzle-loaders.

The Cheyenne were hurling themselves against the soldiers in attack after attack, but the water in some spots came up to the saddles of their horses and the river bottom was slippery. They could not ride up quickly on the enemy, and they faced murderous fire. Their attacks were repulsed, their losses heavy.

Roman Nose prepared for the fight by putting on his finest clothes, war shirt, and leggings. He painted his best horse, with hailstone designs, and he tied the pebble which made him bulletproof into his hair at the back of his head. But an old warrior stepped up to him and said: "You have eaten from an iron kettle with a metal spoon and a steel knife. Your medicine is powerless; you must not fight today. Purify yourself for four days so that your medicine will be good again."

"But the fight is today, not in four days," said Roman Nose. "I must lead my warriors. I will die, but only the mountains and the rocks are forever." He put on his great warbonnet, sang his death song, and then charged. As he rode up to the white's cottonwood breastwork, a bullet hit him in the chest. He fell from his horse; his body was immediately lifted by his warriors, and the Cheyenne retreated with their dead chief. To honor him in death, to give him a fitting burial, was more important than to continue the battle.

All night the soldiers in their fort could hear the Cheyennes' mourning songs, the keening of the women. They too knew that the great chief Roman Nose was dead. He had died as he had lived. He had shown that sometimes it is more important to act like a chief than to live to a great old age.

Working with a classmate who has also read the story about Chief Roman Nose, reread it and together complete the column labeled "Chief Roman Nose" in the data chart in Figure 9.5. When you have filled in that column, read the next legend.

Brave Woman Counts Coup

Over a hundred years ago, when many Sioux were still living in what now is Minnesota, there was a band of Hunkpapa Sioux at Spirit Lake under a chief called Tawa Makoce, meaning His Country. It was his country,

A. *Read about:* As you read, record data in the blocks of the data chart. Use the design of this chart to make similar grids for recording while reading and comparing stories.

Main Characters		
	Chief Roman Nose	**Brave Woman**
Setting: time/place		
Tribe to which he/she belonged		
Personal qualities of the character		
The problem—the core of the legend		
Beginning event of the legend		
Central event in the legend		
Concluding event in the legend		
Meaning of the legend		

B. *Think about:*

1. In what ways are the two legends similar? Use your chart to make comparisons.

   _____

2. In what ways are the two legends different? Use your chart to decide.

   _____

3. Which legend appeals to you more? Give reasons to support your judgment.

   _____

Figure 9.5 *Data-gathering Chart—Comparing Stories*

too—Indian country, until the white soldiers with their cannon finally drove the Lakota tribes across the Mni Shoshay: The Big Muddy, the Missouri.

In his youth the chief had been one of the greatest warriors. Later when his fighting days were over, he was known as a wise leader, invaluable in council, and as a great giver of feasts, a provider for the poor. The chief had three sons and one daughter. The sons tried to be warriors as mighty as their father, but that was a hard thing to do. Again and again they battled the Crow Indians with reckless bravery, exposing themselves in the front rank, fighting hand to hand, until one by one they were all killed. Now only his daughter was left to the sad old chief. Some say her name was Makhta. Others call her Winyan Ohitika, Brave Woman.

The girl was beautiful and proud. Many young men sent their fathers to the old chief with gifts of fine horses that were preliminary to marriage proposals. Among those who desired her for a wife was a young warrior named Red Horn, himself the son of a chief, who sent his father again and again to ask for her hand. But Brave Woman would not marry. "I will not take a husband," she said, "until I have counted coup on the Crows to avenge my dead brothers." Another young man who loved Brave Woman was Wanblee Cikala, or Little Eagle. He was too shy to declare his love, because he was a poor boy who had never been able to distinguish himself.

At this time the Kangi Oyate, the Crow nation, made a great effort to establish themselves along the banks of the upper Missouri in country which the Sioux considered their own. The Sioux decided to send out a strong war party to chase them back, and among the young men riding out were Red Horn and Little Eagle. "I shall ride with you," Brave Woman said. She put on her best dress of white buckskin richly decorated with beads and porcupine quills, and around her neck she wore a choker of dentalium shells. She went to the old chief. "Father," she said, "I must go to the place where my brothers died. I must count coup for them. Tell me that I can go."

The old chief wept with pride and sorrow. "You are my last child," he said, "and I fear for you and for a lonely old age without children to comfort me. But your mind has long been made up. I see that you must go; do it quickly. Wear my warbonnet into battle. Go and do not look back."

And so his daughter, taking her brothers' weapons and her father's warbonnet and best war pony, rode out with the warriors. They found an enemy village so huge that it seemed to contain the whole Crow nation—hundreds of men and thousands of horses. There were many more Crows than Sioux, but the Sioux attacked nevertheless. Brave Woman was a sight to stir the warriors to great deeds. To Red Horn she gave her oldest brother's lance and shield. "Count coup for my dead brother," she said. To Little Eagle she gave her second brother's bow and arrows. "Count coup for him who owned these," she told him. To another young warrior she gave her youngest brother's war club. She herself carried only her father's old, curved coupstick wrapped in otter fur.

At first Brave Woman held back from the fight. She supported the Sioux by singing brave-heart songs and by making the shrill, trembling war cry with which Indian women encourage their men. But when the Sioux, including her own warriors from the Hunkpapa band, were driven back by overwhelming numbers, she rode into the midst of the battle. She did not try to kill her enemies, but counted coup left and right, touching them with her coupstick. With a woman fighting so bravely among them, what Sioux warrior could think of retreat?

Missouri River Region

Figure 9.6   *The Little Big Horn Region*

Still, the press of the Crows and their horses drove the Sioux back a second time. Brave Woman's horse was hit by a musket bullet and went down. She was on foot, defenseless, when Red Horn passed her on his speckled pony. She was too proud to call out for help, and he pretended not to see her. Then Little Eagle came riding toward her out of the dust of battle. He dismounted and told her to get on his horse. She did, expecting him to climb up behind her, but he would not. "This horse is wounded and too weak to carry us both," he said.

"I won't leave you to be killed," she told him. He took her brother's bow and struck the horse sharply with it across the rump. The horse bolted, as he intended, and Little Eagle went back into battle on foot. Brave Woman herself rallied the warriors for a final charge, which they made with such fury that the Crows had to give way at last.

This was the battle in which the Crow nation was driven away from the Missouri for good. It was a great victory, but many brave young men died. Among them was Little Eagle, struck down with his face to the enemy. The Sioux warriors broke Red Horn's bow, took his eagle feathers from him, and sent him home. But they placed the body of Little Eagle on a high scaffold on the spot where the enemy camp had been. They killed his horse to serve him in the land of many lodges. "Go willingly," they told the horse. "Your master has need of you in the spirit world."

Brave Woman gashed her arms and legs with a sharp knife. She cut her hair short and tore her white buckskin dress. Thus she mourned for Little Eagle. They had not been man and wife; in fact he had hardly dared speak to her or look at her, but now she asked everybody to treat her as if she were the young warrior's widow. Brave Woman never took a husband, and she never ceased to mourn for Little Eagle. "I am his widow," she told everyone. She died of old age. She had done a great thing, and her fame endures.

Working with the same classmate, reread the story of Brave Woman and together fill in the column of the data chart in Figure 9.5 labeled "Brave Woman."

Checking for Understanding

Still talking and thinking with a classmate, answer these questions. Use the data chart in Figure 9.5 to help you as you answer.

1. In what ways are the two legends similar? _____
_____

2. In what ways are the two legends different? _____
_____

3. Which legend appeals to you more? Give reasons to support your judgment.
_____
_____

4. What was the most significant difference between Little Eagle and Red Horn?
_____
_____

5. Why did Brave Woman give her oldest brother's lance to Red Horn and her
second brother's bow to Little Eagle, and not vice versa? _____
_____

6. Why did Red Horn pretend not to see Brave Woman? _____
_____

7. Why did Little Eagle give his horse to Brave Woman? _____
_____

8. Do you think Little Eagle realized that by giving away his horse he was also
giving away his life? Explain. _____
_____

9. Why did the Sioux warriors break Red Horn's bow and take his feathers away?
_____
_____

10. Today the deeds of Brave Woman are legendary. Do you believe she did the right
thing when she went into battle with the warriors? Why? Why not? Would
you have done what she did? Explain. _____
_____
_____

11. Do you believe the Sioux were right in killing Little Eagle's horse? Explain.
_____
_____

12. In what ways were Little Eagle and Roman Nose similar? _____

_____

13. Why do you think the whites gave Roman Nose that name? _____

_____

14. Why do you think Roman Nose forgot about the laws of medicine and ate with

metal tools? _____

_____

15. Why did Roman Nose sing his death song before going into battle? What does

this say about the kind of man he was? _____

_____

16. What does honor mean to a Cheyenne or a Sioux? _____

_____

17. What does friendship mean to the Sioux? _____

_____

Reviewing Vocabulary

Select the word from this list that best fits the context of the sentence.

a. abhorred c. extinction e. legendary g. repulsed i. signifies
b. aspires d. keening f. rallied h. scaffold j. vice versa

1. After her death, she became a _____ figure. People told and retold stories of what she had done.

2. They fought until the _____ of their enemies; by the end of the battle, none of the enemy was left alive.

3. That woman _____ cigarette smoking. It was something she hated more than anything else.

4. The Indians _____ the attackers who were trying to take their land; the attackers withdrew in disorder.

5. I will always help my brother, or _____.

6. They erected a _____ to hold all their equipment.

7. His signature on the contract _____ his acceptance of it.

8. During the battle, the troops _____ around their leader and continued to fight.

9. We heard the _____ of the women as they mourned their dead. The noise of it filled the air.

10. She _____ to become a Supreme Court justice. This is her greatest ambition.

Extending Your Understanding Through Writing

What is the most honorable or brave deed that you have read about or seen someone perform? In your notebook, write a paragraph in which you tell about that deed, much in the manner that Jenny Leading Cloud recounted the stories of Brave Woman and Roman Nose to her interviewer.

SELECTION 4: HAYDN AND MOZART (Music)

Expanding Your Vocabulary for Reading

Use context and word-structure clues to figure out the meanings of the italicized terms. Check your predictions in the glossary. Write the meanings in the space provided.

1. The return of the soldiers proved to be a *festive* occasion: Flowers and streamers were everywhere and people danced in the streets.

2. In times gone by, artists had *patrons,* wealthy people who supported them so that they could pursue their artistic endeavors.

3. Just before the exam, there was a *frenzy* of last minute study by the students in the class.

4. He had an *aristocratic* way about him; he held himself as if he were somebody of wealth and position.

5. After her campaign for president, she was left with *staggering* debts—debts so large that no one believed she could ever be free of carrying their weight.

6. It is *degrading* to have to get down on one's knees and beg for support.

7. There were *ominous* rumblings in the earth just before the volcano erupted.

8. By the time he left the presidency, his popularity had *dwindled* to lower than a 25 percent acceptance rate.

9. She was in the *elite* group that was invited to the White House to meet the prime minister of England.

10. He was a child *prodigy;* at age 7, he was writing music and performing it before large audiences.

11. The widow fell into the hands of an *unscrupulous* financial adviser who used every trick to get her money for himself.

12. He received a *commission* from a wealthy patron to write a comic opera.

13. There is *irony* in the fact that he regained popularity just before he died.

Getting Ready to Read

Preview the selection by reading the title, headings, and introduction.

● What is the topic of the selection? _____

● What do you already know about these two men? _____

_____

● What purpose are you setting for yourself as you read? _____

_____

Reading with Meaning

As you read, make comparisons and contrasts between the two men and their music. Try to read between the lines. Think in terms of the meaning, or significance, of the events recounted, and formulate judgments about the rightness and wrongness of acts described.

JOSEPH HAYDN
AND WOLFGANG AMADEUS MOZART

Roger Kamien

The classical period in music extended from 1750 to 1820. Master composers of this period were Joseph Haydn, Wolfgang Amadeus Mozart, and Ludwig van Beethoven. In this selection, you will read about Haydn and Mozart.

Joseph Haydn (1732–1809)

Joseph Haydn was born in a tiny Austrian village called Rohrau. His father made wagon wheels, and until the age of six, Haydn's musical background consisted of folksongs his father loved to sing and the peasant dances that whirled around him on festive occasions. (This early contact with folk music later had an influence on his style.) Haydn's eager response to music was recognized, and he was sent to live with a relative who gave him basic music lessons for two years. At eight, he went to Vienna to serve as a choirboy in the Cathedral of St. Stephen. There, though his good voice was appreciated, he had no chance for composition lessons or for perfecting an instrumental technique. And when his voice changed, Haydn was dismissed from St. Stephen's and turned out on the street without a penny. "I barely managed to stay alive by giving music lessons to children for about eight years," he wrote. Throughout those years he struggled to teach himself composition and also took odd jobs, including playing violin in the popular Viennese street bands that offered evening entertainment.

Gradually, aristocratic patrons of music began to notice Haydn's talent. For a brief time he was music director at the court of a Bohemian count, but the orchestra was dissolved because of his patron's financial problems. At the age of twenty-nine, Haydn's life changed for the better, forever.

In 1761, Haydn entered the service of the Esterhazys, the richest and most powerful of the noble Hungarian families. For almost thirty years, from 1761 to 1790, most of his music was composed for performance in the palaces of the family. Haydn spent much of his time at Esterhaz, a magnificent but isolated palace in Hungary that contained an opera house, a theater, two concert halls, and 126 guest rooms.

As a highly skilled servant, Haydn was to compose all the music requested by his patron, conduct the orchestra of about twenty-five players, coach singers, and oversee the condition of instruments and the operation of the music library. He also was required to "appear daily in the antechamber before and after midday and inquire whether His Highness is pleased to order a performance of the orchestra." The amount of work demanded of Haydn as assistant music director and later as music director was staggering; there were usually two concerts and two opera performances weekly, as well as daily chamber music in the prince's apartment. Since Nicholas Esterhazy played the baryton (a complicated stringed instrument now obsolete), Haydn wrote over 150 pieces with a baryton part.

Though today it seems degrading for a genius to be dependent on the will of a prince, in the eighteenth century patronage was taken for granted. Composers had definite advantages in that they received a steady income and their works were performed. And though Haydn felt restricted by his job from time to time, he later wisely said, "Not only did I have the encouragement of constant approval, but as conductor of an orchestra I could make experiments, observe what produced an effect and what weakened it, and was thus in a position to improve, alter, make additions or omissions, and be as bold as I pleased. I was cut off from the world; there was no one to confuse or torment me, and I was forced to become original."

Despite an unhappy marriage, Haydn was good-humored and unselfish. He was conscientious about professional duties, and he cared about the personal interests of his musicians. Prince Nicholas loved Esterhaz and once stayed at the palace longer than usual. The orchestra members came to Haydn and asked to return to Vienna; they were tired of being isolated in the country, away so long from their wives and children. Haydn obliged by composing a symphony in F-sharp minor, now known as the "Farewell." At its first performance for the prince, the musicians followed the indications in the score: During the last movement, one after another stopped playing, put out his candle, and quietly left the hall. By the time that only Haydn and the first violinist remained, Nicholas took the hint; the next day he ordered the household to return to Vienna.

Haydn met the younger Mozart in the early 1780s and they became close friends. To someone finding fault with one of Mozart's operas, Haydn replied, "I cannot settle this dispute, but this I know: Mozart is the greatest composer the world possesses now."

Over a period of twenty years, word spread about the Esterhazys' composer, and Haydn's music became immensely popular all over Europe. Publishers and concert organizations sent commissions for new works. After the death of Prince Nicholas Esterhazy in 1790, Haydn was free to go to London where a concert series was planned around his compositions. He'd been asked by concert manager Johann Peter Salomon to write and conduct new symphonies for performance at public concerts. Six were composed for a first visit in 1791–1792 and six more for a second visit in 1794–1795. These twelve became known as the "Salomon Symphonies" or "London Symphonies."

Reports of the time say that Haydn's appearances were triumphs. By the end of the eighteenth century, London was the largest and richest city in the world. Its concert life was unusually active and attracted many foreign musicians. Acclaim at Haydn's concerts was so overwhelming that some symphony movements had to be repeated. One listener noted that there was "an electrical effect on all present and such a degree of enthusiasm as almost amounted to a frenzy."

And so, a servant had become a celebrity. Haydn was wined and dined by the aristocracy, given an honorary degree at Oxford, and received by members of the royal family. And, as though to balance out earlier personal unhappiness, he had a love affair with a rich English widow. After thirty years of service to the Esterhazys, Haydn's reception by the English moved him to write, "How sweet is some degree of liberty. The consciousness of no longer being a bond servant sweetens all my toil."

Rich and honored, Haydn returned to Vienna in 1795 and maintained good relations with Esterhaz. The new Prince, Nicholas II, did not have his father's wide musical interests and liked only religious music. Haydn's agreement specified that he would compose a Mass a year. There are six, and all reflect the mature, brilliant writing of the London Symphonies. In this period of his late sixties, Haydn composed two oratorios, *The Creation* (1798) and *The Seasons* (1801). They were so popular that choruses and orchestras were formed at the beginning of the nineteenth century for the sole purpose of performing them.

Haydn died in 1809, at the age of seventy-seven, while Napoleon's army occupied Vienna. A memorial service indicated the wide recognition of Haydn's greatness: Joining the Viennese were French generals and an honor guard of French soldiers.

Working with a classmate who has also read the material about Haydn, reread it and together complete the column labeled "Haydn" in the data chart in Figure 9.7. When you have filled in that column, read the next section about Mozart.

Wolfgang Amadeus Mozart (1756–1791)

One of the most amazing child prodigies in history, Wolfgang Amadeus Mozart was born in Salzburg, Austria, the son of a court musician. By the age of six, he could play the harpsichord and violin, improvise fugues, write minuets, and read music perfectly at first sight. At eight, he wrote a

A. *Read about:* As you read, record data in the blocks of the data chart. Use the design of this chart to make similar grids for recording while reading and for composing life histories.

Composers		
	Haydn	Mozart
Time and place of birth		
Father's background		
Personal qualities		
How he got started in music		
Major events in his musical career 1. 2. 3. 4.		
Concluding events in his life		

B. *Think about:*

1. In what ways were the lives of the two composers similar? Use your chart to make comparisons.

———————————————————————————

2. In what ways were the lives of the two composers different? Use your chart to decide.

———————————————————————————

3. Which composer led the more successful life? Give reasons to support your judgment.

———————————————————————————

Figure 9.7   *Data-gathering Chart—Comparing Life Histories*

symphony; at eleven, an oratorio; and at twelve, an opera. By his early teens, Mozart had behind him many works that would have brought credit to a composer three times his age.

Mozart's father, Leopold, was understandably eager to show him off and went to great lengths to do so. Between the ages of six and fifteen, Mozart spent almost half his life on tour in Europe and England. He played for Empress Maria Theresa in Vienna, for Louis XV at Versailles, for George III in London and for innumerable aristocrats along the way. On his trips to Italy he was able to study and master the operatic style which he later put to superb use. At fourteen, Mozart was in Rome during Holy Week, and he went to the Sistine Chapel to hear the famous choir performing a work that was its treasured property. Anyone caught copying this choral piece was to be punished by excommunication. Mozart heard it once, wrote it out afterward almost completely, returned with his manuscript to make a few additions—and was discovered. That anyone should copy the music was a crime; that Mozart should hear and remember it accurately was incredible. He not only escaped punishment but was knighted by the Pope for his musical accomplishments.

At fifteen, Mozart returned to Salzburg, which was ruled by a new Prince-Archbishop, Hieronymus Colloredo. The Archbishop was a tyrant who did not appreciate Mozart's genius, and he refused to grant him more than a subordinate seat in the court orchestra. With his father's help, Mozart tried repeatedly over the next decade to find a suitable position, but there were never any vacancies.

The tragic irony of Mozart's life was that he won more acclaim as a boy wonder than as an adult musician. His upbringing and personality were partly to blame. As a child, his complete dependence on his father gave little opportunity to develop initiative. Even when Mozart was twenty-two, his mother tagged along when he went to Paris to seek recognition and establish himself. A Parisian observed that Mozart was "too good-natured, not active enough, too easily taken in, too little concerned with the means that may lead him to good fortune."

Unlike Haydn, Mozart began life as an international celebrity, pampered by kings. He could not tolerate being treated like a servant and eating with valets and cooks, and his relations with his patron went from bad to worse. Mozart became totally insubordinate when the Prince-Archbishop forbade him to give concerts or perform at the houses of the aristocracy. Mozart wrote: "He lied to my face that my salary was five hundred *gulden,* called me a scoundrel, a rascal, a vagabond. At last my blood began to boil, I could no longer contain myself, and I said, 'So Your Grace is not satisfied with me?' " He was answered with, "What, you dare to threaten me—you scoundrel? There is the door!" On his third attempt to request dismissal, Mozart was thrown out of the room by a court official and given a kick.

By 1781, when he was twenty-five, Mozart could stand it no longer. He broke free of provincial Salzburg and traveled to Vienna, intending to be a free-lance musician. To reassure his father, he wrote, "I have the best and the most useful acquaintances in the world. I am liked and respected in the best houses, and all possible honors are given me, and moreover I get paid for it. I guarantee you, I'll be successful."

Indeed, Mozart's first few years in Vienna were successful. His German opera *The Abduction from the Seraglio* (1782) was acclaimed. Concerts of his own music were attended by the Emperor and nobility. Pupils paid him high

Figure 9.8   *Joseph Haydn and Wolfgang Amadeus Mozart.*   (Right: Library of Congress)

fees, his compositions were published, and his playing was heard in palace drawing rooms. He even went against his father's wishes by marrying Constanze Weber, who had no money and was as impractical as he. Contributing to the brightness of these years was Mozart's friendship with Haydn, who told his father, "Your son is the greatest composer that I know, either personally or by reputation. . . ."

Then, in 1786, came his opera *The Marriage of Figaro*. Vienna loved it, and Prague was even more enthusiastic. "They talk about nothing but *Figaro*. Nothing is played, sung, or whistled but *Figaro*," Mozart joyfully wrote. This success led a Prague opera company to commission *Don Giovanni* the following year. *Don Giovanni* was a triumph in Prague, but it pushed the Viennese too far. The Emperor Joseph II acknowledged that it was a masterwork, but not appropriate for his pleasure-loving subjects. . . .

Mozart's popularity in Vienna began to decline. It was a fickle city: one was society's darling for a few seasons, then suddenly ignored. And Mozart's music was considered complicated and hard to follow. . . . A publisher warned him: "Write in a more popular style, or else I can neither print nor pay for any more of your music!" His pupils dwindled, and the elite snubbed his concerts. In desperate financial straits, he wrote to friends, "Great god, I would not wish my worst enemy to be in this position. . . . I am coming to you not with thanks but with fresh entreaties."

Many of Mozart's letters have been published. These span his life, and it is sad to move from the colorful, witty, and keenly observant notes of a prodigy on tour through his initial optimism about Vienna to the despair of "I cannot describe what I have been feeling. . . . A kind of longing that is never satisfied."

The events of Mozart's last year would have been good material for a grim opera plot. Though his health was failing in 1791, Mozart was delighted to receive a commission from a Viennese theater for a German comic opera, *The Magic Flute*. While hard at work, Mozart was visited by a stranger dressed entirely in gray who carried an anonymous letter commissioning a Requiem, a Mass for the Dead. Unknown to Mozart, the stranger was a servant of an unscrupulous nobleman who meant to claim the Requiem as his own composition. Mozart's health grew worse, and the Requiem took on ominous implications; he believed it to be for himself and rushed to finish it while on his deathbed. A final bit of happiness came to him two months before his death. *The Magic Flute* was premiered to resounding praise in Vienna. Its success probably would have brought large financial rewards, but it came too late. Mozart died shortly before his thirty-sixth birthday, and the final sections of the Requiem were not his. The work was completed from sketches by Sussmayr, his favorite pupil.

Mozart's funeral was the poorest possible. His body was laid in a common grave assigned to paupers.

Working with a classmate who has also read the selection about Mozart, reread it and together complete the column labeled ''Mozart'' in the data chart in Figure 9.7.

Checking for Understanding

Still talking with a classmate, answer these questions. Use the chart in Figure 9.7 to help you answer.

1. In what ways were the lives of Haydn and Mozart similar? In what ways were they different? _____

   _____

2. Of the two, which one do you believe had the better life? Why?

   _____

   _____

3. Why do you think that Haydn could better accept being dependent on the will of a patron than could Mozart? _____

   _____

4. Haydn called Mozart the greatest composer the world then possessed. What does that tell you about the kind of person Haydn was? _____

   _____

   _____

5. The selection states: "The tragic irony of Mozart's life was that he won more acclaim as a boy wonder than as an adult musician." Irony in this context means an outcome contrary to what might have been expected. Why is Mozart's life an example of tragic irony? _____

   _____

   _____

6. Why was it significant that Mozart married against his father's wishes?

_____

_____

7. As a boy, Mozart played for major rulers of Europe and was knighted by the pope. How do you think this affected him and influenced his later life?

_____

_____

8. Ludwig van Beethoven (1770–1827), who perhaps was the greatest composer of the classical period, came after Mozart. He, too, was a child prodigy, but he was never in the service of the Viennese aristocracy. He succeeded as a free-lance musician, despite deafness that struck him at twenty-nine. Based on what you have read about Mozart, hypothesize why Beethoven succeeded as a free-lancer whereas Mozart had a hard time working without a patron.

_____

_____

9. It is interesting that the three great composers of the classical period—Haydn, Mozart, and Beethoven—lived in central Europe. Do you think this happened by chance? What reasons come to your mind to account for this?

_____

_____

Reviewing Key Vocabulary

Select the word from the list that best fits the context of each sentence. Check the glossary if you need to review the meaning of a word.

a. aristocratic	e. elite	h. irony	k. prodigy
b. commission	f. festive	i. ominous	l. staggering
c. degrading	g. frenzy	j. patron	m. unscrupulous
d. dwindled			

1. The corporation became a _____ of the arts; it gave millions away to support artistic projects.

2. There was a _____ of activity at the end of the year as people did lots of last minute tasks.

3. His friends _____ away until he had none at all.

4. The amount of work required of the man was _____; he could never get it done in a 12-hour workday.

5. We heard an _____ rumble of thunder as we started our picnic.

6. The artist accepted a _____ to paint a portrait of the queen.

7. Some people think it is _____ for women to parade in bathing suits during a beauty contest.

8. There is _____ in the fact that she got what she wanted only after she no longer had use for it.

9. Mozart was a _____; he could compose and play music even as a child.

10. The lords and ladies looked upon themselves as being among the _____, or the privileged.

11. The members of the royal family acted in an _____ way during the coronation.

12. The _____ man lied and cheated on every occasion.

13. The New Year's celebration was a _____ time.

Figure 9.9   *Europe*

Writing About What You Know

In this selection, you learned about the patronage system as it existed during the classical period. In your notebook, write a paragraph in which you state your opinion of the system between patron and musician as it operated at the end of the 1700s. Support your opinion with details. Before writing, jot down your opinion and the details you will use to support it. In short, create a map of the ideas as demonstrated earlier in Figure 5.2.

EXTENDING WHAT YOU HAVE LEARNED

Reviewing Your Reading Strategies

List here a series of questions you should keep in mind as you read beyond the facts given in a selection.

_____

_____

_____

_____

_____

Applying the Strategies to Your Reading

Locate a book of short stories, Greek myths, fables, or legends in the library. Read two stories from the book, and create a data chart for compiling information while reading. Then write a short paragraph in which you compare the two stories and draw a conclusion about them.

Building a Knowledge Base for Reading

Locate the following places on the maps in Figures 9.6 and 9.9:

- Minnesota, the Missouri River, and the Little Bighorn Mts.;
- Vienna and Salzburg in Austria;
- Prague, Czechoslovakia;
- Hungary;
- Rome, Italy; London, England; and Paris, France.

Gaining Ownership over Words

Select several of the words featured in this chapter. Record them in your personal vocabulary list. Try to use them in speaking and writing.

10

Interpreting Style, Tone, and Mood

Before reading the chapter, read the title, the stated objective, and the headings and subheadings. Ask yourself: What is the topic of the chapter? In the space above and beside the chapter number, jot down what you already know about the topic. Then in the space below the number, jot down at least two questions you hope to answer through reading the chapter.

OBJECTIVE

In this chapter, you will develop strategies for interpreting

1. style—the author's overall manner of writing;
2. tone—the way in which an author expresses feelings;
3. mood—the state of feeling in a piece.

STYLE

The term *style* means the way in which authors express themselves—the way they choose and use words, punctuation, sentences, and paragraphs to communicate meanings. Writing can be bare bones, matter of fact, and unembellished: An author uses words sparingly and comes directly to the point. On the other hand, writing can be flowery and dramatic: An author uses colorful and melodious expressions, painting pictures with descriptive words and providing considerable elaboration. Of course, writing style can be somewhere between the plain and the dramatic. And it can be overly matter of fact as well as overly dramatic.

Elements of Style

In *Writer's Guide and Index to English,* Porter Perrin identifies elements to consider in thinking about an author's style. Here are those elements as well as questions to identify an author's style:

1. *Development of ideas:* the way the author develops his or her thought.
   a. Does the writer start with specific information and then develop generalizations based on the specifics? Or does he or she begin with a generalization and then provide details or examples?
   b. Does the writer lay it all out in black and white? Or do you, the reader, have to infer meanings, or put them together based on the data stated?
   c. Is the writer systematic in the way he or she presents ideas?
   d. Does the writer pack in a lot of details in a short space? Does the writer provide considerable visual detail and elaboration?
2. *Qualities of sound:* the way the words sound if read aloud.
   a. Is there a melodious sound to the words, whether they are poetry or prose? Or is there an awkwardness in the way words flow?
   b. Has the writer effectively used alliteration (the repetition of beginning sounds as in "the forest's ferny floor") or rhyme as in

   > Listen, my children, and you shall hear
   > Of the midnight ride of Paul Revere,
   > On the eighteenth of April, in Seventy five;
   > Hardly a man is now alive
   > Who remembers that famous day and year?

   c. Does the writer purposefully repeat words to heighten the message?
   d. How has the writer used punctuation to emphasize sound: for example, the dash to make you pause longer in reading; the exclamation mark to lend excitement?
3. *Visual elements:* the way the author uses space and shape to communicate the message.
   a. Does the piece have the appearance of poetry on the page—laid out in lines and verses?
   b. Does the author use italic type and/or punctuation to heighten the message?
4. *Sentences:* the way the author constructs sentences.
   a. Does the author use short sentences or long? A mix of sentence lengths?
   b. Does the author use complicated sentence patterns? Simple, easy to read sentences?
5. *Words:* the words the author chooses.
   a. Does the author rely on short words? Long words?

b. Does the author rely on familiar words? Unfamiliar words?

6. *Imagery:* the pictures the author paints with words.
   a. Does the author paint pictures that you can see in your mind's eye?
   b. Does the author work with abstractions that are difficult for you to picture?

7. *Figures of speech:* metaphors, similes, unique ways of handling language, and turns of a phrase that an author uses.
   a. Does the author build unusual relationships through metaphor or simile?
      (1) A simile is a creative comparison that relies on the word *like* or *as* to make a connection between two things. Example: "The branches of the tree stretched heavenward like hands reaching for space."

      branches = hands

      (2) A metaphor is a creative comparison without *like* or *as.* Example: "The wind is a deadly dragon, slapping the world with its tail."

      wind = deadly dragon
   b. Does the author use language in unique ways? Does he or she turn a phrase with style?

8. *Literary allusions:* references to other pieces of literature.
   a. Does the author use words, phrases, or sentences from the works of other authors without quoting directly or telling you their source?
   b. Does the author refer in some way to events from other pieces of literature?
   c. Does the author quote directly (with quotation marks) from the works of other authors?

Read aloud this short poem by Nikki Giovanni, a modern-day poet of considerable repute. As you read, listen for sounds and rhythm and consider the creative relationship she has put together:

the drum

Nikki Giovanni

daddy says the world is
a drum tight and hard
and i told him
i'm gonna beat
out my own rhythm

Writing about the world, Giovanni could have described the earth literally as a spinning sphere. She did not. She relied on figurative language—a metaphor—to establish a unique relationship.

the world = a drum

Reading her poem, you must ask, "How is the world like a drum?" You play on a drum; you play on the world. You beat a drum; you beat the world. With a drum, you can make rhythm; with the world, you can make rhythm.

Reread the poem. How does Giovanni use capitalization and punctuation? She does not bother with them. That is a part of her style. What kinds of words does she use? Short, familiar, mostly one-syllable words. She also uses "gonna" rather than the standard "going to." These, too, are elements of her style. What kinds of sentences does she use? One compound sentence comprises the entire piece. What sounds does she build into her poem? The hard sounds of the *b* and *t* in *beat* and *told*—sounds of a drum.

A college junior wrote a poem modeled after Giovanni's. It, too, includes a metaphor, relies on short words and repeating sounds of the *t* as in *tough, told,* and *top,* and dispenses with punctuation and capitalization.

the mountain

daddy says the world is
a mountain that is tough to climb
and i told him
i'd climb it
to the very top

● To what did this writer compare the world? _____

● In what ways are the world and a mountain similar? _____

TONE AND MOOD

A strategy for interpreting tone and mood is to ask: What tone of voice does the author take? What feeling does he or she communicate?

Tone is simply the manner in which a writer communicates feelings; it is closely akin to writing style, and is comparable to tone of voice in speaking. The tone of a piece can be sharp and probing, antagonistic and critical, sarcastic, ironic, humorous, or warm and caring. Both in writing and speaking, tone reflects the attitude of the author toward his or her subject. An author's choice of words often determines the tone.

Mood is the feeling communicated. Both tone and style set the mood, which can be happy or sad, positive or negative, calm or excited, or at times just neutral.

What are the tone and mood of Giovanni's "the drum"? Giovanni speaks in a determined tone of voice. The mood is upbeat. There is no sadness, calmness, humor, or anger. Both the tone and mood are part of the message. It says, "I am determined to make it!" Although Giovanni does not use an exclamation at the end, the exclamation is there—in the determined tone and upbeat mood.

Go back now to Chapter 8, page 175. Reread the essay by Robert Fulghum. As you read, ask: What is the tone of the essay? What kind of mood does the author create? Write a word or two on this line to describe the tone and mood:

_____

In the next part of this chapter, you will read a series of selections for style, mood, and tone—two literary essays, two speeches, and some poems. As you read these, ask: How do the style, mood, and tone differ from the style, mood, and tone of textbook material?

SELECTION 1: FATHERHOOD: BECAUSE IT'S THERE
(Literary Essay)

Expanding Vocabulary for Reading

Use word-structure and context clues to determine the meanings of the italicized words. Check the glossary if you are not certain of the meanings. Record the definition of each highlighted term in the space provided.

1. My *reservations* about the project were overcome when I heard that Magic Johnson was involved. _____

   _____

2. *Impregnation* of the female of the species by the male is necessary if the species is to continue. _____

   _____

3. The fire fighter's *heroic* deed of going into the burning building to save a child won him recognition. _____

   _____

4. She was *nobly* rewarded for her efforts; she received a splendid trophy and a citation from the president. _____

   _____

Getting Ready to Read

Read the title, author, and the first paragraph of the selection.

● What is the article going to be about? _____

● What do you already know about this author? What kind of personality does he have? _____

● What kind of writing do you expect from this writer? A textbook-like piece? A funny piece?_____

Set your purpose for reading.

● Write one question you hope to answer by reading the selection. Make your question relate in some way to the style, tone, or mood of writing.

   _____

   _____

Reading with Meaning

FATHERHOOD: BECAUSE IT'S THERE

Bill Cosby

It's love, of course, that makes us fathers do it—love for the woman we've married and love for every baby we've ever seen, except the one that threw up on our shoes. And so, in spite of all our reservations about this scary business of reproduction, we must admit that people look happy when they're carrying babies. The male looks especially happy because he has someone to carry it for him, his darling packager.

But his wife is happy too, because she feels she's fulfilling herself as a woman. I've heard so many females say that they became mothers because they wanted to feel like women, as if they felt like longshoremen at all other times. And so many others have said, "I had the baby because I wanted to see if I could," which sounds like a reason for climbing Mount Everest or breaking the four-minute mile. If a chimpanzee can have a baby, the human female should realize that the feat is something less than an entry for the Guinness Book of World Records.

The new father, of course, feels that his mere impregnation of his mate, done every day by otters and apes, is Olympic gold medal stuff. Even if he's afraid of garter snakes, he feels positively heroic. He feels that he and his wife have nobly created something that will last. He never thinks that they may have created one of the top underachievers in their town.   [249 words]

Checking for Understanding

1. Why do you think Cosby added the phrase, "except the one that threw up on our shoes"? _____

2. What other phrases does Cosby use for the same reason? _____

   _____

3. What is the overall tone of the essay? _____

4. What is the thesis, or main point, of Cosby's essay? _____

   _____

5. This kind of essay is considered satire. A satirist talks about a serious issue but uses humor and ridicule. Sometimes we call this approach "tongue-in-cheek humor." What other writer—one you have read very recently—uses a similar approach? _____

6. How does Cosby's style differ from textbook writing? _____

   _____

Reviewing Key Vocabulary

Use the following words in sentences so that the meaning of each is rather explicit. Try to add a bit of humor to your sentences. Use the sentences in Expanding Vocabulary for Reading, the selection, and the glossary as models for the sentences you compose. You may collaborate with someone else to write the sentences.

1. heroic

2. impregnation

3. nobly

4. reservations

SELECTION 2: THE GETTYSBURG ADDRESS (Speech)

Expanding Vocabulary for Reading

Use word-structure and context clues to determine the meanings of the italicized words. Check the glossary if you are not certain of the meanings. Record the definition of each highlighted term in the space provided.

1. A *score* of years is twice as long as a decade.

2. He put this *proposition* to me: Every person must do his or her fair share of the work.

3. The priest *consecrated* the site by declaring it a sacred place.

4. "We cannot *hallow* this battlefield; we cannot make it a sacred, or holy place," the president said.

5. Wearing a long skirt does not *detract* from your appearance. It may actually make you look better.

Getting Ready to Read

Read the title, author, and introduction to the selection.

● What do you already know about this selection and its author?

_____

● Setting your purpose for reading: Write one question you hope to answer by reading the selection. _____

_____

Reading with Meaning

As you read the selection or listen to it as your instructor reads it aloud, pretend you are at Gettysburg and are hearing Lincoln deliver the address. Think: How would it have made you feel? What elements of Lincoln's writing style would have led you to feel that way?

ADDRESS AT THE DEDICATION
OF THE GETTYSBURG NATIONAL CEMETERY

Abraham Lincoln

Lincoln delivered this address on November 19, 1863, at Gettysburg, Pennsylvania. The prior speaker, Edward Everett, had just presented a very formal two-hour speech to an audience comprised of 100,000 people. Lincoln had made a rough outline of his own address, wrote it out on paper only shortly before, and scribbled the final sentence in pencil after arriving in Gettysburg. The Gettysburg Address, as we know it today, is one of the best known speeches of all time.

Four score and seven years ago our fathers brought forth on this continent a new nation, conceived in liberty, and dedicated to the proposition that all men are created equal.

Now we are engaged in a great civil war, testing whether that nation, or any nation so conceived and so dedicated, can long endure. We are met on a great battlefield of that war. We have come to dedicate a portion of that field as a final resting-place for those who here gave their lives that this nation might live. It is altogether fitting and proper that we should do this.

But, in a larger sense, we cannot dedicate—we cannot consecrate—we cannot hallow—this ground. The brave men, living and dead, who struggled here, have consecrated it far above our poor power to add or detract. The world will little note nor long remember what we say here, but it can never forget what they did here. It is for us, the living, rather to be dedicated here to the unfinished work which they who fought here have thus far so nobly advanced. It is rather for us to be here dedicated to the great task remaining before us—that from these honored dead we take increased devotion to that cause for which they gave the last full measure of devotion; that we here highly resolve that these dead shall not have died in vain; that this nation, under God, shall have a new birth of freedom; and that government of the people, by the people, for the people, shall not perish from the earth.   [353 words]

Checking for Understanding

1. How did Lincoln's speech make you feel? _____

_____

2. What lines do you particularly like? Write them here and tell why you like the way he turned that particular phrase. _____

_____

3. What words or phrases did Lincoln repeat? Write them here and tell why you think he repeated them. _____

_____

4. How long is four score and seven years? Why did Lincoln not come right out and give the number of years? _____

_____

5. Lincoln used the phrase, "gave the last full measure of devotion." What did he mean by that phrase? Why didn't he come out and say it more clearly?

_____

_____

6. What is the tone of Lincoln's address?
   a. sarcastic   c. humorous
   b. serious   d. light

7. How is the tone of Lincoln's address different from the tone of Cosby's essay?

_____

8. Why do you think that Lincoln's address has become a classic piece of literature, whereas no one remembers the address of the prior speaker, Edward Everett?

_____

_____

Reviewing Key Vocabulary

1. How many years are two *score* and five?
   a. 15   b. 25   c. 35   d. 45
2. We are dedicated to the *proposition* that all people have a right to a free education through the twelfth grade. What is the meaning of *proposition* in the sentence?
   a. evil plan   c. dishonorable proposal
   b. statement of basic belief   c. way of doing something
3. *Hallowed* ground is ground that has been
   a. made sacred.   c. talked about.
   b. dug up.   d. used at Halloween for ghostly purposes.
4. When wine has been *consecrated,* it has been
   a. purified chemically.   c. made impure.
   b. consumed.   d. made holy.
5. Behaving that way will *detract* from your reputation. What is the meaning of *detract* in that sentence?
   a. take away from   c. inhibit
   b. increase   d. clear

SELECTION 3: I HAVE A DREAM (Speech)

Expanding Vocabulary for Reading

Use word-structure and context clues to get the meaning of the italicized words. Check the glossary when you are not sure. Write the definition of the key words in the space provided.

1. After surgery, he *languished* in bed; he got so weak he could not stand up.

2. When Harry got the loan at the bank, he had to sign a *promissory* note.

3. Because of illness, Harry did not have the money to pay back the loan; he had to *default* on it.

4. The prince was the *heir* to a great fortune. At the death of his mother, the queen, he would inherit much money and lands.

5. Having lived amid the hustle and bustle of the city, I was struck by the *tranquillity* of the countryside.

6. His mental health *degenerated* until he no longer could function on his own.

7. Determination and success are *inextricably* bound together. You cannot have one without the other.

8. Arriving at the *oasis* in the desert, we drank from the water there and cooled off under the trees.

9. In her *quest* for fame and fortune, the movie star trampled over the feelings of many others.

10. Do not *wallow* in self-pity like a hippopotamus wallows in the mud. Get up and take action.

Getting Ready to Read

Read the title, author, and the first two paragraphs of the next selection.

● What is the topic of the selection? _____

● What do you know about this topic, about the selection, and about its author?

_____

_____

● Setting your purpose for reading: Write two questions you hope to answer by reading the selection. _____

_____

Reading with Meaning

As you read, pretend you are in the audience on that day in 1963. How do King's words make you feel? What elements of his writing style do you find particularly effective? What words and phrases do you like?

I HAVE A DREAM

Martin Luther King, Jr.

Five score years ago, a great American, in whose symbolic shadow we stand today, signed the Emanicipation Proclamation. This momentous decree came as a great beacon of light and hope to millions of Negro slaves who had been seared in the flames of withering injustice. It came as a joyous daybreak to end the long night of their captivity.

But one hundred years later, the Negro is still not free. One hundred years later, the life of the Negro is still sadly crippled by the manacles of segregation and the chains of discrimination.

One hundred years later, the Negro lives on a lonely island of poverty in the midst of a vast ocean of material prosperity. One hundred years later, the Negro is still languished in the corners of American society and finds himself an exile in his own land. So we have come here today to dramatize a shameful condition.

In a sense we have come to our nation's capital to cash a check. When the architects of our republic wrote the magnificent words of the Constitution and the Declaration of Independence, they were signing a promissory note to which every American was to fall heir. This note was a promise that all men, yes, black men as well as white men, would be guaranteed the unalienable rights of life, liberty, and the pursuit of happiness.

It is obvious today that America has defaulted on this promissory note insofar as her citizens of color are concerned. Instead of honoring this sacred obligation, America has given the Negro people a bad check, which has come back marked "insufficient funds."

But we refuse to believe that the bank of justice is bankrupt. We refuse to believe that there are insufficient funds in the great vaults of opportunity of this nation. So we have come to cash this check—a check that will give us upon demand the riches of freedom and the security of justice.

We have also come to this hallowed spot to remind America of the fierce urgency of now. This is no time to engage in the luxury of cooling off or to take the tranquilizing drug of gradualism. Now is the time to make real the promises of democracy. Now is the time to rise from the dark and desolate valley of segregation to the sunlit path of racial justice. Now is the time to lift our nation from the quicksands of racial injustice to the solid rock of brotherhood. Now is the time to make justice a reality for all of God's children.

It would be fatal for the nation to overlook the urgency of the movement and to underestimate the determination of the Negro. This sweltering summer of the Negro's legitimate discontent will not pass until there is an invigorating autumn of freedom and equality. 1963 is not an end but a beginning. Those who hope that the Negro needed to blow off steam and will now be content will have a rude awakening if the nation returns to business as usual.

Figure 10.1   *Dr. Martin Luther King.*   (UPI/Bettmann Newsphotos)

There will be neither rest nor tranquillity in America until the Negro is granted his citizenship rights. The whirlwinds of revolt will continue to shake the foundations of our nation until the bright day of justice emerges.

But there is something that I must say to my people who stand on the warm threshold which leads into the palace of justice. In the process of gaining our rightful place we must not be guilty of wrongful deeds.

Let us not seek to satisfy our thirst for freedom by drinking from the cup of bitterness and hatred. We must forever conduct our struggle on the high plane of dignity and discipline. We must not allow our creative protest to degenerate into physical violence. Again and again we must rise to the majestic heights of meeting physical force with soul force.

The marvelous new militancy which has engulfed the Negro community must not lead us to a distrust of all white people, for many of our white brothers, as evidenced by their presence here today, have come to realize that their destiny is tied up with our destiny and they have come to realize that their freedom is inextricably bound to our freedom. This offense we share mounted to storm the battlements of injustice must be carried forth by a biracial army. We cannot walk alone.

And as we walk, we must make the pledge that we shall always march ahead. We cannot turn back. There are those who are asking the devotees of civil rights, "When will you be satisfied?" We can never be satisfied as long as the Negro is the victim of the unspeakable horrors of police brutality.

We can never be satisfied as long as our bodies, heavy with fatigue of travel, cannot gain lodging in the motels of the highways and the hotels of the cities. We cannot be satisfied as long as the Negro's basic mobility is from a smaller ghetto to a larger one.

We can never be satisfied as long as our children are stripped of their selfhood and robbed of their dignity by signs stating "for whites only." We cannot be satisfied as long as a Negro in Mississippi cannot vote and a Negro in New York believes he has nothing for which to vote. No, we are not satisfied, and we will not be satisfied until justice rolls down like waters and righteousness like a mighty stream.

I am not unmindful that some of you have come here out of excessive trials and tribulation. Some of you have come from areas where your quest for freedom left you battered by the storms of persecution and staggered by the winds of police brutality. You have been the veterans of creative suffering. Continue to work with the faith that unearned suffering is redemptive.

Go back to Mississippi; go back to Alabama; go back to South Carolina; go back to Georgia; go back to Louisiana; go back to the slums and ghettos of the Northern cities, knowing that somehow this situation can, and will be changed. Let us not wallow in the valley of despair.

So I say to you, my friends, that even though we must face the difficulties of today and tomorrow, I still have a dream. It is a dream deeply rooted in the American dream that one day this nation will rise up and live out the true meaning of its creed—we hold these truths to be self-evident, that all men are created equal.

I have a dream that one day on the red hills of Georgia, sons of former slaves and sons of former slave-owners will be able to sit together at the table of brotherhood.

I have a dream that one day, even the state of Mississippi, a state sweltering with the heat of injustice, sweltering with the heat of oppression, will be transformed into an oasis of freedom and justice.

I have a dream my four little children will one day live in a nation where they will not be judged by the color of their skin but by the content of their character. I have a dream today!

I have a dream that one day, down in Alabama, with its vicious racists, with its governor having his lips dripping with the words of interposition and nullification, that one day, right there in Alabama, little black boys and black girls will be able to join hands with little white boys and white girls as sisters and brothers. I have a dream today!

I have a dream that one day every valley shall be exalted, every hill and mountain shall be made low, the rough places shall be made plain, and the crooked places shall be made straight and the glory of the Lord will be revealed and all flesh shall see it together.

This is our hope. This is the faith that I go back to the south with.

With this faith we will be able to hew out of the mountain of despair a stone of hope. With this faith we will be able to transform the jangling discords of our nation into a beautiful symphony of brotherhood.

With this faith we will be able to work together, to pray together, to struggle together, knowing that we will be free one day. This will be the day when all of God's children will be able to sing with new meaning—"my country 'tis of thee, sweet land of liberty, of thee I sing; land where my fathers died, land of the pilgrim's pride; from every mountainside, let freedom ring"—and if America is to be a great nation, this must become true.

And so let freedom ring from the prodigious hilltops of New Hampshire.

Let freedom ring from the mighty mountains of New York.

Let freedom ring from the heightening Alleghenies of Pennsylvania.

Let freedom ring from the snow-capped Rockies of Colorado.

Let freedom ring from the curvaceous slopes of California.

But not only that.

Let freedom ring from Stone Mountain of Georgia.

Let freedom ring from Lookout Mountain of Tennessee.

Let freedom ring from every hill and molehill of Mississippi, from every mountainside, let freedom ring.

And when this happens, and when we allow freedom to ring, when we let it ring from every village and hamlet, from every state and city, we will be able to speed up that day when all of God's children—black men and white men, Jews and Gentiles, Catholics and Protestants—will be able to join hands and to sing in the words of the old Negro spiritual, "Free at last, free at last; thank God Almighty, we are free at last."   [1,624 words]

Checking for Understanding

Answer the following questions in the space provided.

1. King's purpose for writing is to
   a. give members of his audience hope to continue the fight.
   b. make members of his audience feel badly about their plight.
   c. make members of his audience feel good about themselves.
   d. criticize the past.

2. Why do you think King began with the phrase "five score years"? To what other speech was he alluding, or referring? _____

   _____

3. Part of King's style is using contrasts. For example, he contrasts "a joyous daybreak" with "the long night." Find at least two other contrasts he makes in his speech and record them here. _____

   _____

4. Part of King's style is using sound-filled repetitions. List words and phrases that he repeats and you particularly like. _____

   _____

5. King uses figurative language (metaphors and similes). For example, he speaks of the "storms" of persecution and the "winds" of police brutality. By doing this he is building creative comparisons. Go back and find at least two other examples of figurative language. For each explain the relationship King is pointing out. _____

   _____

   _____

6. King's speech is filled with striking lines. Reread and locate one line that is particularly striking to you. Write it here and tell why you find it effective.

   _____

   _____

7. Do you recognize the phrase "unalienable rights of life, liberty, and the pursuit of happiness"? Do you know the source? If so, write the name of the document

   here. _____

8. Do you recognize the phrase "We hold these truths to be self-evident, that all men are created equal"? Do you know the document where these words are

   found? If so, write its name here. _____

9. Why do you think King used lines from the great documents of America's past?

   _____

   _____

10. What is the source of the lines "my country 'tis of thee, sweet land of liberty . . ."? Why do you think King used those familiar lines in his address?

    _____

    _____

Writing from Reading

What mood did King's speech create? How did it make you feel? Why did the speech make you feel that way? In your notebook, write a paragraph in which you describe your reaction to the address and why you reacted in the way you did.

Reviewing Key Vocabulary

a. defaulted   c. heir   e. languished   g. promissory   i. tranquillity
b. degenerated   d. inextricably f. oasis   h. quest   j. wallowed

From the list, select the word that best fits the context of each sentence. Write it in the blank.

1. The discussion _____ into a barroom brawl. At first the people talked calmly, but at the end they used their fists to make points.

2. The fate of his children was _____ tied to his fate.

3. Her home was an _____ to her at the end of a trouble-filled day.

4. The animals _____ in the heat of the drought, waiting for water.

5. The _____ of the summer evening was disturbed by a thunderstorm.

6. The daughter was named the only _____ under the terms of her mother's will.

7. The business owner signed a _____ note for $50,000.

8. When the business owner _____ on the loan, the bank took away the property that secured it.

9. The prospector panned for gold; his _____ was rewarded when he found a large nugget.

10. The woman who did not receive the award _____ in despair for many months.

SELECTION 4: DREAM POEMS BY LANGSTON HUGHES
(Literature—Poetry)

Expanding Your Vocabulary for Reading

In this selection, comprised of three poems, you will find the word *melody,* as in the sentence "She played the melody on the piano." Write the meaning of *melody* in the space provided. Write its plural form, too.

_____

_____

Getting Ready to Read

The following three poems were written by the twentieth-century African-American poet Langston Hughes. They are all about dreams. Before beginning to read, write down in the web any words that come to mind as you think about dreams. This is a good strategy to use as part of your prereading activity, especially when you are reading poetry. Simply brainstorm words and phrases on the topic.

Reading with Meaning

Now read Langston Hughes's poems. Ask yourself: What is he saying about dreams? What mood is he creating? How does he use words to create that mood?

DREAMS

Langston Hughes

Hold fast to dreams
For if dreams die
Life is a broken-winged bird
That cannot fly.

Hold fast to dreams
For when dreams go
Life is a barren field
Frozen with snow.

THE DREAM KEEPER

Langston Hughes

Bring me all of your dreams
You dreamers,
Bring me all of your heart melodies
That I may wrap them
In a blue cloud cloth
Away from the too-rough fingers
Of the world.

DREAM DUST

Langston Hughes

Gather out of star-dust
Earth-dust
Cloud-dust
Storm-dust
And splinters of hail,
One handful of dream-dust
Not for sale.

Checking Your Understanding

1. What words and phrases from the poems did you particularly like? Record them here. For each tell why it appeals to you. _____

   _____

2. What words or word patterns did Langston Hughes repeat? Write examples of repetitive usage here. _____

   _____

3. Why do you think Langston Hughes repeated words in this way? Did his repetitions help you to enjoy the poems? Explain. _____

   _____

4. Hughes built a creative metaphor (a creative comparison):

   life without dreams = a broken-winged bird

   In what way are life without dreams and a broken-winged bird the same?

   _____

   _____

5. Hughes built a second metaphor in the same poem. Record the parts of it here:

_____ = _____

In what way are the two parts of the metaphor the same? _____

_____

6. Hughes liked to play with opposite meanings. That is part of his style. For example, he contrasted a "blue cloud cloth" to the "too-rough fingers of the world." In what ways are these two things different? _____

_____

7. What mood did Hughes build in his three poems?
   a. despairing   c. impassioned
   b. compassionate   d. languishing

8. How are the Langston Hughes's poems similar to the King speech? What message do they share? What similar elements of style do you find in both?

_____

_____

_____

_____

_____

9. Which of the three poems do you like best? In your notebook, write a short paragraph telling why you like that one. In your topic sentence, name the poem you have chosen. In the following sentences, give your reasons. Give specific words and lines from the poems to support your judgment.

SELECTION 5: SHE SAT STILL (Literary Essay)

Expanding Vocabulary for Reading

Use word-structure and context clues to determine the meanings of the italicized words. Check the glossary if you are not certain of the meanings. Record the definition of each italicized term in the space provided.

1. Jane Fonda is an *activist*. She believes it is important to take action and speak out on controversial issues. _____

_____

2. He was known as a *radical* because of the far-out positions he advocated.

_____

_____

3. Martin Luther King was known for the *eloquent* phrases he used in his speeches.

_____

_____

4. In some churches, baptism of the young is considered a *sacrament*.

5. The young people would *congregate* on the corner in front of the building after school was over for the day. _____

6. The girl was a living *tribute* to her father, who had sacrificed his life so that she might have an education. _____

Getting Ready to Read

Read the title, author, and the first paragraph of the selection.

- What is the article going to be about? _____

- What do you already know about this author? What kind of writing do you expect from this writer? A textbook-like piece? A funny piece? A serious piece?

_____

Set your purpose for reading.

- Write one question you hope to answer by reading the selection. Make your question relate in some way to the style, tone, or mood of writing. _____

_____

Reading with Meaning

Read to answer your purpose-setting question.

SHE SAT STILL

Robert Fulghum

"SIT STILL—JUST SIT STILL!" My mother's voice. Again and again. Teachers in school said it, too. And I, in my turn, have said it to my children and my students. Why do adults say this? Can't recall any child ever really sitting still just because some adults said to. That is why several "sit stills" are followed by "SIT DOWN AND SHUT UP!" or "SHUT UP AND SIT DOWN!" My mother once used both versions back to back, and I, smart-mouth that I was, asked her just which she wanted me to do first, shut up or sit down? My mother gave me that look. The one that meant she knew she would go to jail if she killed me, but it just might be worth it. At such a moment an adult will say very softly, one syllable at a time: "Get-out-of-my-sight." Any kid with half a brain will get up and go. Then the parent will sit very still.

Sitting still can be powerful stuff, though. It is on my mind as I write this on the first day of December in 1988, the anniversary of a moment when someone sat still and lit the fuse to social dynamite. On this day in 1955, a forty-two-year-old woman was on her way home from work. Getting on a public bus, she paid her fare and sat down on the first vacant seat. It was good to sit down—her feet were tired. As the bus filled with passengers, the driver turned and told her to give up her seat and move on back in the bus. She sat still. The driver got up and shouted, "MOVE IT!" She sat still. Passengers grumbled, cursed her, pushed at her. Still she sat. So the driver got off the bus, called the police, and they came to haul her off to jail and into history.

Rosa Parks. Not an activist or a radical. Just a quiet, conservative, churchgoing woman with a nice family and a decent job as a seamstress. For all the eloquent phrases that have been turned about her place in the flow of history, she did not get on that bus looking for trouble or trying to make a statement. Going home was all she had in mind, like everybody else. She was anchored to her seat by her own dignity. Rosa Parks simply wasn't going to be a "nigger" for anybody anymore. And all she knew to do was to sit still.

There is a sacred simplicity in not doing something—and doing it well. All the great religious leaders have done it. The Buddha sat still under a tree. Jesus sat still in a garden. Muhammad sat still in a cave. And Gandhi and King and thousands of others have brought sitting still to perfection as a powerful tool of social change. Passive resistance, meditation, prayer—one and the same.

It works even with little kids. Instead of telling them to sit still, you yourself can sit very still and quiet. Before long they will pay a great deal of attention to you. Students in class are also thrown by silent stillness on the part of a teacher. It is sometimes taken for great wisdom.

And sitting still works with grown-ups. On the very same bus route Rosa Parks used to travel, anybody can sit anywhere on the buses now, and some of the drivers are black—both men and women. The street where she was pulled off the bus has been renamed: Rosa Parks Avenue.

A new religion could be founded on this one sacrament. To belong would be simple. You wouldn't have to congregate on a special day in a special place. No hymns, no dues, no creeds, no preachers, and no potluck suppers. All you have to do is sit still. Once a day, for fifteen minutes, sit down, shut up, and be still. Like your mother told you. Amazing things might happen if enough people did this on a regular basis. Every chair, park bench, and sofa would become a church.

Rosa Parks is in her seventies now, doing most of her sitting in a rocking chair, living in quiet retirement with her family in Detroit. The memorials to her sitting still are countless, but the best ones are the living tributes in the form of millions of people of every color getting on thousands of buses every evening, sitting down, and riding home in peace.

If there is indeed a heaven, then I've no doubt that Rosa Parks will go there. I imagine the moment when she signs in with the angel at the pearly gates.

"Ah, Rosa Parks, we've been expecting you. Make yourself at home—take any seat in the house."   [800 words]

Checking for Understanding

1. Fulghum uses incomplete sentences. They are part of his style. What does this add to his writing? Why is it acceptable here? _____

_____

2. What is the overall tone of the essay? _____

3. What is the thesis, or main point, of Fulghum's essay? _____

_____

4. Of all the authors you have read in this chapter, which one's style is closest to

Fulghum's? _____ Explain why. _____

_____

Reviewing Key Vocabulary

Use the following words in sentences so that the meaning of each is rather explicit. Try to add a bit of humor to your sentences. Use the sentences in Expanding Vocabulary for Reading, the selection, and the glossary as models for the sentences you compose. You may collaborate with someone else to write the sentences.

1. an activist

2. congregate

3. eloquent

4. a radical

5. a sacrament

6. a tribute

EXTENDING WHAT YOU HAVE LEARNED

Building a Knowledge Base for Reading

Circle or plot the following places on the map in Figure 10.2.

Washington, D.C.; the states of New York, Pennsylvania, Colorado, California, Mississippi, Tennessee, Georgia, and Alabama; Gettysburg, Pennsylvania.

Gaining Ownership of Words

Select several words you have studied in this chapter to record in your personal vocabulary list. Try to use those words in speaking and writing.

Applying the Strategies in Independent Reading

Find a piece you feel you would enjoy reading. It can be anything that appeals to you. Think about the way the author is expressing him or herself as you read. When

Figure 10.2 *The United States of America*

you finish, write on a card the name of the author and the title of the selection. Then write down several words, phrases, or sentences that you think are typical of the writer's style, or manner of writing.

Reviewing Elements of Style

When you think of writing style, what elements come to your mind? Record at least three elements of style that particularly affect your reading enjoyment. Next to each, write down an example.

1. _____

_____

2. _____

_____

3. _____

_____

11

*Understanding
Definitions
and Explanations*

Before reading the chapter, read the title, the stated objective, and the headings and subheadings. Ask yourself: What is the topic of the chapter? In the space above and beside the chapter number, jot down what you already know about the topic. Then in the space below the number, jot down at least two questions you hope to answer through reading the chapter.

OBJECTIVE

In this chapter, you will develop strategies for reading different kinds of writing, specifically,

1. writing that has as its purpose to define, and
2. writing that has as its purpose to explain.

INTRODUCTION—
READING DEFINITIONS AND EXPLANATIONS

Not all writing communicates the same kinds of meanings. Some sentences within a selection are definitions. In these sentences, an author states the meaning of a word or phrase by giving qualities associated with it. In contrast, some sentences provide explanations, describe something, give an account of what happened, or express opinions.

Reading different kinds of sentences (definitions, explanations, narrations, descriptions, or opinions), you must shift your purpose and your reading strategies. This chapter focuses on strategies for dealing with the first two kinds of writing—definition and explanation. Later chapters deal with the other three kinds.

DEFINITIONS

Some authors use clue words that tell you they are introducing an important term and are going to define it; they connect a term and a definition using such words as *is, means, refers to, is called,* and *is termed.* Authors may print important words in boldface or italics. A basic strategy for recognizing a definition is to watch out for these clue words.

Study the following sentences from *Human Anatomy and Physiology* by John W. Hole, Jr., and identify the clue words that indicate a term is being defined.

1. "*Plasma* is the straw-colored, liquid portion of the blood in which the various solids are suspended."
   - What is the simple clue word that links the term *plasma* with its definition? _____

2. "The term *hemostasis* refers to the stoppage of bleeding, which is vitally important when blood vessels are damaged."
   - What is the clue phrase that links the term *hemostasis* with its definition?

   _____

3. "If a blood clot forms in a vessel abnormally, it is termed a *thrombus.* If the clot becomes dislodged or if a fragment of it breaks loose and is carried away by the blood flow, it is called an *embolus.*"
   - What is the clue phrase that ties the term *thrombus* to its definition?

   _____

   - What is the clue phrase that ties the term *embolus* to its definition?

   _____

Some textbooks place definitions of technical terms in the margin. When that happens, read the margin definition after reading the paragraph that contains the term.

Strategies for Reading Definitions

Because definitions, especially in the natural sciences, tend to be technical, a first strategy for understanding a definition is to reread the definition when you encounter one and try to picture what is being defined in your mind's eye. This process of mental picturing is called *visualizing.* Visualizing is particularly helpful in grasping definitions when you are dealing with concrete objects. In cases where definitions are really complex, you may find it helpful to sketch your mental image on paper.

A second useful strategy is to paraphrase the definition. By paraphrasing, we mean saying it to yourself in your own words. A related strategy is to devise an equation that puts together the term and its definition and write it in the margin of your text. A good check is to compare your equation to the definition in the glossary of the book.

How do these strategies work? Here is an example. Reading the definition of *plasma* just given, you might picture in your mind's eye the straw-colored liquid without its suspended solids. You might paraphrase by saying to yourself, *plasma* is the liquid part of the blood without the solids. You then might build an equation:

Plasma = liquid part of blood without the suspended solids

If you are studying a textbook section on which you will be tested, you might record that equation in your notebook or in the margin of the text. Finally you compare your equation to the glossary definition.

In sum, your strategy for working with a definition includes these steps:

- Look out for clue words that tell you you are dealing with a definition.
- Reread the definition and picture what is being defined in your mind's eye.
- Paraphrase the definition in your own words.
- Devise an equation that includes the term and its definition.
- Record the equation in a vocabulary section of your notebook or in the margin of the text. This strategy is useful if you are studying a textbook for a college course where you must take a test on what you are learning.
- Verify your equation by comparing it to the definition in the glossary of the book.

Reread the other natural science definitions. In your head, state them in your own words. Then write them in equation form in the space provided.

1. Hemostasis = _____

2. Thrombus = _____

3. Embolus = _____

Practicing the Strategy

Preview each short section by noting the heading and the words in italics. Your purpose in reading is to find out the meaning of the highlighted terms.

1. ANATOMY AND PHYSIOLOGY

John W. Hole, Jr.

Anatomy is the branch of science that deals with the structure of body parts, their forms and arrangements. Anatomists observe body parts grossly and microscopically and describe them as accurately and in as much detail as possible. *Physiology,* on the other hand, is concerned with the functions of body parts—what they do and how they do it. Physiologists are interested in finding out how such parts carry on life processes. In addition to using the

same observational techniques as the anatomists, physiologists are likely to conduct experiments and make use of complex laboratory equipment.
[101 words]

a. Reread the definition of *anatomy.* Tell it to yourself in your own words. Then write an equation with the term and the definition.

Anatomy = _____

b. Reread the definition of *physiology,* paraphrase it, and then write an equation with the term and the definition.

Physiology = _____

2. A HYPOTHETICAL CELL

John W. Hole, Jr.

Because cells vary so greatly in size, shape, and function, it is not possible to describe a "typical" cell. However, for purposes of discussion, it is convenient to imagine that one exists. Such a hypothetical cell would contain parts observed in many kinds of cells, even though some of these cells in fact lack parts included in the imagined structure.

Commonly a cell consists of two major parts, one within the other and each surrounded by a thin membrane. The inner portion is called the *cell nucleus,* and it is enclosed by a *nuclear membrane.* A mass of fluid called cytoplasm surrounds the nucleus and is, in turn, encircled by a *cell membrane.*
[119 words]

a. Reread the sentence that begins "Such a hypothetical cell. . . . " What is a hypothetical cell? Now write an equation that defines one.

Hypothetical cell = a cell that _____

b. Picture, or visualize, a hypothetical cell with its two parts and two membranes. Sketch your mental image here. Label the parts.

c. Reread the sentence that includes the term *cell nucleus.* Put together a definition and record it here in equation form:

Cell nucleus = _____

d. Reread the sentence that includes the term *cytoplasm.* Put together a definition and record it here in equation form:

Cytoplasm = _____

e. Reread the sentence that includes *cell membrane.* Tell yourself a definition of the term and record it here in equation form:

Cell membrane = _____

f. Now reread the sentence that includes *nuclear membrane.* Tell yourself a definition of the term and record it here in equation form:

Nuclear membrane = _____

g. Finally, based on your equations, revisualize the cell. Make any changes in the sketch in "b" that you believe to be necessary based on your definitions.

3. THE CELL MEMBRANE

John W. Hole, Jr.

The *cell membrane* is the outermost limit of the living material within a cell. It is extremely thin—visible only with the aid of an electron microscope—but is flexible and somewhat elastic. Although this membrane can seal off minute breaks and heal itself, if it is damaged too greatly the cell contents are likely to escape and the cell will die.

In addition to its function of maintaining the wholeness of the cell, the membrane serves as a gateway through which chemicals enter and leave. However, this "gate" acts in a special way: it allows some substances to pass and excludes others. When a membrane functions in this way, it is said to be *selectively permeable.* A *permeable* membrane, on the other hand, is one that allows all materials to pass through freely.   [140 words]

a. Picture in your mind's eye a selectively permeable membrane. Then paraphrase the definition and write an equation:

Selectively permeable membrane = a membrane that _____

b. Picture in your mind's eye a permeable membrane. Then paraphrase the definition and write an equation:

Permeable membrane = a membrane that _____

SELECTION 1: DIFFUSION AND OSMOSIS (Biology)

Expanding Your Vocabulary for Reading

The word *concentration* in the next selection you will read applies to the amount of matter in a particular area. For example, where there is a high concentration of people, there would be many people in a particular area; where there is a low concentration of people, there would be relatively few there. Each dot in the following diagrams represents one person. Label the diagrams given here to show areas of high and low concentration. Label one high concentration; label the other low concentration.

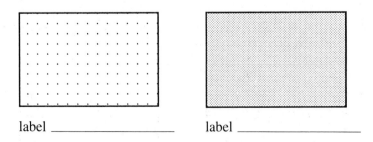

label _____   label _____

A *molecule* is a particle of matter. An *ion* is an electrically charged particle. See if you can figure out the meaning of *haphazard* using context clues as you read.

Getting Ready to Read

Preview the next selection by reading the title and words highlighted by the author.

● What is the topic of the selection? _____

● What do you already know about the topic? To help you answer, think about what happens when you put a teaspoon of sugar into a cup of hot coffee. What

happens to the sugar? _____

_____

Your purpose in reading is to understand the definition of the italicized words.

Reading with Meaning

As you read, apply your reading-for-definition strategy: Record in the margin a sketch of your mental picture of what is going on, an equation that clarifies the definition given at that point in the text, or both. Do not do this after reading the entire passage. Do it as you go along. Read a definition. Stop to visualize, sketch, paraphrase, and write an equation.

Sketch your mental images here. Jot down definition equations as you read. Hint: Write an equation for diffusion. Draw a sketch to show haphazard motion of molecules. Write an equation for osmosis.

DIFFUSION AND OSMOSIS

John W. Hole, Jr.

Diffusion is the process by which molecules or ions scatter or spread from regions where they are in higher concentrations toward regions where they are in lower concentrations. As a rule, this phenomenon involves the movement of molecules or ions in gases or liquids.

Actually, molecules in gases and molecules and ions in body fluids are constantly moving at high speeds. Each of these particles travels in a separate path along a straight line until it collides and bounces off some other particle. Then it moves in another direction, only to collide again and change direction once more. Such motion is haphazard, but it accounts for the mixing of molecules that commonly occurs when different kinds of substances are put together.

For example, if you put some sugar into a glass of water, the sugar will seem to remain at the bottom for a while. Then slowly it disappears into solution. As this happens, the moving water and sugar molecules are colliding haphazardly with one another, and in time the sugar and water molecules will be evenly mixed. This mixing occurs by diffusion—the sugar molecules spread where they are in higher concentration toward the regions where they are less concentrated. Eventually the sugar becomes uniformly distributed in the water. This condition is called *equilibrium.*

Osmosis is a special kind of diffusion. It occurs whenever water molecules diffuse from a region of higher concentration through a selectively permeable membrane, such as a cell membrane.   [259 words]

Checking for Understanding

Select the best response. Refer back to your margin notes to answer.

1. The concentration of a material in an area refers to
   a. the area in which a material is found.
   b. the amount of that material found in a particular area.
   c. the kind of material it is.
   d. the name of the material.
2. The phrase *haphazard motion* as used in this selection means motion that is
   a. orderly.   c. without a pattern or design.
   b. careful.   d. continuous.
3. The process by which molecules or ions move from regions of higher concentrations to regions of lower concentrations is termed
   a. diffusion.   b. equilibrium.   c. osmosis.
4. The process by which water molecules move from regions of higher to regions of lower concentrations across a selectively permeable membrane is called
   a. diffusion.   b. equilibrium.   c. osmosis.
5. The state when a material that is dissolved in another substance becomes uniformly distributed in that substance is known as
   a. diffusion.   b. equilibrium.   c. osmosis.
6. In questions 1 through 5, five different clue words were used to let you know you were dealing with definitions. What are they? Write them here.

   a. _____   d. _____

   b. _____   e. _____

   c. _____

7. What is the purpose of the first sentence in the first paragraph?
   a. to define diffusion   c. to give an opinion of diffusion
   b. to explain diffusion   d. to provide an example of diffusion
8. What is the purpose of the second sentence in the first paragraph?
   a. to elaborate on, or extend, the definition   c. to state the main idea
   b. to give a specific example   d. to give a conclusion
9. Explain what happens when you spray some perfume into the air. Tell a classmate. Use the words *concentration* and *haphazard* in your explanation. Decide if this is an example of diffusion or osmosis. Then together with a classmate, write an explanation in your notebook.

   Before leaving this section, go back and check your answers against the definitions given in the text. This is the same thing you should do when encountering rather difficult terms and definitions in a college text. Remember to make a mental picture for each definition.

SELECTION 2: ENERGY VALUES OF FOOD (Biology)

Expanding Your Vocabulary for Reading

The word *ignited* in the selection means "set on fire." To *oxidize* means "to combine with oxygen." When things burn, they oxidize.

Getting Ready to Read

Preview the following selection by reading the title and italicized terms.

- What is the topic of the selection? _____

- What do you already know about the way we think about the energy value of foods, especially when we are going on a diet? What do you count up when you are on a diet? _____

  _____

- What is your purpose in reading? _____

  _____

Reading with Meaning

As you read, note the italicized words. Visualize where possible and sketch your mental image in the right margin. As you strike a definition, paraphrase it and write an equation in the margin. Do this while reading, not when you finish the entire selection.

Jot equations and mental images here. Hint: Give equations for calorie, large calorie, and bomb calorimeter. Sketch a bomb calorimeter.

ENERGY VALUES OF FOOD

John W. Hole, Jr.

The amount of potential energy contained in a food can be expressed as *calories,* which are units of heat.

Although a *calorie* is commonly defined by a chemist as the amount of heat needed to raise the temperature of a gram of water by one degree Celsius (C), the calorie used in the measurements of food energy is in fact 1,000 times greater. This *large calorie* is equal to the amount of heat needed to raise the temperature of a kilogram (1,000 g.) of water by one degree Celsius (actually from 15 °C to 16 °C). This unit is properly called a *kilocalorie,* but it is customary in nutritional studies to refer to it simply as a "calorie."

The caloric contents of various foods can be determined by using an instrument called a *bomb calorimeter,* which consists of a metal chamber submerged in a known volume of water. The food sample being studied is dried, weighed, and placed inside the metal chamber. The chamber is filled with oxygen gas and is submerged in the water. Then, the food inside is ignited and allowed to oxidize completely. As heat is released from the food, it causes the temperature of the surrounding water to rise, and the change in temperature is noted. Since the volume of the water is known, the amount of heat released from the food sample can be calculated in calories.   [249 words]

Checking for Understanding

Select the best response. You may refer back to your margin notes in making your choice.

1. A chemist defines a *calorie* as the amount of heat needed to raise the temperature of one

a. kilogram of water by one degree Celsius.
b. kilogram of water by 1000 degrees Celsius.
c. gram of water by one degree Celsius.
d. gram of water by 1000 degrees Celsius.

2. A *large calorie* is the amount of heat needed to raise the temperature of one
a. kilogram of water by one degree Celsius.
b. kilogram of water by 1000 degree Celsius.
c. gram of water by one degree Celsius.
d. gram of water by 1000 degrees Celsius.

3. A *kilocalorie* is the amount of heat needed to raise the temperature of one
a. kilogram of water by one degree Celsius.
b. kilogram of water by 1000 degrees Celsius.
c. gram of water by one degree Celsius.
d. gram of water by 1000 degrees Celsius.

4. A *bomb calorimeter* is an instrument for determining
a. the ignition temperature of various foods.
b. the oxidation temperature of various foods.
c. the rise in temperature of foods when burned.
d. the caloric contents of various foods.

5. If you *ignite* a bundle of leaves, you would
a. determine their caloric value.
b. gather them up.
c. set them on fire.
d. put them in a bomb calorimeter.

6. Explain orally to a classmate how scientists determine the calories in a chocolate bar. In your notebook, together write a list of steps that the scientists would use.

SELECTION 3: UNDERSTANDING WHOLE NUMBERS (Mathematics)

Getting Ready to Read

Read the title and the first paragraph. Think briefly about the terms highlighted in bold type.

● What is this selection about? _____

● What do you think you will learn by reading it? _____

_____

Reading with Meaning

Read this selection to learn the meaning of the important mathematical terms used.

UNDERSTANDING WHOLE NUMBERS

Jeffrey Slater

Often we learn a new concept in stages. First comes learning the new *terms* and basic assumptions. Then we have to master the *reasoning,* the logic, behind the new concept. This often goes hand in hand with learning a method for using the idea. Finally, we can move quickly with a *shortcut.*

For example, in the study of stock investments, you must learn the meaning of such terms as *stock, profit, loss,* and *commission* before tackling the question "What is my profit from this stock transaction?" After you learn how to answer this question, you can quickly answer many similar ones.

You can watch your understanding of mathematics grow through this same process. Consider whole numbers. The ideas associated with the whole numbers can be so familiar that you have already jumped to the "shortcut" stage. But with a little patience in looking at the terms, reasoning, and step-by-step methods, you'll find your understanding deepens, even with these very familiar numbers, the whole numbers.

To count a number of objects or to answer the question "How many?" we use a set of numbers called **whole numbers.** These whole numbers are as follows:

$$0, 1, 2, 3, 4, 5, 6, 7, 8, 9, 10, 11, 12, 13, 14, 15, \ldots$$

There is no largest whole number. The three dots . . . indicate that the set of whole numbers goes on indefinitely. Our number system is based on tens and ones and is called the decimal system (or the base 10 system). The numbers 0, 1, 2, 3, 4, 5, 6, 7, 8, 9 are called **digits.** The position, or placement, of the digits in the number tells the value of the digits. For example, in the number 521, the "5" means 5 hundreds (500). In the number 54, the "5" means 5 tens, or fifty. For this reason, our number system is called a **place-value** system.

Consider the number 5643. The four digits are located in four places that are called, from right to left, the ones, tens, hundreds, and thousands place. By looking at the digits and their places, we see that in the number 5643

- the 5 means "5 thousands."
- the 6 means "6 hundreds."
- the 4 means "4 tens," or "forty."
- the 3 means "3 ones."

The *value* of the number is 5 thousand, 6 hundred, 4 tens, 3 ones.

To indicate the value of even greater numbers we can use the following diagram, which shows the names of even more places.

Hundred millions	Ten millions	Millions	Hundred thousands	Ten thousands	Thousands	Hundreds	Tens	Ones

Checking Your Understanding

1. Write equations for each of the following terms. Check the selection as you write.

reasoning =

whole number =

digit =

place-value system =

2. Following the step-by-step method outlined in the article, what does the number 97210 mean?

 ● the 9 means _____

 ● the 7 means _____

 ● the 2 means _____

 ● the 1 means _____

 ● the 0 means _____

3. What is the value of 97210? _____

EXPLANATIONS

As you may have discovered from the selections you just read, definition and explanation go hand in hand; having defined a term, the author moves on to explain it. This happens in the selection on diffusion and osmosis when Hole defines *diffusion* and then explains what happens when the molecules and ions in body fluids travel, collide, and bounce off one another. As Hole explains, haphazard molecular motion of this kind "accounts for the mixing of molecules that commonly occurs when different kinds of substances are put together."

What Is Involved in Reading Explanations

In explaining, an author tells why or how, illustrates with an example, states the conditions under which something happens, clarifies relationships, compares, contrasts, and generalizes. Clues that help you figure out that an author is explaining are words like:

 ● *one, two,* and *three,* that indicate the number of items to be discussed or the steps in a sequence of events.
 ● *for example* and *such as,* that indicate an example.
 ● *also* and *furthermore,* that indicate a continuation of the idea and *but* and *however,* that indicate ideas in opposition.
 ● *similarly* and *on the other hand,* that indicate a comparison/contrast.
 ● *if/then* and *consequently,* that indicate a condition/effect relationship.
 ● *because* and *for this reason,* that indicate a cause/effect relationship.

See Chapter 6 for a full discussion of how to use these clue words to anticipate the direction in which an author is taking you.

The first component of a strategy for reading to understand explanations is to attend to these clue words. Take a moment to reread Selections 1 and 2. As you do, circle the clue words that help you follow the author's explanation and think about what those words are telling you.

A second component is visualizing, or picturing in your mind's eye, what the author is explaining. This is useful when the explanation is about something very concrete. For example, if a passage is explaining how food is digested in the digestive tract, as you read, you might visualize that tract: mouth, esophagus, stomach, small and large intestines, rectum, and associated organs. You hold that picture in your mind, relating what the passage is saying at any one point to the appropriate part of your visual image. Or, if there is a diagram in the text, you refer to it, following the diagram as you read the text.

A third component of a strategy for reading explanations is talking to yourself in your head or (when the passage presents tough ideas) talking to yourself out loud. We call this "thinking along" or "thinking aloud." Here is a really complex passage by John W. Hole, Jr., followed by a *think along*. The think along demonstrates the kinds of thoughts that might come to the mind of a student who is encountering the material for the first time.

To illustrate how diffusion accounts for the movement of various molecules through a cell membrane, let us imagine a container of water that is separated into two compartments by a permeable membrane (Figure 11.1). This membrane has numerous pores that are large enough for water and sugar molecules to pass through. Sugar molecules are placed in one compartment (A) but not in the other (B). As a result of diffusion, we can predict that although the sugar molecules are moving in all directions, more will spread from compartment A (where they are in greater concentration) through the pores in the membrane and into compartment B (where they are in lesser concentration) than will move in the other direction. At the same time, water molecules will tend to diffuse from compartment B (where they are in greater concentration) through the pores into compartment A (where they are in lesser concentration). Eventually, equilibrium will be achieved when there are equal numbers of water and sugar molecules in each compartment.

The Think Along—What Might Go On in Your Head as You Read

"To illustrate" . . . oh, the author is going to give an example. . . . This example shows how different molecules move through a membrane. . . . There is this beaker divided into two parts . . . with a permeable membrane between. . . . I remember about permeable membranes. . . . They let anything through.

"This membrane has pores" . . . There are pores . . . tiny holes . . . like in the skin. These are big ones that let both water and sugar go through to the other side.

From the diagram I can see that they put water and sugar in compartment A but only water in compartment B . . . "As a result of diffusion". . . . What is going to happen? . . . Let's see. There are no sugar molecules in

Figure 11.1   *Diffusion of Molecules Through a Membrane*

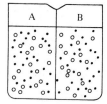

compartment B. . . . There are more water molecules in compartment B than in compartment A. What will happen? . . . I bet the sugar will move from A to B. . . . The water will go from B to A . . . through the pores . . . from areas of high concentration to areas of low concentration . . . through diffusion. . . .

I can see the sugar moving. . . . I'll add arrows to the picture in Figure 11.1 to show the sugar moving from left to right.

There is equilibrium at the end . . . eventually . . . takes time . . . Equilibrium means the same number of water molecules in both compartments . . . same number of sugar molecules in both compartments. . . . This is an example of diffusion. . . .

Reading a very complicated explanation such as this one, you do not just read the words. You must verbalize and visualize the ideas, expressing them in your own words and perhaps in a diagram of your own making. You must relate what is in the passage to what you already know on the topic. Especially helpful is to compare what is stated to something similar; say to yourself, "This is like . . ." (as in the reference to the skin in the think along). You must also constantly predict based on what you already know on the topic and what you already have read. You say to yourself, "I bet. . . ."

In talking to yourself in your head or out loud, you should avoid using vague phrases. Do not just use "this stuff" or "that part." Use, instead, the terms you are learning—in this case, *diffusion, concentration,* and *equilibrium.* Using the terms as you think about the selection reinforces your understanding of them.

In thinking about a passage as you read, you should also raise questions. Examples from the think along are the questions "What is going to happen?" and "What will happen?"

Strategies for Reading Explanations

In summary, here are strategies for reading explanations. They are not steps to be applied in sequence. They are strategies to be applied in the order that best serves your reading purpose.

1. Use clue words (such as *for example, if/then*) to predict where the writer is going and what he or she is going to do.
2. Visualize in your mind's eye what is being explained. Make a sketch if you believe that will clarify the explanation. Refer to the visuals in the text while reading a related explanation.
3. Think along (or talk to yourself aloud or in your head):
   a. Paraphrase the explanation, drawing on what you already know and using any technical vocabulary you know.
   b. Make comparisons between things explained and similar things you know about.
   c. Predict as you read, saying to yourself, "I bet. . . ." Try to keep ahead of the writer and anticipate what he or she is saying.
   d. Ask yourself questions as you read.
   e. Answer your own questions or ones that the author raises in the text. Do this as you read.
4. Reread to clarify points.

In the following sections of this chapter, you will have the opportunity to practice these strategies.

SELECTION 4: PAVLOV'S CONDITIONING EXPERIMENTS
(Experimental Psychology)

Expanding Your Vocabulary for Reading

Use context and word-structure clues to figure out the meaning of each italicized word. Check the glossary to verify your hypotheses. Write the meaning of each term in the margin. Be ready to tell how you deciphered the meaning of the terms.

1. He always had a stomachache after eating because his *digestive* juices were not working as they should.
2. Whenever I see and smell a pizza, I begin to *salivate.* I simply drool in anticipation.
3. The scientist *devised* a way to overcome the effects of that hormone. The procedure she invented was cheered around the world for its lifesaving potential.
4. My receiving a low grade on the test was the *stimulus* that made me settle down and study for the course.
5. The president took a *neutral* position—neither positive nor negative.
6. The judge's entrance into the court was the *cue* for all those in the room to rise.

In the article, you will encounter the word *conditioning.* Conditioning is a scientific term that refers to a form of learning. It is used in reference to the "acquiring of fairly specific patterns of behaviors in the presence of well-defined stimuli." You might say, "I was conditioned at an early age to pick up my belongings before leaving the house. Each day my father made sure I did this before I was allowed to go out."

Getting Ready to Read

Read the title and the subheadings of this section from a college psychology text. Look at the diagram.

- What is the topic of the piece? _____
- What do you already know about conditioning? Can you think of a situation in which you were conditioned to do something? Describe it here. _____

  _____

  _____

- What do you think you might learn from reading the selection given the fact that it is from a psychology text? _____

  _____

  _____

Reading with Meaning

As you read this selection, record in the margin your thoughts while reading. Your think along can include rephrasing ideas in your own words, relating a point to something you already know, asking and answering questions, predicting before the authors make a point, and visualizing by sketching. If you prefer, you may work with a friend and tell him or her your thoughts even as you read the selection paragraph by paragraph together. You may also want to underline words expressing the main idea of each paragraph.

　The names and dates set within parentheses refer to the researchers who proposed the theories and the years they presented their ideas.

PAVLOV'S CONDITIONING EXPERIMENTS

Charles Morris

Write your thoughts here as you read each paragraph.

Classical conditioning was discovered almost by accident by Ivan Pavlov (1849–1936), a Russian physiologist who was studying the digestive processes. Since animals salivate when food is placed in their mouths, Pavlov inserted tubes into the salivary glands of dogs in order to measure how much saliva they produced when they were given food. He noticed, however, that the dogs salivated before the food was in their mouths: The mere sight of food made them drool. In fact, they even drooled at the sound of the experimenter's footsteps. This aroused Pavlov's curiosity. What was making the dogs salivate even before they had the food in their mouths? How had they learned to salivate in response to the sound of the experimenter's approach?

Pavlov's Experiment

In order to answer these questions, Pavlov set out to teach the dogs to salivate when food was not present. He devised an experiment in which he sounded a bell just before the food was brought into the room. A ringing bell does not usually make a dog's mouth water, but after hearing the bell many times just before getting fed, Pavlov's dogs began to salivate as soon as the bell rang. It was as if they had learned that the bell signaled the appearance of food, and their mouths watered on cue even if no food followed. The dogs had been conditioned to salivate in response to a new stimulus, the bell, which would not normally have caused that response (Pavlov, 1927).

The Elements of Classical Conditioning

Generally speaking, *classical conditioning* involves learning to transfer a natural response from one stimulus to another, previously neutral stimulus. Pavlov's experiment illustrates the four basic elements of classical conditioning. The first is an *unconditioned stimulus (US),* like food, which invariably causes a certain reaction—salivation, in this case. That reaction—*the unconditioned response (UR)*—is the second element and always results from the unconditioned stimulus: Whenever the dog is given food (US), its mouth waters (UR). The third element is the neutral stimulus—in this case, the ringing of the bell—which is called the *conditioned stimulus (CS).* At first, the conditioned stimulus does not bring about the desired response. Dogs do not normally salivate at the sound of a bell—unless they have been conditioned to react in this way. Such a reaction is the fourth element in the classical conditioning process: the *conditioned response (CR).* The conditioned response is the behavior that the animal has learned to

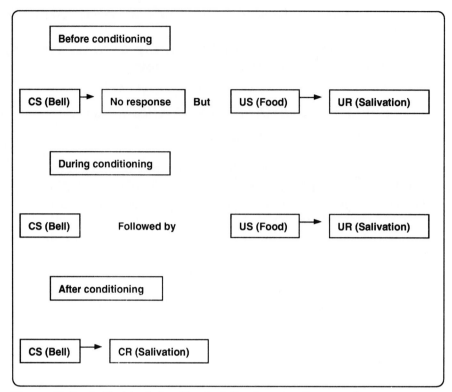

Figure 11.2 *A Model of the Classical Conditioning Process. An arrow means "results in."*

produce in response to the conditioned stimulus. Usually, the unconditioned response—salivation, in our example—and the conditioned response are basically the same. (See Figure 11.2).

Without planning to do so, you may have conditioned your own pet in a way very similar to Pavlov's experiments. Many cats and dogs come running at the sound of a can opener or a certain cupboard door, rubbing around their owner's legs, looking in the dishes in which they are fed, or otherwise preparing for the food that they have learned to associate with particular sounds or activities.

Checking Your Understanding

Answer the questions by writing in the space provided.

1. What did Pavlov observe about dogs' salivation that aroused his curiosity?

   _____

   _____

   _____

2. What did Pavlov condition his dogs to do? _____

   _____

3. How did Pavlov go about conditioning his dogs? In other words, what were the

   steps in his experiment? _____

_____

_____

4. Interpreting definitions is important in understanding explanations. Write equations for the following scientific terms found in the selection.

   a. unconditioned stimulus = _____

   b. conditioned stimulus = _____

   c. unconditioned response = _____

   d. conditioned response = _____

5. Explain why cats and dogs come running when they hear the sound of a can opener. Use the terms *conditioned response* and *conditioned stimulus* in your

   answer. _____

   _____

   _____

Vocabulary Review

Select the word from the list that best completes each sentence.

a. devised   c. cue   e. salivate

b. digestive   d. neutral   f. stimulus

1. I have a very sensitive _____ tract. I get indigestion very easily.

2. Sometimes I _____ so much that I start to drool.

3. Totaling his car was the _____ that made him finally change his driving habits.

4. President Wilson _____ a plan for a world organization that would monitor relations among member states.

5. The stage manager gave the actor a _____ when it was time for her to say her lines.

6. Switzerland remained _____ during World War II. It did not join forces with either side in the combat.

SELECTION 5: CLASSICAL CONDITIONING IN HUMAN BEINGS (Experimental Psychology)

Expanding Your Vocabulary for Reading

Use context and word-structure clues to figure out the meaning of each italicized word. Check the glossary to verify your hypothesis. Write the meaning in the margin. Be ready to tell how you deciphered the meaning of the term.

1. The professor *paired* the students according to their interests. He placed together two students who were interested in investigating the same phenomenon.

2. On each *successive* trial, the athlete did better than he had done previously.

3. My friend is an *asthmatic*. He is allergic to many things and has trouble breathing when in the presence of those things.

4. The governor got himself into a *seemingly* impossible situation. It appeared as if there was no way to resolve the difficulty.

5. Because of her parents' actions, the girl *associated* marriage with fighting. As a result she never married.

Getting Ready to Read

Read the title and the name of the author. Quickly read the subheads.

● What is this selection about? _____

● How does the topic of the selection differ from the topic of the selection that you just read? _____

● What do you now know about conditioning? Can you think of a situation in which you were conditioned to do something? Describe it here. _____

_____

_____

● What do you think you might learn from reading the selection?

_____

_____

Reading with Meaning

As you read, record your thoughts in the margin. Your think along can include rephrasing ideas in your own words, relating a point to something you already know, asking and answering questions, predicting before the author makes a point, and visualizing by sketching.

Write your thoughts here as you read each paragraph.

CLASSICAL CONDITIONING IN HUMAN BEINGS

Charles Morris

So far, we have been focusing on classical conditioning in animals, but humans respond to these same principles. For example, the sight of a menu, the sound of silverware being placed on the dinner table, the ring of the oven timer signaling that a favorite casserole is ready to be served—all of these can cause a hungry person to salivate.

You may also be subject to classical conditioning any time that you watch a television commercial or read a magazine advertisement. Consumer researchers have demonstrated that pairing pleasant or unpleasant music with pictures of a product can lead us to prefer that product even when competing products are otherwise basically the same (Gorn, 1982).

Classical Conditioning in Babies

Classical conditioning can even be used to teach newborn infants. Babies who are only 5 to 10 days old can learn to blink their eyes when they hear a tone (Lipsitt, 1971). Babies blink naturally when a puff of air is blown in their eyes. The puff of air is an unconditioned stimulus. Blinking—the babies' natural reaction—is an unconditioned response. If a tone—a conditioned stimulus—is sounded just before the puff of air is blown into their eyes, the babies soon begin to blink their eyes whenever they hear the tone. By blinking as soon as they hear the tone, the babies are producing a conditioned response.

Strange Kinds of Learning

Classical conditioning can also result in some strange kinds of learning. For example, one group of experimenters conditioned a group of asthma sufferers to react to substances that had not previously affected them. They first exposed the asthmatics to something to which they were allergic, like dust or pollen—an unconditioned stimulus. Of course, the dust or pollen caused an attack of asthma (an unconditioned stimulus). Then the experimenters presented a neutral substance (a conditioned stimulus). Initially, the asthmatics had no reaction to the neutral substance. But when the neutral substance was repeatedly followed by dust or pollen, the asthma sufferers began to wheeze and sniffle as soon as the neutral substance was presented. These attacks were conditioned responses: The subjects had to *learn* to react in this way. In one study, even a picture of the conditioned stimulus could trigger an attack of asthma (Dekker, Pelser, & Groen, 1957). This study and others like it help to explain why asthma attacks are sometimes brought on by such seemingly neutral events as hearing the national anthem, seeing a waterfall, or listening to a political speech.

Well-Known Examples of Conditioning in Humans

One of the best-known examples of classical conditioning in humans is the case of John Watson's experiment with Little Albert, an 11-month-old boy (Watson & Rayner, 1920). The experimenters started by showing Albert a white rat. At first, the child displayed no fear. He crawled toward the rat and wanted to play with it. But every time he approached the rat, the experimenters made a loud noise by striking a steel bar. Since nearly all children are afraid of loud noises, Albert's natural reaction was fear. After just a few times, Albert began to cry and crawl away whenever he saw the rat. This is a simple case of classical conditioning. An unconditioned stimulus—the loud noise—caused the unconditioned response of fear. Next Albert learned to associate the loud noise with the rat, so that the rat (conditioned stimulus) then caused him to be afraid (conditioned response).

Several years later, psychologist Mary Cover Jones demonstrated a method by which children's fears can be unlearned using classical conditioning (Jones, 1924). Her subject was Peter, a 3-year-old boy who, like Little Albert, had a fear of white rats. Jones paired the sight of a rat with a pleasant experience—eating ice cream, Peter's favorite dessert. While Peter sat alone in a room, a caged white rat was brought in and placed far enough away so that he would not be frightened. At this point, Peter was given plenty of ice cream to eat. On each successive day of the experiment, the cage was moved closer and was followed by ice cream, until eventually Peter was not afraid of the rat. In this case, eating ice cream (US) elicited a pleasant response (UR). By pairing the ice cream with the sight of the rat (CS), Jones was able to teach Peter to respond with pleasure (CR) when the rat was present. [736 words]

Checking Your Understanding

Answer the questions as directed.

1. Fill in the blanks.

   Babies blink naturally when a jet of air is puffed into their eyes. In this case, blinking in newborns is a/an _____ response, and the jet of air is a/an _____ stimulus. If a bell is sounded just before the jet of air is puffed into babies' eyes, the babies soon _____ at the sound of the bell. We can say that those babies have been _____ to blink. In this case the conditioned stimulus is the _____; the conditioned response is _____.

2. Tell yourself what the experimenter did and what happened in the Little Albert conditioning experiment. Then on the lines provided, write the names of the unconditioned stimulus, the unconditioned response, the conditioned stimulus, and the conditioned response that were used in the experiment.

   a. Before the conditioning of Little Albert, the unconditioned stimulus, or the _____, caused the unconditioned response, or _____.

   b. Before the conditioning, the conditioned stimulus, or the _____, produced no response.

   c. After the conditioning, the conditioned stimulus, or the _____, produced the conditioned response, _____.

3. Now tell yourself what happened in the experiment conducted by Jones using Peter as the subject. Then write down the steps in the experiment.

   _____

   _____

   _____

4. Are you afraid of something that you wish you were not afraid of? Think about how you may have developed that irrational fear. Then write down a guess, or hypothesis, that may account for your irrational fear. _____

   _____

   _____

5. Suppose you wanted to cure yourself of an irrational fear. Based on what you now know about classical conditioning, what might be a good way of going about

curing your fear? Write your plan of action here. _____

_____

_____

Vocabulary Review

Select the word from the list that best completes each sentence.

a. associate   c. paired   e. successive

b. asthmatic   d. seemingly

1. In the experiment, the investigator _____ an unpleasant stimulus with a pleasant one. By putting the two together, the investigator was able to help her subject overcome an irrational fear.

2. The _____ had an allergic reaction to seafood. The reaction was so severe that the man almost died.

3. The astronaut performed a _____ impossible task by using her last reserves of energy.

4. I always _____ love with marriage. As the old song says, "They go together like a horse and carriage."

5. On each _____ day, the student studied more and more and got higher and higher grades on his quizzes.

SELECTION 6: DAYDREAMING (Psychology)

Expanding Your Vocabulary for Reading

Use context and word-structure clues to figure out the meaning of each italicized word. Check the glossary to verify your hypothesis. Write the meaning in the margin. Be ready to tell how you got the meaning.

1. The *protagonist* in a story or play is the leading character. Opposing him or her is the *antagonist,* the source of conflict in the story.

2. Long John Silver is the *arch* villain of *Treasure Island.* In the story he is cunning and shrewd.

3. As people grow older, they tend to *reminisce* about times gone by; in other words, they enjoy thoughts of what they did in earlier days.

4. He lived a *humdrum* existence, with little variation and almost no excitement to break his everyday, ordinary activity.

In the article you will encounter the term *ASC.* These initials stand for altered states of consciousness, or mental states in which people's thoughts and feelings differ noticeably from those that occur when they are fully awake and reasonably alert. Some altered states are sleeping, dreaming, and daydreaming.

Getting Ready to Read

Read the title and the source of the article. Skim the first paragraph.

● What is the selection about? _____

● Do you daydream? When do you daydream? What do you daydream about? Tell a classmate about your daydreams. Then together make an idea web in which you record the ideas and words that come to mind when you think about your daydreams.

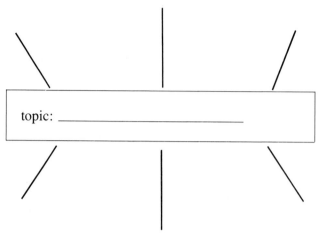

topic: _____

● What do you think you might learn from reading the selection given the fact that

it is from a psychology text? _____

_____

_____

Reading with Meaning

As you read, record in the margin your thoughts while reading. Your think along can include rephrasing ideas in your own words, relating a point to something you already know, asking and answering questions, predicting before the author makes a point, and visualizing by sketching. If you prefer, you may work with a friend and tell him or her your thoughts as you read the selection together. You may also want to underline words expressing the main idea of each paragraph.

Write your thoughts here
as you read each
paragraph.

DAYDREAMING

Charles Morris

1. In James Thurber's book *The Secret Life of Walter Mitty,* the protagonist mentally departs from his humdrum daily existence for a series of fantastic and heroic ventures. In the comic strip "Peanuts," Snoopy is well known for his imaginary adventures as the arch rival of the Red Baron. A college student sitting in psychology class may actually be lost in thoughts of summer sun and fun on the beach. Although it requires deliberate effort to enter an ASC via hypnosis, drugs, or meditation, *daydreaming* is an ASC that occurs seemingly without effort.

2. Typically, daydreaming occurs when you would rather be somewhere else or be doing something else—escaping from the demands of the real world for a moment. You may reminisce pleasantly about last year's vacation or leave the daily college grind behind and fantasize about your future as a business tycoon. And sometimes, as in the case of Walter

Mitty or Snoopy, you may project yourself into fantastic, unlikely adventures. Daydreams provide the opportunity to write, act in, and stage manage a private drama for which you are the only audience.

3. Although daydreaming may seem to be a random and effortless process, psychologists have discovered that people's daydreams tend to fall into a few distinct patterns and that different people tend to prefer different kinds of dreams (Singer, 1975). People who score high on measures of anxiety tend to have fleeting, loosely connected daydreams related to worrying. They take little pleasure in their daydreams. In contrast, people who are strongly achievement oriented tend to have daydreams that concern achievement, guilt, fear of failure, and hostility. These dreams often reflect the self-doubt and competitive envy that accompany great ambition. Still other people derive considerable enjoyment from their daydreams and use them to solve problems, think ahead, or distract themselves. These "happy daydreamers" tend to have pleasant fantasies uncomplicated by guilt or worry. And finally, some daydreamers display unusual curiosity about their environment and place great emphasis on objective thinking. These people tend to have daydreams whose contents are closely related to the objective world and are marked by controlled lines of thought.

4. Intelligence, as well as personality, also affects our daydreaming. One group of researchers discovered that intellectually gifted adolescents—those who have experienced considerable academic success—tend to have daydreams with less guilt and fear of failure than their less gifted peers.

5. If daydreaming is nearly universal, does it serve any useful function? Can Walter Mitty justify his fantasies on a practical basis? Some psychologists argue that daydreams have little or no positive or practical value. These psychologists hold that daydreams are essentially a retreat from the real world that occurs when inner needs cannot be expressed in actual behavior. We daydream, they claim, when the world outside does not meet our needs or when we want to do something but cannot; they suspect that the daydream may actually substitute for more direct and effective behavior.

6. By contrast, other psychologists have stressed the positive value of daydreaming and fantasy. Freudian theorists have traditionally held that daydreams allow us to express and deal with various desires, generally about sex or hostility, that would otherwise make us feel guilty or anxious (Gaimbra, 1974). And Pulaski (1974) suggests that daydreaming can build cognitive and creative skills and help people survive difficult situations. For example, it is difficult to imagine an artist or writer succeeding without an active fantasy life. Pulaski notes that daydreaming has also helped prisoners of war survive torture and deprivation. Her view suggests that daydreaming and fantasy can provide welcome relief from everyday—often

unpleasant—reality and can reduce internal tension and external aggression.

7. Singer goes one step further in proposing that daydreams are not just a substitute for reality or a form of tension-relief, but an important part of our ability to process information. Singer suggests that during the daytime, as we process the vast, potentially overwhelming array of information received through our senses, we single out some of the material for later review and further processing during quieter moments when we have less to do. When the opportunity arises—perhaps during a dull moment—we rework some of this information and transform it into new and more useful forms. Daydreams and dreams provide a window through which we can watch this process of dealing with "unfinished business." In the long run, then, although daydreaming temporarily distracts us from the real world, Singer believes that it also allows us to take care of important unfinished business so that we are in fact *better* able to cope with our environment when the pace of real-world activity quickens again.   [772 words]

Checking Your Understanding—Part I

Reread the selection. Jot in the margin any more thoughts that come to your mind as you reread. Or listen to a friend do a think along. As you listen to him or her read and verbalize aloud, write any new thoughts in the margin. Remember to keep paraphrasing as you read.

Now talk to a classmate about the ideas in the selection. Answer these questions together as you refer back to your margin jottings. Then together write down your explanations.

1. Why do people daydream?

2. Do all people have the same kinds of daydreams? Explain your answer.

3. What kinds of daydreams do you tend to have? Use the categories of daydreams from paragraph 3 to categorize your own dreams.

4. Explain the functions that daydreams serve, according to different researchers.

5. What is Freud's view of daydreams?

6. What is Singer's view of daydreams?

7. How does Morris's discussion of daydreaming differ from the selections on dreams you read in Chapter 10?

Checking Your Understanding of Main and Supporting Ideas—Part II

Refer back to the selection as you answer and collaborate with a classmate. These questions are more difficult than some you have been asked to do; they are similar to questions on some standardized reading tests.

1. The main idea of the first paragraph is that
   a. the protagonist in the Thurber book departs from reality to have a series of imaginary ventures.
   b. ASC means altered state of consciousness.
   c. daydreaming occurs seemingly without effort.
   d. it requires deliberate effort to enter ASC via hypnosis, drugs, or meditation.
2. An example that supports the main idea in paragraph 1 is
   a. the protagonist in the Thurber book departs from reality to have a series of imaginary ventures.
   b. ASC means altered state of consciousness.
   c. daydreaming occurs seemingly without effort.
   d. it requires deliberate effort to enter ASC via hypnosis, drugs, or meditation.
3. Which of the following statements presents a contrast to the main idea?
   a. The protagonist in the Thurber book departs from reality to have a series of imaginary ventures.
   b. ASC means altered state of consciousness.
   c. Daydreaming occurs seemingly without effort.
   d. It requires deliberate effort to enter ASC via hypnosis, drugs, or meditation.
4. Review paragraph 3. Which sentence states the main idea?
   a. Sentence 1   c. The next to last sentence
   b. Sentence 2   d. The last sentence
5. In the remaining sentences in paragraph 3, the author
   a. explains the patterns into which people's dreams fall.
   b. explains when daydreams occur.
   c. explains the function of daydreams.
   d. defines daydreaming.
6. In paragraph 3, the purpose of the third sentence is to
   a. state the main idea.
   b. elaborate on the idea stated in the previous sentence.
   c. give examples relative to the idea stated in the previous sentence.
   d. provide an opinion.
7. In paragraph 4, the phrase "those who have experienced considerable academic success" refers to
   a. daydreamers.
   b. a group of researchers.
   c. intellectually gifted adolescents.
   d. daydreamers who have less fear of failure.
8. The main idea of paragraph 6 is stated in
   a. the first sentence.
   b. the last sentence.

c. one of the middle sentences.

d. none of the above—the main idea is unstated.

9. The second sentence in paragraph 6 provides

a. a definition important in the paragraph.

b. an example in support of the idea in the first sentence of the paragraph.

c. an unrelated detail.

10. The main idea of the last paragraph is that

a. daydreaming is a substitute for reality.

b. daydreaming is a form of tension-relief.

c. daydreaming is an important part of our ability to process information.

11. What view of dreams is given in the last paragraph?

a. Dreams serve little or no practical value.

b. Dreams have a positive value.

c. Dreams have a negative effect on our mental health.

12. The word *us* is used throughout the selection. To whom does it refer?

a. psychologists   c. the author of the selection

b. scientific researchers   d. people in general

13. In the space provided, write down four words from the selection that were key ones in helping you see relationships among ideas within it. Record what meaning you made with each word you select. One example is given as a model.

Word	Meaning
a. *And finally,*	tells that the author is dealing with the last kind of dream.

b.

c.

d.

e.

Summarizing to Increase Comprehension

Research suggests that writing a summary of a passage you have read increases your understanding of what you have read. In your notebook, write a short paragraph in which you sum up the way people use daydreams. The best way to summarize is to start with a sentence that gives the main idea of the complete passage. Then write several sentences that give key details. Use the idea map in Figure 11.3 to plot the main idea and supporting ideas before writing.

Vocabulary Review

Select the word from the list that best completes each sentence.

a. antagonist   c. humdrum   e. reminisce

b. arch   d. protagonist

1. Although I knew I should root for the hero, I could not help but feel sorry for the

   _____.

2. The _____ in the story, the hero, succeeded only after many attempts.

3. By the end of the story his _____ enemy had become his friend.

4. As part of our daydreams, we sometimes _____ about times gone by.

5. Life for him was _____ because he had nothing to break the dullness of his existence.

Figure 11.3 *An Idea Map to Plot Relationships for a Summary before Writing One. First, identify the thesis of the entire selection. Next, identify the supporting ideas. Record the thesis in the top box and the supporting ideas in the connecting boxes. Then use your idea map to write a summary paragraph that includes those points.*

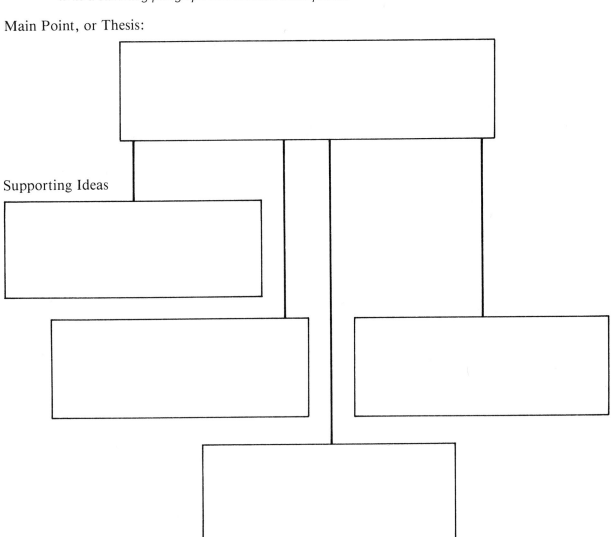

Main Point, or Thesis:

Supporting Ideas

EXTENDING WHAT YOU HAVE LEARNED

Reviewing Strategies for Reading Explanations

List here at least four things you can do as you read explanations to increase your comprehension.

1. _____

2. _____

3. _____

4. _____

Applying the Strategies for Reading Explanations

Read an explanation of some phenomenon in a natural or social science textbook. As you read, apply the strategies for reading explanations as we outlined on page 245. Jot the name of the book and the pages you read on an index card. On the card, list some of the thoughts that came to your mind as you read. Be ready in class to explain orally the phenomenon you read about.

Reviewing the Chapter Vocabulary

Reread the chapter words and the brief definitions given with them. Then select the word from the list that best fits the context of each of the sentences. Add several of these words to your personal vocabulary list.

a.	anatomy	study of the structure of body parts
b.	avid	eager
c.	calorie	a unit of heat often used to indicate the energy value of foods
d.	camouflaged	protected by blending with the environment
e.	concentration	amount of material in an area
f.	diffusion	movement of material from areas of high to areas of low concentration
g.	embryo	the young form of an organism before birth
h.	evolved	changed slowly over time
i.	haphazard	random, or by chance
j.	ignite	set on fire
k.	nucleus	inner portion of the cell, or the core of something
l.	oxidize	combine with oxygen
m.	physiology	study of the way the body functions
n.	plasma	liquid portion of the blood
o.	predators	ones who live by killing and eating others, by preying on others
p.	protagonist	the leading character in a play, the leader of a cause, the opposite of the antagonist
q.	reminisce	think about the past

1. He held a match to the twigs to _____ them.

2. When matter combines with oxygen, it is said to _____.

3. The tiny _____ already resembled its adult parent in many respects.

4. The animal panicked when it realized it was surrounded by _____, which were intent on making a kill.

5. The bird was _____ by its feathers, which allowed it to blend with its surroundings.

6. He was an _____ physiologist. He worked twelve hours a day in his laboratory, conducting experiments on cell functioning.

7. There was such a high _____ of moths in that area that there was not enough food for them.

8. His activity was _____; it was without order or pattern.

9. Chemists define a _____ differently from the way dieters do.

10. Clark is interested in studying the structure of body parts, or what is known as _____. In contrast, Karin is interested in studying the functioning of the body, or _____.

11. The core part of the cell is the _____.

12. His idea slowly _____ over time; by the time he announced it to the world, it was far different from when he began.

13. During the Renaissance, there was a general _____ of ideas—a movement of those ideas from where they originated across most of Europe.

14. As the ex-president got older, he would _____ about the important things that happened during his presidency.

15. Laurence Olivier played the role of the _____ in the play. He took the lead because of the strength of his past performances.

12

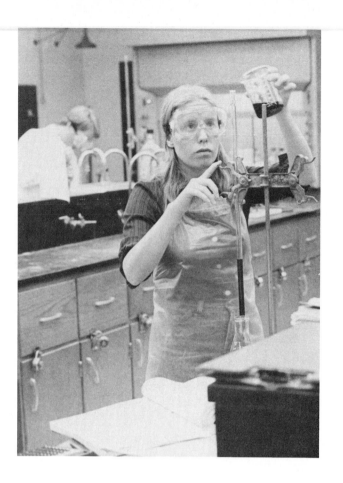

Understanding Descriptions and Narratives

Before reading the chapter, read the title, the stated objective, and the headings and subheadings. What is the topic of the chapter? In the space above and beside the chapter number, jot down what you already know about the topic. Then in the space below the number, jot down at least two questions you hope to answer through reading the chapter.

OBJECTIVE

In this chapter, you will develop strategies for reading descriptions and narratives. Specifically, you will learn to

1. visualize when reading descriptions and narratives;
2. interpret metaphors and similes and create comparisons of your own;
3. grasp sequences and chronology;
4. identify causes of events and influential factors in narratives;
5. compare events and lives to others you know; and
6. get at the ultimate meaning of events and lives.

INTRODUCTION— READING DESCRIPTIONS AND NARRATIVES

Authors write with different purposes in mind. As discussed in Chapter 11, an author's purpose may be to define or explain. In any one paragraph, an author may include statements of definition and explanation, moving from one to the other as the topic demands. The author first may define her terms and then explain relationships.

At other times and sometimes within the same selection, authors write with the intent to describe or to give an account of something. The first kind of writing is *description,* the second, *narrative.* This chapter focuses on these two kinds of writing.

DESCRIPTION

In a description, a writer uses words to paint a picture of something—a person, a scene, or even a feeling. In describing, the writer tells the most significant features, or attributes, of the "thing" he or she is talking about.

Descriptions range from very precise to very creative. In science, descriptions tend to be exact, as when an author describes some apparatus or a particular organism. Descriptions in poetry are more imaginative. In general, descriptions do not occur alone; they blend with definitions and explanations.

A strategy for reading descriptions includes (1) visualizing in your mind what the author is describing, and (2) relating what the author is describing to something you know.

Reading Descriptions

Read the following description of Walden Pond written by Henry David Thoreau in the 1800s. The word *exclusively* as Thoreau uses it means "not including anything else." The *circumference* is "the distance around." As you read, pretend your mind is a camera and take a picture of the pond with it. At the same time in the margin, write phrases that help you snap a picture, or visualize, it in your mind.

WALDEN POND

Henry David Thoreau

Walden Pond is a clear and deep green well, half a mile long and a mile and three quarters in circumference, and contains about sixty-one acres; a perennial spring in the midst of pine and oak woods, without any visible inlet or outlet except by the clouds and evaporation. The surrounding hills rise abruptly from the water to the height of forty to eighty feet, though on the south-east and east they attain to about one hundred and one hundred and fifty feet respectively, within a quarter and a third of a mile. They are exclusively woodland.

The shore is composed of a belt of smooth rounded white stones like paving stones, excepting one or two short sand beaches, and is so steep that in many places a single leap will carry you into water over your head. . . . The stones extend a rod or two into the water, and then the bottom is pure sand.

Write phrases that help you visualize here or draw a picture of the pond.

Reading this, did you picture the green pond with ring of stones and woodland surroundings? Did you visualize the pine and oak trees and the abrupt rise of the hills? Creating a picture in your mind's eye is a first component of a strategy for reading description.

A second component is relating what is being described to something you already know. Sometimes the author of a text helps you to do this by providing an analogy, or creative comparison. For example, Thoreau called the pond a well. Picture a well with its steep sides. Does visualizing a well help you picture how Walden Pond looks?

When Thoreau called Walden Pond a well, he was using a *metaphor*. A metaphor is an expressed comparison between two essentially different things. A metaphor differs from a *simile*, which is an expressed comparison of two different things that relies on the word *as* or *like* to make the comparison. Here is Thoreau's metaphor set in diagram form:

Walden Pond with
its steep banks is
       a well
       with its steep sides.

At times, creating a metaphor or simile of your own when a writer does not supply one can help you to visualize. For example, visualizing a rice field on a windy day, you might think: "The rice field in the wind looked like an ocean with waves moving to and fro." In doing that, you would have created a simile that paints a clearer picture.

The rice field
in the wind is
      like
      an ocean with waves.

Now read this description of an eagle by the nineteenth-century English poet, Alfred Tennyson. As you read, apply these strategies: (1) Visualize the scene, and in the margin write phrases that help you picture it; (2) Create a comparison between what is being described and something you know, or identify the creative comparisons the author has used. The word *azure* means "blue." A *crag* is a "projecting outcropping of rock."

Write phrases that help you visualize here.

THE EAGLE

Alfred Tennyson

He clasps the crag with crooked hands:
Close to the sun in lonely lands,
Ringed with the azure world, he stands.

The wrinkled sea beneath him crawls;
He watches from his mountain walls,
And like a thunderbolt he falls.

Close your eyes for a minute. Visualize the scene—an eagle on a projecting rock high above the sea, the big yellow sun in the background, the blue sky behind, the sea with its ripples below. Then the eagle falls, diving down from his craggy perch.

A key word that helps you paint a picture of the action part of the poem in your mind's eye is *thunderbolt*. Did you think of a thunderbolt, coming loudly and sharply, as you visualized the eagle? The word *thunderbolt* in this context is a simile, for here the word *like* makes the connection between two different things—the diving downward movement of the eagle and the clap of a thunderbolt.

> The eagle falls
>   like
>   a thunderbolt.

Go back now to Chapter 11. Reread the segment about the cell membrane on page 237. Do you recognize the very effective metaphor the author uses to clarify his science content? Hole uses the metaphor of a gate to help you picture a membrane. How are a gate and a membrane the same? Both are barriers between things. Extend the metaphor. Picture a gate with a latch. A man wants to get through. He can do it by lifting the latch. A horse wants to get through. She can not pass through because she cannot operate the latch. Is this "gate" permeable or selectively permeable? This example shows that metaphors are just as important in scientific writing as in poetry and stories.

Practicing Visualizing

Here are a few descriptions that make use of metaphor and simile. Reading them, picture in your mind's eye the object being described, using the metaphor or simile to help you visualize. In the outer margin as you read, jot down the particular words that help you see the picture in your mind.

Practice Exercise 1

Write phrases here that help you visualize.

The lands along the Missouri-Kansas border are a green patchwork of lush creek bottoms and rolling pastures, where eastern forests begin their retreat to western prairies. Farms, small towns, and cities pulse with the strength of the American heartland.

Spring here brings thunderstorms to soak the earth and renew the cycle of life. As dusk comes, cottonwoods stir in the warm breeze, robins pull worms from damp lawns and lightning bugs flash their Morse messages against darkening skies. In overgrown hollows, deer and quail move through groves of hawthorn, oak and walnut, and water moccasins hunt frogs in pristine lotus ponds. The meadows are fringed with daisies, clover and wild rose.

1. What is a patchwork quilt?

2. What picture does the author paint by calling the lands here a green patchwork?

3. What things do you know that pulse?

4. How do farms, towns, and cities pulse?

5. What is the Morse code? How does it work?

6. What picture does the author paint by saying that "lightning bugs flash their Morse messages against darkening skies"?

Practice Exercise 2

Write phrases here that help you visualize.

MOON

Emily Dickinson

The moon was but a chin of gold
A night or two ago,
And now she turns her perfect face
Upon the world below.

7. Draw a picture of the moon when it was "but a chin of gold."

8. What phase of the moon was Dickinson describing with her first metaphor? A metaphor is a creative comparison between two things.

9. Draw a picture of the moon when it has a "perfect face."

10. What phase of the moon was Dickinson describing with her second metaphor?

11. Why didn't Dickinson simply tell the names of the phases of the moon that she was describing? Why did she use the creative comparison of a metaphor?

SELECTION 1: FLORENCE THE MAGNIFICENT (Art)

Expanding Your Vocabulary for Reading

Using context and word-structure clues, figure out the meaning of each italicized word. Jot the meaning in the margin. Check your definition in the glossary. In the selection, you will meet the words palazzi *and* basilicas. *A basilica is a great church. A palazzi is a large dwelling place on the order of a palace.*

1. The crowd was so *unruly* that a dozen police officers were needed to keep order.
2. When the *cornerstone* of the skyscraper was laid, a ceremony was held celebrating the event.
3. She was a *petulant* child, inclined to be irritable whenever she did not get her own way.
4. The faces of the *gargoyles* on the cathedral stared down like avenging demons.
5. After many unsuccessful *forays* into the country to raid, the bandits gave up their plundering.
6. Michelangelo painted the *frescoes* that are on the ceiling of the Sistine Chapel in Rome.
7. The sidewalks were so crowded that I was *jostled* with each step I took and I felt like a puppet on a string.
8. The books were stacked in such a *higgledy-piggledy* way that when I touched them, they came falling down like Humpty Dumpty.

Getting Ready to Read

Preview the selection by reading the title and the headings, and scanning the first paragraph.

- What is the topic of this selection? _____

- Many students choose Italy as the country they would most like to visit and cities such as Rome, Venice, and Florence as ones they would most like to see. Would you like to go to Italy? Write here reasons why you would or would not like to go to Italy. Write down places you would like to see there.

  _____

  _____

  _____

- Write two questions you would hope to answer through reading the selection.

  _____

Reading with Meaning

Read the selection. As you read, visualize what the author is describing. In the margin, write words from the selection that paint pictures for you. Also record equations for the metaphors and similes. The first two items are completed for you. You may wish to do this selection with a classmate. Read silently and stop at the end of each paragraph to complete the margin notes together. Remember that the Renaissance was the great period of learning in Europe during the fourteenth, fifteenth, and sixteenth centuries. It marked the transition from the medieval to the modern world.

Figure 12.1   *Map of Italy*

Write phrases that help
you visualize; write
equations for metaphors
and similes.

1. Simile:

*Ring of hills =
palm of a giant*

2. Simile:

*orange roofs and domes =
bunch of marigolds*

3. Metaphor:

4. Good descriptive
phrase:

5. Good descriptive
phrase:

FLORENCE THE MAGNIFICENT:
THE CITY OF DANTE AND DAVID,
MICHELANGELO AND MACHIAVELLI,
THE MEDICIS, GUCCIS AND PUCCIS

Anne Zwack

"The God who made the hills of Florence was an artist," wrote
Anatole France as he looked down at the city, ringed by hills as
though cupped in the palm of a giant hand, its orange roofs and
domes jumbled like an unruly bunch of marigolds. Not just God,
but centuries of Florentines have been artists. The Florentines
invented the Renaissance, which is the same as saying they invented
the modern world. For nearly three centuries, from Giotto's time to
Michelangelo's, Florence was the hub of the universe, not only
producing palazzi, basilicas and countless art treasures, but also
generating ideas that form the cornerstone of 20th century thought.

Five centuries after the Renaissance, despite neon lights in the
storefronts and swarms of mopeds and Fiats honking petulantly
where horses and carts once rumbled past, Florence remains a
Renaissance city. The streets in the center are still paved with uneven
flagstones, and away from the main throughfares they're so narrow
that the jutting eaves on opposite sides almost touch, keeping you
dry on a rainy day if you hug the ochre-yellow walls. As it is, there
is a war of wills every time you meet someone coming toward you
on a sidewalk no wider than a ledge, and your umbrellas tend to get
into a clinch.

On a sunny day, look up at the skyline, at the leafy terraces,
the square towers, the odd gargoyle or coat of arms worn smooth by
time. The forbidding palazzi, built of massive blocks of brown
stone, still seem to bristle as though in expectation of forays by

bands of Guelfs or Ghibellines, the two warring factions that divided Florence in the Middle Ages. And the faces of today's townspeople come straight out of the frescoes painted centuries ago, when their ancestors were busy building the biggest dome in Christendom.

The City's Pleasures

The most magical walk in Florence is down the Lungarno (literally, "along the Arno," as the streets skirting the river are called). Swallows wheel above the dome of the Church of San Frediano and over the higgledy-piggledy rooftops of houses. Some of the buildings, jostling each other in a hodgepodge of styles, have foundations in the water. The iron lampposts, whose lion's feet grip the parapets all along the river, look as though they were still lighted by gas. Rowers in kayaks occasionally skim over the surface of the fast-flowing yellow river, which gurgles beneath the arches of stone bridges.

6. Good descriptive phrase:

Rebuilt after World War II, the bridges are not as ageless as they appear. Only one remains from early days: the Ponte Vecchio, or Old Bridge, which was so quaint, with its goldsmiths' shops elbowing for room on either side, that Hitler ordered his troops to leave it standing. The present structure dates from 1345, and the tiny jewelers' boutiques that seem stuck to the sides of the bridge like limpets to a rock were once butcher shops.

7. Good descriptive phrase:

8. Good descriptive phrase:

Art and Architecture

Whether you spend a lifetime seeing Florence or a few days, there are a number of things you must not miss. One, in the Accademia, is Michelangelo's *David* (of which there are two copies, one in the Piazza Signoria and one in the Piazzale Michelangelo). Frowning down from his pedestal, his sling over his shoulder and every vein and sinew bursting out of the white marble, David makes the rest of us feel very small. One wonders how Michelangelo would have portrayed Goliath. There's more marble and more Michelangelo in the Medici Chapel behind the Basilica of San Lorenzo: the 16th century genius was responsible for both the architecture and the sculpture of the reclining figures of *Night and Day* and of *Dawn and Dusk.* . . .

9. Good descriptive phrase:

In the days when justice was rough and rudimentary, the building that is now the Bargello Museum was Florence's courthouse, and condemned men were strung out of the windows of its tower. Today the museum houses Renaissance statues. . . . There is also another David, this one by Donatello, and it is said to be the first nude statue of the Renaissance.

10. Good descriptive phrase:

The Pitti Palace crouches like an enormous yellow crab around Pitti Square, one of the few parking areas in Florence. The palace was built by a Renaissance nobleman, Luca Pitti, who wanted his mansion to be bigger and better than anyone else's. It is now divided into five museums. . . .

11. Simile:

Like most Florentine basilicas, the Duomo, or cathedral is striped in a geometric patchwork of different colored marble. It looks huge even by today's standards, let alone those of 1296, when the cornerstone was laid. No one had succeeded in hoisting aloft a

12. Good descriptive phrase:

13. Simile:

14. Metaphor:

massive dome since the building of the Pantheon in Rome. But Brunelleschi, the great Renaissance architect, solved the problem in the early 15th century by building two separate domes, one on top of the other, like two salad bowls of different sizes. If you can face the 463 steps that lead to the very top, you actually can walk between the two layers of the dome. Or you can climb Giotto's bell tower, which Longfellow called "the lily of Florence blossoming in stone."

Another church of striped marble, Santa Croce, could be called Florence's hall of fame, as it contains tombs and monuments that constitute a *Who's Who* of Italy's glorious past. Among the greats memorialized there are Michelangelo, Galileo, Machiavelli and Dante. . . .

The Right and Left Banks

15. Good descriptive phrase:

In the Middle Ages, when Florence flourished as the center of the world's wool trade, the fleeces were washed in the River Arno, which divides the city in two. The Oltrarno, or Left Bank, is my favorite half, with a little maze of streets spreading out from the Pitti Palace and around the Church of Santo Spirito and its neighborhood square, where housewives shop at the morning market, old men doze on benches, and children and dogs tumble over the fountain.

16. Metaphor:

Since the times of the Medicis, the Left Bank has been the city's artisan quarter, a hive of activity where craftsmen in sand-colored overalls bend over their workbenches surrounded by clouds of sawdust and pungent smells of glue. As you wend your way down the little streets, you can peer into the workshops and watch giant picture frames being gilded, antique furniture being restored, metals being forged. Artisans pedal past on their bicycles, the tools of their trade strapped on behind, and it is not unusual to see them stopping traffic as they carry a brass bedstead or an antique commode across the street.

17. Good descriptive phrase:

The other (right) side of the Arno is Florence's more pompous, monumental half, site of most of the museums and churches, banks and offices. Here on wide streets like Via Tornabuoni and Via della Vigna Nuova, chic shoppers flit in and out of designer boutiques. All the big names in Italian fashion are lined up shoulder to shoulder: Gucci, Ferragamo, Armani, . . . You'll also find fun fashion stores and the plushest jewelers in Florence.

18. Simile:

19. Good descriptive phrase:

Perhaps my greatest Florentine pleasure is watching the sun set from Piazzle Michelangelo, with the entire city at my feet. The lights hover like fireflies over the slowly darkening town, and the arches of the bridges show black against the fierce red of a sun that sets twice, once in the waters of the Arno and once in the Tuscan heavens. At this time the light takes on the gossamer texture of a down powder puff, dusting the roofs and domes a hazy apricot, and I find myself sharing with D. H. Lawrence the "feeling of having arrived, of having reached the perfect centre of man's universe."

Checking for Understanding

1. Florence has been described as "a feast for the eyes." Based on your reading of the article, explain the meaning of the metaphor. In what way is Florence a feast? What things do Florence and a feast have in common? _____

   _____

2. Explain the meaning of this simile: Florence is ringed by hills "as though cupped in the palm of a giant." A simile is a creative comparison between two things. The comparison includes the word *like* or *as*. _____

   _____

3. The author writes that Florence's orange roofs and domes are "jumbled like an unruly bunch of marigolds." What two essentially different things is the author comparing through this simile? _____

   What qualities do these two things share? _____

4. A limpet is a small shelled organism that clings to rocks. The author writes, "The tiny jeweler's boutiques that seem stuck to the sides of the bridge like limpets to a rock were once butcher shops." What two essentially different things is the author comparing through this simile? _____

   What qualities do these two things share? _____

5. The author writes, "The Pitti Palace crouches like an enormous yellow crab around Pitti Square." What two essentially different things is the author comparing in this simile? _____

   What qualities do these two things share? _____

6. Describing the domes, the author tells us that they are actually two separate domes, "one on top of the other like two salad bowls of different sizes." What two essentially different things is the author comparing in this simile?

   _____

   What qualities do these two things share? _____

7. When the author describes the artisan section of the city as "a hive of activity,"

   what picture comes to your mind? _____

   _____

8. The author writes, "The lights hover like fireflies over the slowly darkening town." What two things is the author comparing in this simile?

   _____

   What qualities do these two things share? _____

9. The author describes the dusk through a metaphor: "At this time the light takes on the gossamer texture of a down powder puff, dusting the roofs and domes a hazy apricot." What two essentially different things is the author comparing metaphorically? _____

   What qualities do these two things share? _____

10. Longfellow called the bell tower "the lily of Florence blossoming in stone." What two essentially different things is the author comparing through metaphor? _____

    What qualities do these two things share? _____

11. Would you like to travel to Florence? Tell a classmate why or why not. Then in your notebook, write a paragraph in which you give the reasons for your decision. Be ready to share your paragraph with the class.

Making the Writing Connection

Create a metaphor or simile to complete each of the following:

1. The rocket, posed on the launching pad, looked like a

2. In the winter, the bare branches of the trees looked like

3. Blown by the wind, her hair became

4. The islands of Hawaii are

5. The great Rocky Mountain ridge is

Playing with Words

Here are the key words from the selection. Draw a very rough picture, or sketch, to go along with each one to show the meaning that word has for you. The first ones will be relatively easy to do; as you progress, use your imagination in picturing meanings. Check the glossary if you are unsure of the meanings of the words.

1. cornerstone

2. gargoyle

3. fresco

4. higgledy-piggledy

5. unruly

6. jostled

7. petulant

8. foray

NARRATION

A narrative is an account of an event or series of events. It can be fictional (not true) or nonfictional (true). Stories, poems that tell a story, some newspaper reports, history, biography, and autobiography are narrations.

There are four elements in a strategy for successful reading of nonfictional narratives: (1) grasping the chronology of the events, (2) perceiving cause/effect relationships within the events, (3) relating the events to other similar or different events, and (4) understanding the significance of the events. Let us talk about each of these elements.

Grasping the Chronology

An ability to understand time relationships, or chronology, is important in reading narratives, especially biographies (passages that tell about the life of a person), autobiographies (passages that tell about the life of a person written by that person), and historical accounts (passages that tell about sequences of events). To help you comprehend sequence, authors provide two aids: (1) dates and (2) words that indicate sequence.

First, let us consider how to interpret dates. Start by previewing the following paragraph by quickly circling the dates.

> Phyllis Wheatley, the first major African-American poet, was born about 1753. She was taken by slavers from Africa to Boston in 1761 and sold there as a slave to one John Wheatley, a merchant. Wheatley and his wife recognized Phyllis's quickness of mind and ready wit and provided her with an education far beyond what was typically given to black slaves in America. She learned to read and write, began to read the poetry of English writers, and wrote poems of her own. Freed, she traveled to England where she was recognized for her poetry and had a collection of poems published in 1773. The volume was titled *Poems on Various Subjects.*
>
> Returning to America, Phyllis Wheatley sent a copy of one of her poems to George Washington during the period of the American Revolution. It expressed her feelings about the War and made reference to the General. This led to the publishing of one of her poems in the *Pennsylvania Magazine* and gradual recognition of her as the Poet of the American Revolution. Despite this recognition, Wheatley died in virtual poverty in 1784.

1753

1784

In your preview did you note that the selection is organized chronologically in the order in which events occurred? The first event was the birth of Wheatley in 1753. The last was her death in 1784. The intervening events are presented as they happened, in chronological order. Biographies and historical accounts are often structured chronologically. The writers of such selections typically include dates to give a framework to the account.

Having previewed a selection and discovered a sequence of dates embedded in it, you will find it helpful to visualize a time line in your mind as you read. A time line is simply a line on which dates and related events are labeled in chronological order. Reading, you plot each event on your mental time line.

Reading, you also relate the dates mentioned in the selection to significant dates from the past that function as reference points. You think: This happened just after the Civil War. Or this happened even before Columbus made his epic journey. Although you should develop your own series of historical reference points that have meaning to you, here are some markers from the past that you may want to use if you have some knowledge of these events:

Reference Points from History

3500 B.C.	The dawn of civilization (approximate) in the Tigris and Euphrates valleys
3100 B.C.	The unification of Egypt in northern Africa
3000 B.C.	Twelve city-states in Mesopotamia in Asia; civilizations in Crete, India, and China; beginning of Bronze Age
1704–1662 B.C.	The age of Hammurabi in Mesopotamia
1500 B.C.	The collapse of the ancient civilizations
1000 B.C.–A.D. 500	The rise of classical civilizations—Greek, Roman, Indian, Chinese
A.D. 300–400	The collapse of classical civilizations and the beginning of the barbarian invasions of Eurasia
A.D. 600–1000	The rise of Islam
A.D. 1066	The conquest of Britain by William the Conqueror
1400s–1700s	The Renaissance in Europe
1492	Columbus's voyage
1620	Landing of the Pilgrims in Massachusetts
1776	Declaration of Independence
1787	Constitution
1803	Louisiana Purchase, which doubled the country's size
1849	Gold Rush
1861–1865	American Civil War
1914–1918	World War I
1939–1945	World War II

Now reread the passage about Phyllis Wheatley. On the vertical time line in the margin, plot the events of her life as well as two key reference points of history—the Declaration of Independence and the Constitution, 1776 and 1787. In other words, locate each date from the selection on the line and label that date with the event from Wheatley's life. Do the same for the historical reference points.

Based on your time line (which you have just constructed in the margin), answer these questions:

● How old was Phyllis Wheatley when she was enslaved? _____

● How old was she when died? _____

● Was Wheatley alive when the Constitution was written? _____

Often readers make simple calculations based on dates in a selection. They ask themselves questions similar to the three here; in so doing, they are monitoring their own comprehension.

The strategy you have been applying here has four elements:

1. In previewing the selection, check dates given to see if the selection is organized chronologically.
2. In reading a chronologically organized selection, plot times on a mental time line. At times, plot dates sequentially on a time line in the margin.
3. Relate dates to key reference points in history that you know.
4. Make simple calculations based on the dates.

Dates are not the only way a writer expresses time relationships. A writer may use words that signal a passage of time. Sequence words include these:

- first, second, third . . . sixth
- for one year . . . for ten years
- first, next, after that . . . finally
- yesterday, today, tomorrow
- before, while, as, when, after
- then, now
- meanwhile
- soon
- not long after
- later
- in (in the spring), on (on his birthday), during (during her early years)
- childhood, youth, middle years, old age
- pre- and post- as in prewar and postwar periods

Preview the following short selection by skimming it and circling words other than dates that communicate time relationships.

Emily Dickinson, considered by many to be one of the greatest American poets, was born in 1830 in Amherst, Massachusetts. Her childhood was a typical one of that day, filled with friends and parties, church and home activities. For about six years, she attended Amherst Academy. Then she attended Mt. Holyoke Female Seminary for a year. "Valentine Extravaganza," her first poem to appear in print, was published in the *Springfield Republican* when she was 22.   1830

Before she was 30, however, Emily withdrew from Amherst society and increasingly applied herself to the writing of poetry. She would not see friends; and with the death of her father in 1874, she became a virtual recluse. During her lifetime, she had only two other poems published, "The Snake" in 1866 and "Success" in 1878. At her death in 1886, her sister discovered more than a thousand poems that Emily Dickinson had written throughout her life. The poems exhibit a directness of expression and a clarity of image that are apparent even to one who has read little poetry: 1886

To make a prairie it takes a clover and one
bee,—
One clover, and a bee,
And revery.
The revery alone will do
If bees are few.

In this selection, sequence-giving words include *childhood, for about six years, then, for a year, when, before, during,* and *at her death.*

Now reread the Dickinson article. As you read, record key events from Dickinson's life in the margin as a time line. Include a key reference point from history on the line so that you have a general idea of the period in which she lived. Ask as you read: What do the time-sequencing words tell me about the life of Dickinson?

After reading, record your answers to these questions:

● What are the two major periods in Dickinson's life? _____

_____

● How do the organization of the selection and the key sequencing words help you

identify those periods in her life? _____

_____

Did you identify the two periods? The first is Dickinson's childhood; it is discussed in the first paragraph. The second is the period characterized by her reclusive behavior; it is discussed in the second paragraph. Sometimes in reading chronological material about people and events, you may find it helpful to group events into periods or categories: youth, middle years, later years; pre-Darwin, post-Darwin; pre-Reformation, Reformation, post-Reformation. Sometimes, as in this case, the way the writer has organized the material into paragraphs helps you to identify patterns in the events.

Here are two more steps to a reading-for-sequence strategy.

5. Watch for sequencing words such as *first, then, finally* and *before, during,* and *after* that are clues to the passage of time and the sequence of events. Use these words to add events to the time line you visualize during reading.

6. Wherever possible, group events into natural periods or categories, such as childhood, youth, mid-life, prewar and postwar, or pre-Constitution and post-Constitution.

In sum, when working with sequence, think about the dates and words that indicate a passage of time, organizing events into a framework to help you remember when things happened. It is easier to remember that X happened during a person's childhood than to remember that X happened on May 4, 1862.

Analyzing Relationships Within Narratives

A second aspect of reading nonfictional narratives is delving beneath the facts of the account to think about why things came to pass, why they happened. Doing this, you are thinking about cause and effect. For example, reading a biography, you must ask: What were the influences upon this person that made him or her do what he or she did? What were the influences that made him or her become the kind of person he or she was? Reading history, you must ask: What were the events leading up to this? What were the causes? This diagram shows one way to think about causes and effects:

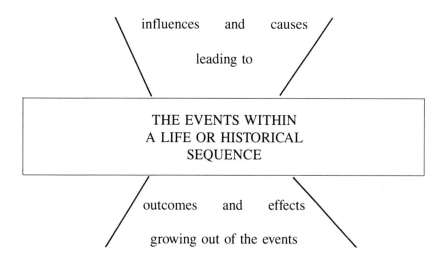

Apply these questions to the lives of Wheatley and Dickinson. What influenced these women to become poets? Write down a few points from each life that you think were important in making them the women they were.

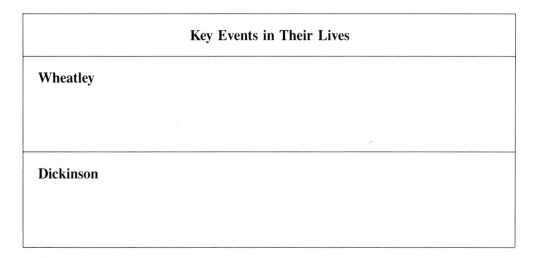

Comparing Events to Other Events

A third element of a strategy for reading historical accounts and biographies is to relate events and lives to other events and lives about which you already know. Reading, you say to yourself: This reminds me of X, Y, and Z that happened several years before. Or this person's life resembles that of Mr. A. Or this is just the opposite of what happened when. . . . Or this person's life started out the same as Ms. B's, but then took a different turn. Essentially, what you are doing is making comparisons and contrasts with things you already know: You are saying "This is like. . . . This is different from. . . ."

Apply these questions to Wheatley and Dickinson. Does the life of either one remind you of the life of someone you know? If so, in what way? In what way are the lives of Wheatley and Dickinson similar? In what way are their lives different?

Determining the Significance of Events

A fourth aspect of a strategy for reading historical accounts and biographies is to consider the significance of individuals and of events. In thinking about the ultimate meaning of a person's life as you read biography, you ask: What influence did this person have on other persons and events? In what ways did he or she change history and affect the future? In thinking about the meaning of a series of events or a period of time in history, you ask: What changes did these events trigger? What were the effects of these events on people and events that were to come?

Reviewing the Strategy for Reading Narratives

In sum, a strategy for reading nonfictional narrative requires that you ask questions that help you

- grasp the sequence of events;
- identify causes of events and factors that influenced people's lives;
- compare and contrast events and lives to other events and lives;
- think about the ultimate meaning, or significance of events and people's lives.

You will have the opportunity to apply this strategy as you read the next selection.

SELECTION 2: MUHAMMAD THE PROPHET (Religion)

Expanding Your Vocabulary for Reading

The selection you will read contains a number of interesting words. Knowing them will help you understand the selection. Read the following sentences, and study the italicized terms. Using context and word-structure clues, hypothesize a meaning for each term and record it in the margin. Check your hypotheses in the glossary.

1. In those days the king was *preeminent*—far above anyone else in authority. (Note: An eminent person is high in rank or is distinguished. How are the words *eminent* and *preeminent* related?)
2. The convict was *consigned* to the warden to begin his prison sentence.
3. "I appreciate your *forbearance*," said the man. "You have been very patient and understanding as you waited for me to pay my debt."
4. "You promised not to *divulge* the secret to anyone," remarked the lawyer. "Yet as soon as you learned it, you told everyone."
5. The *revelation* that she was a member of the CIA surprised us all. We had not known until then that she was working for the government.
6. In that society the king was *paramount*. His preeminence came as a right of birth.
7. To me that situation was *unique*. I had never seen anything like it before.
8. I had a sense of *impending* trouble as I entered the office and saw the principal behind the desk. Something was about to happen.
9. The *Koran* (or Quran), the sacred scriptures of the Islamic religion, affirms the oneness of God. (Note: See also how the word *Koran* is defined within the sentence by a phrase coming after it and set off by commas. You will find this technique for supplying basic information used a number of times in the selection.)
10. The pagans, who lived in Mecca, believed in many Gods. This belief is called *polytheism*. (Remember the meaning of the prefix *poly-*.)

11/12. Muhammad and his *adherents,* or supporters, *migrated* from Medina; they left together because it was unsafe for them there.

13. The leader of the neighboring country tried to *mediate* between the warring parties, but he could do nothing to help them end their struggles.

14. During the *siege* of the city by the enemy, many people were killed.

15. The siege lasted many weeks; yet the results were *inconclusive.* They proved nothing, for nobody came out the victor. (Remember the meaning of the prefix *in-.*)

16. After many hours of work we looked at what we had done and saw that we had made *negligible* progress. We could hardly see what we had done.

17. Only the most eminent persons were allowed *access* to the party; the rest of us were not allowed to enter.

18. The pagans whom Muhammad fought worshipped *idols,* graven images they held in high regard.

19. The Supreme Court generally adheres to the *precedents* set down in previous decisions. What has been decided in the past is a major factor in present cases.

20. Muhammad made an *alliance* with other tribes, an agreement that bound them together as allies.

21. The queen sent an *envoy* with a message to the emperor. The envoy served as the queen's agent and represented her in official talks.

Getting Ready to Read

Preview the selection by studying the title, the first and last paragraphs, the headings, and the map.

● What is the topic of the selection? _____

● Who was Muhammad? Write what you remember here. _____

_____

● The part of the world in which the events in this selection take place is the Middle East. You probably recall that the Middle East was the location of the Gulf War fought in 1991 to free Kuwait from Iraq. You probably heard about Saudi Arabia at that time. Locate these countries on the map in Figure 12.2. Then, talking with a classmate, recall what you remember about the Persian Gulf War of 1991. As you read this article, you may find it interesting to recall that even today, there has been fighting in this area.

● Write two or three questions you hope to answer by reading the selection.

_____

_____

Reading with Meaning

As you read the selection, record a time line of events in the inner margin. Answer the questions in the outer margin as you go along. Keep thinking: What were the causes of this? What is the significance of this? What does this remind me of? It may help to read this selection with a classmate, reading several paragraphs alone and then answering the margin questions together.

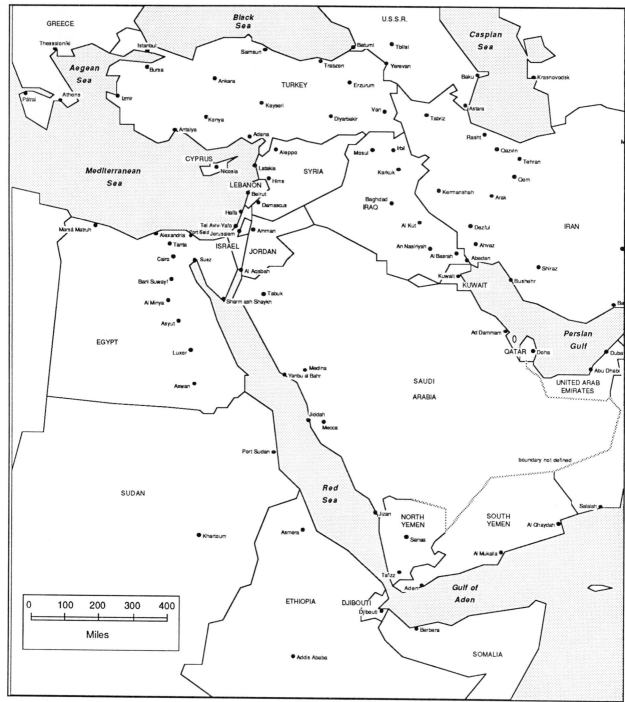

Figure 12.2   *Map of The Middle East*

MUHAMMAD THE PROPHET

Paul Lunde and John A. Sabini

1. Into what kind of family and society was Muhammad born?

In or about the year 570 the child who would be named Muhammad and who would become the Prophet of one of the world's great religions, Islam, was born into a family belonging to a clan of Quraysh, the ruling tribe of Mecca, a city in the Hijaz region of northwestern Arabia.

Originally the site of the Ka'bah, a shrine of ancient origins, Mecca had with the decline of southern Arabia become an important center of sixth-century trade with such powers as the Sassanians, Byzantines, and Ethiopians. As a result the city was dominated by powerful merchant families among whom the men of Quraysh were preeminent.

Muhammad's Early Life

Muhammad's father, 'Abd Allah ibn'Abd al-Muttalib, died before the boy was born; his mother, Aminah, died when he was six. The orphan was consigned to the care of his grandfather, the head of the clan of Hashim. After the death of his grandfather, Muhammad was raised by his uncle, Abu Talib. As was customary, Muhammad as a child was sent to live for a year or two with a Bedouin family that lived a desert life. This custom, followed until recently by noble families of Mecca, Medina, Tayif, and other towns of the Hijaz, had important implications for Muhammad. In addition to enduring the hardships of desert life, he acquired a taste for the rich language so loved by the Arabs, whose speech was their proudest art, and learned the patience and forbearance of the herdsmen, whose life of solitude he first shared and then came to understand and appreciate.

About the year 590, Muhammad, then in his twenties, entered the service of a widow named Khadijah as a merchant actively engaged with trading caravans to the north. Sometime later Muhammad married Khadijah, by whom he had two sons—who did not survive—and four daughters. During this period of his life Muhammad traveled widely.

The Beginnings of Islam

Then, in his forties, Muhammad began to retire to meditate, or think, in a cave on Mount Hira outside of Mecca, where the first of the great events of Islam took place. One day, as he sat in the cave, he heard a voice, later identified as that of the Angel Gabriel, which ordered him to:

Recite: In the name of thy Lord who created,
Created man from a clot of blood.

Three times Muhammad pleaded his inability to do so, but each time the command repeated. Finally, Muhammad recited the words of what are now the first five verses of the 96th surah or chapter of the Quran—words which proclaim God the Creator of man and the Source of all knowledge.

At first Muhammad divulged his experience only to his wife and immediate circle. But as more revelations directed him to proclaim the oneness of God universally, his following grew, at first among the poor and the slaves, but later also among the most eminent men of Mecca. The revelations he received at this time and those he did so later are all incorporated in the Quran, the Scripture of Islam.

Not everyone accepted God's message transmitted through Muhammad. Even in his own clan there were those who rejected his

2. How might this have affected him?

3. What were key events in Muhammad's early life?

4. How might these events have affected Muhammad?

5. What happened to Muhammad next?

6. How could these events have affected him?

7. What happened next to Muhammad?

8. How could these events have affected him?

9. At first how did Muhammad react?

10. Based on your own experiences, suggest why Muhammad reacted in this way.

11. Based on your own experiences, suggest

why opposition sharpened his determination—made him more determined.

12. Based on your own experiences, predict how the Meccans would react.

13. Of what historical event does this persecution remind you?

14. Why did the Meccans not investigate the cave?

15. What is the significance of the Hegira?

16. Why was Muhammad well acquainted with the situation in Medina?

teachings, and many merchants actively opposed the message. The opposition, however, merely served to sharpen Muhammad's sense of mission and his understanding of exactly how Islam differed from paganism. The belief in the unity of God was paramount in Islam; from this all else followed. The verses of the Quran stress God's uniqueness, warn those who deny it of impending punishment, and proclaim His unbounded compassion to those who submit to His will. Because the Quran rejected polytheism and emphasized man's moral responsibility, it presented a grave challenge to the worldly Meccans.

The Hijrah

After Muhammad had preached for more than a decade, the opposition to him reached such a high pitch that, fearful for their safety, he sent some of his adherents to Ethiopia, where the Christian ruler extended protection to them, the memory of which has been cherished by Muslims ever since. But in Mecca the persecution worsened. Muhammad's followers were abused and even tortured. At last, therefore, Muhammad sent seventy of his followers off to the northern town of Yathrib, which was later to be renamed Medina ("The City"). Later, in the early fall of 622, he learned of a plot to murder him and, with his closest friend, Abu Bakr al-Siddiq, set off to join the emigrants.

In Mecca the plotters arrived at Muhammad's home to find that his cousin, 'Ali, had taken his place in bed. Enraged, the Meccans set a price on Muhammad's head and set off in pursuit. Muhammad and Abu Bakr, however, had taken refuge in a cave where, as they hid from their pursuers, a spider spun its web across the cave's mouth. When they saw that the web was unbroken, the Meccans passed by and Muhammad and Abu Bakr went on to Medina, where they were joyously welcomed by the Medinans as well as the Meccans who had gone ahead to prepare the way.

This was the *Hijrah*—or in English the *Hegira*—usually, but inaccurately translated as "Flight"—from which the Muslim era is dated. In fact, the Hijrah was not a flight but a carefully planned migration which marks not only a break in history—the beginning of the Islamic era—but also, for Muhammad and the Muslims, a new way of life. Henceforth, the organizational principle of the community was not to be mere blood kinship, but the greater brotherhood of all Muslims. The men who accompanied Muhammad on the Hijrah were called the *Muhajirun*—"those that made the Hijrah" or the "Emigrants"—while those in Medina who became Muslims were called the *Ansar* or "Helpers."

Muhammad was well acquainted with the situation in Medina. Earlier, before the Hijrah, the city had sent envoys to Mecca asking Muhammad to mediate a dispute between two powerful tribes. What the envoys saw and heard had impressed them and they had invited Muhammad to settle in Medina. After the Hijrah, Muhammad's exceptional qualities so impressed the Medinans that the rival tribes and their allies temporarily closed ranks as, on March 15, 624, Muhammad and his supporters moved against the pagans of Mecca.

Fighting for Islam

The first battle, which took place near Badr, now a small town southwest of Medina, had several important effects. In the first place, the Muslim forces, outnumbered three to one, defeated the Meccans. Secondly, the discipline displayed by the Muslims brought home to the Meccans, perhaps for the first time, the abilities of the man they had driven from their city. Thirdly, one of the allied tribes which had pledged support to the Muslims in the Battle of Badr, but had then proved lukewarm when the fighting started, was expelled from Medina one month after the battle. Those who claimed to be allies of the Muslims, but really opposed them, were thus served warning: membership in the community imposed the obligation of total support.

A year later the Meccans struck back. Assembling an army of three thousand men, they met the Muslims at Uhud, a ridge outside Medina. After an initial success the Muslims were driven back and the Prophet himself was wounded. As the Muslims were not completely defeated, the Meccans, with an army of ten thousand, attacked Medina again two years later but with quite different results. At the Battle of the Trench, the Muslims scored a signal victory by introducing a new defense. On the side of Medina from which attack was expected they dug a trench too deep for the Meccan cavalry to clear without exposing itself to the archers posted behind earthworks on the Medina side. After an inconclusive siege, the Meccans were forced to retire. Thereafter, Medina was entirely in the hands of the Muslims.

The Growth of Islam

The Constitution of Medina—under which the clans accepting Muhammad as the Prophet of God formed an alliance, or federation—dates from this period. It showed that the political consciousness of the Muslim community had reached an important point; its members defined themselves as a community separate from all others. The Constitution also defined the role of non-Muslims in the community. Jews, for example, were part of the community; they were *dhimmis,* that is, protected people, as long as they conformed to its laws. This established a precedent for the treatment of subject peoples during the later conquests. Christians and Jews, upon a payment of a yearly tax, were allowed religious freedom and, while maintaining their status as non-Muslims, were associate members of the Muslim state. This status did not apply to polytheists, who could not be tolerated within a community that worshipped the One God.

Ibn Ishaq, one of the earliest biographers of the Prophet, says it was at about this time that Muhammad sent letters to the rulers of the earth—the King of Persia, the Emperor of Byzantium, the Negus of Abyssinia, and the Governor of Egypt among others—inviting them to submit to Islam. Nothing more fully illustrates the confidence of the small community, as its military power, despite the Battle of the Trench, was still negligible. But its confidence was not misplaced. Muhammad so effectively built up a series of alliances

17. What was the significance of the Battle of Badr?

18. Of what other events do these events remind you?

19. What was the significance of the Constitution of Medina?

20. What do these events tell you about Muhammad's strength at this point?

among the tribes—his early years with the Bedouins must have stood him in good stead here—that by 628 he and fifteen hundred followers were able to demand access to the Ka'bah during negotiations with the Meccans.

21. In 629, Muhammad reentered Mecca. Why was this significant?

This was a milestone in the history of the Muslims. Just a short time before, Muhammad had had to leave the city of his birth in fear of his life. Now he was being treated by his former enemies as a leader in his own right. A year later, in 629, he reentered and, in effect, conquered Mecca without bloodshed and in a spirit of tolerance which established an ideal for future conquests. He also destroyed the idols in the Ka'bah, to put an end forever to pagan practices there. At the same time Muhammad won the allegiance of 'Amr ibn al-'As, the future conqueror of Egypt, and Khalid ibn al-Walid, the future "Sword of God," both of whom embraced Islam and joined Muhammad. Their conversion was especially noteworthy because these men had been among Muhammad's bitterest opponents only a short time before.

22. What do you believe was Muhammad's contribution to world history?

In one sense Muhammad's return to Mecca was the climax of his mission. In 632, just three years later, he was suddenly taken ill, and on June 8 of that year, with his third wife 'Aishah in attendance, the Messenger of God "died with the heat of noon."

Checking on Understanding

Answer these questions based on the selection. Talk out answers with a class-mate. Refer to the selection for evidence to support your answers.

1. How old was Muhammad when he died?
   a. 20   b. 50   c. 62   d. 72

2. Young Muhammad lost his mother and father at a young age, then his grand-father. Propose what influence this might have had in making him the man he became.

3. Muhammad spent a year or two with a Bedouin family in the desert. Propose how this may have influenced him as a person.

4. What were two important effects of the Battle of Badr?

   a.

   b.

5. Why was the Hegira significant, or important?

6. Why was the Constitution of Medina significant, or important?

7. What do you believe was Muhammad's most significant contribution to the world? Give reasons to support your belief.

Writing from Reading

As you read the selection, did you relate the content to other people, places, or times you know about? Of what other events in history does this account remind you? How are the events similar? How are they different? In your notebook, write a short paragraph or two in which you identify a similar event in history and state the similarities and then the differences. Be ready to talk about relationships.

Playing with Words

Here are the featured words from the selection. Match them with their definitions. Place the correct letter on the line at the left.

Adjectives

_____	1. impending	a. standing out above others
_____	2. inconclusive	b. chief in importance
_____	3. negligible	c. being one of a kind
_____	4. paramount	d. about to occur, threatening
_____	5. preeminent	e. so insignificant that it can be disregarded
_____	6. unique	f. not decisive, without a definite outcome

Verbs

_____	7. consigned	g. handed over, delivered
_____	8. divulged	h. served as go-between, acted to bring agreement between groups
_____	9. mediated	i. moved from one place to settle in another
_____	10. migrated	j. made known to others, told something

Nouns

_____	11. access	k. messenger, diplomatic agent
_____	12. adherents	l. union formed by agreement
_____	13. alliance	m. patience, self-control
_____	14. envoy	n. something made known
_____	15. forbearance	o. the scriptures of Islam
_____	16. Koran	p. belief in many gods
_____	17. idols	q. objects or images worshipped as gods
_____	18. polytheism	r. long effort to overcome resistance
_____	19. precedent	s. entrance, admission
_____	20. revelation	t. case that serves as a reason for a later case
_____	21. siege	u. followers, supporters

Using Words in Context

Select from the words just given, and place one in each sentence slot. Place an adjective in each sentence slot. Do not use a word more than once.

1. Graduating from college is of _____ importance to her; all other things are of lesser importance.

2. As a student, her income was _____; she barely had enough money for the basics.

3. The evidence against the prisoner was _____ so they had to release him.

4. He felt a sense of _____ trouble as the test date came closer and closer.

5. The thing that made the house _____ was the way it floated on water.

6. His family held a _____ position in society; they were leaders.

Place a verb in each sentence slot. Do not use a word more than once.

7. During the drought, the Bedouins _____ across the desert in search of a new home.

8. He _____ the information to the police when he heard of the seriousness of the crime.

9. The lawyer _____ between the two angry men.

10. As a child she was _____ to the care of a nurse and never saw her parents.

Place a noun in each sentence slot. Do not use a word more than once.

11. The two nations signed an _____ in which they agreed to assist each other in times of war.

12. The president sent an _____ to talk to the prime minister of that country.

13. It was a _____ to learn that the man she had married was a billionaire.

14. As a child, he read the _____; in that way he learned the important principles of Islam.

15. After a lengthy _____, the city surrendered, for it had been without food for many days.

16. _____ is the belief in many Gods.

17. They denied him _____ into the city because he did not believe as they did.

18. Muhammad had many _____ who followed him when he left the city.

19. "I ask your _____ in this case," the hotel manager said. "There will be a long wait before a room is available for you."

20. They worshipped _____, golden eagles studded with diamonds.

21. Because there is no _____ that we can follow, we must make up
our own minds.

DESCRIPTIONS AND NARRATIVES

In this section you will read a selection that contains elements of both description
and narrative.

SELECTION 3: HUMAN CULTURE—THE YӒNOMAMÖ
(Anthropology)

Getting Ready to Read

Read the title and the first and last paragraphs.

- What is this selection about? _____

- Where does it take place? _____

- What do you know about other anthropologists who studied remote cultures? If
  you remember something, jot a few words or phrases here. _____

  _____

- What do you expect to learn by reading this selection? _____

  _____

Reading with Meaning

*Read the selection, or listen as your instructor reads it aloud to you. As you read
or listen, visualize the scene, and think about the sequence in which events are happening. Keep thinking also about the meaning of what is happening.*

HUMAN CULTURE—THE YӒNOMAMÖ

John Macionis

A small aluminum motorboat chugged steadily along the muddy Orinoco
River, deep in the vast tropical rain forest of southern Venezuela. American
anthropologist Napoleon Chagnon was nearing the end of a three-day journey
to the home territory of the Yӑnomamö, one of the few technologically simple
societies remaining on earth.

Some twelve thousand Yӑnomamö live in scattered villages along the
border between Venezuela and Brazil. Their way of life contrasts sharply with
our own. The Yӑnomamö are spirit worshippers who have no form of writing.
Until recent contact with outsiders, they used hand-crafted weapons such as
the bow and arrow to hunt for food. Thus Chagnon would be as strange to
them as they to him.

By two o'clock in the afternoon, Chagnon had almost reached his
destination. The hot sun made the humid air almost unbearable. The
anthropologist's clothes were soaked with perspiration; his face and hands were
swollen from the bites of innumerable gnats that swarmed around him. But he
hardly noticed, so preoccupied was he with the fact that in just a few moments

he was to come face to face with people unlike any he had ever known.

Chagnon's heart pounded as the boat slid onto the riverbank near a Yanomamö village. Sounds of activity came from nearby. Chagnon and his guide climbed from the boat and walked toward the village, stooping as they pushed their way through the dense undergrowth. Chagnon describes what happened next:

> I looked up and gasped when I saw a dozen burly, naked, sweaty, hideous men staring at us down the shafts of their drawn arrows! Immense wads of green tobacco were stuck between their lower teeth and lips making them look even more hideous, and strands of dark green slime dripped or hung from their nostrils—strands so long that they clung to their [chests] or drizzled down their chins.
>
> My next discovery was that there were a dozen or so vicious, underfed dogs snapping at my legs, circling me as if I were to be their next meal. I just stood there holding my notebook, helpless and pathetic. Then the stench of the decaying vegetation and filth hit me and I almost got sick. I was horrified. What kind of welcome was this for the person who came here to live with you and learn your way of life, to become friends with you? (Chagnon, *Yanomamö: The Fierce People,* 1983)

Fortunately for Chagnon, the Yanomamö villagers recognized his guide and withdrew their weapons. Reassured that he would at least survive the afternoon, Chagnon was still shaken by his inability to make any sense of the people surrounding him. And this was to be his home for a year and a half! He wondered why he had forsaken physics to study human culture in the first place.

All 5 billion people living on our planet are members of but one biological species: *Homo sapiens.* Even so, any of us can be overwhelmed by how different we are from one another, differences not of biology, but of culture. Upon his arrival at the Yanomamö village, Chagnon experienced a severe case of **culture shock:** *the personal disorientation that may accompany exposure to an unfamiliar way of life.* Like most of us, Chagnon had been raised to keep his clothes on, even in hot weather, and to use a handkerchief when his nose was running—especially in front of others. The Yanomamö clearly had other ideas about how to live. The nudity that embarrassed Chagnon was customary to the Yanomamö. The green slime hanging from their nostrils was caused by inhaling a hallucinogenic drug, a practice common among friends. The "stench" from which Chagnon recoiled in disgust no doubt smelled like "Home Sweet Home" to the inhabitants of that Yanomamö village.

Culture The beliefs, values, behavior, and material objects shared by a particular people

Human beings the world over have very different ideas about what is pleasant and unpleasant, polite and rude, true and false, right and wrong. This capacity for startling difference is a wonder of our species: the expression of human culture.

Checking Your Understanding

Collaborate with a classmate to complete the following:

1. Describe to a classmate the scene in the Yanomamö village as Chagnon saw it. Then together record phrases that describe the scene.

2. Listen while a classmate tells you the events that happened to Chagnon. Check that the events are in the correct order. Then together list the events.

3. Give an example from the selection confirming the author's statement that "Human beings . . . have very different ideas about what is pleasant and unpleasant, polite and rude. . . ." Give another example from personal experience.

4. What is the significance of Chagnon's work with the Yanomamö? What have we learned from it?

5. Compare the way of life of the Yanomamö to that of the average person living in your own community. How is it the same? Different?

6. Circle three or four words in the selection that are new or relatively unfamiliar to you. In the margin, write a few words for each giving the meaning based on context and word-structure clues. Be ready to share your definitions.

EXTENDING WHAT YOU HAVE LEARNED

Reviewing Reading Strategies

Write down the strategies you would apply as your read each of these forms of prose:

Description	Narration

Applying Strategies in Independent Reading

1. Read a section from a history book that recounts a sequence of events or tells about the events in a person's life. On a card write down

Figure 12.3   *Map of South America*

● the significant events in the order in which they occurred;
● the factors that brought these events into being;
● the significance of the events;
● another event that you believe to be similar.
2. Read an article from the travel section of the Sunday newspaper or a travel magazine that describes a place you would like to visit. As you read, visualize what is
being described. On an index card, record a few notes about the place. Be ready to
tell about the place you have read about.

Building a Knowledge Base for Reading

Circle Florence, Italy, on the map in Figure 12.1. Locate Medina and Mecca in Saudi Arabia on the map in Figure 12.2. Mark the area between Venezuela and Brazil on the map in Figure 12.3.

Gaining Ownership of Words

Select several words from those featured in this chapter to record in your personal vocabulary list. Include a model sentence for each. Try to use the words you have selected in speaking and writing.

13

Understanding Opinions and Persuasive Writing

Before reading the chapter, read the title, the stated objective, and the headings and subheadings. Ask yourself: What is the topic of the chapter? In the space above and beside the chapter number, jot down what you already know about the topic. Then in the space below the number, jot down at least two questions you hope to answer through reading the chapter.

OBJECTIVE

In this chapter, you will develop strategies for understanding writing in which one of the author's purposes is to express his or her opinions.

INTRODUCTION—READING OPINIONS

At times, authors write with the intention of stating their opinions or judgments and perhaps to persuade you to accept their point of view. Newspaper editorials, syndicated columns, political and social cartoons, and letters to the editor are forums for judgmental and persuasive writing. So are film and book reviews. Reading these pieces, you know you are dealing with opinion even though the authors may include explanations, narrations, and descriptions to support their opinions.

Opinions and judgments are found in a variety of other writing. Authors may have as their primary intent to explain or give an account. However, they color the explanation or account with their feelings. Those feelings give a point of view, or a *bias,* to their writing. Actually it is very difficult for writers to avoid bias and be completely impartial. Writers' personal experiences are sieves through which they filter information as they write.

Reading to Detect Opinion and Bias

What strategies can you use to detect that the author is presenting opinion rather than fact? What strategies can you use to detect an author's personal bias toward the subject? Here are four strategies.

A first strategy is to identify the kind of piece you are reading. Ask: Is this an editorial? A column from the opinion page? A book or film review? If the answer is yes, you are probably reading opinion. A related strategy is to identify the publisher and writer. Ask: Is the publisher an organization or group with a known point of view? Is the author known for supporting a particular view? Is he or she a well-known authority in that field? For example, a selection published by an antiwar group and written by a leading pacifist is likely to contain opinion and reflect an antiwar point of view.

A second strategy is to notice words indicating that an author is giving opinion. Some of these clue words are rather obvious signals of opinion giving. An author states: "I believe. . . ." "I feel. . . ." "I like. . . ." "I think. . . ." Other words that hint the author is advocating a particular course of action are "We should. . . ." "You ought to. . . ." "You should have. . . ." "It would have been better to. . . ." Still other words communicate an evaluative message similar to the message carried by the grades A, B, C, D, and F assigned by professors:

unacceptable	acceptable	more acceptable	
good	better	best	
invalid	least valid	valid	more valid
valuable	very valuable	invaluable	
worthy	worthless	worthwhile	
well done	poorly done		
unique	marvelous	terrible	outrageous

A third strategy is to think about an author's choice of words and what message he or she is sending through the specific words chosen. Words often communicate an implied, or associated, meaning that goes beyond a strict dictionary definition. The implied meaning that a word carries is called *connotation.* The literal dictionary meaning (without the feelings and personal associations that people bring to a word) is *denotation.* Some words communicate a positive connotation, others communicate a negative connotation, and others have no particular connotation.

For example, consider these three common words: *thin, slim,* and *skinny.* Of them, which communicates the most positive view, the most negative view, a rather neutral view? On the lines provided, write the three words from most negative to most positive:

Most Negative Word	Neutral Word	Most Positive Word
1. _____	2. _____	3. _____

Consider these pairs of words. In each case circle the one that carries the more positive message.

egghead	genius
He-man's Shop	Fat-man's Shop
hard worker	grind
changed his mind	waffled on the issues

Consider these sets of words. In each case circle the one that carries the most positive message. There is really no right answer.

beautiful	gorgeous	pretty
fat	obese	chubby
delicious	tasty	scrumptious
steaming	hot	scalding

As you read, you should watch for words such as these that carry particularly positive or negative connotations. They are clues to an author's bias.

A fourth strategy is to ask: Is there another way to view the facts? How would someone on the other side have described the situation, place, or person in question? How would someone on the other side have told the story?

Reading to Assess the Validity of a Judgment

Once you have identified a selection as one expressing an opinion, your next step is to clarify what the author is saying and how he or she is supporting the position he or she is taking. Generally a well-formulated judgment includes both the author's opinion and some support for that opinion. In assessing the validity of a judgment, therefore, you must consider the facts the author musters in support of his or her point of view.

In this context, you must ask: What is this writer advocating? Answering this question helps you identify the main idea of the selection as well as the writer's basic opinion on the topic.

You must also ask: What facts (if any) does the author use to support the judgment? Does he or she clearly organize those facts? Does he or she present a logical argument?

And finally you must ask: How do I feel about this topic? Do I agree? Disagree? Why? Why not? Should I reserve judgment on this issue because the argument is insufficient to convince me either way? In reading opinion and judgment, you should assess your own feelings on the topic. To help you grasp a writer's opinion and supporting facts, you may find it useful to record on a guide such as the one in Figure 13.1.

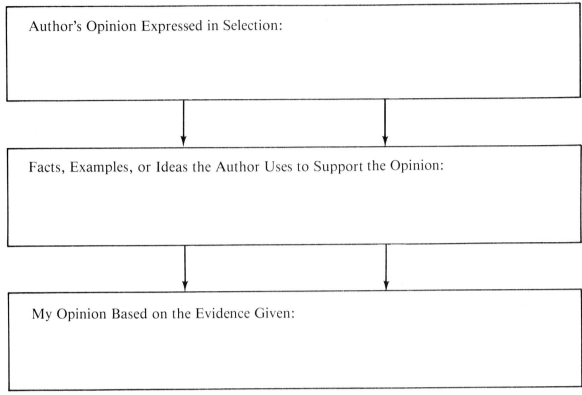

Figure 13.1   *A Guide for Recording Opinions*

Strategies for Understanding Opinions and Judgments

In the selections you read next, keep asking yourself the questions identified in the previous section. Apply these strategies:

● Consider the kind of piece you are reading, the background the author brings to the topic, and the orientation of the publisher;

● Identify words that indicate opinion;

● Note words that communicate positive or negative connotations;

● State to yourself the author's position relative to the topic;

● Assess the argument (if any) that the author presents in support of his or her position;

● Ask yourself if there is another way to view the facts;

● Identify your own feelings on the topic.

In short, as you read, you carry on a conversation with yourself in your head, asking and answering questions as you go along. Do this as you read the next selections.

SELECTION 1: THE EIGHT BEST PRESIDENTS—
AND WHY (Literature—Essay)

Expanding Your Vocabulary for Reading

Using context and word-structure clues, figure out the meaning of the italicized words. Check your ideas in the glossary. Record the meaning of the terms in the margin.

1. By limiting himself to two terms, Washington set a *precedent* that other presidents followed and was not broken for many years.

2. After years of peace and prosperity, people got *complacent* and began to believe that good times would last forever.

3. The rebels were *roundly* beaten by the well-trained troops. Few escaped injury or death.

4. The student took the job out of *economic* necessity; her financial condition required it.

5. That executive was known for his words of *deprecation*. He rarely if ever offered praise to his employees.

6. The business executives formed a *trust*, a combination of companies to control the production and price of goods. This is an illegal economic practice in this country.

7. The Romans built a *pantheon* to honor their gods.

8. I do not want a *synthetic* diamond; I want a genuine one.

9. During the Middle Ages, the lord of the manor was the *sovereign* of the land. He had the power of life and death over all the people who lived on his estate.

Getting Ready to Read

Preview the selection by reading the title, author, and subheadings.

● What is this article about? _____

● What do you know about the author of the selection? _____

_____

● Does the title suggest that the article is going to be mostly fact or opinion? What clue did you use in deciding? _____

_____

● Write one question that you would hope to answer through reading the selection by Truman. _____

_____

Reading with Meaning

Read each section of this selection. Keep asking yourself: What is Truman's judgment of this president? What words does he use that tell me he is presenting his opinion? What facts does he give to support his opinion? Answer the questions in the outer margin after reading each subsection.

THE EIGHT BEST PRESIDENTS—AND WHY

Harry S. Truman

George Washington

1. Truman's opinion of Washington:

_____

_____

There isn't any question about Washington's greatness. If his Administration had been a failure, there would have been no United States. He had all the background that caused him to know how to make it work, because he had worked under the Continental

Congress. Some Presidents have limited their roles to being administrators of the laws without being leaders. But Washington was both a great administrator and a great leader.

I guess, in fact, that the only anti-Washington thing I can say is that he made a mistake when he established the precedent of the two-term Presidency, and even there he had a good personal reason for wanting that, at least for himself. He was attacked viciously by the press of his day; he was called so many terrible things that he told friends even during his first term that he wasn't going to run again. But Thomas Jefferson and James Madison and Alexander Hamilton persuaded him to go ahead and serve a second term and finally he did. After he'd gotten through his second term, though, he made up his mind that he just wouldn't take it anymore, and he quit. That established the precedent. . . .

Thomas Jefferson

Jefferson also had his share of press criticism and people who didn't like him, and I wonder how many people remember our history and realize how close Jefferson came to losing the election in 1800, and how close Aaron Burr came to being our third President. . . .

Jefferson was called a runaway President because he pushed through our purchase of Louisiana over a lot of opposition. I think Jefferson's purchase of Louisiana was one of the best decisions ever made because, if we hadn't taken over Louisiana, then either Britain, France or Spain would have owned it and our country would have ended at the Mississippi River, whereas the greatest part of our development has been our ability to expand beyond the Mississippi. I don't like this talk about runaway Presidents, because the truth is that a President just does what he has to do.

Andrew Jackson

Jackson was elected after a period of what they called in James Monroe's time "the era of good feeling." Well, when the era of good feeling got to feeling too good, meaning that the people and the government became too complacent and too lazy, why, the country went to the dogs, as it has always done. You have got to have opposition if you're going to keep a republic going. Old Jackson remedied that, and he did it in a way that was perfectly satisfactory to all concerned. The economic royalists, the favored few, had control of the government by controlling the finances of the country. A man named Nicholas Biddle and his Bank of the United States had all the government's money, and Jackson took the money away from him and in effect put all the dollar bills back into the Treasury of the United States, where they ought to be, by spreading the funds into various state banks. And, of course, he was roundly abused for doing things of that sort.

James Knox Polk

This choice may surprise some people. Polk isn't much thought about these days. First, he exercised his powers of the Presidency as I think they should be exercised. He was President during the

2. Clue words that tell you are dealing with opinion: _____
_____

3. Reasons Truman gives to support his opinion:
_____
_____
_____
_____

1. Truman's opinion of the Louisiana Purchase:
_____
_____

2. Clue words that tell you are dealing with opinion: _____
_____

3. Reasons Truman gives to support his opinion:
_____
_____
_____
_____

1. Truman's opinion of Jackson: _____
_____

2. Clue words that tell you are dealing with opinion: _____
_____

3. Reasons Truman gives to support his opinion:
_____
_____
_____
_____

1. Truman's opinion of Polk: _____
_____

2. Clue words that tell you are dealing with opinion: _____ _____ _____

3. Reasons Truman gives to support his opinion: _____ _____ _____ _____

1. Truman's opinion of Lincoln: _____ _____

2. Clue words that tell you are dealing with opinion: _____ _____ _____

3. Reasons Truman gives to support his opinion: _____ _____ _____ _____

1. Truman's opinion of Cleveland: _____ _____

2. Clue words that tell you are dealing with opinion: _____ _____

3. Reasons Truman gives to support his opinion:

Mexican War, in an age when the terrible burden of making decisions in a war was entirely in the hands of the President. And when that came about, he decided that that was much more important than going to parties and shaking hands with people.

Second, he bought the Southwest part of the country for just about the same price that Jefferson paid for Louisiana; and third, he did something that most of the rest of us who were Presidents weren't able to do: He decided when he went in there that he would only serve one term, and that's what he did. He knew exactly what he wanted to do in a specified period of time and did it, and when he got through with it he went home. He said a moving thing on his retirement: "I now retire as a servant and regain my position as a sovereign." He was right, absolutely right. I've been through it, and I know.

Abraham Lincoln

Lincoln was a strong executive who saved the government, saved the United States. He was a President who understood people, and, when it came time to make decisions, he was willing to take the responsibility and make those decisions, no matter how difficult they were. He knew how to treat people and how to make a decision stick, and that's why his is regarded as such a great Administration.

Carl Sandburg and a lot of others have tried to make something out of Lincoln that he wasn't. He was a decent man, a good politician, and a great President, and they've tried to build up things that he never even thought about. I'll bet a dollar and a half that if you read Sandburg's biography of Lincoln, you'll find things put into Lincoln's mouth and mind that never even occurred to him. He was a good man who was in the place where he ought to have been at the time important events were taking place, but when they write about him as though he belongs in the pantheon of the gods, that's not the man he really was. He was the best kind of ordinary man, and when I say that he was an ordinary man, I mean that as high praise, not deprecation. That's the highest praise you can give a man, that he's one of the people and becomes distinguished in the service that he gives other people. He was one of the people, and he wanted to stay that way. And he was that way until the day he died. One of the reasons he was assassinated was because he didn't feel important enough to have the proper guards around him at Ford's Theatre.

Grover Cleveland

At least Cleveland was a great President in his first term; in his second term, he wasn't the same Grover Cleveland he was to begin with. Cleveland reestablished the Presidency by being not only a Chief Executive but also a leader. Cleveland spent most of his time in his first term working on bills that came from the Congress, and he vetoed a tremendous pile of bills that were passed strictly for the purpose of helping out people who had voted for the Republican ticket. He also saw to it that a lot of laws passed, if he felt those laws were needed for the good of the general public, even if the laws weren't popular with some members of the Congress.

For the most part, however, Cleveland was a considerably less impressive man in his second term. He had a terrible time with strikes, and he called out the soldiers, and they fired on the strikers. It was also during Cleveland's second term that a number of smaller companies got together and formed great big companies for the suppression of competition. That's why I say Cleveland was a great President only in his first term.

_____
_____
_____
_____

Woodrow Wilson

I've been asked which Presidents served as models for me when I was President myself, and the answer is that there were three of them. Two were Jefferson and Jackson, and the third was Woodrow Wilson. In many ways Wilson was the greatest of the greats. He established the Federal Reserve Board. He established the Federal Trade Commission. He didn't make a great publicity stunt of being a trustbuster, the way Teddy Roosevelt did, but the trust situation was never really met until Wilson became President. Wilson also established the League of Nations, which didn't succeed but which served as a blueprint for the United Nations, which might succeed yet, despite its problems.

All a good President tries to do is accomplish things for the good of the people, and if you want to call that liberal, then I'm with you. I guess the best way to describe Wilson, if I've got to use a label, is to say that he was a common-sense liberal. He wasn't one of these synthetic liberals who aren't very liberal to people who think differently from the way they do. He was a genuine liberal who used his heart and his brain.

1. Truman's opinion of Wilson: _____
_____

2. Clue words that tell you are dealing with opinion: _____
_____

3. Reasons Truman gives to support his opinion:
_____
_____
_____
_____

Franklin Delano Roosevelt

It goes without saying that I was highly impressed by him for a thousand reasons, but a main reason is that he inherited a situation that was almost as bad as the one Lincoln had, and he dealt with it. And he was always able to make decisions. Presidents have to make decisions if they're going to get anywhere, and those Presidents who couldn't make decisions are the ones who caused all the trouble.

It took a President who understood the United States and the world, like Roosevelt, to come along and start to get the country back on its feet again in the Depression, and also to make Americans remember that we're a world power and have to act like a world power.

We also, of course, got the United Nations as a result of Roosevelt's Administration and mine, which is exactly what the League of Nations was supposed to be in the first place. I'm not saying that the United Nations is a perfect organization, or ever will be. It's far from flawless, and it's weak in many ways. But at least it's a start.

1. Truman's opinion of Roosevelt: _____
_____

2. Clue words that tell you are dealing with opinion: _____
_____

3. Reasons Truman gives to support his opinion:
_____
_____
_____
_____

Checking for Understanding

*Place an **F** before statements of fact, an **O** before statements of opinion.*

_____   1. George Washington was the first president of the United States.

_____   2. Thomas Jefferson was elected president in 1800.

_____ 3. Washington was both a great administrator and a great leader.

_____ 4. You have got to have opposition if you're going to keep a republic going.

_____ 5. A good president is going to get criticized.

_____ 6. Jackson remedied the situation in a way that was satisfactory to everyone.

_____ 7. When Polk said, "I now retire as a servant and regain my position as a sovereign," he was right, absolutely right.

_____ 8. The Louisiana Purchase occurred during Jefferson's administration.

_____ 9. Lincoln was a strong executive.

_____ 10. Lincoln was an ordinary man.

_____ 11. Cleveland was a great president during his first term, a poor one in his second term.

_____ 12. Cleveland spent a great deal of time working on bills that came from Congress.

_____ 13. Wilson helped establish the League of Nations.

_____ 14. Wilson was a genuine liberal who used his heart and his brain.

_____ 15. Franklin Roosevelt was a great president because he was always able to make decisions.

_____ 16. The United Nations is far from flawless and weak in many ways.

_____ 17. Truman believed that Woodrow Wilson was a great president.

_____ 18. Truman believed that big companies were not good for the country.

_____ 19. Big companies are not good for the country.

_____ 20. Wilson was the greatest of the greats.

Reviewing Vocabulary

Select several words from the selection vocabulary to include in your personal vocabulary list. Then place the words from this list in the sentence slots. Use each word only once.

a. complacent   d. pantheon   g. sovereign
b. deprecatory   e. precedent   h. synthetic
c. economic   f. roundly   i. trusts

1. Before the exam, the student was far from _____; he had not studied and he feared he would fail.

2. The _____ situation in the country was questionable; interest rates and unemployment were high.

3. I only buy genuine articles. Do not try to sell me something that is

_____.

4. The _____ had many servants to do her bidding.

5. That teacher is not known for praising his students. Rather he has a reputation for making _____ remarks.

6. The tennis star was _____ beaten in the championship match. Right from the beginning, she didn't have a chance.

7. Going into the basilica in Florence, I felt as though I was entering the _____ of the gods.

8. During Cleveland's administration, smaller companies got together to form _____ to suppress competition.

9. That court case set the _____ for the cases to follow. Future judges referred to the case in making their decisions.

Writing from Reading

Of the eight presidents selected by Truman as great, which one do you believe was the greatest? Write a paragraph in which you state your opinion and support that opinion with facts.

Truman is very explicit in the way he expresses his opinions. He also writes in a very clear, straightforward way. You could say that he is up front, which is an opinion and not a fact. You will have to read the next selection more closely, for the author uses a more technical way of writing and you may not be as aware that he is dealing with opinion.

SELECTION 2: THE GENIUS OF MARK TWAIN
(Newspaper Column)

Expanding Your Vocabulary for Reading

Using context clues and word-structure clues, figure out the meaning of each italicized word. Check your ideas in the glossary and record the meaning of the term in the margin.

1. She spoke in a *dialect* of English that I had trouble understanding; it was different from the variety of English I speak.

2. Mark Twain is considered a *literary* giant; he wrote many great books and contributed to our reading pleasure.

3. The sovereign *mandated* that all young people must serve in the military.

4. *Legions* of people flock to the seaside in the summertime to enjoy the sun and the surf; because of this, the beach was crowded.

5. Because he wanted only real, or genuine articles, he bought an *authentic,* eighteenth-century table.

6. That child was *incorrigible;* he would not do anything he was told to do. Regardless of how often he was punished, he kept misbehaving.

7. The woman was *obsessed* with the idea she would win the lottery; as a result, she spent thousands of dollars buying chances.

8. She had the *foresight* to take out insurance in case of accident; as a result, she was prepared when misfortune struck.

9. The council *banned* the sale of the book in the city; they did not want people reading it.

10. The author spent many months writing the *manuscript* for his book. When his book was published, however, the church banned it.

11. He has an *irrepressible* sense of humor; nothing could stop him from telling a joke.

Getting Ready to Read

The article you will read here is from the "Viewpoint" page of a newspaper. It is written by Lawrence Hall, a columnist who is African American. It is similar to the kind of article you can expect to find on the editorial pages of a regional newspaper. You should make it a habit to read a regional newspaper, especially the editorial pages. Preview the article by reading the title and the first, second, and last paragraphs.

● What is the topic of the article? _____

● What do you predict will be Hall's view of Mark Twain and Twain's book *Huckleberry Finn?* _____

● What do you know about Twain and *Huckleberry Finn?* _____

_____

● What purpose will you keep in mind as you read this article? What questions will you try to answer? _____

_____

_____

Reading with Meaning

Read the selection. Keep asking yourself: What is Hall's judgment of Twain and Huck Finn? What words does he use that tell he is dealing with opinion? What facts does he cite to support his judgment? Answer the questions in the outer margin as you go along.

THE GENIUS OF MARK TWAIN: DISCOVERY OF HUCK FINN "DRAFT" UNDERLINES AUTHOR'S GREATNESS

Lawrence Hall   April 12, 1991

1. List one or more words that suggest that Hall is expressing his opinion rather than simply stating facts.

2. What is Hall's opinion of the book, *Huckleberry Finn?*

Recently, I pulled from the bookshelf the *Illustrated Works of Mark Twain* and reread *Huckleberry Finn.* Needless to say, I was so transported back in time that the entire reading—which I accomplished in a day—was mindboggling. It was, truly, an incredible experience. There I was on a raft, on the Mississippi with such characters as the incorrigible, homeless Huck Finn who escaped from "civilization" with the slave Jim. And as they got caught up in funny and violent experiences, Huck and Jim spoke a strange kind of southern dialect which, at first, was difficult to comprehend until my eyes and brain became familiar with the language.

What prompted me to reexperience this book was the announcement by a well-known auction house of a literary find. The first half of the original text of *Huckleberry Finn,* written in longhand, was recently found in a trunk in a Hollywood attic. The second half of the original manuscript is in the custody of the Buffalo, N.Y., public library.

3. Write here a sentence from the paragraph that expresses a fact.

The startling thing about this discovery was the 665-page manuscript differed greatly from the published text which many of us may once have read and loved. For example, the manuscript features a dramatic scene in which Jim discusses his experiences with corpses and ghosts on a stormy night, and a 54-page fight scene aboard the raft.

4. Write here a sentence from the paragraph that expresses a fact.

Rereading this book reminded me of the sad state of humor in this country. There is so much bad, ugly and violent humor in these strange times—so much so that most folks haven't the slightest notion of what humor is all about.

5. Write here a line from the paragraph that expresses an opinion.

The irrepressible Twain, "the Lincoln of our literature," was probably one of the few wits in this nation to employ humor successfully throughout his life. Twain, whose real name was Samuel Langhorne Clemens, held that humor "is only a fragrance, a decoration. Humor must not professedly teach and it must not professedly preach, but it must do both if it would live forever. By forever, I mean 30 years."

6. At what point is Hall expressing an opinion in this paragraph?

7. At what point is Hall expressing a fact in this paragraph?

Much of Twain's literary work has stood the test of time—at least more than his mandated 30 years. H. L. Mencken hailed him as "the one authentic giant of our literature . . . the full equal of Cervantes and Molière, Swift, and Defoe." The proof of Mencken's contention can be seen clearly in *Huckleberry Finn.*

8. Hall states that Mencken hailed Twain as a literary giant. Is this opinion or fact? Why?
9. Mencken wrote that Twain was an equal of Cervantes. Opinion or fact? Why?

Now, I know there are legions of folks—including many black Americans—who look upon *Huckleberry Finn* as nothing more than a racist tract, with Jim stumbling and bumbling through the book, ridiculed and treated as if he were sub-human. But, it's very easy to get hung up reading this book for possible racial slights and in the process miss the fine humor which flows from Twain's pen.

10. Hall writes that it's very easy to get hung up reading this book for racial slights. Opinion or fact? What makes you think so?

This is one of the main points of William Keough, an English professor at Fitchburg State College in Massachusetts in his new book, *Punchlines: The Violence of American Humor.* "*Huckleberry Finn* is a book all African-Americans should insist on; it is a book to make white America blush. Huckleberry Finn still shocks and dazzles . . . *Huckleberry Finn* is certainly not a book without flaws; but as a portrait of frontier American society, warts and all, it has no peer."

11. When Keough calls *Huckleberry Finn* a book that has no peer, is he expressing an opinion or a fact? How do you know?

Twain wrote this book in fits and starts, and tortured himself trying to find a way to end it. But that was the way he normally worked, taking several years to complete a book. When he completed the book, Twain sold it by subscription in advance of publication, and easily collected 40,000 people willing to buy a copy.

12. When Hall writes that Twain normally took several years to complete a book, is he expressing an opinion or a fact?

13. Was the library committee's statement that the book was immoral fact or opinion?

14. In the 1950s CORE sued to have the book banned in Brooklyn. Is this a fact or opinion?

15. The book went on to sell 500,000 copies. Is this a fact or an opinion?

16. When Hall concludes with the statement, "Ah, what riches Twain left for his readers," is he expressing an opinion or a fact?

After it was finally published, the Concord, Mass., public library committee banned the book in 1887, claiming it was subversive, immoral and not wholesome literature for America's reading public.

Ironically, less than a century later, the Congress of Racial Equality (CORE) in the late 1950s successfully sued to have the book banned in Brooklyn because of what it perceived to be racial slurs throughout the book.

Nonetheless, Twain saw a bigger profit in his book being banned by the library. He declared, "That will sell 25,000 copies of our book for sure!" The book went on to sell 500,000 copies then, and today it's difficult to ascertain how many millions of copies have been sold.

One thing is certain, though. The profit from *Huckleberry Finn* helped to feed Twain's obsession with get-rich schemes. For instance, he toyed with investing in, among other things, a carpet-pattern machine and a mechanical organ. Alas, Twain lacked foresight in his investments. He foolishly decided not to invest in Alexander Graham Bell's telephone because he didn't see it as a sound risk. But he lost $300,000 on a new typesetting machine, and other ventures.

Thank goodness, Twain was a better writer than an investor in get-rich schemes. The newly discovered manuscript of *Huckleberry Finn* at least will pay off, with a new version of life on the Mississippi River aboard a raft. Ah, what riches Twain left for his readers.

Checking for Understanding

Complete Figure 13.2 using points you recorded in the margin. Then answer these questions.

1. What is Lawrence Hall's opinion of Mark Twain? Write a complete sentence or two summarizing Hall's opinion.

2. What is Lawrence Hall's opinion of *Huckleberry Finn?* Write a complete sentence or two summarizing Hall's opinion.

3. What words that carry a positive connotation does Hall use to help you see his point of view? List them here.

4. Hall quotes Professor Keough. What is Keough's opinion of *Huckleberry Finn?*

5. Do you agree with Hall and Keough? Explain why or why not.

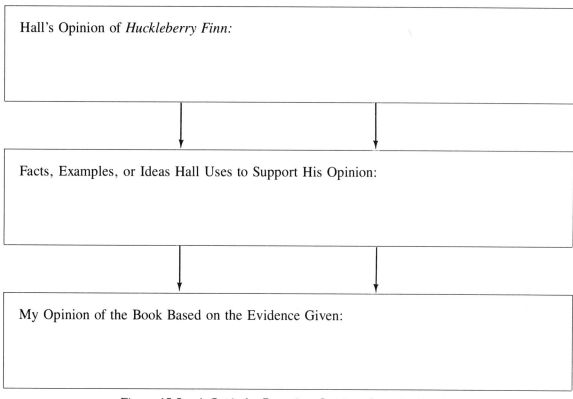

Figure 13.2   *A Guide for Recording Opinions from the Hall Article*

Reviewing Important Vocabulary

Fill in the blanks with words from this list. Use context clues to help you.

a. authentic   d. foresight   g. legions   j. manuscript

b. banned   e. incorrigible   h. literary   k. obsessed

c. dialects   f. irrepressible   i. mandates

1. Shakespeare is considered one of the _____ giants of all times.

2. Twain worked several years completing a _____ for one of his books.

3. The college student was so _____ with keeping thin that he barely ate anything.

4. The writers of the Constitution had the _____ to mandate a government with a system of checks and balances.

5. There are numerous _____ in the English language; where you grow up determines which one you speak.

6. The youngster was _____; he would not obey his parents or his teachers.

7. The countryside was infested with _____ of grasshoppers. The grasshoppers were so numerous that there were no crops left after they arrived.

8. The restaurant _____ anyone from entering who was not dressed in formal attire.

9. I have an _____ first edition of that manuscript. I know it is genuine.

10. Mark Twain had an _____ sense of humor. It showed up in everything he wrote.

11. The law _____ that the police must explain a prisoner's rights to him or her before questioning.

SELECTION 3: MAYA ANGELOU'S SCHOOL THOUGHTS
(Literature—Autobiography)

Expanding Vocabulary for Reading

Use context and word-structure clues to figure out the meaning of each italicized term. Check the glossary if you are unsure. Write the meaning in the margin.

1. The prime minister had an *aura* of authority that made her stand out from the others in the room.

2. The people were so convinced of their *invincibility* that when they lost the war, they could hardly accept it.

3. Until his mother called a halt, the older boy *intimidated* his younger brother, making him fearful and timid.

4. The shopper was struck by the *rarefied,* or very refined, atmosphere in the elite store.

5. I experienced severe *trauma* each time I recalled the appalling accident.

6. His *florid* complexion indicated to me that the man had been drinking.

7. The teacher told me to *elaborate* on what I had said, but I could not think of anything more on the topic.

8. The student's interest *diminished* as the time went on; soon she was asleep.

9. The dollar is the major unit of *currency* in the United States, whereas the pound is the major unit of currency in England.

10. Her behavior was often a bit *frivolous;* as a result, she got a reputation for not being a serious person.

Getting Ready to Read

Preview the title, the name of the author, and the introductory matter before reading.

● What is the selection generally about? _____

● Do you know anything about the author? If so, note it here.

_____

_____

Reading with Meaning

Read the selection to see how Maya Angelou felt about George Washington High School and her teacher there. As you read, think about similar experiences you had in high school.

SCHOOL THOUGHTS
FROM I KNOW WHY THE CAGED BIRD SINGS

Maya Angelou

In this selection Maya Angelou describes her experiences, first in her local high school and then in George Washington High School in San Francisco.

Although my grades were very good (I had been put up two semesters on my arrival from Stamps), I found myself unable to settle down in high school. It was an institution for girls near my house, and the young ladies were faster, brasher, meaner and more prejudiced than any I had met at Lafayette County Training School. Many of the Negro girls were, like me, straight from the South, but they had known or claimed to have known the bright lights of Big D (Dallas) or T Town (Tulsa, Oklahoma), and their language bore up their claims. They strutted with an aura of invincibility, and along with some of the Mexican students who put knives in their tall pompadours they absolutely intimidated the white girls and those Black and Mexican students who had no shield of fearlessness. Fortunately I was transferred to George Washington High School.

The beautiful buildings (of George Washington High) sat on a moderate hill in the white residential district, some sixty blocks from the Negro neighborhood. For the first semester, I was one of three Blacks in the school, and in that rarefied atmosphere I came to love my people more. Mornings as the streetcar traversed my ghetto I experienced a mixture of dread and trauma. I knew that all too soon we would be out of my familiar setting, and Blacks who were on the streetcar when I got on would all be gone and I alone would face the forty blocks of neat streets, smooth lawns, white houses and rich children.

In the evenings on the way home the sensations were joy, anticipation and relief at the first sign which said BARBECUE or DO DROP INN or HOME COOKING or at the first brown faces on the streets. I recognized that I was again in my country.

In the school itself I was disappointed to find that I was not the most brilliant or even nearly the most brilliant student. The white kids had better vocabularies than I and, what was more appalling, less fear in the classrooms. They never hesitated to hold up their hands in response to a teacher's question; even when they were wrong they were wrong aggressively, while I had to be certain about all my facts before I dared to call attention to myself.

George Washington High School was the first real school I attended. My entire stay there might have been time lost if it hadn't been for the unique personality of a brilliant teacher. Miss Kirwin was that rare educator who was in love with information. I will always believe that her love of teaching came not so much from her liking for students but from her desire to make sure that some of the things she knew would find repositories so that they could be shared again.

She and her maiden sister worked in the San Francisco city school system for over twenty years. My Miss Kirwin, who was a tall, florid, buxom lady with battleship-gray hair, taught civics and current events. At the end of a term in her class our books were as clean and the pages as stiff as they had been when they were issued to us. Miss Kirwin's students were never or very rarely called upon to open textbooks.

She greeted each class with "Good day, ladies and gentlemen." I had never heard an adult speak with such respect to teenagers. (Adults usually believe that a show of honor diminishes their authority.) "In today's *Chronicle* there was an article on the mining industry in the Carolinas (or some such distant subject). I am certain that all of you have read the article. I would like someone to elaborate on the subject for me."

After the first two weeks in her class, I, along with all other excited students, read the San Francisco papers, *Time* magazine, *Life* and everything else available to me. Miss Kirwin proved Bailey right. He had told me once that "all knowledge is spendable currency, depending on the market."

There were no favorite students. No teacher's pets. If a student pleased her during a particular period, he could not count on special treatment in the next day's class, and that was as true the other way around. Each day she faced us with a clean slate and acted as if ours were clean as well. Reserved and firm in her opinions, she spent no time in indulging the frivolous.

She was stimulating instead of intimidating. Where some of the other teachers went out of their way to be nice to me—to be a "liberal" with me—and others ignored me completely, Miss Kirwin never seemed to notice that I was Black and therefore different. I was Miss Johnson and if I had the answer to a question she posed I was never given any more than the word "Correct," which was what she said to every other student with the correct answer.

Years later when I returned to San Francisco I made visits to her classroom. She always remembered that I was Miss Johnson, who had a good mind and should be doing something with it. I was never encouraged on those visits to loiter or linger about her desk. She acted as if I must have had other visits to make. I often wondered if she knew she was the only teacher I remembered.

Checking for Understanding

Answer on your own. Be ready to support your answers.

1. What was Angelou's opinion of the "Negro girls straight from the South"?

2. What evidence does the author present in support of her opinion?

3. How did Angelou feel as she rode the streetcar to George Washington High School?

4. Describe when you have felt the same way.

5. What was Maya Angelou's opinion of the "white kids" at George Washington High?

6. What evidence does the author present in support of her opinion?

7. What was Angelou's opinion of her teacher, Miss Kirwin?

8. What evidence does she present to support her opinion?

9. How did the students in Miss Kirwin's class learn if they never opened their books? How do you know this?

10. Someone named Bailey told Angelou that "all knowledge is spendable currency, depending on the market." What did he mean by that? Do you agree? Why? Why not? Support your opinion with reasons.

Reviewing Key Words

Place the words from this list in the appropriate sentence slots.

a. aura   d. elaborate   g. intimidate   i. rarefied
b. currency   e. florid   h. invincibility j. trauma
c. diminished f. frivolous

1. The bully tried to _____ me, but I was not afraid of him.

2. There is an _____ of both strength and gentleness about Maya Angelou; her distinctive air makes her stand out among other writers.

3. If you cannot _____ on that topic, tell me what you know about any other related topic.

4. When the wind _____ and the rain stopped, I knew the storm was over.

5. When I traveled in France, I had to learn to use the French _____ because there are no dollars and cents in that country.

6. Her _____ behavior annoyed us. We wanted to be serious and she acted in the opposite way.

7. She experienced extreme _____ at the death of father.

8. In the _____ atmosphere of that elite college, I grew restless for the ordinary happenings I was accustomed to at home.

9. I was never convinced of the _____ of our army. As a result, I was not surprised by the defeat.

10. The speaker was so angry that his face became _____. I feared he would have a heart attack.

Select several of the new vocabulary words and enter them into your personal vocabulary list to use in writing and speaking.

Writing About Reading

Do you have a teacher you remember from elementary or high school? Following Maya Angelou's model, write a paragraph or two describing that teacher. In your paragraph state your opinion of him or her. To help you get started, first jot down any words that come to mind to describe the teacher. Then build your paragraph using those words.

EXTENDING WHAT YOU HAVE LEARNED

Applying Reading Strategies

Select an editorial or a syndicated column from a newspaper. Record the title, author, date, and newspaper on an index card. Read the column, applying the strategies for reading persuasive writing. On the card, record the main topic of the column, the point of view of the writer, and the evidence the writer cites in support of the point of view. Decide: Does the author make you agree with him or her?

Extending Your Vocabulary

Select several of the words featured in this chapter to record in your personal vocabulary list. Include a model sentence for each. Try to use your chosen words in speaking and writing.

Writing Opinions

1. Think about an issue of current interest. Phrase that issue as a question. For example, Should smoking be banned in all public buildings? Should college tuition be raised? Should candidates for public office be judged on the way they handle their private lives? Decide how you feel about the issue. Write a paragraph or two in which you state your opinion and support that opinion with reasons.

2. Write a brief summary of a book you have read or a film you have seen. Then express your opinion of the book or film and support your opinion by describing specific things about the film or book that you liked.

14

Interpreting Tables, Graphs, and Diagrams

Before reading the chapter, read the title, the stated objective, and the headings and subheadings. Ask yourself: What is the topic of the chapter? In the space above and beside the chapter number, jot down what you already know about the topic. Then in the space below the number, jot down at least two questions you hope to answer through reading the chapter.

OBJECTIVE

In this chapter, you will learn to interpret data presented visually; specifically, you will learn to read tables, graphs, and diagrams.

INTRODUCTION—TABLES, GRAPHS, AND DIAGRAMS

Many textbooks have accompanying figures, or illustrations. You should look at these visuals briefly during your before-reading preview. In previewing, just read the captions to get a rough idea of the data available in the figures. As you later read the text, you should study each figure at the point when it is referenced (for example, "See Fig. 2.5" or "as shown in Fig. 12.4"). Usually figures are indicated numerically; Figure 4.7 is the seventh figure in Chapter 4.

Tables

One way that authors present information is in a table with labeled rows and columns. An example is shown in Figure 14.1.

To interpret a table,

- Read its title and/or caption. The title usually gives the topic—what the table is about.

- Read the labels on the rows and columns, looking particularly at the labels indicating the units that apply to numerical data (for example, area given in square miles, population given in millions, numbers given as percentages).

- Analyze the data to find relationships within them: Which is the biggest? The smallest? Which is the first? The last? Which is the fastest? The slowest? What feature is shared by all the items? Is there a pattern or trend in the data? How do the data relate to the information in the textual part?

Learning the Strategies

Study the table in Figure 14.1. Then answer these questions:

1. The table tells the reader
   a. the way land is used in countries in relation to their populations.
   b. the need for conservation in diverse countries of the world.
   c. the need for population control in different countries of the world.
   d. the relationship between famine and food production in countries of the world.
   e. all of the above.
2. The area of the United States is given as 3,615,104. This means that there are
   a. 3,615,104 people in the United States.
   b. 3,615,104 square miles of territory in the United States.
   c. 3,615,104 acres of territory in the United States.
   d. 3,615,104 people in the United States for every square mile of territory.
   e. 3,615,104 people in the United States for every acre of territory.
3. The cultivated area of the United States is listed as 20. This means that
   a. 20 thousand square miles of territory are under cultivation in the United States.
   b. 20 million square miles of territory are under cultivation in the United States.
   c. 20 percent of the land in the United States is under cultivation.
   d. 20 people live on each square mile of land in the United States.
   e. none of the above.
4. The forested area of the United States is listed as 28. From this and other information in the chart, you can say that the United States has
   a. more land under cultivation than is forested.
   b. less land under cultivation than is forested.
   c. the same amount of land cultivated as is forested.

	Area in Square Miles	Percentage Cultivated	Population in Millions	Percentage Forested
United States	3,615,104	20	243.8	28
Former USSR	8,649,498	10	284.0	42
Netherlands	14,405	23	14.6	8
Brunei	2,228	1	0.2	49
India	1,269,340	51	800.3	21
China	3,705,390	11	1,062.0	14
Egypt	386,660	2	51.9	0
Kenya	224,961	4	22.4	6
Brazil	3,286,475	9	141.5	66

Figure 14.1 *Populations on the Land* (1987)

5. The actual area of the United States that is forested is
   a. 3,615,104 square miles.
   b. 723,020.8 square miles.
   c. 1,012,229.12 square miles.
   d. 48,760,000 millions.
   e. 68,264,000 millions.
6. The population of the United States is listed as 243.8. This means
   a. 243.8 people lived in the United States in 1987.
   b. 243,800 people lived in the United States in 1987.
   c. 2,438,000 people lived in the United States in 1987.
   d. 243,800,000 people lived in the United States in 1987.
   e. 243,800,000,000 people lived in the United States in 1987.

   Now check your answers to 1 through 6.

1. The answer to the first question is "a." The table tells the reader the way the land is used in different countries in relation to their population. You know this from the title of the table and because the labels at the heads of the columns are "Population in Millions," "Area in Square Miles," "Percentage Cultivated," and "Percentage Forested." No data tell you definitively that there is need for conservation or population control. There are no data on famine. If you picked one of the other options in question 1, beware of reading too much into a table.

2. The answer to question 2 is "b." There are 3,615,104 square miles of territory in the United States. You get this fact by reading the data in the row labeled "United States" and the column labeled "Area in Square Miles." The number in this slot of the grid is 3,615,104. In reading that fact, you must affix the numerical label to it—in other words, 3,615,104 square miles. This shows that the numerical labels on the grid are important. The labels tell you how to interpret the data.

3. The answer to question 3 is "c." 20 percent of U.S. land is cultivated. Again you get this information by applying the numerical label at the head of the column ("Percentage Cultivated") to the number in the row labeled "United States."

4. The answer to question 4 is "b." 28 percent of U.S. land is forested. Comparing that datum to 20 percent under cultivation, you can conclude that less land is cultivated than is forested. Since both pieces of data are given as percentages, you can make this kind of comparison.

5. The answer to question 5 is "c." To find out the actual amount of land that is forested, you must multiply the total square miles of land in the United States (3,615,104) by the percentage forested (28 percent or .28). Thus .28 of 3,615,104 square miles is 1,012,229.12 square miles. To multiply by a percentage number, you must first change it to its decimal equivalent. By the term *percentage* we mean "parts of 100." Therefore, you must multiply by .28, which really is 28/100.

Now calculate the amount of land under cultivation in the United States. First convert the percentage to its decimal equivalent. Then multiply the total square miles in the United States by that decimal equivalent. Do not use the population datum given. It does not relate directly to land under cultivation. Do your calculations here:

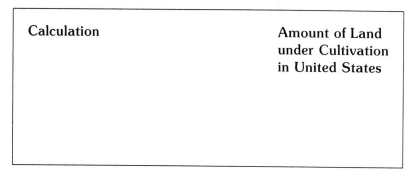

Calculation	Amount of Land under Cultivation in United States

6. The answer to question 6 is "d." The number of people living in the United States in 1987 was 243,800,000. The label on the column marked "Population in Millions" tells you how to handle data in that column. Each population figure given must be multiplied by 1,000,000 (a million), for each number is in millions.

243.8 × 1,000,000 = 243,800,000

Applying the Strategies

Now apply the principles of table reading that you have just learned to answer these questions. Take data from Figure 14.1. Your instructor will help you correct your answers.

7. The population of the Netherlands is
   a. 146,000,000.   d. 144,000,000.
   b. 14,600,000.   e. 1,460,000.
   c. 14,400,000.

8. The number of square miles of land cultivated in Egypt is
   a. 2,000,000 square miles.   d. 7733.2 square miles.
   b. 1,038,000 square miles.   e. 0 square miles.
   c. 386,660 square miles.

9. The number of square miles of land that is forested in Egypt is
   a. 2,000,000 square miles.   d. 7733.2 square miles.
   b. 1,038,000 square miles.   e. 0 square miles.
   c. 386,660 square miles.

10. The population of Brazil is
    a. 3,705,390.   d. 1,415,000.
    b. 2,169,073.   e. 141,500,000.
    c. 1,277,100.

Learning the Strategies

You can also compare countries using the data in Figure 14.1. Questions 11 through 15 are examples of how you can use tables to make comparisons.

11. The country in the table with the greatest land area is
    a. China.
    b. India.
    c. the United States.
    d. the former USSR.
    e. Brazil.

12. The country in the table with the smallest land area under cultivation is
    a. Brunei.
    b. Egypt.
    c. Kenya.
    d. Brazil.
    e. the Netherlands.

13. The country listed in the table with the greatest number of square miles of forest lands is
    a. Brunei.
    b. the former USSR.
    c. Brazil.
    d. the United States.
    e. China.

14. The country listed in the table with the largest total population is
    a. the United States.
    b. the former USSR.
    c. China.
    d. India.
    e. Brazil.

15. The country with the most cultivated land is
    a. India.
    b. the former USSR.
    c. the Netherlands.
    d. China.
    e. the United States.

Now correct questions 11 through 15.

11. The country with the greatest land area is the former USSR, answer "d." The table gives its area as 8,649,498 square miles. Run your eye down the column labeled "Area Square Miles." No other country comes anywhere near to this; the second country in size is China with a land mass of 3,705,390 square miles.

12. The answer to question 12 is "a." Brunei has the smallest total land mass—2,228 square miles, and it is the country on the chart with the smallest percentage of cultivated land (1 percent). Although you can multiply 2,228 square miles by .01 to get 22.28 square miles, you really do not have to do the calculation. If you multiply the smallest land mass by the smallest percentage under cultivation, the number you get will represent the smallest of all the countries listed.

13. The answer to question 13 is "b"—the former USSR. You can use the reasoning in question 12 here, too. The former USSR has the largest total land mass. It also has 42 percent of its land in forests. Brunei has a larger percentage of land in forest—49 percent. But Brunei is very, very small. There is no way it could have more forest land than the USSR. Brazil has a larger percentage (66 percent) of its land in forest, but its total land mass is under half that of the former USSR. Again, although you can multiply 8,649,498 by .42 to get the forest land of the former USSR (3,632,789.16 square miles of forest), and you can multiply 3,286,475 by .66 to get the forest land of Brazil (2,169,073.5 square miles of forest), and you can multiply 2,228 by .49 to get the forest land of Brunei (1091.72), you really don't have to do any calculations. You can reason out the relationships in your head.

14. The answer to question 14 is "c." The population of China is one billion, sixty-two million (1,062,000,000)! India is second with a population of a little more than eight hundred million.

15. The answer to question 15 is "b." The former USSR has the largest land mass dedicated to agriculture. You can calculate it by multiplying the total land mass of the former USSR (8,649,498 square miles) by the percentage under cultivation. The result is 864,949.8—one tenth of the total land. Although India has 51 percent under cultivation, its land mass is considerably smaller than the former USSR's; India has only 647,363.4 square miles of cultivated land—a little more than half its total mass. Again if you are mentally able to juggle numbers, you can estimate rather than do the multiplication.

You can also get another kind of information from the table in Figure 14.1—the population density, the population per square mile of territory for each nation listed. To find the number of people per square mile of land mass, you divide the total population by the total area. For example, the population per square mile in Brazil is 43.06.

$$\frac{\text{population}}{\text{area in square miles}} \quad \frac{141,500,000}{3,286,475} = 43.06 \text{ people}$$

Thus 43.06 is the number (on average) living within each square mile of Brazil. Of course, there is a problem with that figure; the population is not spread out evenly across the land mass of Brazil. Many people live tightly together in the cities, while those vast forest regions of Brazil are sparsely populated.

What is the population density of these countries? Use a calculator to do the arithmetic.

Brunei $\dfrac{\text{population 200,000}}{\text{area 2,228 square miles}} =$

India $\dfrac{\text{population 800,300,000}}{\text{area 1,269,340 square miles}} =$

China $\dfrac{\text{population 1,062,000,000}}{\text{area 3,705,390 square miles}} =$

the Netherlands $\dfrac{\text{population 14,600,000}}{\text{area 14,405 square miles}} =$

16. Of the countries listed, which has the greatest average population density?
    a. Brunei   c. China
    b. India   d. the Netherlands
17. Of the countries listed, which has the smallest average population density?
    a. Brunei   c. China
    b. India   d. the Netherlands

SELECTION 1: LAND AND POPULATIONS (Geography)

Figure 14.2 presents data on other countries of the world, similar to what you have been considering already. Use those data to answer these questions.

18. The country listed in Figure 14.2 with the largest population is
    a. Australia.   d. Mexico.
    b. Bangladesh.   e. the United Kingdom.
    c. Canada.
19. The country in Figure 14.2 with the smallest population is
    a. Australia.   d. Ethiopia.
    b. the United Kingdom.   e. Poland.
    c. Djibouti.

	Area in Square Miles	Percentage Cultivated	Population in Millions	Percentage Forested
Ethiopia	471,776	11	46.0	23
Bangladesh	55,598	63	107.1	15
Canada	3,851,792	5	25.9	33
Mexico	761,602	13	81.9	23
United Kingdom	94,525	29	56.8	9
Poland	120,726	47	37.8	28
Australia	2,967,896	6	16.2	14
Djibouti	8,494	0	0.3	0

Figure 14.2 *Land and Populations* (1987)

20. The country with the smallest land mass under cultivation is
    a. Australia.   d. Ethiopia.
    b. the United Kingdom.   e. Poland.
    c. Djibouti.
21. The country with the smallest amount of forest lands is
    a. Australia.   d. Ethiopia.
    b. the United Kingdom.   e. Poland.
    c. Djibouti.
22. The country with the largest number of square miles dedicated to farming is
    a. Ethiopia.   d. Mexico.
    b. Bangladesh.   e. Australia.
    c. Canada.
23. The country with the largest number of square miles in forest is
    a. Ethiopia.   d. Mexico.
    b. Poland.   e. Australia.
    c. Canada.
24. The country with the greatest number of people per square mile is
    a. Ethiopia.   d. Mexico.
    b. Bangladesh.   e. the United Kingdom.
    c. Canada.

SELECTION 2: THE FIFTY STATES
OF THE UNITED STATES (Geography)

Figure 14.3 contains data on the states within the United States. Use it to answer the following questions. Read the title and the labels on the rows and columns before answering.

25. The largest state in land area is
    a. Alaska.   d. Montana.
    b. California.   e. Texas.
    c. Colorado.

26. The smallest state in area is
    a. Connecticut.   d. New Jersey.
    b. Delaware.   e. Rhode Island.
    c. Hawaii.

27. The first state to enter the Union was
    a. Delaware.   d. South Carolina.
    b. Georgia.   e. Florida.
    c. New York.

Figure 14.3   *A Data Chart on the States of the United States*

State	Area in Sq. Miles	Rank in Area	Entered Union	Entry Order	Population 1990	Pop. Rank 1990	Pop. per Sq. Mile
Alabama	51,609	29	1819	22	4,040,587	22	78.3
Alaska	589,757	1	1959	49	550,043	49	0.9
Arizona	113,909	6	1912	48	3,665,228	24	32.2
Arkansas	53,104	27	1836	25	2,350,725	33	44.3
California	158,693	3	1850	31	29,760,021	1	187.5
Colorado	104,247	8	1876	38	3,294,394	26	31.6
Connecticut	5,009	48	1783	5	3,287,116	27	656.2
Delaware	2,057	49	1787	1	666,168	46	323.9
Florida	58,560	22	1845	27	12,937,926	4	220.9
Georgia	58,876	21	1788	4	6,478,216	11	110.0
Hawaii	6,450	47	1959	50	1,108,229	41	171.8
Idaho	83,557	13	1890	43	1,006,749	42	12.0
Illinois	56,400	24	1818	21	11,430,602	6	202.7
Indiana	36,291	38	1816	19	5,544,159	14	152.8
Iowa	56,290	25	1846	29	2,776,755	30	49.3
Kansas	82,264	14	1861	34	2,477,574	32	30.1
Kentucky	40,395	37	1792	15	3,685,296	23	91.2
Louisiana	48,523	31	1812	18	4,219,973	21	87.0
Maine	33,215	39	1820	23	1,227,928	38	37.0
Maryland	10,577	42	1788	7	4,781,468	19	452.1
Massachusetts	8,257	45	1788	6	6,016,425	13	728.6
Michigan	58,126	23	1837	26	9,295,297	8	159.9
Minnesota	84,068	12	1858	32	4,375,099	20	52.0
Mississippi	47,716	32	1817	20	2,573,216	31	53.9
Missouri	69,686	19	1821	24	5,117,073	15	73.4

28. The first states to enter the Union were generally located
    a. along the Pacific Coast.
    b. along the Atlantic Coast.
    c. along the Gulf of Mexico.
    d. along the Mississippi River.
    e. outside the continental United States.
29. The last two states to enter the Union were located
    a. along the Pacific Coast.
    b. along the Atlantic Coast.
    c. along the Gulf of Mexico.
    d. along the Mississippi River.
    e. outside the continental United States.
30. The most densely populated state is
    a. Connecticut.
    b. New Jersey.
    c. New York.
    d. Massachusetts.
    e. Rhode Island.
31. The most densely populated states tend to be those admitted to the Union
    a. between 1787 and 1788.
    b. between 1800 and 1850.
    c. between 1851 and 1900.
    d. between 1901 and 1950.
    e. after 1950.
32. The state with the greatest number of people is
    a. Alaska.
    b. California.
    c. New York.
    d. New Jersey.
    e. Pennsylvania.

Figure 14.3   *cont.*

State	Area in Sq. Miles	Rank in Area	Entered Union	Entry Order	Population 1990	Pop. Rank 1990	Pop. per Sq. Mile
Montana	147,138	4	1889	41	799,065	44	5.4
Nebraska	77,227	15	1867	37	1,578,385	36	20.4
Nevada	110,540	7	1864	36	1,201,833	39	10.9
New Hampshire	9,304	44	1788	9	1,109,252	40	119.2
New Jersey	7,836	46	1787	3	7,730,188	9	986.5
New Mexico	121,666	5	1912	47	1,515,069	37	12.5
New York	49,576	30	1788	11	17,990,455	2	362.9
North Carolina	52,586	28	1789	12	6,628,637	10	126.1
North Dakota	70,665	17	1889	39	638,800	47	9.0
Ohio	41,222	35	1803	17	10,847,115	7	263.1
Oklahoma	69,919	18	1907	46	3,145,585	28	45.0
Oregon	96,981	10	1859	33	2,842,321	29	29.3
Pennsylvania	45,333	33	1787	2	11,881,643	5	262.1
Rhode Island	1,214	50	1790	13	1,003,464	43	826.6
South Carolina	31,055	40	1788	8	3,486,703	25	112.3
South Dakota	77,047	16	1889	40	696,004	45	9.0
Tennessee	42,244	34	1796	16	4,877,185	17	115.5
Texas	267,338	2	1845	28	16,986,510	3	63.5
Utah	84,916	11	1896	45	1,722,850	35	20.3
Vermont	9,609	43	1791	14	562,758	48	58.6
Virginia	40,817	36	1788	10	6,187,358	12	151.6
Washington	68,192	20	1889	42	4,866,692	18	71.4
West Virginia	24,181	41	1863	35	1,793,477	34	74.2
Wisconsin	56,154	26	1848	30	4,891,769	16	87.1
Wyoming	97,914	9	1890	44	453,588	50	4.6

33. The state with the smallest number of people is
    a. Alaska.   d. North Dakota.
    b. Arizona.   e. Wyoming.
    c. Hawaii.

PICTOGRAPHS

A pictograph is a graph that uses pictures as symbols. Each picture symbol represents a fixed amount as given in the key. For example, study Figure 14.4. It is a pictograph that shows the population of the major land masses of the world. At the bottom is the key. It tells you that each person symbol on the pictograph stands for 100 million (100,000,000) people. Incomplete person symbols stand for a part of that number. A half a person symbol stands for 50 million, a quarter of one for 25 million, and so on.

An advantage of a pictograph is that you can make comparisons at a glance because the data are presented visually. A disadvantage is that, when there are parts of a picture symbol, you must estimate the amounts for which they stand. Your answer, therefore, is an approximation, not as exact as an answer based on a table.

Interpreting a Pictograph

Study the pictograph in Figure 14.4. What is the population of North America, which includes the countries of Canada and the United States? Count the number of symbolic people. There are two people plus a part of a person symbol. That part appears to be larger than a half. Because each person symbol stands for 100 million people, you could estimate that the population of North America in 1990 was about 275 million.

Now read the pictograph to find the following data:

1. The population of Africa _____

2. The population of Latin America _____

3. The population of Asia _____

4. The population of Europe _____

5. The population of the former USSR _____

Figure 14.4 *Pictograph of Population of Major Land Masses of the World in 1990*

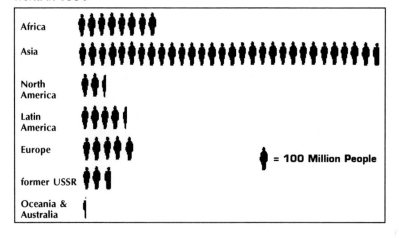

6. The population of Oceania
   (including Australia and New Zealand) _____

7. The land mass with the greatest population _____

8. The land mass with the smallest population _____

Figure 14.5 presents data on the per capita (per person) gross national product for seven countries in 1988. Each money bag stands for $2,000. Gross national product (GNP) is the total worth of goods and services produced. Given that information, you can see that the per capita GNP (which gives a rough idea of the annual wealth of an area) of Mexico is in the neighborhood of 2,000 U.S. dollars. Using Figure 14.5, supply the data required:

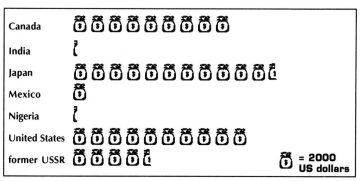

Figure 14.5   *Pictograph of Gross National Product (GNP) of Major Countries of the World in 1988*

9. The per capita GNP of Japan _____

10. The per capital GNP of Canada _____

11. The per capita GNP of India _____

12. The per capita GNP of the United States _____

13. The per capita GNP of the former USSR _____

14. The country on the pictograph with the highest per capita GNP _____

15. The country on the pictograph with the lowest per capita GNP _____

Making a Pictograph

Make a pictograph using the data in Figures 14.1 and 14.2. To do this, select a symbol to represent what you want to show—perhaps the percentage of forested land in a group of countries chosen from the chart. A good symbol in this case is a pine tree. Decide on the percentage of forested land each symbol is to represent. In this case, one pine tree might represent 10 percent forested land. Draw your pictograph in your notebook.

CIRCLE (OR PIE) GRAPHS

A pie graph is a picture that shows percentages. It is based on a circle. The whole circle stands for 100 percent of the data. The individual wedges (or pieces of the pie) give information about the parts that make up the entire pie, or circle.

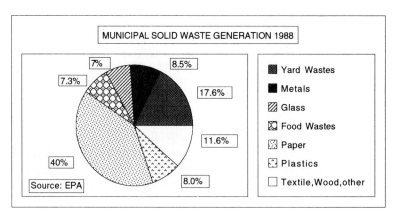

Figure 14.6   *Municipal Solid Waste Generation—A Pie Graph*

Study Figure 14.6. The title (which you should read first when studying a visual) tells you what the graph is about—municipal solid waste generation in 1988. The total circle represents 100 percent of the U.S. waste generation. If you add the percentages shown around the pie, you get 100 percent. To work effectively with a circle graph, you must understand percentages and realize that each percentage gives you "parts of 100."

Think about Figure 14.6 and answer these questions.

1. The kind of waste municipalities produce the most of: _____

2. The kind of waste municipalities produce the least of: _____

3. The percentage of total waste contributed by plastic: _____

4. The percentage of total waste contributed by metals: _____

5. Hypothesize: Why do U.S. municipalities produce so much paper wastes?

   _____

6. Hypothesize: Why do U.S. municipalities produce so much yard wastes?

   _____

7. Problem solving: What can individuals do to cut back on paper and glass

   wastes? _____

   _____

As these questions demonstrate, sometimes the reader can go beyond the data presented in a table or graph to hypothesize and solve problems.

BAR GRAPHS

Another way that data are represented visually is the bar graph. Each bar on the graph presents a piece of information. Bars can be arranged vertically or horizontally.

Study Figure 14.7. Start by reading the title. What does the graph show? Give the topic of the graph here:

1. _____

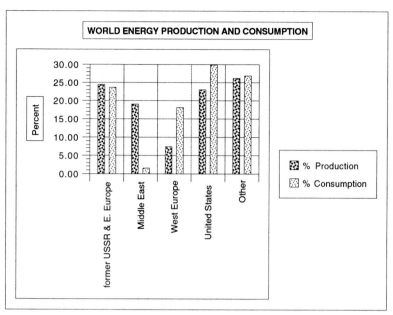

Figure 14.7   *World Energy Production and Consumption—A Bar Graph*

Now consider the data. Across the bottom on the horizontal axis are labels that identify the areas of the world for which data are given. Down the left-hand side of the graph on the vertical axis are the numbers (in this case, percentages) that guide you in interpreting each bar. For each area, there are two bars. The darker one gives data on energy production. The lighter one gives data on energy consumption.

Here is how you read the graph. Western Europe produces about 7 percent of the world's energy. It uses about 18 percent of the world's production of energy. A good hypothesis to make at this point is that Western Europe probably has to import sources of energy to make up the difference between its production and consumption.

Answer these questions based on the graph.

2. What percentage of the world's energy production comes out of the Middle East?

   _____

3. What percentage of the world's energy is consumed in the Middle East?

   _____

4. Is the Middle East more likely to be an energy importer or exporter?

   _____

   Explain _____

5. Does the United States produce all the energy it uses? _____

6. Where does the United States probably get some of the energy it uses?

   _____

7. Are the former USSR and East Europe countries likely to be big exporters of

   energy? _____

   Explain _____

8. Hypothesize: What problems do you see when countries use more energy than they produce? _____

SELECTION 3: IMMIGRATION TO THE UNITED STATES
(History)

Read the graph given in Figure 14.8 to get the information to answer the questions.

1. What kind of information is given in the graph?
   a. world immigration patterns
   b. immigration to the United States, 1850–1899
   c. emigration from Europe to the United States, 1850–1899
   d. emigration from Europe and Asia, 1850–1899
   e. All of the above are true.
2. How many people immigrated to the United States from 1890 to 1899?
   a. 2,000,000 people   d. 3,650,000 people
   b. 2,750,000 people   e. 5,250,000 people
   c. 3,200,000 people
3. During which decade did the greatest number of people immigrate to the United States?
   a. 1850–1859   d. 1880–1889
   b. 1860–1869   e. 1890–1899
   c. 1870–1879
4. During which decade did the smallest number of people come to the United States from other countries?
   a. 1850–1859   d. 1880–1889
   b. 1860–1869   e. 1890–1899
   c. 1870–1879

Figure 14.8   *Immigration to the United States—A Bar Graph*

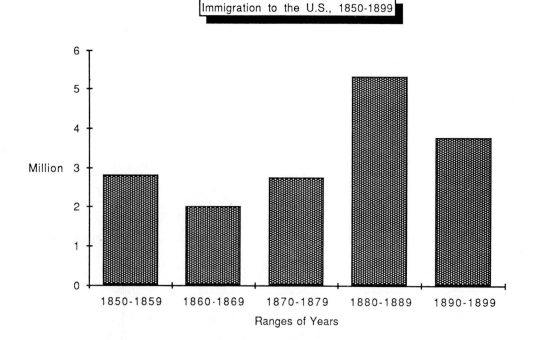

Immigration to the U.S., 1850-1899

5. How did the number of immigrants to the United States during 1890–1899 compare to the number during 1880–1889?
   a. The number during 1890–1899 was less than that during 1880–1889.
   b. The number during 1890–1899 was greater than that during 1880–1889.
   c. The number during both periods was approximately the same.
6. How did the number of immigrants to the United States during 1850–1859 compare to the number during 1870–1879?
   a. The number during 1850–1859 was much less than that during 1870–1879.
   b. The number during 1850–1859 was much greater than that during 1870–1879.
   c. The number during both periods was approximately the same.
7. Think about the decade in which immigration to the United States was the lowest. Can you account for the low that occurred during that decade? If you can, write a sentence that explains why there was a drop in immigration during that period.

_____

_____

LINE GRAPHS

A line graph is another way of representing numerical data visually. A line graph has two labeled axes—vertical and horizontal. Figure 14.9 is a line graph showing the same data as the bar graph in Figure 14.8. Notice that the number of immigrants is given on the vertical axis, the time periods on the horizontal axis, as in Figure 14.8. Notice, too, that it is easy to see the ups and downs in immigration on this simple line graph.

Figure 14.10 is another line graph. Preview it by reading the title. The topic of the graph is Pesticide Production in the United States. Look at the labels on the points marked on the vertical axis. They start at the bottom with 100 million pounds of pesticide and extend to 1,600 million pounds of pesticide in even increments of 200 million pounds. That means that there is the same distance on the axis between 200

Figure 14.9   *Immigration to the United States—A Line Graph*

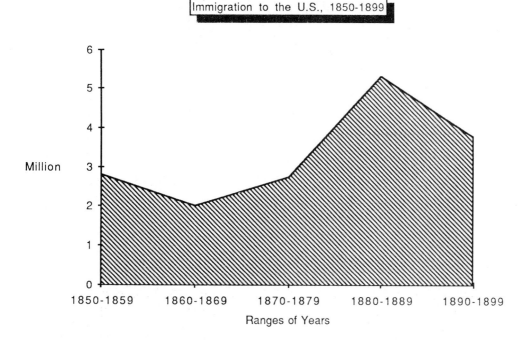

and 400 million pounds as between 1,400 and 1,600 pounds. Notice that the unit (millions of pounds) is given. The author of the graph did not write out the big numbers (e.g., 200,000,000), but used only 200 with the label that it means "millions of pounds."

Now think about the horizontal axis. It indicates the years for which data are given—in this case, 1947 to 1985. Notice that in general the years are given in increments of five years (1970, 1975, 1980), and the labeled years are placed beneath marked points on the horizontal axis. Notice again that the space between each marked year point (e.g., between 1970 and 1975 and between 1975 and 1980) is the same.

Before trying to get information from a line graph, you should read the title and the labels on the axes, including any units indicated.

Now answer these questions based on Figure 14.10.

1. The topic of the graph is
   a. the millions of pounds of pesticides.
   b. the United States between 1947 and 1985.
   c. the pesticide production in the United States from 1947 to 1985.
2. The 800 written on the vertical axis refers to
   a. 800 people.   c. 800,000,000 people.
   b. 800,000,000 pounds of pesticide.   d. 800 pounds of pesticide.
3. The year in which the greatest amount of pesticide was produced in the United States was
   a. 1950.   c. 1974.
   b. 1965.   d. 1980.
4. The amount of pesticide produced each year in the United States from 1947 to 1985 tended to
   a. decrease.   b. increase.   c. stay the same.

Figure 14.10 *Pesticide Production in the United States— A Line Graph*

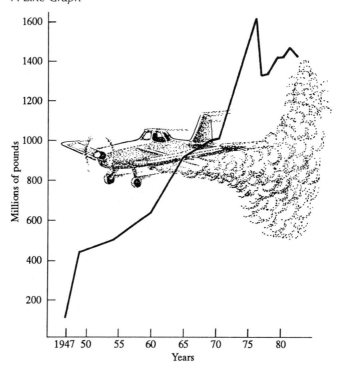

5. The amount of pesticide produced in the United States from 1947 to 1985
   a. went down once during the period.
   b. went down twice during the period.
   c. went down three times during the period.
   d. never went down during the period.

SELECTION 4: WEATHER IN NEW DELHI AND SANTIAGO (Climatology)

    Preview the two graphs in Figure 14.11. Read the titles and the labels on the vertical and horizontal axes. Note that each graph has two lines. The top solid line gives the average high temperature in that location. The bottom solid line gives the average low temperature there. Note again that the units on the vertical axis increase in equal increments.

    Now study the graphs and answer these questions.

1. During what month does the temperature reach its highest point in New Delhi?
   a. April   d. July
   b. May   e. August
   c. June
2. During what month does the temperature reach its lowest point in New Delhi?
   a. November   d. February
   b. December   e. March
   c. January
3. What is the average high temperature in New Delhi during the month of October?
   a. 65 Fahrenheit   d. 97 Fahrenheit
   b. 93 Fahrenheit   e. 102 Fahrenheit
   c. 105 Fahrenheit

Figure 14.11 *Temperature Highs and Lows in Two Parts of the World—India and Chile*

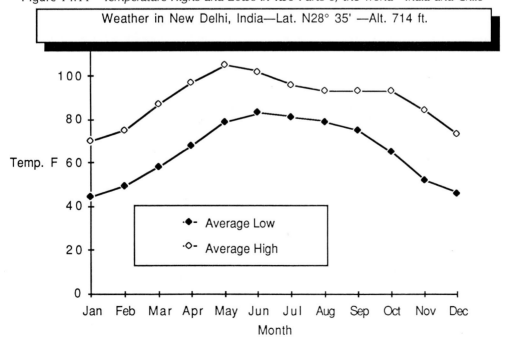

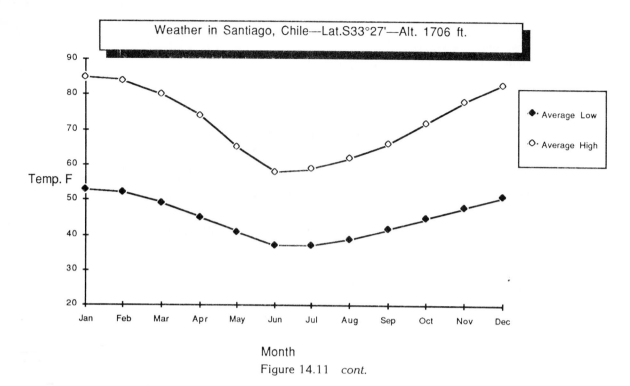

Month

Figure 14.11   cont.

4. Is New Delhi in the Northern or Southern Hemisphere?
   a. Northern   b. Southern
5. During what month does the temperature reach its highest point in Santiago, Chile?
   a. January   d. April
   b. February   e. December
   c. March
6. During what month does the temperature reach its lowest point in Santiago?
   a. May   d. August
   b. June   e. September
   c. July
7. What is the average high temperature in Santiago during October?
   a. 45 Fahrenheit   d. 75 Fahrenheit
   b. 66 Fahrenheit   e. 83 Fahrenheit
   c. 72 Fahrenheit
8. Is Santiago in the Northern or Southern Hemisphere?
   a. Northern   b. Southern

LINE DRAWINGS

As you may have discovered when you tried to answer questions 4 and 8, some geographical understanding may be helpful in reading and comprehending graphs. To answer those questions correctly, you had to know that the hottest months are June, July, and August in the Northern Hemisphere. The hottest months are December, January, and February in the Southern Hemisphere. In short, the Northern and Southern hemispheres experience summer at opposite times of the year.

Study Figure 14.12. It is a line drawing that shows why there are seasons. Answer these questions based on it.

THE SEASONS

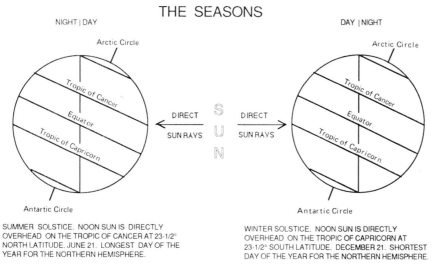

NIGHT | DAY   DAY | NIGHT

Arctic Circle   Arctic Circle

Tropic of Cancer   Tropic of Cancer

DIRECT   S   DIRECT

Equator   SUN RAYS   U   SUN RAYS   Equator

Tropic of Capricorn   N   Tropic of Capricorn

Antartic Circle   Antartic Circle

SUMMER SOLSTICE. NOON SUN IS DIRECTLY OVERHEAD ON THE TROPIC OF CANCER AT 23-1/2° NORTH LATITUDE. JUNE 21. LONGEST DAY OF THE YEAR FOR THE NORTHERN HEMISPHERE.

WINTER SOLSTICE. NOON SUN IS DIRECTLY OVERHEAD ON THE TROPIC OF CAPRICORN AT 23-1/2° SOUTH LATITUDE. DECEMBER 21. SHORTEST DAY OF THE YEAR FOR THE NORTHERN HEMISPHERE.

Figure 14.12   *Diagram Showing the Seasons*

1. When it is summer in the Northern Hemisphere, the direct rays of the sun strike the
   a. Arctic Circle.   d. Tropic of Capricorn.
   b. Tropic of Cancer.   e. Antarctic Circle.
   c. Equator.
2. When it is winter in the Northern Hemisphere, the direct rays of the sun strike the
   a. Arctic Circle.   d. Tropic of Capricorn.
   b. Tropic of Cancer.   e. Antarctic Circle.
   c. Equator.
3. Figure 14.12 indicates that
   a. the earth rotates on its axis.   c. the earth is tilted on its axis.
   b. the earth revolves around the sun.   d. All of the above are true.

There is no one strategy to use to understand line drawings. Each drawing has characteristics that make it unique. However, general steps to take include these:

● Read the title.
● Carefully study all labels.
● Explain the drawing to yourself in your own words.

SELECTION 5: ROSE VS. COBB/HALL OF FAME BANS ROSE (Popular Sports)

Expanding Your Vocabulary for Reading

You will find the word *era* in this selection. An era is the period of time to which something belongs. For example, you could say that a particular time period was the rock and roll era. Another term you will encounter is *vs.* It stands for the word *versus,* which in sports is used to denote a contest between two players. The word is also used in reference to court cases, such as the case *Brown* v. *Board of Education, 1954.* In this case, versus is abbreviated as *v.*

The word *incongruous* in the second half of the selection means "inappropriate." The word *eligible* means "properly qualified, fit to be chosen." An ineligible person is unfit to be chosen.

Getting Ready to Read

This selection consists of two articles. Preview the selection by reading the two titles and looking over the graphs in Figure 14.13.

Reading with Meaning

ROSE VS. COBB

**Samuel C. Certo, Max E. Douglas,
and Stewart W. Husted**

On September 11, 1985, Pete Rose won a permanent spot in baseball history by breaking Ty Cobb's mark of 4,191 career hits. Rose broke the record with two hits (a single and a triple), giving him 4,193 in his twenty-third major league season.

But the career-hit record is just one statistic. How does Rose compare to Cobb in other statistics? The bar charts below highlight a few of the major areas of comparison. These data were gathered just before Rose broke Cobb's record.

Rose certainly had more opportunities to hit, since he played over 400 more games and was at the plate 2,334 more times than Cobb. Cobb's batting average of .367 seems far greater than Rose's .305. Cobb also surpassed Rose in RBI's.

Figure 14.13   *Rose vs. Cobb*

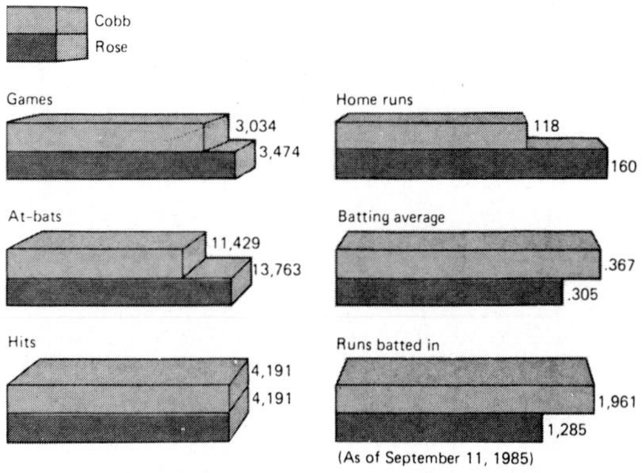

Many baseball historians claim that you cannot accurately compare players from different eras. It is like comparing Bing Crosby to Bruce Springsteen. For example, in Cobb's era, players' gloves were mittens—compare to the "baskets" that are used today. How many diving catches were made in the 1920s? Today's professional baseball player may face four or five pitchers, since relief specialists have become a vital part of the game. In Cobb's day, relief pitchers were considered mop-up men. Rose also pointed out that he faced the best players of his era, but in Cobb's time black players were excluded from the game.

Needless to say, the comparison of the bar charts needs to be framed in proper perspective. What about the effect of night games? Longer travel schedule? Better training techniques? This list could go on. How do *you* interpret these statistics?   [282 words]

Now read the following related article from the sports section of a regional newspaper. The article appeared in 1991. Remember that Pete Rose was suspended from baseball for gambling and received a jail sentence for income tax irregularities.

HALL OF FAME BANS ROSE

Dan Castellano

It is official. Unless and until he is reinstated to baseball's good graces, Pete Rose can forget about the Hall of Fame.

That body's board of directors on February 4, 1991, put a rubber stamp on the recommendation of the special committee that voted 7–3, January 10, 1991, to add a new rule to Hall of Fame eligibility, prohibiting any player permanently suspended from baseball from being considered for election. With 12 members of the 16-member board on hand at a meeting in a New York hotel, a voice vote was held and the measure was passed unanimously. . . .

"The directors felt it would be incongruous to have a person (who is) declared ineligible by baseball to be eligible for election to the Hall of Fame," said Hall of Fame president, Ed Stack. "It follows that if such an individual is reinstated by baseball, he would then be a candidate for election."

Another member of the board of directors, Milwaukee Brewers' owner Bud Selig, said what the board was worried about was "the integrity of the game."

Rose completed a five-month federal prison sentence for two income tax felonies January 8, 1991, and had to serve a three-month term in a halfway house performing community service in Cincinnati. According to the Associated Press, Rose did not appear surprised by the decision. "I'm not in control of that, so there's not much I can do about it," he said. . . .

Rose, baseball's all-time hit leader, . . . can apply for reinstatement to baseball, but it's unlikely the commissioner would grant that at this time. Thus, the Hall of Fame, which seemed a sure thing for Rose during his playing days, now seems like an impossibility.

This decision does not affect the Rose memorabilia already in Cooperstown. "The Hall of Fame has two focuses," Stack said, "the Hall of Fame Gallery, where the plaques hang, and the National Baseball Museum, which is two large buildings containing many thousands of artifacts depicting the timeline of baseball history. There are many artifacts from Pete Rose's career in the museum itself and this is part of baseball history and this will always be, not to be removed or changed."   [367 words]

Checking for Comprehension

1. Who had the greater number of home runs?
   a. Rose   b. Cobb
2. In terms of one statistic, at the time the graphs were compiled Rose and Cobb had comparable records. What statistic was that?
   a. games played   c. hits
   b. runs batted in   d. at-bats
3. At the time the graphs were compiled, Cobb had batted in more runs than Rose. How many more?
   a. 42   c. 676
   b. 440   d. 62

4. Who was the greater player, Rose or Cobb? You decide. Then in your notebook write a paragraph in which you use data from the graphs, as well as information from the news report about Rose. Start with a topic sentence in which you state your opinion as the main idea. Use your follow-up sentences to give data to support your opinion.

5. Was it right for Pete Rose to be banned from the Baseball Hall of Fame? Write a second paragraph in which you state your own opinion and support that opinion with data from the selection and any other information you know.

Reviewing Key Vocabulary

Select the word that fits in each sentence.

a. eligible   b. era   c. incongruous   d. vs.

1. During that _____, human beings began to rely on the computer.

2. It seemed a bit _____ that the winner of the peace award had been a fighter in his younger years.

3. Only those with a 3.5 average are _____ for the merit scholarship.

4. During the 1992 New Hampshire primary, the Republican contest was Bush _____ Buchanan.

EXTENDING WHAT YOU HAVE LEARNED

Going from Visuals to Words—Tables

Locate a table. Study it. Then write a paragraph in which you summarize what the table is saying. Be ready to share what you have written.

Going from Visuals to Words—Graphs

Locate a bar or line graph. Study it. Then write a paragraph in which you summarize what the graph is saying. Be ready to share what you have written.

Going from Visuals to Words—Line Drawings

Locate a line drawing. Study it. Then write a paragraph in which you summarize the data presented in the drawing. Be ready to share what you have written.

Summation

Reading
with Meaning

What have you learned about reading with meaning? In the area surrounding the title on this page, record words, phrases, sentences, and reading strategies that come to your mind.

Appendix

Calculating Your Reading Rate: Reading Rate Tables and Explanations

To calculate your reading rate:

1. Record your starting time in hours, minutes, and seconds; for example, you might have started at

10 o'clock   55 minutes   31 seconds

2. Read the selection and record your ending time; for example, you might have finished reading at

11 o'clock   5 minutes   10 seconds

3. Subtract your starting time from your ending time to find the time it took you to read the selection:

11 o'clock	5 minutes	10 seconds
10 o'clock	55 minutes	31 seconds
	9 minutes	39 seconds

4. Convert your time to a decimal by rounding up to the nearest quarter of a minute, as follows:

60 seconds = 1 minute
45 seconds = .75 minutes
30 seconds = .50 minutes
15 seconds = .25 minutes

In this case, 9 minutes and 39 seconds becomes 9.75 minutes.

5. To find your reading rate, divide the number of words in the selection by your reading time given in minutes—for example:

$$\frac{750 \text{ words}}{9.75 \text{ minutes}} = 77 \text{ reading rate (words per minute)}$$

Or use Table A to find your reading rate. To use the table,

- Locate your reading time in the left-hand column.
- Locate the number of words in the selection in the top row.
- Find your reading rate at the intersection of the selected column and row on the chart.

	NUMBER OF WORDS																													
TIME IN DECIMAL MINUTES	140	160	180	200	220	240	260	280	300	320	340	360	380	400	420	440	460	480	500	520	540	560	580	600	620	640	660	680	700	720
2	70	80	90	100	110	120	130	140	150	160	170	180	190	200	210	220	230	240	250	260	270	280	290	300	310	320	330	340	350	360
2.25	62	71	80	89	98	107	116	124	133	142	151	160	169	178	187	196	204	213	222	231	240	249	258	267	276	284	293	302	311	320
2.50	56	64	72	80	88	96	104	112	120	128	136	144	152	160	168	176	184	192	200	208	216	224	232	240	248	256	264	272	280	288
2.75	51	58	65	73	80	87	95	102	109	116	124	131	138	145	153	160	167	175	182	189	196	204	211	218	225	233	240	247	255	262
3.00	47	53	60	67	73	80	87	93	100	107	113	120	127	133	140	147	153	160	167	173	180	187	193	200	207	213	220	227	233	240
3.25	43	49	55	62	68	74	80	86	92	98	105	111	117	123	129	135	142	148	154	160	166	172	178	185	191	197	203	209	215	222
3.50	40	46	51	57	63	69	74	80	86	91	97	103	109	114	120	126	131	137	143	149	154	160	166	171	177	183	189	194	200	206
3.75	37	43	48	53	59	64	69	75	80	85	91	96	101	107	112	117	123	128	133	139	144	149	155	160	165	171	176	181	187	192
4.00	35	40	45	50	55	60	65	70	75	80	85	90	95	100	105	110	115	120	125	130	135	140	145	150	155	160	165	170	175	180
4.25	33	38	42	47	52	56	61	66	71	75	80	85	89	94	99	104	108	113	118	122	127	132	136	141	146	151	155	160	165	169
4.50	31	36	40	44	49	53	58	62	67	71	76	80	84	89	93	98	102	107	111	116	120	124	129	133	138	142	147	151	156	160
4.75	29	34	38	42	46	51	55	59	63	67	72	76	80	84	88	93	97	101	105	109	114	118	122	126	131	135	139	143	147	152
5.00	28	32	36	40	44	48	52	56	60	64	68	72	76	80	84	88	92	96	100	104	108	112	116	120	124	128	132	136	140	144
5.25	27	30	34	38	42	46	50	53	57	61	65	69	72	76	80	84	88	91	95	99	103	107	110	114	118	122	126	130	133	137
5.50	25	29	33	36	40	44	47	51	55	58	62	65	69	73	76	80	84	87	91	95	98	102	105	109	113	116	120	124	127	131
5.75	24	28	31	35	38	42	45	49	52	56	59	63	66	70	73	77	80	83	87	90	94	97	101	104	108	111	115	118	122	125
6.00	23	27	30	33	37	40	43	47	50	53	57	60	63	67	70	73	77	80	83	87	90	93	97	100	103	107	110	113	117	120
6.25	22	26	29	32	35	38	42	45	48	51	54	58	61	64	67	70	74	77	80	83	86	90	93	96	99	102	106	109	112	115
6.50	22	25	28	31	34	37	40	43	46	49	52	55	58	62	65	68	71	74	77	80	83	86	89	92	95	98	102	105	108	111
6.75	21	24	27	30	33	36	39	41	44	47	50	53	56	59	62	65	68	71	74	77	80	83	86	89	92	95	98	101	104	107
7.00	20	23	26	29	31	34	37	40	43	46	49	51	54	57	60	63	66	69	71	74	77	80	83	86	89	91	94	97	100	103
7.25	19	22	25	28	30	33	36	39	41	44	47	50	52	55	58	61	63	66	69	72	74	77	80	83	86	88	91	94	97	99
7.50	19	21	24	27	29	32	35	37	40	43	45	48	51	53	56	59	61	64	67	69	72	75	77	80	83	85	88	91	93	96
7.75	18	21	23	26	28	31	34	36	39	41	44	46	49	52	54	57	59	62	65	67	70	72	75	77	80	83	85	88	90	93
8.00	18	20	23	25	28	30	33	35	38	40	43	45	48	50	53	55	58	60	63	65	68	70	73	75	78	80	83	85	88	90
8.25	17	19	22	24	27	29	32	34	36	39	41	44	46	48	51	53	56	58	61	63	65	68	70	73	75	78	80	82	85	87
8.50	16	19	21	24	26	28	31	33	35	38	40	42	45	47	49	52	54	56	59	61	64	66	68	71	73	75	78	80	82	85
8.75	16	18	21	23	25	27	30	32	34	37	39	41	43	46	48	50	53	55	57	59	62	64	66	69	71	73	75	78	80	82
9.00	16	18	20	22	24	27	29	31	33	36	38	40	42	44	47	49	51	53	56	58	60	62	64	67	69	71	73	76	78	80
9.25	15	17	19	22	24	26	28	30	32	35	37	39	41	43	45	48	50	52	54	56	58	61	63	65	67	69	71	74	76	78
9.50	15	17	19	21	23	25	27	29	32	34	36	38	40	42	44	46	48	51	53	55	57	59	61	63	65	67	69	72	74	76
9.75	14	16	18	21	23	25	27	29	31	33	35	37	39	41	43	45	47	49	51	53	55	57	59	62	64	66	68	70	72	74
10.00	14	16	18	20	22	24	26	28	30	32	34	36	38	40	42	44	46	48	50	52	54	56	58	60	62	64	66	68	70	72
10.25	14	16	18	20	21	23	25	27	29	31	33	35	37	39	41	43	45	47	49	51	53	55	57	59	60	62	64	66	68	70
10.50	13	15	17	19	21	23	25	27	29	30	32	34	36	38	40	42	44	46	48	50	51	53	55	57	59	61	63	65	67	69
10.75	13	15	17	19	20	22	24	26	28	30	32	33	35	37	39	41	43	45	47	48	50	52	54	56	58	60	61	63	65	67
11.00	13	15	16	18	20	22	24	25	27	29	31	33	35	36	38	40	42	44	45	47	49	51	53	55	56	58	60	62	64	65
11.25	12	14	16	18	20	21	23	25	27	28	30	32	34	36	37	39	41	43	44	46	48	50	52	53	55	57	59	60	62	64
11.50	12	14	16	17	19	21	23	24	26	28	30	31	33	35	37	38	40	42	43	45	47	49	50	52	54	56	57	59	61	63
11.75	12	14	15	17	19	20	22	24	26	27	29	31	32	34	36	37	39	41	43	44	46	48	49	51	53	54	56	58	60	61
12.00	12	13	15	17	18	20	22	23	25	27	28	30	32	33	35	37	38	40	42	43	45	47	48	50	52	53	55	57	58	60
12.25	11	13	15	16	18	20	21	23	24	26	28	29	31	33	34	36	38	39	41	42	44	46	47	49	51	52	54	56	57	59
12.50	11	13	14	16	18	19	21	22	24	26	27	29	30	32	34	35	37	38	40	42	43	45	46	48	50	51	53	54	56	58
12.75	11	13	14	16	17	19	20	22	24	25	27	28	30	31	33	35	36	38	39	41	42	44	45	47	49	50	52	53	55	56
13.00	11	12	14	15	17	18	20	22	23	25	26	28	29	31	32	34	35	37	38	40	42	43	45	46	48	49	51	52	54	55
13.25	11	12	14	15	17	18	20	21	23	24	26	27	29	30	32	33	35	36	38	39	41	42	44	45	47	48	50	51	53	54
13.50	10	12	13	15	16	18	19	21	22	24	25	27	28	30	31	33	34	36	37	39	40	41	43	44	46	47	49	50	52	53
13.75	10	12	13	15	16	17	19	20	22	23	25	26	28	29	31	32	33	35	36	38	39	41	42	44	45	47	48	49	51	52
14.00	10	11	13	14	16	17	19	20	21	23	24	26	27	29	30	31	33	34	36	37	39	40	41	43	44	46	47	49	50	51
14.25	10	11	13	14	15	17	18	20	21	22	24	25	27	28	29	31	32	34	35	36	38	39	41	42	44	45	46	48	49	51
14.50	10	11	12	14	15	17	18	19	21	22	23	25	26	28	29	30	32	33	34	36	37	39	40	41	43	44	46	47	48	50
14.75	09	11	12	14	15	16	18	19	20	22	23	24	26	27	28	30	31	33	34	35	37	38	39	41	42	43	45	46	47	49
15.00	09	11	12	13	15	16	17	19	20	21	23	24	25	27	28	29	31	32	33	35	36	37	39	40	41	43	44	45	47	48
15.25	09	10	12	13	14	16	17	18	20	21	22	24	25	26	28	29	30	31	33	34	35	37	38	39	41	42	43	45	46	47
15.50	09	10	12	13	14	15	17	18	19	21	22	23	25	26	27	28	30	31	32	34	35	36	37	39	40	41	43	44	45	46
15.75	09	10	11	13	14	15	17	18	19	20	22	23	24	25	27	28	29	30	32	33	34	36	37	38	39	41	42	43	44	46
16.00	09	10	11	13	14	15	16	18	19	20	21	23	24	25	26	28	29	30	31	33	34	35	36	38	39	40	41	43	44	45
16.25	09	10	11	12	14	15	16	17	18	20	21	22	23	25	26	27	28	30	31	32	33	34	36	37	38	39	41	42	43	44
16.50	08	10	11	12	13	15	16	17	18	19	21	22	23	24	25	27	28	29	30	32	33	34	35	36	38	39	40	41	42	44
16.75	08	10	11	12	13	14	16	17	18	19	20	21	23	24	25	26	27	29	30	31	32	33	35	36	37	38	39	41	42	43
17.00	08	09	11	12	13	14	15	16	18	19	20	21	22	24	25	26	27	28	29	31	32	33	34	35	36	38	39	40	41	42
17.25	08	09	10	12	13	14	15	16	17	19	20	21	22	23	24	26	27	28	29	30	31	32	34	35	36	37	38	39	41	42
17.50	08	09	10	11	13	14	15	16	17	18	19	21	22	23	24	25	26	27	29	30	31	32	33	34	35	37	38	39	40	41
17.75	08	09	10	11	12	14	15	16	17	18	19	20	21	23	24	25	26	27	28	29	30	32	33	34	35	36	37	38	39	41
18.00	08	09	10	11	12	13	14	16	17	18	19	20	21	22	23	24	26	27	28	29	30	31	32	33	34	36	37	38	39	40
18.25	08	09	10	11	12	13	14	15	16	18	19	20	21	22	23	24	25	26	27	28	30	31	32	33	34	35	36	37	38	39
18.50	08	09	10	11	12	13	14	15	16	17	18	19	21	22	23	24	25	26	27	28	29	30	31	32	34	35	36	37	38	39
18.75	07	09	10	11	12	13	14	15	16	17	18	19	20	21	22	23	25	26	27	28	29	30	31	32	33	34	35	36	37	38
19.00	07	08	09	11	12	13	14	15	16	17	18	19	20	21	22	23	24	25	26	27	28	29	31	32	33	34	35	36	37	38
19.25	07	08	09	10	11	12	14	15	16	17	18	19	20	21	22	23	24	25	26	27	28	29	30	31	32	33	34	35	36	37
19.50	07	08	09	10	11	12	13	14	15	16	17	18	19	21	22	23	24	25	26	27	28	29	30	31	32	33	34	35	36	37
19.75	07	08	09	10	11	12	13	14	15	16	17	18	19	20	21	22	23	24	25	26	27	28	29	30	31	32	33	34	35	36
20.00	07	08	09	10	11	12	13	14	15	16	17	18	19	20	21	22	23	24	25	26	27	28	29	30	31	32	33	34	35	36
20.25	07	08	09	10	11	12	13	14	15	16	17	18	19	20	21	22	23	24	25	26	27	28	29	30	31	32	33	34	35	36
20.50	07	08	09	10	11	12	13	14	15	16	17	18	19	20	20	21	22	23	24	25	26	27	28	29	30	31	32	33	34	35
20.75	07	08	09	10	11	12	13	13	14	15	16	17	18	19	20	21	22	23	24	25	26	27	28	29	30	31	32	33	34	35
21.00	07	08	09	10	10	11	12	13	14	15	16	17	18	19	20	21	22	23	24	25	26	27	28	29	30	30	31	32	33	34
21.25	07	08	08	09	10	11	12	13	14	15	16	17	18	19	20	21	22	23	24	24	25	26	27	28	29	30	31	32	33	34
21.50	07	07	08	09	10	11	12	13	14	15	16	17	18	19	20	20	21	22	23	24	25	26	27	28	29	30	31	32	33	33
21.75	06	07	08	09	10	11	12	13	14	15	16	17	17	18	19	20	21	22	23	24	25	26	27	28	29	29	30	31	32	33
22.00	06	07	08	09	10	11	12	13	14	15	15	16	17	18	19	20	21	22	23	24	25	25	26	27	28	29	30	31	32	33
22.25	06	07	08	09	10	11	12	13	13	14	15	16	17	18	19	20	21	22	22	23	24	25	26	27	28	29	30	31	31	32
22.50	06	07	08	09	10	11	12	12	13	14	15	16	17	18	19	20	20	21	22	23	24	25	26	27	28	28	29	30	31	32
22.75	06	07	08	09	10	11	11	12	13	14	15	16	17	18	18	19	20	21	22	23	24	25	25	26	27	28	29	30	31	32
23.00	06	07	08	09	10	10	11	12	13	14	15	16	17	17	18	19	20	21	22	23	23	24	25	26	27	28	29	30	30	31
23.25	06	07	08	09	09	10	11	12	13	14	15	15	16	17	18	19	20	21	22	22	23	24	25	26	27	28	28	29	30	31
23.50	06	07	08	09	09	10	11	12	13	14	14	15	16	17	18	19	20	20	21	22	23	24	25	26	26	27	28	29	30	31
23.75	06	07	08	08	09	10	11	12	13	13	14	15	16	17	18	19	19	20	21	22	23	24	24	25	26	27	28	29	29	30
24.00	06	07	08	08	09	10	11	12	13	13	14	15	16	17	18	18	19	20	21	22	23	23	24	25	26	27	28	28	29	30
24.25	06	07	07	08	09	10	11	12	12	13	14	15	16	16	17	18	19	20	21	21	22	23	24	25	26	26	27	28	29	30
24.50	06	07	07	08	09	10	11	11	12	13	14	15	16	16	17	18	19	20	20	21	22	23	24	24	25	26	27	28	29	29
24.75	06	06	07	08	09	10	11	11	12	13	14	15	15	16	17	18	19	19	20	21	22	23	23	24	25	26	27	27	28	29
25.00	06	06	07	08	09	10	10	11	12	13	14	14	15	16	17	18	18	19	20	21	22	22	23	24	25	26	26	27	28	29

NUMBER OF WORDS

TIME IN DECIMAL MINUTES	740	760	780	800	820	840	860	880	900	920	940	960	980	1000	1020	1040	1060	1080	1100	1120	1140	1160	1180	1200	1220	1240
2	370	380	390	400	410	420	430	440	450	460	470	480	490	500	510	520	530	540	550	560	570	580	590	600	610	620
2.25	329	338	347	356	364	373	382	391	400	409	418	427	436	444	453	462	471	480	489	498	507	516	524	533	542	551
2.50	296	304	312	320	328	336	344	352	360	368	376	384	392	400	408	416	424	432	440	448	456	464	472	480	488	496
2.75	269	276	284	291	298	305	313	320	327	335	342	349	356	364	371	378	385	393	400	407	415	422	429	436	444	451
3.00	247	253	260	267	273	280	287	293	300	307	313	320	327	333	340	347	353	360	367	373	380	387	393	400	407	413
3.25	228	234	240	246	252	258	265	271	277	283	289	295	302	308	314	320	326	332	338	345	351	357	363	369	375	382
3.50	211	217	223	229	234	240	246	251	257	263	269	274	280	286	291	297	303	309	314	320	326	331	337	343	349	354
3.75	197	203	208	213	219	224	229	235	240	245	251	256	261	267	272	277	283	288	293	299	304	309	315	320	325	331
4.00	185	190	195	200	205	210	215	220	225	230	235	240	245	250	255	260	265	270	275	280	285	290	295	300	305	310
4.25	174	179	184	188	193	198	202	207	212	216	221	226	231	235	240	245	249	254	259	264	268	273	278	282	287	292
4.50	164	169	173	178	182	187	191	196	200	204	209	213	218	222	227	231	236	240	244	249	253	258	262	267	271	276
4.75	156	160	164	168	173	177	181	185	189	194	198	202	206	211	215	219	223	227	232	236	240	244	248	253	257	261
5.00	148	152	156	160	164	168	172	176	180	184	188	192	196	200	204	208	212	216	220	224	228	232	236	240	244	248
5.25	141	145	149	152	156	160	164	168	171	175	179	183	187	190	194	198	202	206	210	213	217	221	225	229	232	236
5.50	135	138	142	145	149	153	156	160	164	167	171	175	178	182	185	189	193	196	200	204	207	211	215	218	222	225
5.75	129	132	136	139	143	146	150	153	157	160	163	167	170	174	177	181	184	188	191	195	198	202	205	209	212	216
6.00	123	127	130	133	137	140	143	147	150	153	157	160	163	167	170	173	177	180	183	187	190	193	197	200	203	207
6.25	118	122	125	128	131	134	138	141	144	147	150	154	157	160	163	166	170	173	176	179	182	186	189	192	195	198
6.50	114	117	120	123	126	129	132	135	138	142	145	148	151	154	157	160	163	166	169	172	175	178	182	185	188	191
6.75	110	113	116	119	121	124	127	130	133	136	139	142	145	148	151	154	157	160	163	166	169	172	175	178	181	184
7.00	106	109	111	114	117	120	123	126	129	131	134	137	140	143	146	149	151	154	157	160	163	166	169	171	174	177
7.25	102	105	108	110	113	116	119	121	124	127	130	132	135	138	141	143	146	149	152	154	157	160	163	166	168	171
7.50	99	101	104	107	109	112	115	117	120	123	125	128	131	133	136	139	141	144	147	149	152	155	157	160	163	165
7.75	95	98	101	103	106	108	111	114	116	119	121	124	126	129	132	134	137	139	142	145	147	150	152	155	157	160
8.00	93	95	98	100	103	105	108	110	113	115	118	120	123	125	128	130	133	135	138	140	143	145	148	150	153	155
8.25	90	92	95	97	99	102	104	107	109	112	114	116	119	121	124	126	128	131	133	136	138	141	143	145	148	150
8.50	87	89	92	94	96	99	101	104	106	108	111	113	115	118	120	122	125	127	129	132	134	136	139	141	144	146
8.75	85	87	89	91	94	96	98	101	103	105	107	110	112	114	117	119	121	123	126	128	130	133	135	137	139	142
9.00	82	84	87	89	91	93	96	98	100	102	104	107	109	111	113	116	118	120	122	124	127	129	131	133	136	138
9.25	80	82	84	86	89	91	93	95	97	99	102	104	106	108	110	112	115	117	119	121	123	125	128	130	132	134
9.50	78	80	82	84	86	88	91	93	95	97	99	101	103	105	107	109	112	114	116	118	120	122	124	126	128	131
9.75	76	78	80	82	84	86	88	90	92	94	96	98	101	103	105	107	109	111	113	115	117	119	121	123	125	127
10.00	74	76	78	80	82	84	86	88	90	92	94	96	98	100	102	104	106	108	110	112	114	116	118	120	122	124
10.25	72	74	76	78	80	82	84	86	88	90	92	94	96	98	100	101	103	105	107	109	111	113	115	117	119	121
10.50	70	72	74	76	78	80	82	84	86	88	90	91	93	95	97	99	101	103	105	107	109	110	112	114	116	118
10.75	69	71	73	74	76	78	80	82	84	86	87	89	91	93	95	97	99	100	102	104	106	108	110	112	113	115
11.00	67	69	71	73	75	76	78	80	82	84	85	87	89	91	93	95	96	98	100	102	104	105	107	109	111	113
11.25	66	68	69	71	73	75	76	78	80	82	84	85	87	89	91	92	94	96	98	100	101	103	105	107	108	110
11.50	64	66	68	70	71	73	75	77	78	80	82	83	85	87	89	90	92	94	96	97	99	101	103	104	106	108
11.75	63	65	66	68	70	71	73	75	77	78	80	82	83	85	87	89	90	92	94	95	97	99	100	102	104	106
12.00	62	63	65	67	68	70	72	73	75	77	78	80	82	83	85	87	88	90	92	93	95	97	98	100	102	103
12.25	60	62	64	65	67	69	70	72	73	75	77	78	80	82	83	85	87	88	90	91	93	95	96	98	100	101
12.50	59	61	62	64	66	67	69	70	72	74	75	77	78	80	82	83	85	86	88	90	91	93	94	96	98	99
12.75	58	60	61	63	64	66	67	69	71	72	74	75	77	78	80	82	83	85	86	88	89	91	93	94	96	97
13.00	57	58	60	62	63	65	66	68	69	71	72	74	75	77	78	80	82	83	85	86	88	89	91	92	94	95
13.25	56	57	59	60	62	63	65	66	68	69	71	72	74	75	77	78	80	82	83	85	86	88	89	91	92	94
13.50	55	56	58	59	61	62	64	65	67	68	70	71	73	74	76	77	79	80	81	83	84	86	87	89	90	92
13.75	54	55	57	58	60	61	63	64	65	67	68	70	71	73	74	76	77	79	80	81	83	84	86	87	89	90
14.00	53	54	56	57	59	60	61	63	64	66	67	69	70	71	73	74	76	77	79	80	81	83	84	86	87	89
14.25	52	53	55	56	58	59	60	62	63	65	66	67	69	70	72	73	74	76	77	79	80	81	83	84	86	87
14.50	51	52	54	55	57	58	59	61	62	63	65	66	68	69	70	72	73	74	76	77	79	80	81	83	84	86
14.75	50	52	53	54	56	57	58	60	61	62	64	65	66	68	69	71	72	73	75	76	77	79	80	81	83	84
15.00	49	51	52	53	55	56	57	59	60	61	63	64	65	67	68	69	71	72	73	75	76	77	79	80	81	83
15.25	49	50	51	52	54	55	56	58	59	60	62	63	64	66	67	68	70	71	72	73	75	76	77	79	80	81
15.50	48	49	50	52	53	54	55	57	58	59	61	62	63	65	66	67	68	70	71	72	74	75	76	77	79	80
15.75	47	48	50	51	52	53	55	56	57	58	60	61	62	63	65	66	67	69	70	71	72	74	75	76	77	79
16.00	46	48	49	50	51	53	54	55	56	58	59	60	61	63	64	65	66	68	69	70	71	73	74	75	76	78
16.25	46	47	48	49	50	52	53	54	55	57	58	59	60	62	63	64	65	66	68	69	70	71	73	74	75	76
16.50	45	46	47	48	50	51	52	53	55	56	57	58	59	61	62	63	64	65	67	68	69	70	72	73	74	75
16.75	44	45	47	48	49	50	51	53	54	55	56	57	59	60	61	62	63	64	66	67	68	69	70	72	73	74
17.00	44	45	46	47	48	49	51	52	53	54	55	56	58	59	60	61	62	64	65	66	67	68	69	71	72	73
17.25	43	44	45	46	48	49	50	51	52	53	54	56	57	58	59	60	61	63	64	65	66	67	68	70	71	72
17.50	42	43	45	46	47	48	49	50	51	53	54	55	56	57	58	59	61	62	63	64	65	66	67	69	70	71
17.75	42	43	44	45	46	47	48	50	51	52	53	54	55	56	57	59	60	61	62	63	64	65	66	68	69	70
18.00	41	42	43	44	46	47	48	49	50	51	52	53	54	56	57	58	59	60	61	62	63	64	66	67	68	69
18.25	41	42	43	44	45	46	47	48	49	50	52	53	54	55	56	57	58	59	60	61	62	64	65	66	67	68
18.50	40	41	42	43	44	45	46	48	49	50	51	52	53	54	55	56	57	58	59	61	62	63	64	65	66	67
18.75	39	41	42	43	44	45	46	47	48	49	50	51	52	53	54	55	57	58	59	60	61	62	63	64	65	66
19.00	39	40	41	42	43	44	45	46	47	48	49	51	52	53	54	55	56	57	58	59	60	61	62	63	64	65
19.25	38	39	41	42	43	44	45	46	47	48	49	50	51	52	53	54	55	56	57	58	59	60	61	62	63	64
19.50	38	39	40	41	42	43	44	45	46	47	48	49	50	51	52	53	54	55	56	57	58	59	61	62	63	64
19.75	37	38	39	41	42	43	44	45	46	47	48	49	50	51	52	53	54	55	56	57	58	59	60	61	62	63
20.00	37	38	39	40	41	42	43	44	45	46	47	48	49	50	51	52	53	54	55	56	57	58	59	60	61	62
20.25	37	38	39	40	40	41	42	43	44	45	46	47	48	49	50	51	52	53	54	55	56	57	58	59	60	61
20.50	36	37	38	39	40	41	42	43	44	45	46	47	48	49	50	51	52	53	54	55	56	57	58	59	60	60
20.75	36	37	38	39	40	40	41	42	43	44	45	46	47	48	49	50	51	52	53	54	55	56	57	58	59	60
21.00	35	36	37	38	39	40	41	42	43	44	45	46	47	48	49	50	50	51	52	53	54	55	56	57	58	59
21.25	35	36	37	38	39	40	40	41	42	43	44	45	46	47	48	49	50	51	52	53	54	55	56	56	57	58
21.50	34	35	36	37	38	39	40	41	42	43	44	45	46	47	47	48	49	50	51	52	53	54	55	56	57	58
21.75	34	35	36	37	38	39	40	40	41	42	43	44	45	46	47	48	49	50	51	51	52	53	54	55	56	57
22.00	34	35	35	36	37	38	39	40	41	42	43	44	45	45	46	47	48	49	50	51	52	53	54	55	55	56
22.25	33	34	35	36	37	38	39	40	40	41	42	43	44	45	46	47	48	49	49	50	51	52	53	54	55	56
22.50	33	34	35	36	36	37	38	39	40	41	42	43	44	44	45	46	47	48	49	50	51	52	52	53	54	55
22.75	33	33	34	35	36	37	38	39	40	40	41	42	43	44	45	46	47	47	48	49	50	51	52	53	54	55
23.00	32	33	34	35	36	37	37	38	39	40	41	42	43	43	44	45	46	47	48	49	50	50	51	52	53	54
23.25	32	33	34	34	35	36	37	38	39	40	40	41	42	43	44	45	46	46	47	48	49	50	51	52	52	53
23.50	31	32	33	34	35	36	37	37	38	39	40	41	42	43	43	44	45	46	47	48	49	49	50	51	52	53
23.75	31	32	33	34	35	35	36	37	38	39	40	40	41	42	43	44	45	45	46	47	48	49	50	51	51	52
24.00	31	32	33	33	34	35	36	37	38	38	39	40	41	42	43	43	44	45	46	47	48	48	49	50	51	52
24.25	31	31	32	33	34	35	35	36	37	38	39	40	40	41	42	43	44	45	45	46	47	48	49	49	50	51
24.50	30	31	32	33	33	34	35	36	37	38	38	39	40	41	42	42	43	44	45	46	47	47	48	49	50	51
24.75	30	31	32	32	33	34	35	36	36	37	38	39	40	40	41	42	43	44	44	45	46	47	48	48	49	50
25.00	30	30	31	32	33	34	34	35	36	37	38	38	39	40	41	42	42	43	44	45	46	46	47	48	49	50

	NUMBER OF WORDS																						
TIME IN DECIMAL MINUTES	1260	1280	1300	1320	1340	1360	1380	1400	1420	1440	1460	1480	1500	1520	1540	1560	1580	1600	1620	1640	1660	1680	1700
2	630	640	650	660	670	680	690	700	710	720	730	740	750	760	770	780	790	800	810	820	830	840	850
2.25	560	569	578	587	596	604	613	622	631	640	649	658	667	676	684	693	702	711	720	729	738	747	756
2.50	504	512	520	528	536	544	552	560	568	576	584	592	600	608	616	624	632	640	648	656	664	672	680
2.75	458	465	473	480	487	495	502	509	516	524	531	538	545	553	560	567	575	582	589	596	604	611	618
3.00	420	427	433	440	447	453	460	467	473	480	487	493	500	507	513	520	527	533	540	547	553	560	567
3.25	388	394	400	406	412	418	425	431	437	443	449	455	462	468	474	480	486	492	498	505	511	517	523
3.50	360	366	371	377	383	389	394	400	406	411	417	423	429	434	440	446	451	457	463	469	474	480	486
3.75	336	341	347	352	357	363	368	373	379	384	389	395	400	405	411	416	421	427	432	437	443	448	453
4.00	315	320	325	330	335	340	345	350	355	360	365	370	375	380	385	390	395	400	405	410	415	420	425
4.25	296	301	306	311	315	320	325	329	334	339	344	348	353	358	362	367	372	376	381	386	391	395	400
4.50	280	284	289	293	298	302	307	311	316	320	324	329	333	338	342	347	351	356	360	364	369	373	378
4.75	265	269	274	278	282	286	291	295	299	303	307	312	316	320	324	328	333	337	341	345	349	354	358
5.00	252	256	260	264	268	272	276	280	284	288	292	296	300	304	308	312	316	320	324	328	332	336	340
5.25	240	244	248	251	255	259	263	267	270	274	278	282	286	290	293	297	301	305	309	312	316	320	324
5.50	229	233	236	240	244	247	251	255	258	262	265	269	273	276	280	284	287	291	295	298	302	305	309
5.75	219	223	226	230	233	237	240	243	247	250	254	257	261	264	268	271	275	278	282	285	289	292	296
6.00	210	213	217	220	223	227	230	233	237	240	243	247	250	253	257	260	263	267	270	273	277	280	283
6.25	202	205	208	211	214	218	221	224	227	230	234	237	240	243	246	250	253	256	259	262	266	269	272
6.50	194	197	200	203	206	209	212	215	218	222	225	228	231	234	237	240	243	246	249	252	255	258	262
6.75	187	190	193	196	199	201	204	207	210	213	216	219	222	225	228	231	234	237	240	243	246	249	252
7.00	180	183	186	189	191	194	197	200	203	206	209	211	214	217	220	223	226	229	231	234	237	240	243
7.25	174	177	179	182	185	188	190	193	196	199	201	204	207	210	212	215	218	221	223	226	229	232	234
7.50	168	171	173	176	179	181	184	187	189	192	195	197	200	203	205	208	211	213	216	219	221	224	227
7.75	163	165	168	170	173	175	178	181	183	186	188	191	194	196	199	201	204	206	209	212	214	217	219
8.00	158	160	163	165	168	170	173	175	178	180	183	185	188	190	193	195	198	200	203	205	208	210	213
8.25	153	155	158	160	162	165	167	170	172	175	177	179	182	184	187	189	192	194	196	199	201	204	206
8.50	148	151	153	155	158	160	162	165	167	169	172	174	176	179	181	184	186	188	191	193	195	198	200
8.75	144	146	149	151	153	155	158	160	162	165	167	169	171	174	176	178	181	183	185	187	190	192	194
9.00	140	142	144	147	149	151	153	156	158	160	162	164	167	169	171	173	176	178	180	182	184	187	189
9.25	136	138	141	143	145	147	149	151	154	156	158	160	162	164	166	169	171	173	175	177	179	182	184
9.50	133	135	137	139	141	143	145	147	149	152	154	156	158	160	162	164	166	168	171	173	175	177	179
9.75	129	131	133	135	137	139	142	144	146	148	150	152	154	156	158	160	162	164	166	168	170	172	174
10.00	126	128	130	132	134	136	138	140	142	144	146	148	150	152	154	156	158	160	162	164	166	168	170
10.25	123	125	127	129	131	133	135	137	139	140	142	144	146	148	150	152	154	156	158	160	162	164	166
10.50	120	122	124	126	128	130	131	133	135	137	139	141	143	145	147	149	150	152	154	156	158	160	162
10.75	117	119	121	123	125	127	128	130	132	134	136	138	140	141	143	145	147	149	151	153	154	156	158
11.00	115	116	118	120	122	124	125	127	129	131	133	135	136	138	140	142	144	145	147	149	151	153	155
11.25	112	114	116	117	119	121	123	124	126	128	130	132	133	135	137	139	140	142	144	146	148	149	151
11.50	110	111	113	115	117	118	120	122	123	125	127	129	130	132	134	136	137	139	141	143	144	146	148
11.75	107	109	111	112	114	116	117	119	121	123	124	126	128	129	131	133	134	136	138	140	141	143	145
12.00	105	107	108	110	112	113	115	117	118	120	122	123	125	127	128	130	132	133	135	137	138	140	142
12.25	103	104	106	108	109	111	113	114	116	118	119	121	122	124	126	127	129	131	132	134	136	137	139
12.50	101	102	104	106	107	109	110	112	114	115	117	118	120	122	123	125	126	128	130	131	133	134	136
12.75	99	100	102	104	105	107	108	110	111	113	115	116	118	119	121	122	124	125	127	129	130	132	133
13.00	97	98	100	102	103	105	106	108	109	111	112	114	115	117	118	120	122	123	125	126	128	129	131
13.25	95	97	98	100	101	103	104	106	107	109	110	112	113	115	116	118	119	121	122	124	125	127	128
13.50	93	95	96	98	99	101	102	104	105	107	108	110	111	113	114	116	117	119	120	121	123	124	126
13.75	92	93	95	96	97	99	100	102	103	105	106	108	109	111	112	113	115	116	118	119	121	122	124
14.00	90	91	93	94	96	97	99	100	101	103	104	106	107	109	110	111	113	114	116	117	119	120	121
14.25	88	90	91	93	94	95	97	98	100	101	102	104	105	107	108	109	111	112	114	115	116	118	119
14.50	87	88	90	91	92	94	95	97	98	99	101	102	103	105	106	108	109	110	112	113	114	116	117
14.75	85	87	88	89	91	92	94	95	96	98	99	100	102	103	104	106	107	108	110	111	113	114	115
15.00	84	85	87	88	89	91	92	93	95	96	97	99	100	101	103	104	105	107	108	109	111	112	113
15.25	83	84	85	87	88	89	90	92	93	94	96	97	98	100	101	102	104	105	106	108	109	110	111
15.50	81	83	84	85	86	88	89	90	92	93	94	95	97	98	99	101	102	103	105	106	107	108	110
15.75	80	81	83	84	85	86	88	89	90	91	93	94	95	97	98	99	100	102	103	104	105	107	108
16.00	79	80	81	83	84	85	86	88	89	90	91	93	94	95	96	98	99	100	101	103	104	105	106
16.25	78	79	80	81	82	84	85	86	87	89	90	91	92	94	95	96	97	98	100	101	102	103	105
16.50	76	78	79	80	81	82	84	85	86	87	88	90	91	92	93	95	96	97	98	99	101	102	103
16.75	75	76	78	79	80	81	82	84	85	86	87	88	90	91	92	93	94	96	97	98	99	100	101
17.00	74	75	76	78	79	80	81	82	84	85	86	87	88	89	91	92	93	94	95	96	98	99	100
17.25	73	74	75	77	78	79	80	81	82	83	85	86	87	88	89	90	92	93	94	95	96	97	99
17.50	72	73	74	75	77	78	79	80	81	82	83	85	86	87	88	89	90	91	93	94	95	96	97
17.75	71	72	73	74	75	77	78	79	80	81	82	83	85	86	87	88	89	90	91	92	94	95	96
18.00	70	71	72	73	74	76	77	78	79	80	81	82	83	84	86	87	88	89	90	91	92	93	94
18.25	69	70	71	72	73	75	76	77	78	79	80	81	82	83	84	85	87	88	89	90	91	92	93
18.50	68	69	70	71	72	74	75	76	77	78	79	80	81	82	83	84	85	86	88	89	90	91	92
18.75	67	68	69	70	71	73	74	75	76	77	78	79	80	81	82	83	84	85	86	87	89	90	91
19.00	66	67	68	69	71	72	73	74	75	76	77	78	79	80	81	82	83	84	85	86	87	88	89
19.25	65	66	68	69	70	71	72	73	74	75	76	77	78	79	80	81	82	83	84	85	86	87	88
19.50	65	66	67	68	69	70	71	72	73	74	75	76	77	78	79	80	81	82	83	84	85	86	87
19.75	64	65	66	67	68	69	70	71	72	73	74	75	76	77	78	79	80	81	82	83	84	85	86
20.00	63	64	65	66	67	68	69	70	71	72	73	74	75	76	77	78	79	80	81	82	83	84	85
20.25	62	63	64	65	66	67	68	69	70	71	72	73	74	75	76	77	78	79	80	81	82	83	84
20.50	61	62	63	64	65	66	67	68	69	70	71	72	73	74	75	76	77	78	79	80	81	82	83
20.75	61	62	63	64	65	66	67	67	68	69	70	71	72	73	74	75	76	77	78	79	80	81	82
21.00	60	61	62	63	64	65	66	67	68	69	70	70	71	72	73	74	75	76	77	78	79	80	81
21.25	59	60	61	62	63	64	65	66	67	68	69	70	71	72	72	73	74	75	76	77	78	79	80
21.50	59	60	60	61	62	63	64	65	66	67	68	69	70	71	72	73	73	74	75	76	77	78	79
21.75	58	59	60	61	62	63	63	64	65	66	67	68	69	70	71	72	73	74	74	75	76	77	78
22.00	57	58	59	60	61	62	63	64	65	65	66	67	68	69	70	71	72	73	74	75	75	76	77
22.25	57	58	58	59	60	61	62	63	64	65	66	67	67	68	69	70	71	72	73	74	75	76	76
22.50	56	57	58	59	60	60	61	62	63	64	65	66	67	68	68	69	70	71	72	73	74	75	76
22.75	55	56	57	58	59	60	61	62	62	63	64	65	66	67	68	69	69	70	71	72	73	74	75
23.00	55	56	57	57	58	59	60	61	62	63	63	64	65	66	67	68	69	70	70	71	72	73	74
23.25	54	55	56	57	58	58	59	60	61	62	63	64	65	65	66	67	68	69	70	71	71	72	73
23.50	54	54	55	56	57	58	59	60	60	61	62	63	64	65	66	66	67	68	69	70	71	71	72
23.75	53	54	55	56	56	57	58	59	60	61	61	62	63	64	65	66	67	67	68	69	70	71	72
24.00	53	53	54	55	56	57	58	58	59	60	61	62	63	63	64	65	66	67	68	68	69	70	71
24.25	52	53	54	54	55	56	57	58	59	59	60	61	62	63	64	64	65	66	67	68	68	69	70
24.50	51	52	53	54	55	56	56	57	58	59	60	60	61	62	63	64	64	65	66	67	68	69	69
24.75	51	52	53	53	54	55	56	57	57	58	59	60	61	61	62	63	64	65	65	66	67	68	69
25.00	50	51	52	53	54	54	55	56	57	58	58	59	60	61	62	62	63	64	65	66	66	67	68

TIME IN DECIMAL MINUTES	NUMBER OF WORDS																						
	1720	1740	1760	1780	1800	1820	1840	1860	1880	1900	1920	1940	1960	1980	2000	2020	2040	2060	2080	2100	2120	2140	2160
2	860	870	880	890	900	910	920	930	940	950	960	970	980	990	1000	1010	1020	1030	1040	1050	1060	1070	1080
2.25	764	773	782	791	800	809	818	827	836	844	853	862	871	880	889	898	907	916	924	933	942	951	960
2.50	688	696	704	712	720	728	736	744	752	760	768	776	784	792	800	808	816	824	832	840	848	856	864
2.75	625	633	640	647	655	662	669	676	684	691	698	705	713	720	727	735	742	749	756	764	771	778	785
3.00	573	580	587	593	600	607	613	620	627	633	640	647	653	660	667	673	680	687	693	700	707	713	720
3.25	529	535	542	548	554	560	566	572	578	585	591	597	603	609	615	622	628	634	640	646	652	658	665
3.50	491	497	503	509	514	520	526	531	537	543	549	554	560	566	571	577	583	589	594	600	606	611	617
3.75	459	464	469	475	480	485	491	496	501	507	512	517	523	528	533	539	544	549	555	560	565	571	576
4.00	430	435	440	445	450	455	460	465	470	475	480	485	490	495	500	505	510	515	520	525	530	535	540
4.25	405	409	414	419	424	428	433	438	442	447	452	456	461	466	471	475	480	485	489	494	499	504	508
4.50	382	387	391	396	400	404	409	413	418	422	427	431	436	440	444	449	453	458	462	467	471	476	480
4.75	362	366	371	375	379	383	387	392	396	400	404	408	413	417	421	425	429	434	438	442	446	451	455
5.00	344	348	352	356	360	364	368	372	376	380	384	388	392	396	400	404	408	412	416	420	424	428	432
5.25	328	331	335	339	343	347	350	354	358	362	366	370	373	377	381	385	389	392	396	400	404	408	411
5.50	313	316	320	324	327	331	335	338	342	345	349	353	356	360	364	367	371	375	378	382	385	389	393
5.75	299	303	306	310	313	317	320	323	327	330	334	337	341	344	348	351	355	358	362	365	369	372	376
6.00	287	290	293	297	300	303	307	310	313	317	320	323	327	330	333	337	340	343	347	350	353	357	360
6.25	275	278	282	285	288	291	294	298	301	304	307	310	314	317	320	323	326	330	333	336	339	342	346
6.50	265	268	271	274	277	280	283	286	289	292	295	298	302	305	308	311	314	317	320	323	326	329	332
6.75	255	258	261	264	267	270	273	276	279	281	284	287	290	293	296	299	302	305	308	311	314	317	320
7.00	246	249	251	254	257	260	263	266	269	271	274	277	280	283	286	289	291	294	297	300	303	306	309
7.25	237	240	243	246	248	251	254	257	259	262	265	268	270	273	276	279	281	284	287	290	292	295	298
7.50	229	232	235	237	240	243	245	248	251	253	256	259	261	264	267	269	272	275	277	280	283	285	288
7.75	222	225	227	230	232	235	237	240	243	245	248	250	253	255	258	261	263	266	268	271	274	276	279
8.00	215	218	220	223	225	228	230	233	235	238	240	243	245	248	250	253	255	258	260	263	265	268	270
8.25	208	211	213	216	218	221	223	225	228	230	233	235	238	240	242	245	247	250	252	255	257	259	262
8.50	202	205	207	209	212	214	216	219	221	224	226	228	231	233	235	238	240	242	245	247	249	252	254
8.75	197	199	201	203	206	208	210	213	215	217	219	222	224	226	229	231	233	235	238	240	242	245	247
9.00	191	193	196	198	200	202	204	207	209	211	213	216	218	220	222	224	227	229	231	233	236	238	240
9.25	186	188	190	192	195	197	199	201	203	205	208	210	212	214	216	218	221	223	225	227	229	231	234
9.50	181	183	185	187	189	192	194	196	198	200	202	204	206	208	211	213	215	217	219	221	223	225	227
9.75	176	178	181	183	185	187	189	191	193	195	197	199	201	203	205	207	209	211	213	215	217	219	222
10.00	172	174	176	178	180	182	184	186	188	190	192	194	196	198	200	202	204	206	208	210	212	214	216
10.25	168	170	172	174	176	178	180	181	183	185	187	189	191	193	195	197	199	201	203	205	207	209	211
10.50	164	166	168	170	171	173	175	177	179	181	183	185	187	189	190	192	194	196	198	200	202	204	206
10.75	160	162	164	166	167	169	171	173	175	177	179	180	182	184	186	188	190	192	193	195	197	199	201
11.00	156	158	160	162	164	165	167	169	171	173	175	176	178	180	182	184	185	187	189	191	193	195	196
11.25	153	155	156	158	160	162	164	165	167	169	171	172	174	176	178	180	181	183	185	187	188	190	192
11.50	150	151	153	155	157	158	160	162	163	165	167	169	170	172	174	176	177	179	181	183	184	186	188
11.75	146	148	150	151	153	155	157	158	160	162	163	165	167	169	170	172	174	175	177	179	180	182	184
12.00	143	145	147	148	150	152	153	155	157	158	160	162	163	165	167	168	170	172	173	175	177	178	180
12.25	140	142	144	145	147	149	150	152	153	155	157	158	160	162	163	165	167	168	170	171	173	175	176
12.50	138	139	141	142	144	146	147	149	150	152	154	155	157	158	160	162	163	165	166	168	170	171	173
12.75	135	136	138	140	141	143	144	146	147	149	151	152	154	155	157	158	160	162	163	165	166	168	169
13.00	132	134	135	137	138	140	142	143	145	146	148	149	151	152	154	155	157	158	160	162	163	165	166
13.25	130	131	133	134	136	137	139	140	142	143	145	146	148	149	151	152	154	155	157	158	160	162	163
13.50	127	129	130	132	133	135	136	138	139	141	142	144	145	147	148	150	151	153	154	156	157	159	160
13.75	125	127	128	129	131	132	134	135	137	138	140	141	143	144	145	147	148	150	151	153	154	156	157
14.00	123	124	126	127	129	130	131	133	134	136	137	139	140	141	143	144	146	147	149	150	151	153	154
14.25	121	122	124	125	126	128	129	131	132	133	135	136	138	139	140	142	143	145	146	147	149	150	152
14.50	119	120	121	123	124	126	127	128	130	131	132	134	135	137	138	139	141	142	143	145	146	148	149
14.75	117	118	119	121	122	123	125	126	127	129	130	132	133	134	136	137	138	140	141	142	144	145	146
15.00	115	116	117	119	120	121	123	124	125	127	128	129	131	132	133	135	136	137	139	140	141	143	144
15.25	113	114	115	117	118	119	121	122	123	125	126	127	129	130	131	132	134	135	136	138	139	140	142
15.50	111	112	114	115	116	117	119	120	121	123	124	125	126	128	129	130	132	133	134	135	137	138	139
15.75	109	110	112	113	114	116	117	118	119	121	122	123	124	126	127	128	130	131	132	133	135	136	137
16.00	108	109	110	111	113	114	115	116	118	119	120	121	123	124	125	126	128	129	130	131	133	134	135
16.25	106	107	108	110	111	112	113	114	116	117	118	119	121	122	123	124	126	127	128	129	130	132	133
16.50	104	105	107	108	109	110	112	113	114	115	116	118	119	120	121	122	124	125	126	127	128	130	131
16.75	103	104	105	106	107	109	110	111	112	113	115	116	117	118	119	121	122	123	124	125	127	128	129
17.00	101	102	104	105	106	107	108	109	111	112	113	114	115	116	118	119	120	121	122	124	125	126	127
17.25	100	101	102	103	104	106	107	108	109	110	111	112	114	115	116	117	118	119	121	122	123	124	125
17.50	98	99	101	102	103	104	105	106	107	109	110	111	112	113	114	115	117	118	119	120	121	122	123
17.75	97	98	99	100	101	103	104	105	106	107	108	109	110	112	113	114	115	116	117	118	119	121	122
18.00	96	97	98	99	100	101	102	103	104	106	107	108	109	110	111	112	113	114	116	117	118	119	120
18.25	94	95	96	98	99	100	101	102	103	104	105	106	107	108	110	111	112	113	114	115	116	117	118
18.50	93	94	95	96	97	98	99	101	102	103	104	105	106	107	108	109	110	111	112	114	115	116	117
18.75	92	93	94	95	96	97	98	99	100	101	102	103	105	106	107	108	109	110	111	112	113	114	115
19.00	91	92	93	94	95	96	97	98	99	100	101	102	103	104	105	106	107	108	109	111	112	113	114
19.25	89	90	91	92	94	95	96	97	98	99	100	101	102	103	104	105	106	107	108	109	110	111	112
19.50	88	89	90	91	92	93	94	95	96	97	98	99	101	102	103	104	105	106	107	108	109	110	111
19.75	87	88	89	90	91	92	93	94	95	96	97	98	99	100	101	102	103	104	105	106	107	108	109
20.00	86	87	88	89	90	91	92	93	94	95	96	97	98	99	100	101	102	103	104	105	106	107	108
20.25	85	86	87	88	89	90	91	92	93	94	95	96	97	98	99	100	101	102	103	104	105	106	107
20.50	84	85	86	87	88	89	90	91	92	93	94	95	96	97	98	99	100	100	101	102	103	104	105
20.75	83	84	85	86	87	88	89	90	91	92	93	93	94	95	96	97	98	99	100	101	102	103	104
21.00	82	83	84	85	86	87	88	89	90	90	91	92	93	94	95	96	97	98	99	100	101	102	103
21.25	81	82	83	84	85	86	87	88	88	89	90	91	92	93	94	95	96	97	98	99	100	101	102
21.50	80	81	82	83	84	85	86	87	87	88	89	90	91	92	93	94	95	96	97	98	99	100	100
21.75	79	80	81	82	83	84	85	86	86	87	88	89	90	91	92	93	94	95	96	97	97	98	99
22.00	78	79	80	81	82	83	84	85	85	86	87	88	89	90	91	92	93	94	95	95	96	97	98
22.25	77	78	79	80	81	82	83	84	84	85	86	87	88	89	90	91	92	93	93	94	95	96	97
22.50	76	77	78	79	80	81	82	83	84	84	85	86	87	88	89	90	91	92	92	93	94	95	96
22.75	76	76	77	78	79	80	81	82	83	84	84	85	86	87	88	89	90	91	91	92	93	94	95
23.00	75	76	77	77	78	79	80	81	82	83	83	84	85	86	87	88	89	90	90	91	92	93	94
23.25	74	75	76	77	77	78	79	80	81	82	83	83	84	85	86	87	88	89	89	90	91	92	93
23.50	73	74	75	76	77	77	78	79	80	81	82	83	83	84	85	86	87	88	89	89	90	91	92
23.75	72	73	74	75	76	77	77	78	79	80	81	82	83	83	84	85	86	87	88	88	89	90	91
24.00	72	73	73	74	75	76	77	78	78	79	80	81	82	83	83	84	85	86	87	88	88	89	90
24.25	71	72	73	73	74	75	76	77	78	78	79	80	81	82	82	83	84	85	86	87	87	88	89
24.50	70	71	72	73	73	74	75	76	77	78	78	79	80	81	82	82	83	84	85	86	87	87	88
24.75	69	70	71	72	73	74	74	75	76	77	78	78	79	80	81	82	82	83	84	85	86	86	87
25.00	69	70	70	71	72	73	74	74	75	76	77	78	78	79	80	81	82	82	83	84	85	86	86

Glossary

EXPLANATION:

- The guide words at the top of each page indicate which words are located on that page. For example, the guide words for this first page are *aa* and *aura*. Words that come alphabetically after *aa* but before *aura* are found on the page.

- Within parentheses after each entry, the word is marked to show pronunciation. Use the marks (called diacritical marks) to help you pronounce the words.

ă	act, cat	o͞o	ooze
ā	ace, cape	ou	out, cloud
â	air, care	ŭ	up
ä	arm	ū	use, flute
ĕ	egg, fed	û	urn, turn
ē	equal, feed	ə	occurs in unaccented
ĭ	it, lit		syllables and is
ī	ice, line		pronounced as follows:
ŏ	fox, lot	a	aloud
ō	over, so	e	item
ô	order	i	pencil
oi	oil, toy	o	atom
o͝o	took, put	u	circus

The symbol (ˊ) as in **freˊdəm** marks the primary stress, or accent. The syllable preceding it is pronounced with greater emphasis than other syllables. The symbol (ˊ) as in **telˊə fonˊ** marks the secondary stress, or accent. The syllable preceding the secondary accent (ˊ) is pronounced with less emphasis than the one marked (ˊ).

A

a•a (ä´ä´), *noun,* blocky, angular lava. Some Hawaiian lava fields are made of *aa.* (Chap. 6)

ab•hor (ăb hôr´), *verb,* loathe; feel disgust for. The talented artist *abhorred* the cheap copies of his paintings. (Chap. 9)

ac•cess (ăk´sĕs), *noun,* approach to something or somebody; admittance. The reporters were unable to gain *access* to the private meeting. (Chap. 12)

ac•ti•vist (ăk´tə vĭst), *noun,* one who supports political or national interests by every means, including force. The *activists* stormed into the hall and shouted the speaker down. (Chap. 10)

ad•her•ent (ăd hĭr´ənt), *noun,* supporter or follower of a cause or leader. Jesse Jackson had many *adherents* during his presidential campaign. (Chap. 12)

aes•thet•ic (ĕs thĕt´ ĭk), *adjective,* artistic; having a sense of beauty. The graceful ballet appealed to her *aesthetic* sensitivity. (Chap. 2)

a•gil•i•ty (ə jĭl´ə tē), *noun,* ability to move quickly and easily. The horse showed its *agility* as it jumped over the wall. (Chap. 2)

a•kin (ə kĭn´), *adjective,* related; similar. We like Dixieland; our tastes in music are *akin* to one another. (Chap. 5)

al•le•vi•ate (ə lē´vē āt´), *verb,* lessen; mitigate; make easier to bear. The rescue squad was able to *alleviate* the patient's pain. (Chap. 2)

al•li•ance (ə lī´əns), *noun,* a connection or agreement between nations or parties for some special purpose. During World War I, The United States made an *alliance* with Great Britain and France against Germany. (Chap. 12)

al•loy (ăl´oi), *noun,* a composition of two or more metals melted together. Stainless steel is an *alloy* of steel and chromium that resists rust. (Chap. 6)

a•nat•o•my (ə năt´ə mē), *noun,* the structure of a plant, animal, or its parts. The biology class studied the *anatomy* of the heart. (Chap. 11)

an•tag•o•nist (ăn tăg´ə nĭst), *noun,* an opponent in any kind of contest. The candidate for office had several *antagonists* running against him. (Chap. 7)

an•te•date (ăn´tə dāt´), *verb,* to be an older date than; happen before in time. The arrival of Columbus in the New World *antedates* that of the pilgrims in Plymouth. (Chap. 3)

an•thro•pol•o•gist (ăn´thrə pŏl´ə jĭst), *noun,* one who studies the origins, development, cultures, and beliefs of human beings. The *anthropologist* was able to rebuild a clay bowl from the fragments she unearthed. (Chap. 3)

an•ti•bi•ot•ic (ăn´ti bī ŏt´ ĭk), *noun,* a substance produced by molds, yeast, or bacteria that kills or weakens germs. The *antibiotic* was put directly on the infection to kill the bacteria. (Chap. 3)

an•ti•war (ăn´tĕ wôr´), *adjective,* against; opposed to war. Pacifists are *antiwar.* (Chap. 3)

an•to•nym (ăn´tə nĭm), *noun,* a word that means the opposite of another word. The word "large" is an *antonym* for the word "small." (Chap. 3)

aq•ua•pho•bi•a (ăk´wə fō´bĭ ə), *noun,* a fear of water. His *aquaphobia* prevented his learning to swim. (Chap. 3)

arch (ärch), *adjective,* most important; sly, cunning. Among several, he was the *arch* rival. (Chap. 11)

ar•chae•ol•o•gy (är´kē ŏl´ə jē), *noun,* the study of customs, life, and things of ancient times by excavating the remains of structures and cities. Because she wanted to know more about Greek buildings, she studied *archaeology.* (Chap. 3)

a•ris•to•crat•ic (ə rĭs´tə krăt´ ĭk), *adjective,* belonging to an upper class; considered superior. Because of his intelligence, fame, and culture, he appeared *aristocratic* to some. (Chap. 9)

ar•tic•u•la•tion (är tĭk´yə lā´shən), *noun,* a jointed state, a state of being connected. The House and Senate committees worked smoothly together; they had good *articulation.* (Chap. 3)

as•pire (ə spīr´), *verb,* seek; aim for. We *aspire* to achieve our dreams. (Chap. 9)

as•so•ci•ate (ə sō´shē āt´), *verb,* to join as partner, to bring together, to connect with other parts. The dog *associated* his leash with going out for a walk. (Chap. 12)

a•ssump•tion (ə sŭmp´shən), *noun,* something taken for granted; a supposition. The customer's *assumption* was that the goods would be ready on the date promised. (Chap. 5)

asth•ma•tic (ăz măt´ ĭk), *adjective* or *noun,* a condition of difficult breathing with gasping or coughing; a person with asthma. The *asthmatic* patient was using an oxygen mask. (Chap. 12)

as•tro•nom•i•cal (ăs´trə nŏm´ək əl), *adjective,* having to do with astronomy, very high. Galileo made *astronomical* measurements with his telescope. The price was *astronomical;* there was no way I could pay. (Chap. 3)

au•ra (ôr´ə), *noun,* distinctive character or manner. The procession had an *aura* of beauty and dignity. (Chap. 13)

au•then•tic (ô thĕn´tĭk), *adjective,* worthy of belief, not copied or imitation, genuine. The ten-dollar bill was not *authentic;* it was counterfeit. (Chap. 13)

au•to•crat (â´tə krăt´), *noun,* a ruler who holds absolute power. Some kings were *autocrats* who thought their power was a given right. (Chap. 6)

av•id (ăv´ĭd), *adjective,* extremely eager, keen. Many writers start out as *avid* readers. (Chap. 11)

awe•some (ô´səm), *adjective,* bringing a feeling of power, dread, terror, or reverent wonder and respect. The sight of Niagara Falls was *awesome.* (Chap. 6)

B

banned (bănd), *verb,* forbidden or not allowed by law or social pressure. The judge *banned* the jury from speaking to reporters. (Chap. 14)

bi•cam•er•al (bī kăm´ər əl), *adjective,* having two chambers. The U.S. Congress is *bicameral.* (Chap. 4)

bi•cen•ten•ni•al (bī sĕn tĕn´ē əl), *noun,* a 200th anniversary. In 1977 the United States celebrated the *bicentennial* of the Constitution. (Chap. 3)

brac•ing (brās´ĭng), *verb,* preparing; putting oneself in readiness. They were *bracing* the tent against the expected winds. (Chap. 2)

brood (brüd), *verb,* dwell moodily in thought; to ponder at length. He had the tendency to *brood* about his errors; he could not, however, bring himself to correct them. (Chap. 2)

C

cam•ou•flage (kăm´ə fläzh´), *verb,* coloring or screening objects so that they blend into their background. The spots on the bird's eggs *camouflaged* them so that the predator walked by without seeing them. (Chap. 11)

ca•price (kə prēs´), *noun,* change of mind with no apparent reason. Because directions were given by *caprice,* and not by reason, the workers did not know what to do next. (Chap. 11)

car•ni•vore (kär´nə vōr´), *noun,* an animal that eats meat. The eagle is a *carnivore* that eats fish. (Chap. 3)

cen•ten•ni•al (sĕn tĕn´ē əl), *noun,* a 100th anniversary. A parade and fireworks marked the town's *centennial.* (Chap. 3)

cir•cum•nav•i•gate (sûr´kəm năv´ə gāt´), *verb,* sail around. In the early 1400s, Chinese ships *circumnavigated* Southeast Asia and sailed to India and the Persian Gulf. (Chap. 3)

clar•i•fy (klăr´ə fī), *verb,* make clear. His summary will *clarify* what he said. (Chap. 3)

cleave (klēv), *verb,* split open; split or cut with a blow. The cook will *cleave* the chops off the roast one by one. (Chap. 2)

co•los•sal (kə lŏs´əl), *adjective,* huge; gigantic. The pyramids of Egypt are *colossal* structures. (Chap. 1)

co•los•sus (kə lŏs´əs), *noun,* anything huge or gigantic. The legendary statue of Apollo, known as the *Colossus* of Rhodes, was one of the seven wonders of the world. (Chap. 1)

com•mis•sion (kə mĭsh´ən), *noun,* a task or job; a grant of authority. Goethals received a *commission* to engineer the building of the Panama Canal. (Chap. 9)

com•pla•cent (kŏm plā´sənt), *adjective,* self-satisfied with one's advantages. *Complacent* citizens may find their rights become limited if they ignore the self-serving acts of officials. (Chap. 13)

con•cen•tra•tion (kŏn´sən trā´shən), *noun,* the amount of a substance in a given area or volume. His soft drink had a high *concentration* of sugar. (Chap. 11)

con•cep•tu•al (kən sĕp´choo əl), *adjective,* pertaining to concepts. He arranged his thoughts into a *conceptual* scheme. (Chap. 6)

con•gre•gate (kŏng´grə gāt´), *verb,* to come together, gather, assemble. The students *congregated* in the schoolroom. (Chap. 10)

con•se•crate (kŏn´sə krāt´), *verb,* declare sacred, dedicate for a purpose. The ceremony *consecrated* the new temple. (Chap. 10)

con•sign (kən sīn´), *verb,* hand over; deliver. His arrest forced him to *consign* his expensive car to the courts. (Chap. 12)

con•tempt (kən tĕmpt´), *noun,* the feeling one has about something or someone regarded as unworthy or mean; scorn; disdain. She felt *contempt* for the selfish group who only thought of themselves. (Chap. 2)

con•ti•nen•tal di•vide (kŏn´tə nən´təl dĭ vīd´), *noun,* a line of mountaintops across a continent that separates stream flows to oceans on either side. The pioneers found passes across the *continental divide.* (Chap. 5)

con•tra•dic•tion (kŏn trə dĭk´shən), *noun,* act or statement of disagreement or direct opposition;

inconsistency. The sloppy paper was a direct *contradiction* of the careful work she always had done. (Chap. 5)

con•verge (kən vûrj´), *verb,* tend to meet in a point, to come together; tend to common result. Their efforts *converged* to get the job done. (Chap. 9)

con•vey (kən vā´), *verb,* to carry, transport; to make known. This paper will *convey* the message to the president. (Chap. 2)

cor•ner•stone (kôr´nər stōn´), *noun,* stone built into the corner of an important building and usually hollowed out to contain documents. Before it was cemented in place, newspapers and pictures were placed in the *cornerstone.* (Chap. 12)

coup (kōō), *noun,* unexpected achievement. It was a *coup* to achieve an A in that difficult course. (Chap. 9)

crust (krŭst), *noun,* the solid outer rock layers of the earth. The oil well drill penetrated deep into the earth's *crust.* (Chap. 2)

cue (kyōō), *noun,* a signal, prompt, or hint. The raised hand was a *cue* that the children should be quiet. (Chap. 11)

cur•ren•cy (kûr´ən sē), *noun,* money; medium of exchange. The *currency* he tried to deposit was counterfeit. (Chap. 13)

D

dazz•le (dăz´əl), *verb,* to overpower with bright light; to excite the imagination. His description of traveling in the Grand Canyon *dazzled* the audience. (Chap. 2)

de•ba•cle (dĭ bä´kəl), *noun,* a rout; sudden collapse or overthrow. The battle turned into a complete *debacle:* everything went wrong for the invading armies. (Chap. 5)

de•fault (dĭ fôlt´), *noun,* failure to pay a financial debt. If its obligations are not paid, the bank will *default.* (Chap. 10)

de•gen•er•ate (dĭ jĕn´ə rāt´), *verb,* decline, deteriorate. Drugs made him *degenerate* mentally and physically. (Chap. 10)

de•grad•ing (dĭ grā´dĭng), *adjective,* lowering in dignity. Being pushed to the rear was a *degrading* experience. (Chap. 9)

del•e•gate (dĕl´ə gāt), *verb,* to give authority to another. The president will *delegate* authority to the committee chairperson. (Chap. 4)

de•lib•er•ate (dĭ lĭb´ər ĭt), *adjective,* carefully

considered; done on purpose. His *deliberate* noise spoiled the performance. (Chap. 2)

dep•re•ca•tion (dĕp´rə kā´shən), *noun,* disapproval of; protestation against. No one likes his or her work to be subject to *deprecation* by others. (Chap. 13)

de•rive (dĭ rĭv´), *verb,* obtain from some source. The musician will *derive* pleasure from the concert. (Chap. 6)

der•ma•tol•o•gy (dûr´mə tŏl´ə jē), *noun,* the science of the skin and its diseases. The *dermatologist* gave him an antibiotic for his rash. (Chap. 3)

des•ig•nate (dĕz´ig nāt), *verb,* point out; mark. The girl was told to park her car in the zone *designated* for students. (Chap. 2)

de•tract (dē trăkt´), *verb,* take away; withdraw value or reputation. All the nasty remarks did not *detract* from his fine reputation. (Chap. 10)

dev•as•tate (dĕv´ə stāt´), *verb,* destroy; lay waste. The arsonist *devastated* the buildings with fire. (Chap. 5)

de•vise (dĭ vīz´), *verb,* to invent, to form in the mind new applications of ideas. He was able to *devise* a new part to repair the machine. (Chap. 11)

di•a•lect (dī´ə lĕkt´), *noun,* a variety of a language. Their *dialect* had special words we did not understand. (Chap. 14)

dif•fu•sion (dĭ fū´zhən), *noun,* a spreading widely, a scattering. The leak caused the *diffusion* of the fluid throughout the lake. (Chap. 11)

di•gest•ive (dĭ jĕs´tĭv), *adjective,* relating to the process of breaking down foods into simpler chemical forms. The stomach is part of the *digestive* tract. (Chap. 11)

di•min•ish (dĭ mĭn´ ĭsh), *verb,* make smaller; reduce. You cannot *diminish* my enthusiasm with your negative comments; I will continue to persist. (Chap. 13)

dis•crep•an•cy (dĭs krĕp´ən sē´), *noun,* difference; inconsistency. There was a large *discrepancy* between what she said and what she meant. (Chap. 13)

disk (dĭsk), *noun,* a flat circular object. The sun looks like a bright yellow *disk* even though we know it is a sphere. (Chap. 6)

di•vulge (dĭ vŭlj´), *verb,* reveal; make known. The mechanic cannot *divulge* her technique for repairing the special part. (Chap. 12)

du•el (dōō´əl), *noun,* fight or contest between two persons, usually prearranged. Alexander Hamilton was killed by Aaron Burr in a *duel* on the bluffs of Weehawken, New Jersey. (Chap. 9)

dwin•dle (dwĭn´dəl), *verb,* become smaller and smaller. The student sat and did nothing; as a result, his vacation time *dwindled* away. (Chap. 9)

E

e•clipse (ē klĭps´), *noun or verb,* the moving into the shadow of a planet or moon; to darken, hide, or obscure. The *eclipse* of the sun frightened the illiterate people. (Chap. 6)

e•col•o•gy (ē kŏl´ə jē), *noun,* the branch of biology that deals with living things and their relationships to the environment. *Ecologists* have found that weeds can tolerate poor environmental conditions. (Chap. 3)

e•co•nom•ic (ē´kə nŏm´ ĭk), *adjective,* having to do with production, distribution, and use of wealth. Adam Smith formulated *economic* principles in the 1700s. (Chap. 13)

ed•i•fice (ĕd´ə fĭs), *noun,* large or imposing building. The Lincoln Memorial in Washington is a grand *edifice.* (Chap. 6)

e•ject (ĭ jĕkt´), *verb,* expel; force out. The unruly were *ejected* from the meeting. (Chap. 6)

e•lab•or•ate (ĭ lăb´ə rāt´), *verb,* add details. Dickens could *elaborate* on all the characters in his novels. (Chap. 13)

el•ig•i•ble (ĕl´ ĭ jə bəl), *adjective,* qualified; worthy of being chosen. She was *eligible* for the award. (Chap. 14)

e•lite (ĭ lēt´), *noun,* select; best part. The nobility thought they were *elite* persons. (Chap. 9)

el•o•quent (ĕl´ə kwənt), *adjective,* having fluent, expressive, forceful speech. The preacher's *eloquence* held the audience in rapt attention. (Chap. 10)

e•mas•cu•late (ĭ măs´kyə lāt´), *verb,* castrate; remove testes or ovaries; weaken. Steers are bulls that have been *emasculated.* The governor was *emasculated* by the overwhelming vote of no confidence. (Chap. 6)

em•bo•lus (ĕm´bəl əs), *noun,* clot or undissolved mass carried in the circulatory system. Sometimes the body can dissolve an *embolus* in the bloodstream. (Chap. 11)

em•bry•o (ĕm´brē ō´), *noun,* an organism in early stages of development. The organs of the *embryo* were not yet all developed. (Chap. 11)

en•dorse (ĕn dôrs´), *verb,* to approve, support. The politician *endorsed* his friend during the primaries. (Chap. 2)

en•sure (ĕn shur´), *verb,* make sure; make certain. Her special care *ensured* the safety of her children. (Chap. 4)

en•voy (ĕn´voi), *noun,* a diplomatic representative. An *envoy* is next in rank below an ambassador. (Chap. 12)

er•a (ĭr´ə), *noun,* a significant period of time or history. The industrial revolution occurred during the *era* from the mid-1700s to the mid-1800s. (Chap. 14)

es•chew (ĕs choo´), *verb,* avoid, shun. The shy couple *eschewed* publicity. (Chap. 4)

e•volve (ĭ vŏlv´), *verb,* develop or change gradually. Fossils indicate that horses *evolved* from ancestors the size of dogs. (Chap. 11)

ex•pec•ta•tion (ĕk spĕk tā´shən), *noun,* anticipation; something looked forward to. The child's *expectation* was for far more than Santa would bring. (Chap. 5)

ex•plic•it (ĕk splĭs´ ĭt), *adjective,* clearly stated; definite. Her directions were *explicit;* no one misunderstood. (Chap. 2)

ex•tinc•tion (ĭk stĭngk´shən), *noun,* dying out of a biological line. We have caused the *extinction* of many plant and animal species. (Chap. 9)

F

fes•tive (fĕs´tĭv), *adjective,* merry, lively. The family gathering was a *festive* reunion. (Chap. 9)

flaunt (flônt), *verb,* to show off; to display boastfully. The boys skated very close to the girls to *flaunt* their skills. (Chap. 2)

flick•er (flĭk´ər), *verb,* to flutter, waver, give off unsteady light. The lamp lights *flickered* during the electrical storm. (Chap. 6)

flor•id (flôr´ ĭd), *adjective,* ruddy in cheeks or complexion. Their faces were *florid* from exposure to the intense sun. (Chap. 13)

for•ay (fôr´ ā), *noun,* a raid for plunder. The horse troop made a *foray* through the town to take food and livestock. (Chap. 12)

for•bear•ance (fôr bâr´əns), *noun,* patience. The mother had *forbearance* as the child struggled to dress himself without help. (Chap. 12)

fore•sight (fôr´sīt), *noun,* a forward view; ability to foresee. She had the *foresight* to carry her umbrella because the weather prediction was rain. (Chap. 13)

for•tu•i•tous•ly (fôr tū´ ə təs lē), *adverb,* by chance; accidentally. *Fortuitously,* the rain stopped in time for the outdoor ceremonies. (Chap. 4)

fren•zy (frĕn´zē), *noun,* wild agitation; excitement. The fox caused a *frenzy* in the chicken coop. (Chap. 9)

fres•co (frĕs´kō), *noun,* a picture painted in wet plaster. *Frescoes* allow the paint to become embedded in the plaster. (Chap. 12)

friv•o•lous (frĭv´ə ləs), *adjective,* with lack of sense; trivial; of little importance. His objections were *frivolous;* people paid no attention. (Chap. 13)

fu•ror (fyo͞or´ôr), *noun,* outburst of excitement; rage. The referee's poor decision caused a *furor* in the grandstand. (Chap. 2)

G

gar•goyle (gär´goil), *noun,* a rainspout on a roof gutter often made in the shape of an ugly animal or human head. When it rained, the *gargoyles* spouted water from their mouths. (Chap. 12)

gen•er•ate (jĕn´ə rāt´), *verb,* to produce; to bring into existence. Their kindness will *generate* a lot of goodwill. (Chap. 2)

ge•net•ic (jə nĕt´ ĭk), *adjective,* dealing with genetics, the science of heredity. Mendel worked with *genetic* traits but did not use the word *gene.* (Chap. 3)

ge•ol•o•gy (jē ŏl´ə jē), *noun,* the science that deals with the earth, the rocks that compose it, and its changes. In *geology* class, we identified rocks that we collected. (Chaps. 2, 3)

graph•ic (grăf´ ĭk), *adjective,* lifelike; vivid; pertaining to drawing or painting. The *graphic* description of the scene was so realistic, we felt we were actually there viewing the scene ourselves. (Chap. 3)

H

hal•low (hăl´ ō), *verb,* make holy; consecrate. Lincoln did not think he could *hallow* a battlefield. (Chap. 10)

hand•some•ly (hăn´səm lē), *adverb,* generously, impressively, skillfully. The artist *handsomely* crafted a beautiful silver bowl. (Chap. 2)

hap•haz•ard (hăp´hăz´ərd), *adjective,* at random; by chance. His notes were *haphazard;* he had trouble organizing them for study. (Chap. 11)

hard-liner (härd-lī´nər), *noun,* a person taking a very conservative or orthodox view, usually in politics. The *hard-liners* did their best to obstruct democratic moves in China. (Chap. 9)

heir (âr), *noun,* one who inherits property of a deceased person. She was the *heir* to her mother's few keepsakes. (Chap. 10)

he•mo•sta•sis (hē´mə stā´sĭs), *noun,* condition of blood stoppage. Two Greek words meaning "blood" and "standing" are put together to make the word *hemostasis.* (Chap. 11)

herb•i•vore (hûr´bĭv ôr), *noun,* an animal that eats plants. Cows and horses are *herbivores.* (Chap. 3)

her•o•ic (hĭ rō´ ĭk), *adjective,* of or suitable to a hero; having qualities of a hero. With *heroic* effort, the men lifted the car off the child. (Chap. 10)

hi•er•o•glyph•ic (hī´ər ə glĭf´ ĭk), *adjective,* pertaining to a picture writing system where symbols stand for words. Egyptian *hieroglyphic* writing includes pictures of birds and tools. (Chap. 7)

hig•gle•dy-pig•gle•dy (hĭg´əl dē-pĭg´əl dē), *adverb,* confused jumble. After the crowd left, the chairs were left scattered *higgledy-piggledy* around the room. (Chap. 12)

hor•rif•ic (hô rif´ĭk), *adjective,* causing horror. Being caught in a fire is an *horrific* experience. (Chap. 5)

hy•per•ac•tive (hī´pər ak´tĭv), *adjective,* overactive; easily excited. The *hyperactive* child was constantly moving about. (Chap. 3)

hy•po•thet•i•cal (hī´pə thĕt´ə kəl), *adjective,* not well supported by evidence; conditional; supposed. His argument was *hypothetical;* it was not based on fact. (Chap. 2)

I

i•dol (ī´dəl), *noun,* an image representing a diety. Some *idols* are worshipped, fed, and clothed as if they were alive. (Chap. 10)

ig•ne•ous (ĭg´nĭ əs), *adjective,* fire-formed; produced under intense heat. *Igneous* rocks form from molten material. (Chap. 6)

ig•nite (ĭg nīt´), *verb,* to set on fire; to begin to burn. The hot coals fell on the dry grass and *ignited* it. (Chap. 11)

im•pend•ing (ĭm pĕn´ding), *adjective,* about to happen. We ran inside to avoid the *impending* thunderstorm. (Chap. 12) im•per•cep•ti•ble (ĭm´pər sĕp´tə bəl), *adjective*, not noticeable; very slight. Any defects in the fine carving were *imperceptible*. (Chap. 4)

im•preg•na•tion (ĭm prĕg nā´shən), *noun*, process of making pregnant; fertilization. The *impregnation* resulted in twins. (Chap. 10)

im•prov•i•sa•tion (ĭm´prəv ĭ zā´shən), *noun*, something provided on the spur of the moment. The musician did an *improvisation* when the song title was announced. (Chap. 2)

in•au•di•ble (ĭn ô´də bəl), *adjective*, not capable of being heard. The machinery was so quiet that it was *inaudible* to the workers. (Chap. 2)

in•con•clu•sive (ĭn´kən klōō´sĭv), *adjective*, not settled. The experiment did not settle anything; it had *inconclusive* results. (Chap. 12)

in•con•gru•ous (ĭn kăng´grə wəs), *adjective*, not harmonious, inconsistent within itself. The nasty behavior was *incongruous* with his usual even temper. (Chap. 14)

in•cor•rig•i•ble (ĭn kor´ə jə bəl), *adjective*, uncorrectable, unmanageable. His lengthy criminal record indicated he was *incorrigible*. (Chap. 14)

in•cum•bent (ĭn kŭm´bənt), *noun*, the holder of an office. The newcomer challenged the *incumbent* president in the election. (Chap. 5)

in•dis•crim•in•ate•ly (ĭn´dĭs krĭm´ə nĭt lē), *adverb*, not discriminately; not making a distinction; not observing a difference. The madman fired his gun *indiscriminately*, hitting bystanders as well as his intended target. (Chap. 9)

in•ex•tri•ca•bly (ĭn eks´trə kə blē), *adverb*, cannot be taken apart. The cables were tangled *inextricably*. (Chap. 10)

in•no•va•tion (ĭn´ə vā´shən), *noun*, something new or different that is introduced. The invention of the transistor was an *innovation* that made modern computers possible. (Chap. 3)

in•sur•rec•tion (ĭn´sə rĕk´shən), *noun*, a revolt; open resistance against civil authority. Shay's Rebellion in 1676 was an *insurrection* by farmers to prevent debt judgments against them. (Chap. 6)

in•ten•si•ty (ĭn tĕn´sə tē), *noun*, great strength; power; violence. The heat *intensity* of the furnace burned their faces. (Chap. 2)

in•ter•ac•tion (ĭn´tər ăk´shən), *noun*, action on each other. The *interaction* among the members of the team showed fine team spirit and cooperation. (Chap. 5)

in•ter•state (ĭn´tər stāt´), *adjective*, between states. The railroad carrying goods from Missouri to California was involved in *interstate* commerce. (Chap. 3)

int•er•val (ĭnt´ər vəl), *noun*, a period between events, a pause; a space between objects. The game had fifteen-minute *intervals* between quarters. (Chap. 4)

in•ter•vene (ĭn´tər vēn´), *verb*, come between; be between. The referee *intervened* in the dispute between the two teams. (Chap. 4)

in•tim•i•date (ĭn tĭm´ə dāt´), *verb*, make timid, cow. The others were *intimidated* by his outspoken sureness. (Chap. 13)

in•tra•state (ĭn´trə stāt´), *adjective*, within one state. The inspector's duties were *intrastate;* he took water samples only in Georgia. (Chap. 3)

in•un•date (ĭn´ən dāt´), *verb*, overflow; flood; overwhelm. The water broke through the dam and *inundated* the valley below. (Chap. 5)

in•vin•ci•bil•i•ty (ĭn vĭn´sə bĭl´ə tē), *noun*, status of not being able to be conquered or overcome. The ignorant soldiers were told their *invincibility* protected them against bullets. (Chap. 13)

i•ron•y (i´ər nē´), *adjective*, outcome of events opposite to that expected. There was *irony* in that the journalist who advocated gun control used an unregistered pistol. (Chap. 9)

ir•re•press•i•ble (ĭr ĭ prĕs´ə bəl), *adjective*, impossible to control or restrain. The team had an *irrepressible* spirit that carried them to victory. (Chap. 13)

isth•mus (ĭs´məs), *noun*, narrow neck of land connecting two larger land areas. The *isthmus* of Suez connects Asia and Africa. (Chap. 5)

J

jos•tle (jŏs´əl), *verb*, push or shove rudely against. The pickpocket *jostled* the victim to draw his attention away from the thieving action. (Chap. 10)

K

keen (kēn), *verb*, wail for the dead. They *keened* loudly and made everyone aware of the tragedy. (Chap. 9)

Ko•ran (Kō rän´), *noun*, Islamic sacred scripture. The *Koran* is believed by Muhammadans to contain revelations by Allah. (Chap. 10)

L

lan•guish (lăng´gwĭsh), *verb,*   lose vigor, strength; become weak. The battle survivors *languished* from their wounds. (Chap. 10)

leg•end•ar•y (lĕj´ən dĕ rē), *adjective,*   in regard to a story handed down by tradition. Although *legendary* exploits have no proof of truth, they are often accepted as having happened. (Chap. 9)

le•gions (lē´jəns), *noun,*   large numbers, multitudes, armies. There were *legions* who followed his great leadership. (Chap. 13)

leg•is•la•tive (lĕj´ ĭs lā´tĭv), *adjective,*   having the function of making laws. Our national *legislative* body sits in Washington. (Chap. 4)

lei•sure•ly (lē´zhər lē), *adjective,*   without haste; taking plenty of time. The couple strolled *leisurely* along the beach. (Chap. 2)

lit•e•rar•y (lĭt´ə rĕr´ ē), *adjective,*   relating to books, literature, writing. It was a *literary* family; they enjoyed reading books and writing stories. (Chap. 13)

lu•cra•tive (lōō´krə tĭv), *adjective,*   profitable, yielding gain. Selling goods in heavy demand is *lucrative* work. (Chap. 2)

M

man•date (măn´dāt), *noun,*   a formal order or command. They had no choice; the order to vacate was a *mandate* from the court. (Chap. 13)

man•u•script (măn´yə skrĭpt´), *noun,*   something handwritten, typewritten, or in computer rough draft as opposed to final printed copy. Some libraries have collections of *manuscripts* written by famous authors. (Chap. 14)

mar•ket (mär´kĭt), *verb,*   to buy or sell; to deal. The tradesman *markets* his wares at the mall. (Chap. 2)

me•di•ate (mē´dĭ āt´), *verb,*   try to bring agreement between disputing groups or persons. The mediator was called to *mediate* the differences between labor and management. (Chap. 12)

mem•o•ra•ble (mĕm´ər ə bəl), *adjective,*   worthy of remembering; notable. For the Pearl Harbor survivor, December 7 is a *memorable* day. (Chap. 3)

met•a•mor•phic (mĕt´ə môr´fĭk), *adjective,*   having change in form or structure. Heat and pressure can change sedimentary rocks into *metamorphic* rocks. (Chap. 6)

mi•grate (mī´grāt), *verb,*   move from one country or region to settle in another. Many of us have ancestors that *migrated* here from another country. (Chap. 12)

mil•len•ni•um (mĭ lĕn´ ē əm), *noun,*   one thousand years. There are trees that have lived more than a *millennium.* (Chap. 3)

mire (mīr), *noun,*   soft, deep mud or slushy snow. Spinning the wheels only *mired* the car more deeply. (Chap. 5)

mul•ti•tude (mŭl´tə tōōd), *noun,*   a crowd; a great many. The hungry *multitude* gathered around the food truck. (Chap. 3)

mus•ter (mŭs´tər), *verb,*   summon; gather together. The new miners *mustered* their courage before entering the deep mine shaft. (Chap. 5)

N

nat•ur•al•ist (năch´ər ə lĭst), *noun,*   a person who studies plants and animals. John Muir was a *naturalist* who crusaded for national parks and nature reservations. (Chap. 6)

neg•li•gi•ble (nĕg´lə jə bəl), *adjective,*   can be neglected. Because their differences were *negligible,* they agreed on the contract. (Chap. 12)

neu•tral (nōō´trəl), *adjective,*   not taking either side. The fans were not *neutral;* they cheered for their own teams. (Chap. 11)

niche (nĭch), *noun,*   in ecology, the role or position and function of an animal or plant in the natural community. The monkey's *niche* was to live and feed in the tops of trees. (Chap. 3)

no•bly (nō´blē), *adjective,*   in a noble manner; splendidly. The musician stood in front of a very critical audience and performed *nobly.* (Chap. 10)

nov•ice (nŏv´ ĭs), *noun,*   one without experience; one new to the position. He was a *novice* with hammer and saw but the carpenter would train him. (Chap. 2)

O

o•a•sis (ō ā´sĭs), *noun,*   a desert place where water is available. In an *oasis,* groundwater comes near or to the surface and allows some plants to thrive. (Chap. 10)

ob•jec•tive (əb jĕk´tĭv), *adjective,*   unbiased; free from personal feelings. While interpreting the data, the chemist made an effort to be *objective. Noun,* something toward which effort is directed. The pioneers' *objective* was to get the shelter finished before winter arrived. (Chap. 4)

ob•liv•i•on (ə blĭv´ ĭ ən), *noun,* condition of being forgotten by the world. Some early civilizations have passed into *oblivion.* (Chap. 6)

ob•scu•ri•ty (əb skyōōr´ə tē), *noun,* condition of being unknown; dimness. The original meanings of the markings on the monument have fallen into *obscurity.* (Chap. 7)

ob•sessed (əb sĕssd´), *verb,* holding an idea or feeling to an intense degree. Churchill was *obsessed* with the idea of defending Britain from the Nazis. (Chap. 13)

ob•ses•sion (əb sesh´ən), *noun,* a persistent idea or dominating influence that a person cannot escape. Columbus was driven by an *obsession* to reach India by sailing westward. (Chap. 7)

o•men (ō´ mən), *noun,* an occurrence believed to be a sign of a future event. Early peoples saw the appearances of certain animals as *omens* of good hunting. (Chap. 6)

om•in•ous (ŏm´ə nəs), *adjective,* threatening; portending evil. The funnel-shaped cloud was *ominous;* it meant a tornado. (Chap. 9)

om•nip•o•tent (ŏm nĭp´ə tənt), *adjective,* having unlimited power or authority. Many ancient kings were *omnipotent* in their kingdoms. (Chap. 3)

om•ni•pres•ent (ŏm´nə prĕz´ənt), *adjective,* all present; being or existing everywhere. God, in many religions, is thought to be *omnipresent.* (Chap. 3)

op•er•a•tive (ŏp´ər â´tĭv), *adjective,* exerting influence; being in effect. The rules *operative* when he played the game have since been changed. (Chap. 2)

o•ver•all (ō´vər ôl´), *adjective,* from one extreme of a thing to the other. The *overall* length of the car was fifteen feet. (Chap. 2)

P

pa•ho•e•ho•e (pä hō´ ā hō´ ā), *noun,* lava that looks like coils of heavy rope. Some Hawaiian lava fields are made of *pahoehoe.* (Chap. 6)

pair (pâər), *verb,* to arrange two parts for use together. He *paired* the two straps so that together they held the case firmly on his back. (Chap. 11)

pa•le•on•tol•o•gy (pâ´lē ən tŏl´ə jē), *noun,* the science of extinct forms of life as represented by fossil plants and animals. We have learned about dinosaurs through *paleontology.* (Chap. 3)

pan•the•on (păn´thĭ ŏn´), *noun,* temple dedicated to the gods. Hadrian erected a domed *pantheon* that today is used as a church. (Chap. 13)

par•a•mount (păr´ə mount´), *adjective,* above all; superior in authority. His *paramount* concern was to make his car payment. (Chap. 12)

par•tial (pär´ shəl), *adjective,* relating to a part or piece of the whole. The money she earned made only a *partial* payment for her coat. (Chap. 6)

pa•tron (pā´trən), *noun,* one who supports art, music, scientific, or other worthy endeavors. The *patron* covered the cost of the free concert. (Chap. 9)

per•il•ous•ly (pĕr´əl əs lē), *adverb,* in a dangerous manner. The surefooted goats walked *perilously* close to the edge of the cliff. (Chap. 2)

per•ti•na•cious (pûr´tə nā´shəs), *adjective,* holding tightly to a course of action, purpose, or belief. The *pertinacious* writer kept revising the article until it was accepted. (Chap. 6)

pet•u•lant (pĕch´ə lənt), *adjective,* showing irritation. The *petulant* crowd shouted and booed when the player made slight errors. (Chap. 12)

pho•tom•e•ter (fō tŏm´ə tər), *noun,* an instrument for measuring light intensity. The camera had a built-in *photometer.* (Chap. 3)

pic•to•graph (pĭk´tə grăf´), *noun,* a chart or record that has amounts shown by picture symbols. The three bundles of wheat in the *pictograph* stood for 3,000 bushels. (Chap. 14)

plas•ma (plăz´mə), *noun,* liquid part of blood in which blood cells are suspended. Blood *plasma* is about 90 percent water. (Chap. 11)

pol•y•the•ism (pŏl´ ĭ thē isəm), *noun,* belief in many gods. The ancient Greeks believed in *polytheism.* (Chap. 12)

post•war (pōst´wôr´), *adjective,* after a war. The *postwar* period was a time for rebuilding. (Chap. 3)

pre•ce•dent (prĕs´ə dənt), *noun,* a preceding example that may serve as justification for a later case. The lawyer cited *precedent* to support his case. (Chap. 13)

pre•da•tion (prē dā´shən), *noun,* act of hunting and seizing animals for food. The reptile's act of *predation* was necessary for its survival. (Chap. 11)

pre•em•i•nent (prē ĕm´ə nənt), *adjective,* superior to others; distinguished above others. The *preeminent* authors and scientists were honored at the ceremony. (Chap. 12)

pre•side (prĭ zīd´), *verb,* hold the place of authority; have charge of a meeting. The committee chairperson will *preside* at the meeting. (Chap. 4)

pres•tige (prĕs tēzh´), *noun,* distinction; reputation, based on abilities, achievements, or rank. Those awarded the Nobel Prize have great *prestige* in the world. (Chap. 4)

pri•or•i•ty (prī ŏr´ə tē), *noun,* a precedence in order, rank, or attention; being earlier in date or time. They gave *priority* to getting the work done before they sat down to relax. (Chap. 4)

prod•i•gy (prŏd´ə jē), *noun,* person having extraordinary talents. Isaac Newton was a *prodigy* in mathematics. (Chap. 9)

prom•is•so•ry note (prŏm´ə sōr ē nōt), *noun,* a written promise. A *promissory note* may be written with payment due at a certain time or on demand. (Chap. 10)

pro•mote (prə mōt´), *verb,* to encourage, further; to develop or establish. The ad agency is in business to *promote* products. (Chap. 2)

prop•o•si•tion (prŏp´ə zĭsh´ən), *noun,* proposal; plan; scheme. The business *proposition* meant a large order for the salesperson. (Chap. 10)

pro•tag•o•nist (prō´tăg´ə nĭst), *noun,* leading character in a play. Macbeth was both *protagonist* and title of a tragedy written by Shakespeare in 1606. (Chap. 11)

pro•to•type (prō´tə tīp´), *noun,* a model or example from which something is formed. Others copied the *prototype* that he had developed. (Chap. 3)

pseu•do•sci•ence (sōō´dō sī´əns), *noun,* false; sham science. Astrology is a *pseudoscience;* it is not based on systematic truths showing general laws. (Chap. 3)

pum•ice (pŭm´ ĭs), *noun,* porous, glassy form of lava. Fine ground *pumice* is used as an abrasive cleanser. (Chap. 6)

py•ro•clas•tic (pī´rə klăs´tĭk), *adjective,* fire-made from volcanoes. The *pyroclastic* rock fragments made a cone around the volcano. (Chap. 6)

Q

quad•ri•cen•ten•ni•al (kwŏd´rĕ sĕn tĕn´ ē əl), *noun,* a 400th anniversary. A *quadricentennial* marks the completion of 400 years. (Chap. 3)

quest (kwĕst), *noun,* a search or pursuit. Don Quixote made a number of unsuccessful *quests.* (Chap. 10)

quin•tu•plet (kwĭn´tə plĭt), *noun,* one of five offspring born at a birth. If identical *quintuplets* are born, all five are of the same sex. (Chap. 3)

quo•rum (kwôr´əm), *noun,* number of members of a body required to be present for business to be conducted legally. In the House and Senate, a majority constitutes the *quorum* to do business. (Chap. 4)

R

rad•i•cal (răd´ə kəl), *adjective,* drastic; thoroughgoing. Moving from stagecoach to railroad was a *radical* change in transportation. (Chap. 3)

rad•i•cal (răd´ə kəl), *noun,* one favoring extreme changes or reforms in government, views, or existing conditions. The *radicals* plotted the overthrow of the government. (Chap. 10)

ral•ly (răl´ ē), *verb,* bring together; bring to order. Washington *rallied* his dispirited troops at Valley Forge. (Chap. 9)

rar•e•fied (râr´ə fīd´), *adjective,* less gross; refined. The stunning furnishings gave the room a *rarefied* appearance. (Chap. 13)

re•form•er (rē fôrm´ər), *noun,* a person who attempts improvement of what is wrong; a person who reforms, restores. Martin Luther was a *reformer* of religion. (Chap. 9)

rel•e•vant (rĕl´ə vənt), *adjective,* connected to, or bearing upon the matter at hand. His directions were *relevant* to repairing the broken chair. (Chap. 2)

rem•i•nisce (rĕm´ə nĭs´), *verb,* to recall past experiences. The World War II veterans *reminisced* about the battles in Normandy. (Chap. 11)

re•press•ion (rē prĕsh´ən), *noun,* condition of curbing, keeping under control; putting down. The military *repression* kept down the overt complaints. (Chap. 9)

res•er•va•tion (rez´ər vā´shən), *noun,* a keeping back, a withholding; a setting aside of a tract of land; a doubt; a travel accommodation. The woman had *reservations* about whether to report the crime to the police. (Chap. 10)

res•o•nant (rĕz´ə nənt), *adjective,* echoing; resounding. The sounds of the organ were *resonant;* they filled the cathedral. (Chap. 4)

rev•e•la•tion (rĕv´ə lā´shən), *noun,* act of revealing, disclosing. His *revelation* indicated that undercover agents had been checking on the criminal's activities. (Chap. 12)

rev•er•ie (rĕv´ə rē), *noun,* daydream; dreamy musing. Her *reveries* brought back pleasant memories of childhood. (Chap. 6)

round•ly (round´lē), *adverb,* severely; vigorously. He beat the rug *roundly* to get the dirt out. (Chap. 13)

S

sac•ra•ment (săk´rə mənt), *noun,* something looked on as being sacred; an oath or pledge. Marriage to her is a *sacrament.* (Chap. 10)

sa•gac•i•ty (sə găs´ə tē), *noun,* soundness of judgment; sharpness of mind. Albert Einstein was admired for his *sagacity.* (Chap. 6)

sa•li•ent (sā´le ənt), *adjective,* prominent; conspicuous. The fireworks were the *salient* event in the celebration. (Chap. 4)

sal•i•vate (săl´ə vāt), *verb,* drool, produce excess saliva. The dog *salivated* as it smelled its food dish. (Chap. 12)

scaf•fold (skăf´əld), *noun,* temporary platform structure. A *scaffold* might be erected for workers and materials or to serve as a stage for exhibits. (Chap. 9)

score (skōr), *noun,* set of twenty. Lincoln spoke of four *score,* or eighty years. (Chap. 10)

sco•ri•a (skōr´ĭ ə), *noun,* volcanic rock with saclike holes. The *scoria* has the appearance of a mass of hardened bubbles. (Chap. 6)

scru•tin•y (skrōō´tə nē), *noun,* a careful examination; a detailed search. The people crossing the border came under the *scrutiny* of the guards. (Chap. 2)

sed•i•men•ta•ry (sĕd´ə mĕn´tər ē), *adjective,* formed from deposits of sediment. Some *sedimentary* rocks show layers of different colors. (Chap. 6)

seem•ing•ly (sē´ming lē), *adverb,* apparently, at first sight or view. *Seemingly* they were very pleasant, but in reality they were two-faced. (Chap. 12)

siege (sēj), *noun,* the surrounding of a fortified place to capture it by cutting off supplies or help. The army kept bombarding the fort while keeping it under *siege.* (Chap. 12)

sig•ni•fy (sĭg´nə fī´), *verb,* be a sign of. The arrow in the road sign *signifies* a curve. (Chap. 9)

sit•u•a•tion (sĭch´ə wā´shən), *noun,* state of affairs, or plight, at any given time. In winter camp at Valley Forge, Washington's men were in a desperate *situation.* (Chap. 5)

soar (sôr), *verb,* to climb, rise, fly upward. When crude oil prices *soar,* gasoline prices quickly follow. (Chap. 2)

sov•er•eign (sŏv´ĭ rĭn), *noun,* monarch; king or queen. The *sovereign* had her portrait put on all the coins and stamps. (Chap. 13)

spate (spāt), *noun,* sudden onset or outpouring. Desert flowers bloom after a *spate* of rain. (Chap. 6)

spec•ter (spĕk´tər), *noun,* ghost; visible spirit. In Dickens's *A Christmas Carol,* Scrooge was frightened by a series of *specters.* (Chap. 6)

spew (spū), *verb,* to discharge contents; to vomit. Old Faithful geyser *spewed* water and steam into the air. (Chap. 2)

stag•ger•ing (stăg´ər ĭng), *adjective,* heavy as to cause falling or tottering. The *staggering* load on his back made him fall down the stairs. (Chap. 9)

stal•wart (stôl´wərt), *adjective,* strongly built; firm; steadfast. The defenders of the Alamo were *stalwart* to the end. (Chap. 4)

stim•u•lus (stĭm´yə ləs), *noun,* something that excites or arouses. A scratch on the frog's nose was the *stimulus* that made him jump. (Chap. 12)

struc•tur•al (strŭk´chər əl), *adjective,* having to do with structure; pertaining to how parts are put together. *Structural* steel made up the framework of the building. (Chap. 3)

sub•tle (sŭt´l), *adjective,* delicate; likely to avoid perception. The mouse never noticed the *subtle* movements of the owl. (Chap. 2)

suc•cess•ive (sək sĕs´ĭv), *adjective,* following in order without interruption. The medicine was to be taken for ten *successive* days. (Chap. 12)

su•per•in•ten•dent (sōō´pər ĭn tĕn´dənt), *noun,* one who directs or oversees an institution or enterprise. The *superintendent* was in charge of the blueprints for the new bridge. (Chap. 3)

sur•vive (sər vīv´), *verb,* continue to live or exist. The plant *survived* through the extreme cold spell. (Chap. 2)

syn•the•sis (sĭn´thə sĭs), *noun,* a building of simpler parts into a complex organization. Plants make sugar by *synthesis* of small molecules. (Chap. 6)

syn•thet•ic (sĭn thĕt´ĭk), *adjective,* made by putting components together; made, rather than formed naturally. *Synthetic* fabrics take the place of cotton and wool. (Chap. 13)

T

te•di•ous (tē´dĭ əs), *adjective,* lengthy and

tiresome. Westward pioneers made *tedious* journeys. (Chap. 6)

tel•e•graph (tĕl´ə grăf), *noun,* a device for sending coded messages over long distances. Marconi invented a wireless *telegraph* and was the first to send a message across the Atlantic Ocean. (Chap. 3)

ter•ror•ize (tĕr´ər īz), *verb,* to create fear, to coerce violently. The volcanic eruption *terrorized* the people living on the mountain slopes. (Chap. 6)

tes•ta•ment (tĕs´tə mənt), *noun,* a formal declaration or statement, usually written. The Declaration of Independence was a *testament* of the Founders' beliefs. (Chap. 4)

the•o•ret•i•cal (thē´ə rĕt´ək əl), *adjective,* dealing with theories; not practical. *Theoretical* knowledge of the universe is obtained from examining changes in stars. (Chap. 3)

throm•bus (thrŏm´bəs), *noun,* blood clot. Fibrin molecules of the plasma together with blood cells make a clot called a *thrombus.* (Chap. 11)

tran•quil•li•ty (trăng kwĭl´ə tē), *noun,* peacefulness; calmness. They rested in the *tranquillity* of the early morning. (Chap. 10)

trans•con•ti•nen•tal (trăns´kŏn tə nən´təl), *adjective,* extending across a continent. When tracks from the Pacific coast and from Omaha were joined near Ogden, Utah, in 1769, the first *transcontinental* railroad was completed. (Chap. 3)

trans•form (trăns fôrm´), *verb,* to change in form, character, appearance. The dirty travelers were *transformed* by their hot bath and change into fresh clothes. (Chap. 2)

trau•ma (trô´mă), *noun,* violent bodily injury; shock. The word *trauma* can mean physical harm or severe shock to mental well-being. (Chap. 13)

trea•tise (trē´tĭs), *noun,* a formal book or paper on some subject. Asa Gray wrote a *treatise* on plant identification. (Chap. 6)

trib•ute (trĭb´ ūt), *noun,* an offering of gratitude or esteem; a forced gift or valuable paid in submission. In *tribute,* the people laid hundreds of flowers at their leader's feet. (Chap. 10)

tri•lat•er•al (trī lăt´ər əl), *adjective,* having three sides. The three electric companies have a *trilateral* agreement to share power when one has a shortage. (Chap. 3)

triv•i•al (trĭv´ ĭ əl), *adjective,* unimportant; commonplace. His problems were *trivial;* he soon forgot them. (Chap. 6)

trust (trŭst), *noun,* a monopoly; an organization in restraint of trade. Antitrust laws now regulate the powers of *trusts.* (Chap. 13)

tur•moil (tûr´moil), *noun,* a state of disturbance, commotion, agitation. The attack came from two directions and put the defenders in *turmoil.* (Chap. 9)

U

u•nan•i•mous (ū năn´ə məs), *adjective,* agreed, in complete accord. They all agreed; the vote was *unanimous.* (Chap. 4)

u•nique (ū nēk´), *adjective,* sole; being the only one of its kind. Because something *unique* has no like or equal, we should not say something is very unique. (Chap. 12)

un•prec•e•den•ted (ŭn prĕs´ə dĕn´tid), *adjective,* never known or done before. The record high jump was *unprecedented.* (Chap. 9)

un•ru•ly (un rü lē), *adjective,* difficult to control; not conforming to rule. The chairperson had difficulty in maintaining order when the members became *unruly.* (Chap. 12)

un•scru•pu•lous (ŭn skrōō´pyə ləs), *adjective,* having no principles; no conscience. The *unscrupulous* salesperson took advantage of their ignorance. (Chap. 9)

V

ver•i•ta•ble (vĕr´ə tə bal), *adjective,* genuine; real; true. He was a *veritable* jack-of-all-trades; there was nothing he could not do. (Chap. 6)

ver•sus (vûr´ səs), *preposition,* against, in contrast. Studying to do well *versus* having a good time was the freshman's decision. (Chap. 14)

ves•i•cle (vĕs´ə kəl), *noun,* cavity; sac; small bladder. The sponge was filled with *vesicles.* (Chap. 6)

vice ver•sa (vī´sə vûr´sə), *adverb,* the other way round. She was going first to Denmark and then to Norway, or *vice versa.* (Chap. 9)

vir•tu•al (vûr´chōō əl), *adjective,* being in force or in effect but not actually expressed as such. The general was the *virtual* power behind the throne; he told the king what to do. (Chap. 5)

vis•cous (vĭs´kəs), *adjective,* sticky; gummy. The *viscous* grease dripped from the roasting pan. (Chap. 6)

vis•i•bil•i•ty (vĭz ə bĭl´ə tē), *noun,*   capacity of being seen. The fog made the *visibility* very poor. (Chap. 2)

W

wal•low (wŏl´ ō), *verb,*   roll the body around in; indulge in. The children contentedly *wallowed* in the new snow. (Chap. 10)

wrest (rĕst), *verb,*   pull away by force. The thief tried to *wrest* the jewelry from the woman. (Chap. 2)

Glossary compiled by George Hennings

Credits

Reading on page

6 and 142 Bob Rosefsky, *Money Talks* (New York: McGraw-Hill, 1989). Used by permission.

9 Henry Graff, *This Great Nation.* Copyright 1985 by Riverside Publishing Company. Reprinted by permission of the publisher.

14 Pat Sleem, "For Heaven's Sakes, Choose a Job You Enjoy!" Reprinted with permission from *Careers and the College Grad* (Holbrook, MA: Bob Adams, Inc.), p. 16.

18 Adapted from Helena Curtis and N. Sue Barnes, *Invitation to Biology,* Copyright 1985 by Worth Publishers. Reprinted by permission of the publisher.

21 Emma Lazarus, "The New Colossus," from the pedestal of the Statue of Liberty.

27 Sentences are from Leo Fay, et al., *Riverside Reading Program, Level 15.* Copyright 1989 by Riverside Publishing Co. Reprinted by permission of the publisher.

28 Charles Cazeau, Robert Hatcher, and Francis Siemankowski, *Physical Geology: Principles, Processes, and Problems.* Copyright © 1976 by Harper and Row Publishers, Inc. Reprinted by permission of Harper & Row, Publishers, Inc.

30 Excerpt pp. 6–7 from *Living with Computers* by Patrick G. McKeown, copyright © 1986 by Harcourt Brace Jovanovich, Inc., reprinted by permission of the publisher.

33, 247, 250, and 254 Charles G. Morris, *Psychology: An Introduction,* 6th ed., © 1988, pp. 177–180, 340–341. Reprinted by permission of Prentice Hall, Englewood Cliffs, New Jersey.

36 Philip Kotler and Gary Armstrong, *Principles of Marketing,* 5th ed., © 1991, p. 614. Reprinted by permission of Prentice Hall, Englewood Cliffs, New Jersey.

51 and 173 Alan Mandell, *The Language of Science.* Copyright 1974 by the National Science Teachers Association. Reprinted by permission of the National Science Teachers Association.

55 Stefi Weisburd, "Brushing Up on Dinosaurs," *Science News,* 130 (October 4, 1986), pp. 216–220. Reprinted with permission from *Science News,* the weekly newsmagazine of science, copyright 1986 by Science Service Inc.

72 The ten paragraphs on this and following pages are from Hubert Pryor, "Summer of Destiny," *Modern Maturity* (February/March 1987), p. 60. Copyright 1987 by American Association of Retired Persons. Reprinted by permission.

76 William Ecenbarger, "James Michener," *Modern Maturity* (February-March 1985), pp. 24–26. Reprinted with permission. Copyright 1985 American Association of Retired Persons.

83 From *The Constitution of the United States of America* by Sam Fink. Foreword copyright © 1985 by James Michener. Reprinted by permission of Random House, Inc.

86 Stephen Robbins, *Management,* 2nd ed., © 1988, pp. 199–201. Reprinted by permission of Prentice Hall, Englewood Cliffs, New Jersey.

92 The paragraphs on this and following pages are from William Ecenbarger, "James Michener," *Modern Maturity* 28 (August/ September 1985), p. 24.

96, 189, and 287 John Macionis, *Sociology,* 3rd ed., © 1991. Reprinted by permission of Prentice Hall, Englewood Cliffs, New Jersey.

98 Karl Case and Ray Fair, *Principles of Economics,* 2nd ed., © 1992, pp. 538–539. Reprinted by permission of Prentice Hall, Englewood Cliffs, New Jersey.

101 George Cruys, "The Dream of Panama," *Skald* (Spring/Summer 1986), pp. 2–7. Copyright 1986 by Royal Viking Line. Reprinted by permission of the Royal Viking Line.

115 The seven paragraphs quoted on pages 115–124 are from Chester R. Longwell, Adolph Knopf, and Richard Flint, *Physical Geology* (New York: John Wiley, 1948), pp. 347–348.

126 Kathryn Kelley and Donn Byrne, *Exploring Human Sexuality,* © 1992, pp. 259–265. Reprinted by permission of Prentice Hall, Englewood Cliffs, New Jersey.

134 The four paragraphs quoted on pages 134–136 are from Jay Pasachoff, Maomi Pasachoff, Roy Clark, and Marlene Westermann, *Physical Science Today.* Copyright 1987 by Prentice Hall. Reprinted by permission of the publisher.

147 and 330 Samuel C. Certo, Max E. Douglas, and Stewart W. Husted, *Business,* Second Edition. Copyright year date © 1984. Reprinted with permission of Allyn and Bacon.

150 Daniel Politoske, *Music,* 4th ed. © 1988, pp. 510–512. Reprinted by permission of Prentice Hall, Englewood Cliffs, New Jersey.

154 From *Hunger of Memory* by Richard Rodriguez. Copyright © 1982 by Richard Rodriguez. Reprinted by permission of David R. Godine, Publisher.

161 Nila Smith and H. Alan Robinson, *Reading Instruction for Today's Children,* 2nd ed. Copyright 1980 by Prentice Hall. Reprinted by permission of the publisher.

165 and 166 Thomas Brock, David Smith, and Michael Madigan, *Biology of Microorganisms,* 4th ed. Copyright 1984 by Prentice Hall. Reprinted by permission of the publisher.

169 Eudora Welty, *One Writer's Beginnings* (Cambridge, Mass.: Harvard University Press, 1984), pp. 29–30. Copyright 1983, 1984 by Eudora Welty. Reprinted by permission of the publisher.

172 Robert Wiggins, "Complex Insecurity: Big Brother Is Watching You," *MacUser,* 4 (April 1988), p. 47. Reprinted from MacUser, April 1988. Copyright © 1988 Ziff Communications Company.

175 From *All I Really Need to Know I Learned in Kindergarten* by Robert Fulghum. Copyright © 1986, 1988 by Robert Fulghum. Reprinted by permission of Villard Books, a division of Random House, Inc.

179 Jean Berko Gleason, *The Development of Language.* Copyright 1985 by Charles E. Merrill. Reprinted by permission of the publisher.

184 Lee Sheridan, "The Bridge They Said Couldn't Be Built." *In Concert,* published 1989 by Riverside Publishers, Chicago. Reprinted with permission of Carole Palmer and Riverside Publishing.

193 Richard Erdoes and Alfonso Ortiz, ed., *American Indian Myths and Legends.* Reprinted by permission of Pantheon Books, a division of Random House, Inc.

201 Roger Kamien, *Music: An Appreciation,* 3rd ed. (New York: McGraw-Hill, 1984), pp. 220-223, 231-234. Used by permission.

213 "the drum," from *Spin a Soft Black Song,* by Nikki Giovanni. Copyright © 1971, 1985 by Nikki Giovanni. Reprinted by permission of Farrar, Straus & Giroux, Inc.

215 From *Fatherhood* by Bill Cosby. Copyright © by William H. Cosby, Jr. Used by permission of Doubleday, a division of Bantam Doubleday Dell Publishing Group, Inc.

218 Abraham Lincoln, "Address at the Dedication of the Gettysburg National Cemetery," November 19, 1863.

221 Martin Luther King, Jr., "I Have a Dream." Copyright 1963 by Martin Luther King, Jr., copyright renewed 1991 by Coretta Scott King. Reprinted by permission of The Joan Daves Agency.

226 Langston Hughes, "Dreams" and "The Dream Keeper," *The Dream Keeper and Other Poems* (New York: Alfred Knopf, 1932). Copyright 1932 and renewed 1960 by Langston Hughes.

227 "Dream Dust," *The Panther and the Lash* (New York: Alfred Knopf, 1947). Copyright 1947 by Langston Hughes. Reprinted from *The Panther and the Lash* by Langston Hughes by permission of Alfred A. Knopf.

229 From *It Was on Fire When I Lay Down on It* by Robert Fulghum. Copyright © 1989, 1989 by Robert Fulghum. Reprinted by permission of Villard Books, a division of Random House, Inc.

235 Excerpts on pages 235 and 238 are from John W. Hole, Jr., *Human Anatomy and Physiology.* Copyright 1979 by William C. Brown. Reprinted by permission of the publisher.

241 Jeffrey Slater and John Tobey, *Basic College Mathematics,* © 1991, p. 3. Reprinted by permission of Prentice Hall, Englewood Cliffs, New Jersey.

265 William Tracy, "Middle West Meets Middle East," *Aramco World Magazine,* 38:5 (September-October 1987), p. 3. Used by permission.

268 Anne Marshall Zwack, "Florence, the Magnificent," *Travel and Leisure,* 17:4 (April 1987), pp. 103-114, 162. Reprinted by permission of *Travel and Leisure* and of the author.

280 Paul Lunde and John A. Sabini, *ARAMCO and Its World: Arabia and the Middle East.* Copyright 1980 by Arabian American Oil Company. Reprinted by permission of ARAMCO.

296 Harry Truman, "The 8 Best Presidents—and Why," *Parade Magazine,* April 3, 1988, pp. 4-5. From *More Plain Speaking,* by Harry S. Truman, edited by Margaret Truman and Scott Meredith. Reprinted by permission of the author and Scott Meredith Literary Agency, Inc., 845 Third Avenue, New York, NY 10022 and with permission from *Parade.* Copyright © 1988.

302 From *The Star Ledger* (Newark, NJ), April 12, 1991.

307 Maya Angelou, *I Know Why the Caged Bird Sings,* Copyright © 1969 by Maya Angelou. Reprinted by permission of Random House, Inc.

331 From *The Star Ledger* (Newark, NJ), February 5, 1991.

Index

Names of authors of selections are given in italics. Names of selections are in bold.